Locked in Place

Locked in Place

STATE-BUILDING AND LATE
INDUSTRIALIZATION IN INDIA

Vivek Chibber

PRINCETON UNIVERSITY PRESS

PRINCETON AND OXFORD

Copyright © 2003 by Princeton University Press
Published by Princeton University Press, 41 William Street, Princeton, New Jersey 08540
In the United Kingdom: Princeton University Press, 3 Market Place, Woodstock, Oxfordshire OX20 1SY

Library of Congress Cataloging-in-Publication Data

Chibber, Vivek, 1965–
Locked in place: state-building and late industrialization in India/Vivek Chibber.
p. cm.
Includes bibliographical references and index.
ISBN 0-691-09659-7 (alk. paper)
1. Industrial policy—India—History—20th century. 2. Industrialization—India—History—20th century. 3. India—Economic conditions—20th century. 4. Industrial policy—Korea (South)—History—20th century. I. Title.

HD3616.I42C45 2003
338.0954′09′045—dc21   2002192489

British Library Cataloging-in-Publication Data is available

This book has been composed in Sabon

Printed on acid-free paper. ∞

www.pupress.princeton.edu

Printed in the United States of America

10 9 8 7 6 5 4 3 2 1

Contents

FOR ABBA AND AMMA

Preface

THIS BOOK SETS out to examine, and to explain, some central elements of the post-colonial Indian state. In particular, I ask why it was that Jawaharlal Nehru and his colleagues failed in what they regarded as perhaps their central mission — to build what we now would call a developmental state. This is not a matter of mere historical interest. The Nehru years were absolutely pivotal for the half-century following Independence, since the basic institutional apparatus bequeathed by him remained in place, through the decades, until the onset of liberalization in the 1990s. The dynamics of these early years are therefore critical to understanding the subsequent arc of the Indian political economy.

Interestingly, the recent spate of research on the role of the state in late development has largely sidestepped the Indian experience. There has undoubtedly been some work on India in this regard, but, when compared to the outpouring of scholarship on East Asia and South America, the work on India shrinks almost to insignificance. This is surprising. In the halcyon days of development planning, stretching roughly from the 1950s to the early 1970s, many commentators considered the subcontinent as perhaps the most ambitious attempt at state-led development in the South. And, for a while, India was the object of considerable attention in the scholarly world. But by the late 1970s the attention shifted, and it has not recovered since.

While the scholarship on developmentalism has tended to set aside the Indian experience, the research on post-colonial India has produced very little historically informed work on the region's political economy, especially the matter of the state. This, too, is puzzling. Since the explosion of Marxist scholarship in the 1970s, debates in Indian academic and Left circles have frequently visited the problem of state power and the political basis of development policy — yet this has failed to generate original research on those critical formative years which form the focus of this book. As a result, much of the scholarship of recent vintage has had to base its appraisal of the early, more foundational years on work that is by now more than a quarter of a century old, and which was written without access to archival material. As I show in the body of the book, this has led to some quite profound misconceptions about the dynamics that underlay state building in India.

It is my hope that this book contributes toward mending this state of affairs. India is far too significant a case to be ignored in the developmental state debates, and the post-colonial state is far too critical a matter to be left out of India scholarship. Of course, some may wonder as to the relevance of a book on the developmental state, since not only India, but also much of East Asia and Latin America, appear to have abjured state-led development strategies. That the era of full-blown *dirigisme* may be over, I do not dispute. But it is far from clear that some kind of state intervention at the sectoral or firm level is also a thing of the past. Indeed, it is hard to imagine that state intervention in the economy can ever be avoided under capitalism, for reasons I enumerate in chapter 2. This being the case, it is of some interest to study the conditions under which states can, or cannot, make such interventions successfully. In any event, I believe that the dearth of scholarship on the post-colonial Indian state provides sufficient warrant for this book.

Partly owing to the paucity of scholarship on state building in the post-colonial years, I have relied almost entirely on original and, for the most part, previously unused, archival material, as well as a large number of published government documents. But the turn to archival material is also motivated by a methodological imperative. A book such as this seeks to analyze how social groups organized around their interests and the extent to which these interests were, in fact, responsible for shifts in state policy. In such inquiries, social scientists typically proceed by drawing up the interests of relevant actors, and then making an *inference* about their role in shaping outcomes by mapping the policy outcomes onto the *ex ante* demands made by social groups. Hence, if capitalists are demanding higher tariffs, and if tariffs are in fact raised, then it is inferred that the latter was brought about by the former. But this is problematic. For it could, of course, have been that state managers settled on that very policy independently of social pressure. To cash out the claim that social pressure was important, it is critical to open up the "black box" of the policy process, so to speak — to establish a causal chain, if there is one, between the political pressure exercised by the group and the ultimate shift in policy. In recent years social scientists have made use of manuscript collections in one significant debate around the state, namely, on the origins of the welfare state in advanced capitalist countries. Access to the private correspondence of key players has been instrumental in establishing their actual intentions, as distinct from their public pronouncements. The series of questions now raised in research on the developmental state calls for a similar methodology.

Having said this, I feel compelled to offer a brief description of the sources that have proved relevant, and, more important, the conditions under which I was able to gain access to them. In part, this is simply to follow convention; but it is also intended to help future scholars navigate the rough waters of archival research on the post-colonial Indian state. When I began work on this book, I had expected to spend no more than eight to ten months in the archives. It, in fact, took me close to four years to complete the research. How and why this happened may be of interest.

A Note on Sources

The fundamental problem confronting any researcher of post-colonial state policy is the dearth of manuscript sources. Officially India operates with a thirty-year gag rule on government files, after which they are to be transferred from Central Ministries to the National Archives. When I arrived in Delhi in 1994, I had expected to have at my disposal all relevant files up to 1965. What I found, instead, was that the National Archives did not have any such files or at least were not aware of them. Through the grapevine, I learned that one small series of files from the Cabinet Secretariat had been transferred and might be available. It took two months of detective work to discover from Archives officials that this was indeed the case. Thereafter, a few dozen files were handed over to me for use. But what happened to the thousands of other files from the various ministries? Again, after several weeks of bouncing back and forth from one official to another, the consensus that emerged was that, if they existed, they would be in the storage rooms at the respective ministries.

Then began a months-long process of investigation at the ministries. My first tactic, utterly naïve, was to approach the librarians and clerks at the ministries directly and seek permission to peruse the records. The foolhardiness of this was brought home in a chastening experience at the Planning Commission, where the clerk in charge of documents informed me, "We don't have any records from those years, and even if we did, I would not show them to you." When I reminded the clerk of the thirty-year rule, his response was a quizzical look: "Those rules mean nothing to me." When I persisted, now somewhat idiotically, in asking why, he shrugged and said, "If I give permission to anyone who walks in, what is left of me?" Good point.

So I began to seek access the old-fashioned way — by using family connections to gain an audience with top ministry officials and, where possible, with the Ministers themselves. Naturally this took months. But in the end I was able to examine the records rooms of the Planning Commission (completely bypassing my old friend in the library), the Finance Ministry, the Industry Ministry, and the Commerce Ministry. What emerged was deeply depressing. In all the ministries save one, I made two discoveries: first, that no one in fact knew if the old records existed and, if they did, where they would be; second, on investigating — which usually meant being taken on long peregrinations around moldy, dusty rooms — we discovered that most old files had simply been thrown away or burned. It seems that in the 1960s, when ministries were running out of storage space and were interested in transferring records to the Archives, the latter informed them that it did not have the space to receive the ministerial files. So, after a point, clerks decided simply to destroy them — or so I was told. In any case, in one ministry after another, over the course of months of trying, I came up with nothing. Now, it could be that there are files somewhere in the bowels of these buildings and the officials just do not know of their existence; or perhaps I was simply lied to. We can only hope. But I came up with nothing.

The exception turned out to be fortuitous. The Industry Ministry also destroyed most of its old records, but a few files central to industrial policy from the 1940s were saved — and these turned out to be gems. And in the Commerce Ministry, I stumbled onto what appeared to be gold — literally thousands of files, in a dank, dusty room, lining rows of shelves. But after spending more than eight weeks, going through each file and inhaling lots of dust (they were un-catalogued and un-indexed), I again came up with nothing. Over 90 percent of the files pertained to bilateral trade negotiations or to proceedings at the GATT (General Agreement on Tariffs and Trade) — relevant for some other researcher, perhaps, but not for me. Again, wasted months, but many exciting trips to the pharmacist.

The most difficult acquisition of all, but one that I felt would be crucial, was Jawaharlal Nehru's personal papers housed at the Nehru Memorial Museum and Library. This collection has been closed to scholars for more than two decades, and access to it requires the personal permission of the prime minister of India and a member of the Nehru family (at that time, Sonia Gandhi). Though initially rebuffed, I managed, after about six months of efforts, to secure permission from Prime Minister I. K. Gujral and Sonia Gandhi in 1999. The Nehru collection turned out to be somewhat surprising. For research on economic policy, it is of great interest around one issue, the origins and subsequent dynamics of the Second Five-Year Plan, especially its heavy industry strategy. But interestingly, although it is extremely rich for the years 1954 to 1959, its materials pertaining to economic policy in the last five years of Nehru's life — the years of the Third Plan — are so thin as to be almost nonexistent. And for the period of the First Plan, the collection has some, but not a great deal, of material. In the end, I decided not to incorporate the material from the Nehru papers into the book. For one thing, the basic manuscript was already prepared; but, more important, the information gathered from these papers would have added more texture to the second half of the book (especially chapter 7) but would not have changed the argument even in a minor capacity. Since this book is intended as a historical inquiry, but not as a work of history, I decided to refrain from rewriting the text to accommodate the new material. Instead, I intend to use it in a separate series of articles for specialist journals.

The final source that turned out to be of use was the rich records of the U.S. embassies and consulates, kept in the State Department Central Files in the U.S. National Archives. The idea of using this source came to me while I was reading Ayesha Jalal's wonderful book on Pakistan, *The State of Martial Rule* (Cambridge: Cambridge University Press, 1990), which is based mostly on American and British embassy records. I would urge researches to take advantage of this source, which turned out to be extremely useful. Especially helpful are the many "Memoranda of Conversation" between embassy officials and prominent political and business leaders. A trip to the Public Records Office in Kew during the summer of 2001 turned out to be less rewarding. Surprisingly, the U.S. collections are richer for Indian issues than the British — something I had not expected.

Between the Indian material and that in the U.S. National Archives, I managed, in the end, to collect more than enough to make a credible argument around state building in the years after Independence. I can only hope that this book contributes to the start of serious historical scholarship on post-colonial India, which is, at present, almost nonexistent. I have described my efforts to acquire sources, in part to alert scholars to the labors that await them should they decide to undertake similar projects. But it is also my hope that this account of my experience will make the process easier for those who follow, pointing them to promising sources and helping them to avoid dead ends.

Acknowledgments

THE RESEARCH for this book was funded by a grant from the American Institute for Indian Studies and a research grant from the University of Wisconsin. I am grateful to both. An earlier version of chapter 3 appeared in *Politics and Society* (September 1999), as "Building a Developmental State: The Korean Case Reconsidered"; parts of chapter 7 appeared in the *American Journal of Sociology* (January 2002), as "Bureaucratic Rationality and the Developmental State." I am grateful to Sage Press and the University of Chicago Press, respectively, for permission to use them here.

The bulk of the work leading up to this book was done while I was a student in the doctoral program in sociology at the University of Wisconsin–Madison. I owe a debt of gratitude to my professors and fellow students while there — I cannot imagine a better, more vibrant and collegial culture for students. I would like to thank Stephen Bunker, Joe Elder, Denis O'Hearn, Joel Rogers, and Gay Seidman for their patience and guidance. From a distance, Robert Brenner befriended me and provided much intellectual and moral support. I will spend a lifetime aspiring to his combination of commitment and scholarly rigor. Among my friends, special mention goes to Sara Abraham, Joel Shoemaker, John Roosa, Raka Ray, Didacus Jules, Jose Padin, Stephanie Luce, Alair McLean, Elizabeth Katz, Glen Rosselli, and, of course, the "ubiquitous" Allen Ruff. My friends and comrades at Rainbow, and in Solidarity, provided me with the wherewithal to keep my eyes on the prize. A special debt of gratitude is owed to Patrick Barrett, who served happily as a close interlocutor for several years.

In Delhi I was exceptionally fortunate to have a circle of friends and relatives to make my "research trip" more a homecoming than anything else. The linchpins, of course, were my father and my aunt, Sudesh Vaid. My father is probably the only parent in the subcontinent who was *relieved* when he discovered that his son was abandoning the pursuit of a medical career — and that, too, for a dubious future as a sociologist in American academia. His dedication to his own academic responsibilities, and to his activism in the democratic rights movement in India, have been formative influences. I remember still how excited and proud I was to discover that the University of Wisconsin library carried the book that emerged from his dissertation, written some four decades earlier. With this book I will now proudly double the number of Chibbers in the library.

It is my greatest regret that Sudesh did not live to see this book come to fruition. After a lifetime fighting for democratic rights and social justice, she succumbed to cancer in the winter of 2001–2002. She was a profound influence on my intellectual and political development, more than she imagined, I suspect. So, too, was C.V. Subba Rao, who passed away at an unconscionably young age in 1994. I know Subba would have loved my conclusions about the orientation of the Indian capitalist class, about the real motives behind the Bombay Plan. I also know that we would have sat up long hours arguing about it. For depriving me of that, I will never forgive him.

In the wider circle of Delhi came the rest of the group — Harish Dhavan, Joseph Mathai, Snehlata Gupta, Rohan D'Souza, Rajesh Gupta, Shahana Bhattacharya, Ramaa Vasudevan, Ashok Prasad, Nagaraj Adve, Daman Deep Singh, Tommie Matthews, Bela Malik, and, of course, my buddy, Sharmila Purkayastha. To all of you — you made Delhi, surely the most uncivil city in India, something very special.

Also in Delhi the late professor Ravinder Kumar, Shri Rajindar Sacchar, Amrik Singh, and Suman Dube helped me enormously in my quest for the Nehru papers. And, of course, I must thank Mrs. Sonia Gandhi and Prime Minister I. K Gujral for the penultimate permission. Arun Shouri generously directed me to Arun Bharat Ram, who, in turn, allowed me access to the Shri Ram archives; Suman Dube was again very helpful in shepherding me to Shri P. Chidambaram, the Minister of Commerce, who allowed me entry into the ministry's collection room; and E.A.S. Sharma, then Additional Secretary in the Industry Ministry, helped in getting access to that ministry's records, which turned out to be of crucial importance. I am grateful to one and all.

Two people in Madison deserve special mention. Robert McChesney came to Madison the same year I arrived as a Ph.D. student. Soon thereafter we became fast friends and have remained so ever since. Bob has been a constant source of encouragement and sustenance, not to mention a shining example of committed scholarship. Erik Wright was the reason I went to Madison for graduate work at all. It turned out to be the best decision I have ever made. Everyone who has ever come across him knows very well just how brilliant a mind he possesses. But brilliant minds do not always make good teachers. Erik is easily the best combination of scholar and teacher I have ever seen. May everyone who goes through a Ph.D. program have an adviser as generous, supportive, rigorous, and trusting as Erik.

The Department of Sociology at New York University has provided a wonderful home while I turned my dissertation into a book. I extend special thanks to Craig Calhoun and Doug Guthrie for helping me with the practicalities of finding a publisher. At Princeton University Press

Ian Malcolm has been a superb editor—always prompt, never remote, and scrupulously professional. I am also grateful to Terry Byres and Craig Calhoun for very helpful comments on the manuscript. Finally, as a reviewer for Princeton, Peter Evans made some extremely valuable suggestions, prompting me to substantially rewrite the concluding chapter. And, in New York, Elliot Podwill and Avis Lang have been like an extended family since the day I arrived.

My mother has not only given me the kind of support that makes a long process such as this one possible at all, but she is also responsible for imbuing me with the intellectual excitement that motivates my work. Whatever sense of moral and intellectual commitment I have today stems mainly from her. In almost every respect, she has set the example to which I have aspired. Gogi, my sister, is easily the most courageous person I know, battling her disability her whole life with fierce determination. I hope she sees fit to read this book some day. And, lastly, the best thing of all about this project is that it led me to Nivedita, who agreed to take a plunge into another land, another reality, and start a life with me. I would probably have been able to write the book in her absence, but I can only imagine how much less fulfilling it would have been.

Abbreviations

APB	Advisory Planning Board	EDC	Economic Development Council
AITUC	All-India Trade Union Congress (Affiliated with Communist Party of India)	EPB	Economic Planning Board
		ELI	export-led industrialization
		FDI	Foreign Direct Investment
ASSOCHAM	Associated Chambers of Commerce	FEER	*Far Eastern Economic Review*
CSP	Congress Socialist Party	FICCI	Federation of Indian Chambers of Commerce and Industry
CACI	Central Advisory Council for Industry	FKI	Federation of Korean Industries
CII	Confederation of Indian Industries	GATT	General Agreement on Trade and Tariffs
		HMS	Hind Mazdoor Sabha (Affiliated with Socialist Party)
CITU	Congress of Indian Trade Unions (Affiliated with Communist Party of India (Marxist)	IDRA	Industries Development and Regulation Act
		IMC	Indian Merchants Chamber
CPM	Communist Party of India (Marxist)	INC	Indian National Congress
DSR	Department of State Records, U.S. National Archives	INTUC	Indian National Trade Union Congress
		IPS	Industrial Policy Statement
ECLA	Economic Commission for Latin America	ISI	import-substituting industrialization
		JNSW	*Jawaharlal Nehru Selected Works*
ECC	Economic Committee of the Cabinet	KBA	Korean Businessmen's Association

LDC	less-developed country	NPC	National Planning Committee
MITI	Ministry of International Trade and Industry	OECD	Organization for Economic Cooperation and Development
MNC	Multinational Corporations		
NAI	*National Archives of India*	PC	Planning Commission
NIC	Newly Industrializing Country	PMS	Prime Minister's Secretariat
NMML	Nehru Memorial Museum and Library	QIMSD	Quit India Movement — Select Documents

PART I

The Issues and the Argument

CHAPTER 1

Introduction

AMID THE ENORMOUS diversity of experience across developing countries since the Second World War, India has managed to stand out. At mid-century, in the years following its independence from British rule, there was a tremendous sense of anticipation as the nation embarked on its first development plan, perhaps the most ambitious yet witnessed in poor countries. Despite the grinding poverty of the bulk of the population, the expectations were that India had some of the basic ingredients required for a great leap forward economically: a rich stock of natural resources, an industrial base which, by the standards of the South, was fairly broad and advanced; a bureaucratic and administrative apparatus which was—again by the standards of the developing world—quite competent; and, lastly, a political leadership genuinely committed to launching an industrial transformation.

Adding to the sense of drama was that this massive nation of four hundred million, with its enormous diversity and history of conflict, was choosing to push forward within a bourgeois democratic framework—a fact of some significance in a continent that already boasted two large nations committed to Communism, hence making the Indian experiment all the more significant to the capitalist world. India was to be an exemplar, demonstrating the possibility that planning need not presuppose the abolition of property, but could, in fact, be harnessed to the engine of capital accumulation.

Fifty years later India still stands out, but only as a lesson in disappointment. Development planning, once seen as the instrument that would launch the country onto a path of industrial dynamism, is now regarded as having been an impediment toward that same end. The 1990s have witnessed a turning away from the statist economic policy of previous decades, ushering in a process of concerted liberalization, a dismantling of the vast panoply of controls and regulations that had slowly accumulated over the years. But the sense of ennui had, in fact, set in much earlier, during the 1970s, when the economy slowed down perceptibly, settling into the famous "Hindu rate of growth."[1] It had become clear that the state's ambition of pushing the country into the front ranks of the developing world had fallen far short of its target, with seemingly few prospects of changing in the near future. By the time liberalization set in during the 1990s, India had fallen from being the prospective beacon for the developing world to what one scholar has called "the most dramatic case of a failed developmental state."[2]

This book seeks to explain why the Indian state failed so conspicuously in its mission to transform India into an industrial dynamo. It does not pretend to offer a complete analysis of the development experience since 1947. My focus is quite narrower: I wish to provide an explanation of why the Indian state failed in the specific domain of industrial planning and policy. Why, when it boasted a political leadership of considerable quality and commitment, the apparent administrative wherewithal, and the requisite industrial base, did India not succeed in propelling a successful industrial transformation? To Jawaharlal Nehru and the Indian National Congress (INC), the path to development was virtually synonymous with industrialization. That they met with relatively limited success in achieving it merits an explanation.

That the failure was a *relative* one needs to be emphasized at the outset. My intention is not, by any means, to portray the Indian experience as an embodiment of the caricatures that populate neoliberal strictures against interventionist economic policy. State intervention, whatever its shortcomings, did manage to widen and deepen the country's industrial base considerably and to move the economy along the technological ladder. India today can boast significant competence in many of the cutting-edge sectors of the world economy. This is an achievement that ought not to be slighted, especially in light of the numerous, and quite spectacular, development disasters that decorate the international landscape. But while the Indian state did manage to oversee a somewhat respectable industrial transformation, it cannot be denied that its performance as a developmental agency fell far short not only of the expectations of policy elites but also of the standards set by the states of other countries — in particular, those of Northeast Asia.

Asking why the Indian state failed in its ambitions presumes having some idea of what kinds of policies or choices *would* have been more successful. Toward this end, my examination of the Indian experience is framed by a comparison with South Korea, perhaps the exemplar developmental state in the postwar period. The fortunes of industrial policy and planning in Korea stand in glaring contrast to those of India: whereas in the latter case the state's efforts to promote a dynamic industrial sector fell prey to the twin evils of bureaucratic paralysis and capitalist rent-seeking, Korean efforts were rewarded by unprecedented success. What makes the comparison interesting and possible are not just the divergent outcomes; there are similarities in background conditions that make it possible to draw meaningful comparisons. Both countries started their development efforts soon after World War II, making their experiences largely concurrent; both were at broadly similar levels of industrial

TABLE 1.1

Share of Manufacturing and Allied Activities in GNP, India (1950) and Korea (1960–62)

Sector	Share of GNP India (1950) (%)	Share of GNP Korea 1960–62 (%)
Manufacturing and Construction	15.4	17.1
Utilities	a	1.1
Mining and Quarrying	0.7	2.0
Total	16.1	20.2

[a]Included in the figure for Manufacturing and Construction.

Sources: For India: Raymond Goldsmith, *The Financial Development of India, 1869–1977* (New Haven: Yale University Press, 1977), table 3.2. For Korea: Edward Mason et al., *The Economic and Social Modernization of the Republic of Korea* (Cambridge, Mass.: Harvard University Press, 1980), table 13.

development at the start of their rapid industrialization programs, as shown in table 1.1; in both countries, the industrial sector was dominated by a small number of business houses, which accounted for a disproportionate share of output and investment;[3] in both cases, the policy design was heavily interventionist, relying on extensive government intervention in, and regulation of, the private sector; and in each case industrial policy was directed by the central government, and nominally concentrated in a few key ministries and agencies. Hence, despite many differences in other dimensions, these similarities allow for a meaningful comparison, and indeed have generated some efforts in this direction in recent years.[4]

The enormous success of Korea in making its traversal to a dynamic and efficient industrial economy has generated significant rethinking in development studies. When I first began thinking about the political economy of development in the late 1980s, the dominant trend among scholars evinced a strong suspicion of statist or *dirigiste* economic strategies. The decade had witnessed the derailment of several prominent experiments in state-led development, most notably in Latin America but also in India, Turkey, and other countries.[5] Although there were many reasons for the downturn in these countries, it was impossible to ignore the fact that their maladies were at least partly generated by the domestic political economy. And most heavily implicated in this drama was the state itself. With a public sector that was often operating with large losses, a private sector bloated from state subsidies and virtually immune from competition, and bureaucracies rife with corruption and venality, the ground was laid for the suspicion that it was state intervention in the economy itself that lay at the heart of the crisis in these countries.[6] The natural conclusion flowing from this position would have been that India's mistake was its very turn toward development planning in the first place, an economic strategy that relied so centrally on state intervention in markets.[7]

At around this same time, a series of studies began to emerge that demanded a rethinking of the reigning consensus. Led most notably by Alice Amsden and Robert Wade, whose case studies have quickly acquired classical status, a number of scholars pointed to the extraordinary growth of the (North)East Asian economies, which they insisted was a fact of great significance for development theorists.[8] For these economies—Japan, Taiwan, and South Korea—had engineered their spectacular success not through any fidelity to free-market policies but with a reliance on highly interventionist industrial planning. The Korean and Taiwanese states had actively manipulated trade and exchange rates,[9] the allocation of finance,[10] as well as the price structure of the domestic economy;[11] it was also shown that both countries not only had developed a large public enterprise sector[12] but had also been active in directing the structure of private investment.[13]

These studies have triggered a disintegration of the consensus on the role of the state in development. It can no longer be argued confidently that a reliance on an interventionist state in developing countries was a mistake. State intervention is a phenomenon that has been common *across* the development experience, in the successful cases as well as the failures. This fact has led several prominent scholars to conclude that the East Asian experience differed from that of other developing areas, not in the *fact* of state involvement in the economy but rather in its *quality*.[14] The state in the newly industrializing countries (NICs) intervened in the domestic economy just as its counterparts did elsewhere, and even toward the same ends; however, it managed to succeed in prodding local industry toward greater efficiency and productivity, whereas others, like the Indian state, did not. States in these regions thus differ not so much in their orientation toward the economy—for in both cases they were committed to "governing" the market[15]—but in their *capacity* to bring about the desired results. This is not to say that the chief responsibility for the extraordinary growth rates in Taiwan and Korea goes to development planning. Observed rates of economic growth are driven by a combination of a host of factors—cultural, institutional, economic, geographical, and so on.[16] What the scholarship under discussion stresses is that the state has turned out to be one of those factors after all, and a significant one at that.

The debate on the developmental state has thus come to a conclusion much like the one reached about capitalist welfare states a decade before: that much of the interesting variation in outcomes (in this case, success in fostering industrial development) depends on the state's having the capacity to fulfill the tasks assigned to it. *State capacity* itself has been decomposed into two broad dimensions: an intrinsic component, namely, the state's *cohesiveness* as a strategic actor, which can formulate and implement policy in a coherent fashion;[17] and an extrinsic component, which is the state's ability to *extract performance* from private firms — setting standards, monitoring performance, and influencing the direction of investment — in exchange for the subsidies that are doled out to them. Alice Amsden, who has argued this more forcefully than anyone else, puts it aptly:

> All governments know that subsidies are most effective when they are based on performance standards. Nevertheless state power to *impose* such standards, and bureaucratic capability to implement them, vary from country to country. . . . The state in Korea, Japan, and Taiwan has been more effective than other late-industrializing countries *because it has had the power to discipline big business.*[18]

The difference in quality of intervention is thus explained in large measure by the state's ability to formulate and implement policy in a coherent fashion, and to impose discipline on private firms. Where Korea and Taiwan succeeded in this task, the states in South Asia and Latin America typically did not.

Hence, in answer to the question posed above — namely, what kind of policies or choices would have been more successful in India — the recent literature does provide us with some guidance, pointing to the centrality of adequate state capacity. And the arguments about East Asia, particularly Korea, certainly do contrast in appropriate ways with what we know about the Indian state: its excessively bureaucratic style, lack of coherence in policy, and utter inability to discipline domestic business are well known.[19] But while I affirm this understanding of the Indian case in the analysis to come (in chapters 7 and 8), I direct much of my attention to two other questions, which flow immediately from the recognition of the state's inadequacies.

THE INSTALLATION OF THE DEVELOPMENTAL STATE

First, if the Indian state lacked the capacity to succeed in its developmental tasks, how do we explain this? In other words, why did Indian political leaders and bureaucrats fail to build the institutions adequate to the task? After all, the idea that policy needs to be coherent and that governments have to be able to impose discipline on firms is hardly a deep, arcane truth known only to intrepid social scientists. It is common knowledge to every politician and state functionary, and mid-century Indians should have been no exception; indeed, as I show in chapters 4 and 6, they were keenly aware of the issue, and the idea of building such institutions was very much on the immediate political agenda. That the state ended up without the requisite institutional capacity, despite the national leadership's awareness of its necessity, and despite the leadership putting it on the agenda, requires explanation.

Let us call this—the lack of success in putting a developmental state in place—the question of the *installation of the state*. It is surprising that, on this issue, there has been very little discussion in the recent work on development.[20] This is perhaps a measure of the extent to which the neoliberal challenge has been able to set the terms of the debate of late. Scholars doing empirical work on East Asia have put considerable effort into showing that states need not fall prey to the pathologies their critics predict.[21] It is for this reason that we have accumulated so much detail on just what these states did in their "miracle" decades, and what kinds of institutions their success required. But one consequence of the dedication to this research agenda is that the anterior issue, of why the East Asian regimes were able to build such states in the first place, has suffered from relative neglect.[22]

In the chapters that follow I offer an account of the Indian experience that seeks to explain why the political leadership did not install a developmental state, despite the fact that they were aware of the need to do so. This is set in contrast to the Korean experience, examined in chapter 3, where the outcome was very different, in that a state with the appropriate institutional backbone was put into place. It needs to be noted here that, despite the comparative frame, questions such as this—in which the concern is to explain the absence of particular institutions— are often more easily posed than answered. Such questions have rightly drawn criticism from some quarters as subtly teleological, in that they presume that there is a "normal" end state (in this case, a developmental state) toward which all paths lead, so that the divergence from such a path requires explanation. But why presume, the criticism goes, that any such end state exists, and why presume that the absence of particular institutions, or types of institutions, requires explanation? There are instances where such worries have proven to be justified; I hope to show, however, that this study is not one of them.

Two conditions suffice to defuse the charge of teleology in analyses such as this one. First, it must be shown that the institutions in question—which were not, in the end, installed—were, in fact, on the political agenda at some critical juncture;[23] second, it needs to be shown that the actors in the drama were aware of this agenda and acted in cognizance of its implications. If these conditions hold, then we are fully justified in asking why, despite being among the menu of options, the desired institutions were not installed. The Indian case meets these conditions handily. The years immediately following Independence, 1947 to 1951, constituted just this kind of critical juncture, in which a strong developmental state was very much on the political agenda. It is therefore an ideal setting to examine the constraints that exist in actualizing the project of installing such states, and I devote chapters 5 and 6 to its examination.

The argument I offer as an explanation for why Indian elites failed to actualize their state-building agenda while their Korean counterparts succeeded departs somewhat from the dominant tendency in the literature. More through default than by dint of theoretical commitment, the prevailing approach to the study of state building in development studies has been statist in orientation. Scholars have been primarily concerned to show that, given the requisite state capacity, patterns of intervention in the economy need not fall prey to neoliberal worries. The process of how such states were installed often serves as a quick, and hence somewhat perfunctory, narrative of the sequential implementation of policies. The focus therefore remains on political elites and dynamics within the governmental apparatus, giving the overarching impression that what matters is the goings-on *within* the state. This has been reinforced by some scholars who do, in fact, have a theoretical commitment to statism, taking the view that, indeed, it is the state that is the main actor in this drama; and it is the main player because it is more powerful than any other.[24]

I argue, in contrast, that the critical conflicts for building state capacity occur not *within* the state but *between* the state and societal actors, particularly the capitalist class. I show this through a detailed analysis of the Indian case, but it is also strengthened through a new interpretation of the relevant period in Korean history. The explanation itself consists of two nested claims. First, the divergence in outcomes with respect to state capacity depended crucially on the orientation of the business class toward the state: the Indian state managers' agenda was frustrated by a well-organized offensive launched by domestic capitalists, whereas in the Korean case the state was able to harness capitalists to its project. Indian capitalists in the years immediately after Independence refused to countenance a state with wide-ranging regulatory and interventionist powers, and organized effectively against it. In so doing, they reduced the autonomy and power of political elites to build the institutions they had proposed. Conversely, it was the success in striking an alliance of sorts with its domestic business class that gave the Korean political elite the space to build appropriate state institutions. Naturally, having the autonomy to put the institutions in place was not sufficient for success;

for this, the facts internal to the state, on which much of the literature has focused, were of great importance. The argument presented in this book does suggest, however, that the antecedent autonomy garnered by the alliance with business was necessary for the state-level processes to be effective.

So the first argument states that the state-building project is critically mediated by the nature of state-capitalist relations. But this, in turn, raises a question, to which the second argument is addressed: why did the capitalist classes in the two countries react differently to the idea of a strong developmental state? Was the difference generated by contingent historical factors, or was there, in fact, a deeper, structural factor that might explain it? In other words, could we specify the circumstances in which business classes would react favorably or unfavorably to building a developmental state? I argue that, indeed, it is possible to adduce a deeper mechanism that was responsible for the diverging reactions by domestic capitalists to the state-building agenda. This mechanism is, for lack of a better term, the development model the respective regimes chose to adopt. In India the state opted for import-substituting industrialization (ISI), whereas in Korea greater emphasis was placed on export-led industrialization (ELI).[25] I suggest that the two models generated different political incentive structures for the capitalist classes: ISI made it possible, and even rational, for Indian capitalists to resist the effort to build a state that could impose discipline on private firms; ELI, on the other hand, made it rational for Korean business to acquiesce to its own disciplining by a developmental state.

The emphasis on the autonomy of the state from the capitalist class brings into our analysis the same categories and concerns that have framed the discussion of the welfare state in past decades. I believe that this is to be welcomed. For too long, discussions of the state in developing countries have been bracketed off from the analytical concerns that animate the study of advanced capitalist states.[26] A central concern of the latter debates has been to uncover the constraints that social forces impose on state action, and the conditions that govern the variation of these constraints. Of particular interest has been the manner in which capitalist class interests, and class organizational power, limits the autonomy of the state.[27] While these questions do enter concretely into discussions of the state in developing countries, they are not commonly conceptualized in a self-conscious fashion. Hence the possibility of research in the two settings being used for the advancement of a common framework is not fully utilized. This book is intended to contribute toward bridging this divide and bring discussions of the developmental state into the broader theoretical ambit of the capitalist state.

THE REPRODUCTION OF THE STATE

Thus the argument about the installation of the state is that it is governed in the first instance by the state's relation to the capitalist class, which is, in turn, conditioned by the adopted development model. This brings us to the second question: even if an adequate developmental state is not installed initially, why is it not reformed once its inadequacies are discovered? Why is an unsatisfactory state reproduced over time? Analyses focusing on the origins of particular institutional configurations sometimes leave their subsequent reproduction unexplained, and into this analytical vacuum step such notions as "bureaucratic inertia" or "historical momentum" in place of real explanations. This is regrettable in any setting, but in the analysis of state failure it is especially so. So long as political elites are at least nominally committed to a genuinely developmental agenda, and aware that the existing state apparatus lacks the capacity to serve this function, it is of some interest to ask why, despite their commitments, elites abide by a weak state.

This is the issue around which the last two chapters revolve, and the issue that dictates the historical end point of the book. Why the state was not restructured to better serve the purpose of industrial transformation is most easily answered if, like in the case of state installation, we can find a point at which reform was on the agenda but did not ultimately come to fruition. In India, such a window of opportunity opened in the mid-sixties, when, after the death of Jawaharlal Nehru, calls were made within the political elite as well as the bureaucracy for overhauling the planning institutions, in clear recognition of their inadequacy. Methodologically this presents an excellent opportunity to examine the hurdles, which, in the end, made state transformation a non-starter. The reform episode turned out not only to be fleeting but also one in which the very meaning of reform took on a particular cast: from making the state better at industrial planning to considerably reducing the scope of development planning itself. I offer explanations for both phenomena — the construal of reform as liberalization, as well as the squelching of even this impulse.

Once the reform episode was past, Indian development policy continued within the old groove for another decade and a half, until liberalization was initiated haltingly in the 1980s, and then on an accelerated pace in the decade that followed. The lapsing of the initial opportunity for reform was thus of some historical importance, in two ways: first, because another such window did not open again for another fifteen years; and second, because it showed that, even if reform were to occur in the future, it would not be toward *better* state intervention but *less* intervention. The analysis of the mid-sixties conjuncture thus provides a convenient point at which to terminate the story. A close analysis of why the state and economic elites finally did undertake a path toward dismantling the policy regime in the 1980s is a task I intend to undertake in future work. For now, I hope it is enough to explain why India became saddled with an inadequate developmental state, and how, once installed, it became locked in place.

The architecture of the book is structured around answering the three main questions that have been introduced in this chapter: What do developmental states do? Why was Korea able to install a state with the ability to carry out the required tasks, while India was not? And, lastly, why was the Indian state not reformed in appropriate ways after its inadequacies became clear? Chapter 2 probes more deeply into the nature of the developmental state and into existing approaches to its study. It also presents a summary of the basic argument developed in the chapters to come. We then enter part 2 of the book, which is concerned with the installation of the state: chapter 3 examines the origins of the Korean state, in order to frame the subsequent examination of India, and chapters 4 to 6 present an argument as to why, in the Indian case, the attempt to put a developmental apparatus in place failed. Part 3 of the book attempts to answer why the state was not reformed: chapter 7 examines how its institutional structure generated a particular pattern of intervention in the economy, and chapter 8 argues that this pattern of intervention affected both the power of the planning authorities and the legitimacy of the planning process itself, which, in turn, affected their ability to fight for reform.

CHAPTER 2

Late Development and State-Building

THE PHENOMENON OF late development in the capitalist world economy has typically been associated with an important role for the state. This was, of course, true for the initial batch of countries, such as Germany and Japan, attempting to catch up with their more advanced competitors;[1] it has been even more so for what Albert Hirschman called the "late late developers" — the nations across the South in the postwar twentieth century that undertook programs of development planning.[2] In fact, it would not be an exaggeration to suggest that it was in this period that state-led development really emerged as a well-theorized strategy and a political project, so much so that it became, for a spell, the "common sense" of political elites and their advisers.

This surface continuity with respect to the state, however, should not be allowed to mask some significant divergences between the two periods. State intervention during the latter half of the twentieth century differed from that preceding it in several respects: it extended into a wider range of activities; its subsidization of industry relied less extensively on tariffs in comparison with nineteenth-century efforts and more on direct provision of credit and finance;[3] but perhaps the most conspicuous difference is that it is really during the postwar development efforts that the state has made a concerted effort not only to subsidize industrialization, or to create a favorable climate for it, but actually to coordinate the activities of firms as a means of accelerating its progress. Perhaps the hallmark of "late late development" is the appearance of *development planning* in its various forms: in its weaker form, simply in the guise of industrial policy, and, in its most pointed expression, as the ubiquitous five-year plans that so many countries proudly displayed for decades.

The changing form of intervention is of considerable analytical importance, because with it come different responsibilities, which, in turn, necessitate correspondingly different capacities on the part of the state. Attempts to foster industrialization by manipulating structural conditions — through land reforms or increasing national savings — will demand a different kind of state than those that rely on micro-level intervention at the level of the sector or firm, the hallmark of industrial policy. This chapter delves into the specifics of postwar development strategies in order to bring into relief the particular demands that they made on the state. Once we locate just what kind of institutional capacity is required for industrial policy to succeed, it becomes possible to analyze why it was successfully acquired in some countries and not in others. It therefore sets the stage for examining why Korean political elites were able to build a state with the necessary qualities, while their Indian counterparts were not.

THE TWO DIMENSIONS OF INDUSTRIAL POLICY

There is, no doubt, something misleading in the proposition that late development is distinguished by the important role that is played by the state or, even more pointedly, by its intervention in markets. The very creation and reproduction of a society that is fully commodified has demanded, from the start, extensive state manipulation. This is nowhere more apparent than in the labor market, an institution that secured its moorings only after early modern governments closed off the exit options for laborers — through, in Marx's memorable phrase, "bloody legislation against the expropriated."[4] And if the initial stabilization of the labor market relied on state support, its reproduction has been no less dependent on regulation and public intervention, as famously documented by Karl Polanyi.[5] It was Polanyi who insisted that the very existence of a market in labor power was unthinkable but for constant and ubiquitous public regulation.[6] Similar stories can be told in the case of trade — both internal and external — and the management of currency.[7] In all these spheres, Polanyi argued, intervention is necessitated by a basic fact about capitalist markets: their inherent instability, and the welfare effects of this instability, generates a constant pressure on the state toward their management.[8] Capitalism creates an endogenous pressure for its own regulation.

The noteworthy feature of late development is not that states regulate markets but that their focus shifts from *managing the effects* of accumulation to *accelerating its pace*. This is, of course, a stylized characterization of the phenomenon, and, like all such renderings, admits to qualifications and exceptions. But there is no gainsaying the fact that, in the past century and a half, less-developed countries (LDCs) have structured their economic policies around the task of catching up with their more advanced rivals.[9] Toward this, the core strategy has been to hasten the transition from agricultural to industrial economies and, within that, to ratchet upward the pace and quality of capital accumulation. Perhaps the most well-known form of state intervention toward this end, especially in the earlier wave of late developers, was land reform, which was intended at once to deepen the spread of commodity production within agriculture, increase the production of raw materials and wage goods for industry, and, in turn, provide a larger domestic market for the latter's goods.[10] Land reforms belong to a class of state actions aimed at speeding up the pace of industrialization by manipulating the environment in which firms function, while leaving the firms themselves more or less untouched. From the start, however, there has been another kind of state policy, increasing in significance, which has been geared toward more directly influencing the industrial sector itself — the public subsidization of domestic enterprises.

The turn to subsidies has become an increasingly important aspect of state intervention in late developing countries. Alice Amsden has gone so far as to refer to it as the defining element of development strategy in the current era.[11] And, indeed, when examining the historical record of national development policies in the twentieth century, it is easy to see that state subsidization has been at the very heart of it all. First, where capital is simply uninterested in investing, the state has directly substituted for private firms through public enterprises: this has been most conspicuous in infrastructure and the capital goods sectors. Second, when capital has shown an interest in investing in particular sectors but lacked the resources to do so, public monies have been used to socialize the costs of the undertaking by providing cheap finance and, in some cases, guaranteeing acceptable rates of return. Lastly, where capital is on precarious footing in relation to international competition, governments have provided protection from such threats through the erection of trade barriers.[12]

The institutional capacities demanded of the state flow from the tasks it assumes; if its responsibilities in late developers were defined by the supply side of the subsidization process, then the chief concern of political elites ought to have been to add to the state's extractive ability — in order to collect the resources to be doled out to capital — and its managerial expertise — in order to manage those enterprises that substitute for private firms. And it is no surprise that, since the provision of subsidies has been a core component of industrialization programs, states in LDCs have placed a great deal of emphasis on these aspects of state strength. To take one prominent example, tax reform has been taken as an indispensable component of economic strategy, precisely in order to acquire the resources needed to fund development programs.[13]

In the halcyon days of development economics after the Second World War, it was this dimension of state capacity that attracted the most attention. Experts and politicians frequently considered increasing the available investable resources as the key to rapid development — as captured, for example, in W. Arthur Lewis's dictum that the central problem of economic development is to raise the savings of an economy from 5 percent of national income, to 15 percent.[14] Not surprisingly, the problem of state strength was understood mainly as relating to its *fiscal* capacity, the accretion of which was seen as the most pressing immediate task. It is no exaggeration to say that, at an overarching level, the impressive increase in the fiscal capacity of LDCs in the twentieth century has been driven, in substantial measure, by a perceived need to increase and streamline the flow of resources toward the investment process.[15]

But the subsidization process also brings with it another set of responsibilities, which carry in train the need for an attendant set of state institutional capabilities. As the complement to the provision of subsidies, states have also, to varying degrees, attempted to ensure that they are put to productive use. This has been motivated by the realization that providing domestic industry with greater resources is no guarantee that they will be invested in ways conducive to rapid growth. Development literature has highlighted two broad reasons why a policy of rapid industrialization may require more than just an increase in the level of financial resources at firms' disposal. First, the complementarity of investment decisions can create a variety of *coordination failures*.[16] In sectors involving economies of scale, firms will be hesitant to sink funds into projects that may not command a sufficiently large market; in basic and intermediate goods sectors, this market is frequently the investment projects of downstream enterprises.[17] On the other hand, downstream firms will not undertake new investments unless there is an assured stream of inputs coming from more basic industry, or from imports. Unless the appropriate coordination is effected among related investment projects, the subsidies made available to firms will very likely be directed to other, less risky lines. But this will simply mean a perpetuation of the very industrial structure that policy makers are trying to alter through their industrialization program.

Hence, in such cases, the provision of subsidies is accompanied by an explicit move to coordinate the investment decisions of the firms themselves. Perhaps the most well-known institutional mechanism or this has been French-style indicative planning, described with such admiration by Andrew Shonfield in his classic study of postwar capitalism.[18] One of the key components of indicative planning was for the state to collect the disparate investment plans of domestic enterprises and, through an iterative process, bring them into line with one another. In developing countries, indicative planning has often been conjoined with efforts to organize firms into collective bodies — cartels or associations — which, in tandem with state planners, monitor and regulate the sectoral spread of investment.[19] Both mechanisms are designed to reduce the uncertainty of the investment process by, among other things, allowing firms in complementary lines to communicate — either directly or through the state.

A second reason why subsidies may not be enough to generate rapid industrialization stems from the fact that the highest *private* returns to firms may come from investments that do not generate correspondingly high *social* returns.[20] In such situations, if the resources channeled to domestic capitalists are fungible (which they often are), there is a high likelihood that they will be invested in projects that bring high profits but do nothing to alter the industrial structure in the intended direction. States have therefore designed a variety of mechanisms to *regulate* the actual flow of capital into the desired sectors. Some of these are formal: firms may be required to secure an investment license from planning agencies before they can enter into a particular line;[21] they may have to show proof of success in particular high-priority lines before they are allowed to expand into others; entire sectors may be declared off-limits for a period, hence forcibly closing them off to new investment; firms may be forcibly merged in order to reduce excess capacity; and, most important, they may be punished if they ignore policy signals or if they do not abide by stipulated agreements — through, for example, being refused a renewal of an investment license. States also use less formal techniques to influence investment decisions: the phone call to the managing director, the subtle threat of an especially close inspection of tax returns, and the like.

Coordination is important because, without it, firms may find themselves unable to undertake projects they find desirable; or, in other cases, it may induce them to alter investment plans in light of new information about the designs of other firms. Compulsion, of the kind described in the preceding paragraph, is important because simple coordination may not be enough. The gap between private returns and social returns may be such that firms simply do not have the desired investment on their agenda, with or without the state-sponsored collective action. Therefore developmental states in the twentieth century have typically deployed some combination of both. Together, they have functioned to turn state-sponsored industrialization from the simple provision of subsidies — which was much more the case with late-nineteenth-century late developers — to a more organized strategy of industrial policy and planning.[22] This process of ensuring that subsidies do not turn into outright gifts and giveaways is what Alice Amsden has referred to as the "disciplining" of capital.[23] So for a developmental state, subsidization and discipline are two sides of the same coin.

INDUSTRIAL POLICY AND STATE CAPACITY

Just as the commitment to subsidies requires adequate extractive capacity from the state, so the turn to discipline makes its own demands on state structure and capability. To coordinate the investment strategies of a large number of firms — or even a small number, for that matter — is no simple task. More difficult still is the goal of monitoring their performance, establishing clear and dependable lines of communication, and devising mechanisms to hold their feet to the fire in case of noncompliance with prescribed standards.[24] Add to these the need to ensure that the information collected about targeted sectors is processed and distributed adequately *within* the state, and then utilized to revise policy prescriptions. It goes without saying that such responsibilities call for states that have formidable organizational resources at their disposal. So just as it cannot be assumed that states will have the fiscal capacity needed for funding development projects, we cannot be certain that they will be endowed with structures adequate for organizing the investment strategies of firms. If anything, the organizational capacity for industrial policy is more problematic. The simple existence of a state implies that it has a respectable ability to extract resources from the society that supports it. If this ability is found inadequate, it often simply calls for the intensification of existing extractive practices or for their extension to new sectors of the economy. The move toward industrial planning in the postwar period, however, called for the state to take on functions that were historically unprecedented. It is not simply a matter of extending old methods to new domains — it often demands the creation of entirely new bureaucratic and inter-agency structures, and new forms of expertise.

The upshot is that states attempting to foster rapid industrialization cannot be assumed to possess the institutional capacities that the task requires. It is somewhat extraordinary, therefore, to observe how recently the problem of state capacity, on this front, has come to occupy the attention of development scholars. It is not that the importance of disciplining firms per se was lost on them or, for that matter, on state functionaries. As the preceding discussion suggests, the effort to coordinate the strategies of local capitalists was a fairly natural outgrowth of the subsidization process. Policy analysts and bureaucrats in the postwar years routinely gave a nod to imposing performance standards on firms.[25] But what was not appreciated as fully was how difficult it would be to carry out such commitments successfully. In the Indian case, for which considerable evidence will be presented in this book, it is difficult to escape the impression that policy planners often thought that, once the orders were handed down to the relevant agencies, the heavy lifting was finished. This is even more evident when examining the work of economists and other experts of the time, who were keenly aware of the important role to be played by the state in industrial policy but were far less concerned about its capacity to actually carry out its responsibilities. The state was not only assumed to be standing above the sectional pressures of civil society, but, perhaps even more damaging, it was assumed to possess the institutional capacity required to turn its policy pronouncements into actual achievements.[26]

The debt crisis of the 1980s is something of a watershed in this regard. Its onset brought into relief the insufficiency of simply channeling funds toward the private sector, since the countries that were hardest hit had been awash in liquidity for years, only to see it flowing into relatively unproductive projects.[27] This is not to say that the crisis was seen immediately as proof positive of the importance of state discipline. In fact, in many quarters it was — and still is — adduced as evidence for the futility of *any* kind of state-led industrialization strategy.[28] In certain respects the travails of the 1980s in many developing countries were seen as a necessary outcome of the turn away from free markets, and therefore as reason to embrace neoliberalism. *Politically* the momentum certainly swung in the direction of the critics, and has remained with them, though the Mexican crisis of 1994 and then the East Asian collapse of 1997–98 abated it somewhat. But *intellectually* the early victories gave way to a series of counterblows coming from the new scholars of East Asia. This body of work made it abundantly clear that it was not the fact of state intervention that plunged the debt-ridden countries into crisis but rather its quality. And this quality, in turn, depended to a significant degree on the kind of state that was presiding over the development process.[29] In the wake of this scholarship, the possibility of state-led development has witnessed a resurrection of sorts. But it does not constitute a return to the heady optimism that seemed to blind scholars of the immediate postwar era. Instead of the *omnipotent* planner, the recent scholarship has offered us the *embattled* planner, whose success depends very much on the environment in which he functions — both within the state and without.

The Elements of State Capacity

So what is the institutional environment that allows for industrial planning to turn into disciplinary planning? There is no particular mystery to the ingredients.

A RATIONAL BUREAUCRACY

First and foremost, the state needs to be endowed with a coherent, internally coordinated policy apparatus. And the necessary condition for attaining such coherence, as Peter Evans has so forcefully argued, is that policy agencies be guided by norms of bureaucratic rationality.[30] The importance of bureaucratic traditions has come to light partly from the study of East Asia, but it is safe to say that its real significance has been brought home by the disastrous experience of countries such as Zaire and the Philippines. In these latter regions the absence of any kind of rational state tradition generated political economies in which public functionaries simply used their office as a mechanism for predation (Zaire), or, at the other extreme, economic elites colonized and then bled policy agencies for personal enrichment (the Philippines).[31]

The virtue of a well-oiled bureaucracy is that it prevents both the slide into individualistic predation as well as the easy colonization of state agencies. First, a bureaucratic tradition generates norms of comportment for state functionaries and, in doing so, channels their actions away from individualistic practices. It does this by putting into place abstract and clearly specified rules, and ensuring that functionaries' decisions are guided by such rules, rather than by their own private interests.[32] The effects of rule-following are compounded by a second mechanism crucial for state cohesiveness, namely, the adherence to clearly specified norms of recruitment and career mobility.[33] The establishment of such criteria for bureaucratic promotion reinforces one of the effects of proper rule-following: they orient functionaries away from personal gain and toward the duties attached to their station. They also, however, generate a kind of esprit de corps within the bureaucracy: the knowledge that they belong to a highly select "club," with similar qualifications and rare skills, creates a corporate culture among functionaries, which in turn secures state cohesiveness.[34] This sense of exclusiveness helps to repel attempts at colonization by economic elites, insofar as it generates a sense of purpose and of a collective, exalted enterprise.

Nodal Agencies

But for the kind of coherence needed for developmental states, bureaucratic rule-following per se will most likely be insufficient.[35] Economic agencies within the state — ministries, lending institutions, and so on — can often be saddled with responsibilities that are in conflict with one another and, more important, with the requirements of rapid industrialization. It is very common, for example, to find conflicts erupting between planning agencies, which typically favor easy credit policy and are willing to tolerate inflation, and central banks, which are responsible for monetary stability.[36] This is not the fallout of an administrative culture that is inattentive to the importance of rules; it is a conflict generated by the rules of the agencies themselves. Furthermore, the very functioning of the state, which involves inter-agency wrangling and competition for resources, generates conflicts within the administrative structure. And in these conflicts the rules of bureaucratic procedure easily become a weapon that agencies use against one another — as a means of protecting territory, hoarding information, and so forth[37] In such situations a fragmented state apparatus, rather than a cohesive one, results.

The problem is that formal bureaucratic rationality can only assure that state functionaries attend to the duties of their station; it cannot make the stations themselves cohere. A developmental state certainly requires the formal rationality that a culture of rule-following delivers; but, above that, it requires a *strategic* rationality, one that is geared toward a *particular* end.[38] Policy agencies not only have to be administratively functional, they have to be arranged and rearranged as the surrounding environment changes in order to attain a specified goal, namely, rapid industrialization. For this, the micro-level rationality that bureaucracy allows has to be supplemented with a more meso-level *inter-agency coordination*.

Typically this has been provided by the creation of some kind of nodal agency, which has real, institutionalized authority within the state to coordinate the ministries and policy agencies connected with economic policy. The importance of a nodal agency was initially brought to light by Chalmers Johnson in his classic study of the Japanese experience, in which the Ministry of International Trade and Industry played a pivotal policy role;[39] in the intervening years, however, it is Korea's Economic Planning Board (EPB) that has stolen the spotlight and emerged as the exemplar nodal agency.[40] I shall have more to say about the EPB, and how it functioned in Korean industrial policy, in chapters 3 and 7. For now, let us simply note that its importance lies in its role as — to borrow a term from our Althusserian past — the *factor of cohesion* in the developmental state. This was the agency which, in the exemplar developmental states, made certain that the disparate responsibilities of the economic ministries cohered around the project of rapid industrialization.[41]

EMBEDDEDNESS

A well-functioning bureaucracy and inter-agency coordination are two features that secure the cohesiveness of the developmental state. But aside from its internal cohesion, the state also needs to be endowed with instruments through which policy makers and administrators can communicate with firms around the strategy of industrialization. State managers cannot discipline firms if they lack information about performance and productivity; they can hardly organize coordinated investment, backward and forward linkages, and provide public goods, if they are isolated from market dynamics; in turn, firms cannot be expected to abide by performance standards or surrender required information if they are not provided with access to planners. The construction of structured interactions with market actors has come to be referred to as the state's "embeddedness" in the economy, specifically, in the industrial sector.[42] This task can be fulfilled by any variety of concrete institutions: in East Asia, a common one was the state-sponsored trade association, which acted as the conduit to firms in a particular sector or industry;[43] in India, this role was to be played by "development councils," which were sector-specific consultative bodies of state functionaries, industry representatives, and sometimes union officials;[44] variants can also be found in European-style "social corporatism," with its state-sponsored tripartite bargaining structures.[45]

Whatever the particular institutional form it takes, this dimension of state structure has proven to be of central importance in the construction and implementation of disciplinary industrial policy.[46] This is not to say, however, that institutional variations are without significance. As I argue in chapters 7 and 8, there is a big difference between institutions that serve as genuine forums for bargaining and reportage, and those that are basically "talking shops." In the latter, industrialists are present not in any official capacity as representatives of their sector but simply as advisers drawing on their own experience. This is not without its use — eliciting the opinions of experienced businessmen can be of considerable assistance to policy makers. But it has distinct disadvantages relative to a more corporatist setting, in which firms are organized into some kind of association, and industrialists in policy bodies represent the sector in an official capacity.[47] Not only is a "talking shop" of less use to planners, but it can quickly lose legitimacy with domestic industry, as it is not organically linked to the actual policy process.[48]

A proper bureaucracy, a nodal policy agency, and dense ties to the industrial sector — together these three elements go a considerable distance toward providing the state with the capabilities it needs for disciplinary industrial policy. The first two appear crucial for the state's internal cohesiveness, and the third secures for it the external links required to discipline firms. They do not, by any means, exhaust the list of possibilities. But these are perhaps the mechanisms that exercise the greatest marginal impact, and whose importance is the most widely acknowledged. They are now just about universally recognized as being necessary for successful industrial policy, regardless of the analyst's attitude toward state-led development. Furthermore, confining ourselves in this fashion to a small list of components also has a distinct analytical payoff, in that it becomes easier to trace the conditions that may be responsible for particular states being weaker than others.[49]

The upshot of the preceding arguments is that the variation in the quality of state intervention is governed, in substantial measure, by the variation in the strength of these institutions. I argued in the beginning of this section that most states did not find themselves endowed with these instruments when they embarked on their development programs. Therefore the onset of these programs was, in many cases, *coeval* with state building, rather than being preceded by it. Political elites were forced to create appropriate state institutions as they crafted industrial policy, building them in tandem with it, and in reaction to it. But is this kind of state-building project historically realistic? There is certainly room to argue that it is not, and that, in many respects, simple inertial forces govern the whole matter. A bureaucratic tradition, for example, cannot be created overnight, and a state embarking on an industrial policy will, to some degree, be bound by its particular traditions of statecraft—however strong they may be. But the argument from "historical momentum" ought not to be overdrawn. Even if a functioning bureaucracy cannot be created overnight, it can certainly be strengthened and reformed where it *does* exist. And this kind of reform can have quite a dramatic impact, as we will observe in the discussion of Korea. Further, other instruments are much more amenable to rapid institutionalization, even if they cannot be created ex nihilo. Nodal agencies, for example, have sometimes evolved somewhat slowly, as in the case of MITI, but they have also been created and consolidated virtually overnight, as in the case of the Economic Planning Board in Korea. The institutional capacity of the state economic apparatus can therefore be built up rapidly, as new challenges appear on the horizon. Whether state managers can, in fact, succeed in this task is, of course, a different matter. But it is important to recognize that their failure—if it should so materialize—is not to be prejudged simply on the basis of inherited historical traditions.

So the task of building state institutions for promoting rapid industrialization is formidable but ought to be within reach of many aspirants. Indeed, that such states were built in Taiwan and Korea, two countries that were not even considered candidates for success in the 1950s, underscores this point. But this only serves to make the rarity of successful state building all the more puzzling. Why, if the mission was so pressing, were the successful efforts not more common? Why did so many political elites find themselves encumbered with state institutions unsuited to the task of disciplinary industrial policy?

STATE CAPACITY AS DILEMMA

The Appearance of Consensus

On the face of it, there ought not to have been prohibitively strong structural forces blocking the process of state building in the postwar era. Starting at least from the 1930s, there emerged in many LDCs a powerful consensus around the desirability of state-led rapid industrialization. Since the collapse of world markets during the Great Depression, powerful political impulses emerged in developing countries for governments to come to the aid of "their" local capitalists. This was especially true in Latin America but was also the case in parts of the colonized world, like India.[50] The motor behind this political pressure was provided by business groups, who saw the Depression as a challenge as well as an opportunity. Three issues in particular animated local capitalists: first, and predictably, the need for protection from international competition, for which they drew on the venerable arguments in favor of "infant industry protection";[51] second, the need for state assistance in the acquisition of inputs, especially finance and raw materials;[52] and lastly, and somewhat surprisingly, business groups argued in favor of some central coordination of economic policy, as against its dispersal across provincial governments.[53] Such demands were initiated as early as the 1920s and continued to grow into the postwar period.

Capitalist pressure was an important component of the impulse toward state-coordinated industrial development. Complementing this was the fact that political elites, too, found it in their interest to argue for such policies. Most immediately, they provided a tremendous avenue for the advancement of a stratum of bureaucratic functionaries and political managers, who were the most advanced section of the newly emerging middle class. The growth of the state translated into greater power for this very articulate and visible section of developing societies.[54] This is not to say that political elites were driven by sectional interests alone. Certainly many among them were motivated by a genuine commitment to national development. But there can be little doubt that the nationalist aspirations of these groups found wider purchase at least in part because of the avenues they opened up for the material advancement of new middle classes. Hence, as Peter Evans has observed, rapid industrialization under state aegis emerged as a "shared project" between the state and capital, for "neither can implement the project on their own, and each brings something to the task."[55]

Which brings us again to the puzzle: if there was a consensus around this project, then how did it transpire that so many attempts at state building ended as failures? After all, insofar as rapid industrialization required appropriate interventions by the state, the process of installing the needed state institutions ought to have been seen as a necessary accompaniment to industrialization itself—indeed, even as a precondition of it. The most common answer to this puzzle places emphasis on conflicts within the political elite. On this view, state-building was successful in those cases where political elites were able to organize *them-*

selves for the job: by forming strong parties, overcoming resistance within the state, recognizing the need for centralized administration, creating networks of ties with firms, and so on.[56] And the reason that state building failed in many cases, despite the historic opportunity presented by the coalition with capital, was supposedly that political elites were unable to get their house in order. This, indeed, is a prominent explanation for the outcome in India: despite the alliance of the Indian National Congress with domestic capital, the argument goes, the Congress, because of internal squabbles, and because of its dogmatic commitment to a socialist economy, built a state that only served to stifle local entrepreneurial initiative.[57]

There is absolutely no doubt that intra-state conflicts played an important part in many such cases. But there is another explanatory avenue open to investigation, which, if conjoined with the statist approach, could also yield rich dividends. This is to reexamine the whole question of there being a "shared project" between political elites and local industrialists. It is not that the putative consensus around state-led industrialization did not exist—it very much did. But scholars have tended to elide the difference between an agreement around the *fact* of state intervention and an agreement around its *modalities*. While there was indeed a consensus around the former, we ought not to presume that it extended to the latter. In fact, there is good reason to predict that there would have been significant controversy around it. And this goes to the very heart of the question being examined here, namely, why so many political elites were unable to install appropriate institutions for disciplinary industrial policy. If indeed there was conflict around the modalities of state intervention, then, in all likelihood, this would have extended to the institutions being built to enable such intervention. This being the case, the relative failure of many state-building projects may very well have been produced by conflicts between the state and industrialists, and not simply through conflicts within, or predilections of, the political elites.

The Possibility of Conflict

What is it about the modalities of state intervention that might generate conflict, and hence impede the installation of a genuinely developmental state? The problem arises from the fact that the commitment to subsidization brings with it, for state managers, an impulse to impose *discipline*. Industrialists in developing countries can be expected to enthusiastically support the commitment to subsidize and protect local enterprise. They can therefore be expected to embrace many aspects of state building that are required purely for the subsidization of their profits[58]—this

has extended in many cases even to such measures as the nationalization of banks and the extension of the public sector.[59] What such measures have in common is that, for the most part, they manipulate the
environment in which private capital functions—boosting its profits
and increasing its liquidity—while leaving the actual disposition of
funds to owners and managers. This relation between state institutions
and capitalists changes, however, when planners move to actually ensure that firms are willing and able to invest in ways that conform to
policy priorities.

Earlier in the chapter I described the disciplining process as consisting, broadly, of two parts: coordination and compulsion. Although the
two differ in significant ways, they have a feature in common: both
elements entail, for the state, a shift from manipulating the environment
in which firms function to manipulating the firms themselves. This is
important because, in doing so, the state has to rely, to varying degrees,
on the use of coercion to ensure the desired outcomes. Even in the case
of the state's role as coordinator, there is call for the occasional, judi-
cious use of arm-twisting and cajoling. To take the paradigmatic case:
while the state's role in French indicative planning was, in theory, restricted to coordinating investment by collating firms' disparate investment plans into an aggregate model, it was always backed up by the
coercive use of credit and state finance.[60] French planners did not simply
try to increase the pace of investment by reducing the uncertainty that
firms faced; they also pushed managers into making the desired investments by using finance in a carrot and stick policy. Hence, even though
indicative planning—the exemplar of hands-off, purely consultative industrial policy—supposedly restricted the state's role to simply providing managers with information about market conditions and then letting them adjust their own investment plans, it actually shaded into
measures that looked a good bit like simple compulsion.[61] This should
not be surprising: even in the process of collecting information, planners
might have to resort to coercing it from recalcitrant managers fearful
that their competitors might use it against them or simply suspicious of
any governmental encroachment;[62] or when coordinating vertically
linked or complementary investment chains, planners might find themselves confronted with a firm that prefers a different course of action.
So while coordination need not rely on coercion, it sometimes has to
resort to it, and it may in fact work best when the threat of force can be
reliably invoked.

Needless to say, the second component of the disciplinary process—
simple compulsion—only amplifies the state's intrusion into the domain
of firms' management. Whether it is in a negative form—as when sectors of the market are closed off to new investments—or more direct—

as when planners organize mergers in oversubscribed sectors or require firms to invest in targeted lines—this instrument amounts to a forcible encroachment on the independence of private investors. Hence, if the state's role is to extend beyond the provision of subsidies to undertaking measures designed to extract adequate performance from firms, then a degree of coercive intrusion into the investment prerogative would seem unavoidable.

Of course, such intrusion brings with it some very real benefits to capitalists collectively, as well as individually. If successful, the channeling of investment flows and the imposition of performance standards can accelerate the traversal to greater competitiveness, thereby increasing the profitability and enhancing the long-term viability of local enterprises. Therefore, at an important, albeit general level, it is certainly consistent with capitalist interests. But it also brings some real costs. First, there is no avoiding the fact that measures such as those under discussion mean that capitalists lose a significant amount of freedom over where, when, and how much to invest. Since many regard the control over investment decisions to be an essential element of private property, these measures require that capitalists willingly accept a limitation of their own class prerogative.[63] Second, at a more mundane level, it means having to deal with an intrusive bureaucracy as a matter of course in a very wide range of decisions. Even under the aegis of the most conservative administration, this amounts to industrialists having to "haggle" over investments with career bureaucrats. Third, the hard fact is that ceding such power to the state runs the risk of having it fall into the wrong hands—there is no guarantee that the intrusive and meddling planning apparatus will always remain in the hands of parties that are ideologically acceptable;[64] nor is there a guarantee that the bureaucrats actually administering industrial policy will be above using their power to line their pockets or to favor their particular clients.

In sum, if policy makers want to avoid letting the subsidization of industry turn into giveaways, they will have to build institutions that give them some power over firms. But this brings with it new problems. While there are good reasons for industrialists to support disciplinary industrial policy, in so far as it could, if successful, strengthen their competitive position, there are also good reasons for them to oppose it, since it could leave them vulnerable to a meddlesome and grasping state bureaucracy.[65] The upshot is that there is no reason to assume that capitalist support for state-led development will go "all the way down," encompassing both its disciplinary as well as its subsidizing activities. The process of building institutions for the implementation of such industrial planning could very well elicit opposition from local capital— and quite rational opposition—not to the idea of state subsidization of industrial development — for that, we should expect to see widespread support — but to the idea that the state has the right, and ought to have the power, to make demands on enterprises in exchange for the subsidies channeled their way. This is the manner in which the modalities of industrial policy could very well lead to conflict between the state and local capital, despite the shared commitment to subsidizing industrial development.

Why It Matters

Here, then, is a possible clue as to why, despite the alliance between industrialists and political elites around industrial development, the construction of state capacity to promote this mission was so uneven. State managers, at mid-century and after, faced a pointed dilemma. The commitment to subsidizing domestic enterprises was taken as binding, but the ability to coax adequate performance from them was limited. This latter ability would depend on building, fairly quickly, adequate institutions within the state, such as those enumerated in the preceding section. But the very project of adding to the state's capacity for this purpose might elicit concerted opposition from domestic industrialists wary of bureaucrats' intrusion into their most prized domain. The end result, therefore, could very well be a process of state formation in which these crucial institutions remained underdeveloped, rendering state managers unable to carry out the tasks for which the institutions are required. Whether the whole process culminated in this fashion would depend on which of the consequences that discipline brought in train motivated domestic capital — the possibility of greater competitiveness or of becoming burdened with an intrusive state. If the former, then the project of industrialization would be a genuinely shared endeavor, and the project of state building could proceed smoothly; if the latter, then the outcome would be far less certain, for the appropriate state institutions would have to be installed over the opposition of domestic capitalists.

This gives us a framework for understanding the divergent outcomes in state formation, which does not rely on the statist premise that the critical mechanism is the quality of, or conflicts within, the political elite. While the orientations of state managers and political leaders are indeed important, the preceding arguments suggest that their ability to successfully install developmental states may be mediated by the reactions of local firms to the project. The analytical focus, therefore, needs to shift from an exclusive focus on the state to a consideration of its relations with local classes. The same arguments, however, also call for modifying the characterization of "late industrialization" as a joint project between the state and firms. Nothing in my arguments calls for rejecting this view. Rather, I contend that, although there may be a consensus around the *fact* of state intervention, it may coexist with considerable tension around its *character* — in particular, around whether it should or should not be disciplinary. This is crucial, because a large part of the puzzle regarding the developmental state has to do with this very issue — why the ability to impose discipline has been so uneven across cases.

That being said, we are now in a position to approach the facts. In what follows I summarize the chapters to come in a fashion that ties them to the arguments of the preceding section. The arguments are broken up into two broad sections. The first summarizes part 2 of the book, which are the chapters on the *installation* of the state apparatus in India and Korea. Here the animating issue is, why were political elites in Korea able to put a developmental state into place while their Indian counterparts were not? I show that the divergent outcomes are quite consistent with the arguments developed so far. Then, in the second section, I summarize part 3 of the book, the chapters dealing with the *reproduction* of the state. There are two main issues in this regard. First, how did the different capacities of the two states, once installed, matter? And, just as important, if the quality of the state did matter, and the Indian state was in fact unable to perform the tasks required of it, then why did political elites not reform it in an appropriate fashion? The arguments of part 2 explain how India became saddled with a substandard developmental state; those of part 3 explain why, having put such a state in place, Indian elites then had to learn to live with it.

Installing the Developmental State: Four Theses

Thesis 1: *State building in India was stunted because of a highly organized and concerted offensive launched by the business class against the idea of disciplinary planning, whereas it was successful in Korea because state managers were able to harness a leading segment of the business class to the developmental agenda.*

In both countries, political elites came to power with a firm commitment to building developmental states. If anything, the project was more clearly enunciated and conceptualized in the Indian case. The difference was that, in the latter, state managers met with concerted opposition from domestic capital, whereas in Korea they did not. This is, it should be noted, a revisionist view of the Indian case, perhaps even in the extreme. It is a matter of almost unanimous agreement among students of Indian development that the onset of industrial planning was underwritten by solid support, even enthusiasm, on the part of the business class. According to the accepted view, India was just about unique in the developing world in having a bourgeois class that had announced its support of capitalist planning even before the attainment of Independence in 1947. This support found its most visible expression in a two-part document published in 1944–45, in which six of the leading industrialists in the country not only declared their enthusiasm for industrial planning but even laid out the rudiments of what such a plan might look like. This document, which has become known as the Bombay Plan (after the city where the authors convened), is typically seen as the template on which future plans were constructed. The support from capital was, in turn, balanced by a deep commitment to planning on the part of the Indian National Congress as well, particularly Jawaharlal Nehru, who instituted the new developmental state soon after Independence. Given this putative level of support among relevant actors, explanations of state failure in India typically come to rest on the failure of state managers to take *advantage* of their opportunity. Instead of instituting a regime that could take advantage of bourgeois enthusiasm for planning, they built a leviathan that stifled business initiative, over-extended the administrative capacity of the state, and lost coherence in a dense web of bureaucratic red tape. The failure of the developmental state thus rests on the failure of state managers.

Against this venerable view, I argue that the Indian capitalist class did not support a developmental state *in the relevant sense*. The appearance of agreement between state managers and industrialists on the issue of "planning" was a mirage. Underlying it were two very different conceptions of what it entailed: for business, it meant support for the *subsidization* process: that is, that the state should do everything it can to encourage the development of domestic firms, while leaving the actual disposition of investable funds to the firms themselves; for state managers, its meaning was closer to a regime of *disciplinary* planning. Naturally, this difference brought with it sharply divergent ideas of the institutions through which planning would be carried out. So when the Congress government proposed legislation that would not only grant industry the protection and subsidies it sought but would also regulate the flow of investment and impose punishment on noncompliant firms, this triggered a massive offensive by the class against the new state. This offensive took the form of an investment slowdown, on the one hand, and, on the other, a concerted campaign in public and private against the proposed legislation.

The business offensive also had the effect of sharpening fissures *within* the Congress government on relevant issues. A natural consequence of disciplinary planning would have been the subordination of various economic policy agencies to the new Planning Commission, so that planners could impose discipline within the state as well as without. The economic downturn and organized outcry by business provided an opening to forces *within* the state to beat back the ambitious planning agenda. Thus the business offensive was joined by a group of ministers and bureaucrats—most notably those in the Finance Ministry—who now saw the new regime as a threat to their own power inside the state. The result was that planners were forced to make one concession after another, until the end product was one that was simply incapable of implementing disciplinary planning.

Conversely, in Korea, the new regime was able to successfully harness the leading segments of the industrial class to its project. Most of the literature on the Korean case has assumed that the project of state building was successful because the state was simply dominant over its industrial class. The need for a "pact" with the bourgeoisie is therefore underplayed. This makes for an interesting contrast with the Indian case: whereas in the latter it is the putative *existence* of a "pact" that leads analysis to statist conclusions, in Korea such an analysis is encouraged by the apparent *absence* of a "pact." But just as I show that, in fact, there was no appropriate alliance between the state and capital in India, I will show that, in Korea, it *did* obtain. Once this alliance was cemented around a clearly defined economic strategy, state managers could build institutions not only for doling out subsidies to firms but also for disciplining them. This coalition was an important precondition for Korea's success in state building; for even if state managers and some firms did harbor resentment against planners, it could not find expression in an organized wide-scale attack.

Thus the first lesson we gain from the India-Korea comparison is that, as argued in the previous section, the commitment to industrial planning *as such* from capitalists need not extend to *disciplinary* planning. When it does not, as in the Indian case, then state managers either have to refashion their agenda so that the objectionable elements are removed, making planning more amenable to the business class, or find some way to overcome their resistance and impose the new state on them—regardless of their preferences. On the other hand, if leading segments of the class can be brought onboard, then a pact can translate into a consistent and successful arc of state-building—as in the Korean case. The project of building state capacity is thus centrally mediated by the relation of the state to the capitalist class.

But this raises an interesting question: if the capitalists had such different orientations with regard to planning in India and Korea, what explains this difference? The argument that business power has a decisive effect on state building is not a trivial one, to be sure. As I have observed above, it is given little analytical play in the current literature. Nevertheless, the argument does seem incomplete without some investigation of the causes of this divergent orientation. Were there structural reasons for Indian capitalists to oppose disciplinary planning? If so, why were they absent in Korea? If there were such mechanisms, can they be theorized at a general level, so that India and Korea are seen as exemplars of certain *types*, and not just two diverging cases? I contend that there were indeed structural reasons for the different orientations, and this is presented in the next thesis.

Thesis 2: *Indian capital opposed disciplinary planning because, in the import-substituting model that India was undertaking, it was rational for capital to do so; conversely, Korean capitalists offered greater support to it because Korea embarked on a very different development model—an export-led one—which made it in capital's interest to support a developmental state.*

Throughout the book I refer to import-substituting industrialization (ISI) and export-led industrialization (ELI) as two contrasting development models. There is no novelty in this; students of the subject commonly recognize the two as such. For our purposes, development models are important because they imply quite different conditions for capital accumulation; more precisely, they generate distinct capitalist accumulation strategies. These accumulation strategies, in turn, generate a different incentive structure for firms vis-à-vis the state-building project. One makes it rational to reject the idea of a disciplinary state, whereas the other induces its acceptance.

The Incentive Structure of Import-Substituting Industrialization

Why should import-substituting industrialization generate incentives to resist the disciplinary side of the state-building project? Two facts about this development model are relevant here: the nature of its economic benefits to domestic firms and the general market conditions in which it was implemented.

At the core of ISI was the doctrine of infant industry protection, which aimed to nurture domestic business undertakings to ready them for the rigors of the world market.[66] This had two sides to it. One was protection from foreign competition, through the erection of tariff barriers, quantitative restrictions on imports, and other such measures. These were intended to create a space for the products of local capitalists, which otherwise, it was felt, would not survive long enough to mature. The second side of infant-industry protection was the funneling of public funds to local firms—often the same ones that enjoyed protection — as subsidies, incentives, credit, and the like.[67] This second component was not only intended to assist firms in their investments and growth, although that was certainly an important motivation. It was also driven by another conviction, namely, that domestic firms would not spontaneously take up the kinds of investments that were required for development. Domestic firms were more prone to venture into sectors that offered quick and high returns, like luxury consumer goods; but future development would require investment in projects that initially would not render high yields and carried greater risks. Private capital was to be drawn to these sectors by the offer of considerable subsidies and safe markets.

An important consequence of this development model was that it also typically generated a monopoly or oligopoly in the sectors targeted for growth. The first step toward this was, of course, the insulation from international competition. But competition among domestic producers was also attenuated, because of two factors. First, the small size of the market meant that it was easy for the first entrant to secure a dominant position. Since market and product diversification was still very narrow, there was a direct benefit of being the first mover into new areas and establishing market control. This would not be the case, of course, if each producer was very small, as in neoclassical models. But the fact about late developers is that firms are quite often very large, part of larger conglomerates, and can easily establish control over a considerable portion of the market.[68] A second route to monopoly or oligopoly was that policy makers themselves intentionally limited the number of producers in each sector, for fear of allowing over-investment and hence idle capacity. In a developing country, with its severe constraints, planners often saw excess capacity as an unconscionable waste of precious resources.

Development theorists have recognized these economic consequences of ISI; what has not been adequately appreciated are its *political* consequences, particularly with regard to the project of building disciplinary developmental states. The intention of political elites and economic planners in these countries was not only to offer local industrialists safe profit-making opportunities, but also to regulate and monitor the flow of capital, to ensure it went into targeted areas, and that it was used efficiently. Investment licenses and credit agreements were therefore typically granted with certain conditions attached to them, which stipulated the sector in which investment was to occur, the scale of operations, and so on. The agreements were, to the policy agencies, a kind of contract.

But for the recipients of the largesse, there was ample reason to resist the *terms* of these contracts. While state policy agencies granted subsidies to firms on the basis of a development plan with particular priorities, business houses made their own investment plans, based on their prognoses and their priorities — which often did not coincide with those of planners.[69] Domestic industrialists rightly saw ISI as a tremendous opportunity for growth and profits, because of the sectors being literally handed over to them free of international competition. But for this very reason, they also regarded the disciplinary component of ISI as an unacceptable encumbrance; in order to exploit their opportunities fully, firms would need maximum latitude to make their own decisions as to which sectors they would expand into, where new investments would be made. The best way to use ISI was to encourage the state's commitment to subsidies while insisting that private capital have the maximum latitude in their actual disposition. Again, this was all the more attractive because of the highly diversified character of many business houses.[70] Funds given by the state for one project could easily be diverted to other, more attractive projects being taken up by an enterprise in the business group — if the group could escape the state's monitoring apparatus.[71] Capitalists therefore had an interest in supporting the subsidizing side of ISI, while strenuously opposing the state's power to regulate and monitor the flow and utilization of investment.

This has a direct bearing on the orientation of business groups toward the state-building project. Since their preference is for the state to offer its assistance, but without the right, or the ability, to make demands on them, firms will have an incentive to oppose the project of building a disciplinary planning apparatus. This is not to say that they will oppose state intervention in the economy; after all, the offer of subsidies and protection can hardly be regarded as an instance of laissez faire. The opposition will be to a particular *kind* of intervention, one that seeks to regulate the flow and disposition of investment. The political consequences of ISI, therefore, are that capitalists will support the idea of planning as state subsidization of industry but not the project of building the institutional basis for a *disciplinary* planning regime. They will support building the means to mobilize and distribute funds to the private sector but oppose the state's moves to monitor and regulate their use.

The critical factor underlying this resistance to discipline is the attenuation of competitive pressures in ISI. One may wonder why firms would resent demands made by the state to perform at competitive standards, which, in many respects, is certainly in their interests. The reason is that, with the entry of international competitors blocked by protectionist measures, and with internal competition muted owing to the small size of the market, firms are under no systematic pressure to constantly upgrade their operations.[72] With each influx of newly acquired credit, managers do not feel compelled to increase the efficiency of existing undertakings, since there is no imminent threat of losing market share. Instead, as long as their market positions are secure, there is an incentive to enter new lines, new market niches, as first movers, and secure a dominant position.[73] The state's insistence on operating at certain warranted levels of efficiency are thus resisted in favor of diversifying their position into new, lucrative fields.[74] The way that ISI thus generates a peculiar political incentive structure for firms can be appreciated better by turning now to the political consequences of export-led industrialization.

The Incentive Structure of Export-Led Industrialization

Most developing countries in the aftermath of the Second World War resorted to ISI as the nucleus of their development strategy.[75] But starting in the late 1950s, and especially in the early 1960s, many countries began placing a greater emphasis on exports in their economic policies; in a very few cases, this push for export promotion was carried even further, so that exports came to occupy the strategic core of the development policy.[76] This was the case most famously in Korea and Taiwan, which are rightly considered the exemplars of an export-led path of industrialization. Two features of ELI need to be highlighted before proceeding to examine its incentive structure in order to avoid misunderstandings.

First, The ELI model I refer to in this discussion and throughout the book ought not to be confused with its forerunner in the nineteenth century. During that period many developing countries adopted growth paths heavily dependent on exports—this, of course, was the case in South America but was also true for much of the colonial world, including India.[77] This initial brand of ELI differed from that which emerged after the Second World War in that it was almost entirely based on the export of raw materials and agricultural commodities; the emphasis in the latter variety, however, has been not only on manufactured goods but also on continually moving up the value chain to products of increasing technical sophistication. So it is not simply the turn to exports that concerns us but rather exports of modern manufactured goods.

Second, it is important to note that the turn to this more contemporary variety of ELI was not symptomatic of a broader commitment to an open trade regime, as some commentators have suggested. The turn to ELI was not tantamount to the adoption of free trade. Indeed, in Korea, imports continued to be subject to strict controls and the domestic market, through the 1980s, to be carefully protected.[78] Nevertheless, exports grew at phenomenal rates starting in the 1960s, until they accounted for a substantial part of the domestic economy. Further, aside from the quantitative importance of exports, they exercised a critical qualitative impact on the economy, as the regime used firms' export success as a condition for access to further subsidies.[79]

With these caveats in mind, we can turn to the incentive structure of the development model. Unlike the case of ISI, where investment plans of local firms were shaped by the easy opportunities of the domestic market, firms in ELI had to adapt to the rigors of international competition. And from this difference in economic challenges came the difference in political incentive structures. Recall that the resort to import controls and protection across the developing world—including Korea—came because of the apprehension that competitors from more advanced economies would decimate local producers. If local firms could not be expected to withstand international competition at home, they hardly stood a chance as exporters to the markets of the industrialized countries. Indeed, the difficulty of entry and survival there would be even greater. First, they would have to secure funds to make the minimum scales of investment individually; but a more important obstacle was that these investments would have to be in technologies that the firms had no experience and training with; worse yet, any given investment would typically require complementary investment by other firms, either upstream or downstream, if it were to bear fruit.

In addition to these investment-related obstacles, there was also the overhead cost of establishing marketing and sales networks in countries where the firms had no history of success, a barrier which, as Gary Gereffi and others have pointed out, is perhaps the most important one for producers in textiles and other light industry—precisely those lines in which LDCs first enter as exporters.[80] Success thus involved overcoming the paucity of funds, acquiring and mastering new technology, solving the problem of investment coordination, and gathering the information and contacts needed for marketing. These problems, of course, are present in any capitalist market, whether local or external. What made such problems pressing and forbidding for exporters, however, was that they had to be solved in a context of intense competition with producers who had access to far greater funds, who not only had experience with new technology but had, in fact, *developed* it, and who had a massive advantage in sales networks.[81] This placed severe pressure on exporting firms not only to solve the problems just outlined but to do so rapidly and on a continuing basis.

The severity of these conditions makes for a different kind of relation with the state, as compared to that in ISI. First, state managers now have far greater leverage against firms, since the latter must depend on the former to solve many of the problems just mentioned. So long as firms are willing to hazard the export market, and hence must survive in that market, they have to depend on the state to provide a steady stream of finance, help acquire and unpack technology and its attendant supports, establish sales and marketing networks, and, perhaps most important, coordinate investment in complementary lines. This gives state managers the bargaining power to make demands on firms in return for the subsidization and support they provide.

But just as crucial is a second aspect of the state-business relation: under ELI, not only does the state's role assume greater importance, but firms have a greater incentive to *comply* with state managers' demands for performance. Under ISI, the ability of firms to secure dominant positions in particular lines and deter entry in them tends to sever the link between high profits and efficient production; businesses can take loans or credits granted for a particular project and divert them to other lines, with no great worry about losing market share. But when firms have to perform in the more competitive external markets, they have a direct incentive to adhere to the state's demands for increasing the efficiency of production in a line, because the firm's survival in that line depends in steadily increasing its productivity.

It is this second effect of ELI that most sharply distinguishes its incentive structure from that of ISI. In both models the state provides firms with assistance and support; in both models, as a conditionality of that support, it demands certain standards of performance in return. But in pure import-substituting regimes, the economic environment gives firms an incentive to take the subsidies the state offers while rejecting its prerogative to regulate their flow and utilization. Hence firms will also have a political incentive to resist the agenda to build a state with the institutional capacity to impose disciplinary industrial policy. In ELI, however, because of the more extreme competitive pressure, firms have a greater reason to take the subsidies and channel them into upgrading productive efficiency. Further yet, they have an interest in having a state that has the capacity to effectively coordinate and monitor investment in order to more ably assist their expansion into external markets. The more stringent competitive conditions, the greater uncertainty, the tenuous relations with customers, and so on, all decrease the margin for error that firms can take for granted in safer domestic markets. While slow and maladroit coordination of investment may not be a serious problem in protected domestic markets, where firms do not face strong competitive threats, it poses a considerable threat in export markets, where firms have to be able to respond rapidly to new entrants, new technologies, and the like. In addition, matters such as quality standards, which are almost a non-issue in monopolistic domestic markets, become exceedingly important under more competitive conditions.

Here, too, state monitoring and imposition of such standards is not only unlikely to elicit firms' objections but is, in fact, more likely to be welcomed. The upshot is that in export-led strategies capitalists have no reason to oppose the project of building a disciplinary developmental state; indeed, they have good reason to support it — so long as such a state is a precondition for export success.

The different environment established by the two development models thus calls for quite distinct accumulation strategies for local firms, and the latter, in turn, generate different incentives with regard to the state. If the preceding argument is correct, then we have an explanation for why the two capitalist classes reacted differently to the state-building project. For Indian industrialists, the knowledge that future policy would be framed around the protection of domestic industry meant that they could make easy profits without the whip of market competition. On top of this was the promise of other kinds of subsidies — cheap credit, inputs, and the like — which would only further grease the wheels of local accumulation. Lastly, adding to this was a fact peculiar to the Indian case. In the immediate postwar scenario, British firms were evacuating segments of the Indian market, leaving open vistas for Indian capital's entrance. It was therefore in the interest of the largest business houses to demand the widest possible latitude regarding the disposition of their funds, so they could swiftly move into the vacated sectors — at least some of which would be low priority for economic planners. With such opportunities already on tap, what did the disciplinary components of development policy have to offer, other than a meddlesome and overweening bureaucracy? With easy profits virtually guaranteed, a disciplinary state was only an encumbrance. For Korean capitalists, however, having a state with considerable capacity to monitor, coordinate, and even coerce firms made eminent sense — for it was an essential precondition for surviving in export markets. It is not that the Chaebols, the few enormous conglomerates dominating the Korean industrial structure, relished the idea of an intrusive state; rather, they considered it an acceptable encumbrance since the rewards it brought were so handsome. For firms coming from small, developing economies, success in the massive markets of the West meant almost limitless expansion and growth. Hence, far from an encumbrance, a disciplinary state was a needed ally in the competitive battle.

This takes us some distance toward understanding why the installation of a developmental state met with such different degrees of success in the two cases. The Indian capitalist class had a very strong incentive to reject any such agenda, because of the incentives generated by the ISI model. This did not necessarily make the prospect of installing a disciplinary planning apparatus impossible. It did imply, however, that if such a state were to be a real possibility, it would either have to be *imposed* on the class against its preferences or somehow the ordering of preferences itself would have to be changed. To accomplish the latter, the Indian state would have had to move rapidly to ELI, which, if the arguments in this section are correct, would have made local firms much more amenable to the state-building agenda. So why did the Indian state not take either of these alternatives? The next thesis examines the problem of adopting ELI, and the following one explores why state managers could not simply impose a strong planning apparatus on the class against its will.

Thesis 3: *Korea was able to switch from ISI to ELI because certain conditions virtually unique in the world economy were available to Korea, conditions that simply were not available to other LDCs. Absent such conditions, business classes throughout the developing world resisted attempts by governments to turn to an export-led strategy, and this was true in India as well.*

Why India chose to turn to ISI as the first step in its development strategy is not a mystery. The fact is that in the countries which undertook rapid industrialization programs after the Great Depression, it was simply taken for granted that the road to success involved a period of import-substitution. This premise was common to political and economic elites throughout the developing world at the time — including Korea and Taiwan — and was the basis for the "shared project," as discussed above. It was the immediate and perhaps most important reason why, in the aftermath of the Second World War, a turn to exports was simply not on India's agenda — for it was not the agenda anywhere. But other, more structural reasons also made the commitment to ISI attractive, and hence perhaps overdetermined.

The most important inducement to ISI, and deterrent to ELI, in the 1950s may have been the nature of the international trade regime. This decade is often presented as the time when trade barriers were removed throughout the world, in contrast to the protectionism of the interwar period. What this overlooks, however, is that the removal of barriers was limited mainly to trade within countries belonging to the Organization for Economic Cooperation and Development (OECD). The provisions of the GATT regime that allowed for freer trade did not apply to all trade, only trade within Europe and between Europe and North America. Imports from developing countries were subject to differential and higher tariffs relative to those faced by imports from other advanced industrial countries. In effect, this put the threshold level of productivity required for success beyond the reach of developing countries.[82] Developing countries have often been criticized for their "export pessimism" in these years, and it may be true that a concerted commitment to exports may have allowed for a greater degree of success in foreign markets. But it seems far-fetched indeed to suppose that strategies which placed exports at the core of the development process, as ELI did, could have been possible at this stage for newly industrializing economies.

A third and less recognized reason for the reliance on ISI was the influence of the U.S. aid conditions on LDCs. In an important but still unpublished dissertation, Yeonmi Ahn has described the myriad ways in which, throughout the 1950s, countries receiving grants from the United States for the purchase of capital goods were prohibited from exporting commodities produced through their use.[83] Since foreign assistance in the 1950s was mainly in the form of grants, and not commercial loans, this meant that U.S. restrictions applied to any country receiving American aid. This acted as a powerful deterrent to ELI, given that almost all developing countries lacked a capital goods industry of their own; most of the semi-developed nations were heavily dependent on the United States for machinery, parts, and raw materials for their manufacturing activities. It was not until the next decade, Ahn argues, that changes in U.S. law made it legal for recipient countries to use materials acquired in aid packages for exports.[84]

As a result of these three factors, almost the entire developing world embraced ISI during the 1950s, including Korea and India. Only in the early 1960s was there a turn to exports, and, again, this was partly occasioned by a change in the attitude of the United States. The passing of the Foreign Assistance Act of 1961 made economic aid subject to disbursement as loans instead of grants, which meant, in turn, that recipients would have to generate exports to repay the loans.[85] American advisers in LDCs thus began urging their hosts to put greater emphasis on exports. Partly as a response to this advice, and partly as a reaction to their own need for greater foreign exchange, a large number of countries in the 1960s turned to export-promotion — including India and Korea.

But only Korea and Taiwan not only maintained a commitment to export-orientation but took the policy even further, to ELI.[86] In country after country, state managers found that local industrialists refused to treat export markets as anything but an outlet for excess capacity in their plants. Committing to exports as the center of their investment strategy was something that business classes refused to countenance. The reasons are not hard to fathom: as discussed earlier, export markets were the site of fierce competition and hence uncertainty, whereas firms in domestic markets were virtually assured high and safe profits. Furthermore, the commodities that LDCs were capable of exporting in large quantities—light manufacturing goods—were ones that were highly dependent on ready links to sales and marketing outlets, which is precisely what firms in LDCs lacked.[87] This meant that the start-up costs of success in the markets of the industrialized countries were considered too high, especially when compared to the ready alternative of domestic markets.

Why, then, did Korean firms take the plunge? Commentators suggest that there were two predominant factors: pressure by the United States to place greater emphasis on exports[88] and the steadily approaching saturation of the Korean domestic market.[89] Whereas the former induced the *state* to orient its *policies* toward export promotion, the latter generated a willingness among *firms* to orient their *production* in the same direction. Added to this was the recognition by Park Chung-Hee himself that the massive import needs of his development plans could not be sustained unless the country also generated correspondingly impressive gains in export revenues. Hence, by the early 1960s, there was a switch from a pure ISI strategy to one reliant on ELI.

Although these three factors undoubtedly played an important role in Korea's adoption of an export-led model of industrialization, it is highly unlikely that they *sufficed* in themselves to actually produce the turn. In fact, by the 1960s, the two crucial conditions adduced to be the impulse behind ELI—U.S. pressure and a sated domestic market—*were present in a large number of developing countries*. We have already seen that the switch to aid in the form of loans induced American advisers to press for export promotion among virtually all their clients. It is also true that domestic markets were rapidly becoming saturated across the developing world—in South America, South Asia, and the Middle East. Despite this, when state managers attempted to initiate a turn to export promotion, they found stiff resistance from local firms. In one country after another, firms continued to use foreign markets as outlets for inventory buildup during the business cycle rather than as the primary destination for local manufactures.[90] As I show in chapter 8, India was no exception to this dynamic when it launched its own export program in the late 1950s and found little interest among local capitalists. But the range of examples extends far beyond the subcontinent; indeed, in discussions of the Korean and Taiwanese cases, it is often forgotten that attempts at ELI were quite common in the 1960s.[91]

External pressure and slumping local markets cannot have been sufficient, therefore, to push Korean firms outward (though these two conditions may have been necessary). I suggest that the turn to ELI emerged because another factor came into the picture, one that was absent in most other cases but played a crucial, enabling role in Korea, and it was this: during the 1960s Korea fell within the ambit of Japan's industrial strategy, which had as one of its components the *relinquishing of markets in the United States to Korean firms*. In other words, Japanese firms were vacating markets in the United States and bequeathing them to Korean firms, along with their marketing and sales outlets.[92] In addition to this demand-side bounty, Japanese trading companies — the Sogo Shosha — also secured critical finance and machinery for Korean firms, which was essential to building the muscle required for competitive success. Japanese firms, for their part, were able to secure a captured market in Korea for their capital goods and other inputs, as well as a lucrative outlet for their excess savings.[93] In any case, this meant that Korean capitalists were able to circumvent the most important entry barriers to the markets of the industrial world, the very barriers that acted as a powerful deterrent to all the other developing countries. A similar dynamic occurred in Taiwan, and also at about the same time, in the early 1960s.[94]

The Korean state-building effort was thus the beneficiary of an enormous bit of good luck in terms of timing: Park came to power in 1961, just as Japanese capital was moving to make its switch in its industrialization strategy and establish ties with Korean capital. Of course, this was not sufficient to produce a developmental state; the Chaebol's partnership with Japanese capital simply gave the new regime an opening it could exploit. That it did exploit it successfully was not preordained. This was a genuine achievement of Park Chung-Hee's developmental state, and the statist literature has traced its vicissitudes with admirable thoroughness. Indeed, it is difficult to imagine that Korean firms would have committed themselves to competing in export markets for anything but the most rudimentary manufactures, had they not had credible signals from the political elite that the state, too, would be restructured around the ELI strategy, just as firms were restructuring themselves. Japanese patronage was critical to securing *entry* into export markets; *remaining* in them successfully would depend on the state fulfilling its role with respect to the provision of subsidies and coordination. It was therefore of central significance that Park's restructuring of the state around the demands of developmentalism was concurrent with the arrival of Japanese patron firms into Korea.

Korean ELI was thus made possible by a combination of luck and genuine effort. It was plain good fortune that, as Park initiated a turn to export-promotion, Japanese firms were looking for regional partners to whom they could off-load their low-end export lines: this was crucial in *lowering* a critical set of entry costs into world markets. But also critical was that Park, at the same time, launched his program of transforming the state in a developmental direction: this added to the momentum toward ELI by further *socializing* another set of costs to firms, as well as solving basic coordination problems. So while the Japanese partners lowered some costs of entry, the state socialized others and also provided services essential to export success. This was a combination of inducements that states in other countries simply could not muster.

In the rest of the developing world, ISI remained the order of the day. This had the effect of turning local capital against the idea of disciplinary planning, because state discipline was not required for garnering high profits. If political elites were to install a developmental state, it would have to be through a route that was different from the Korean one—there was no developmental pact in the offing, at least not of an appropriate kind. The new state apparatus, therefore, would have to be installed *over the resistance* of domestic capital. And this brings us to the next, final issue, that frames the structure of politics during the critical years after Independence.

Thesis 4: *A full explanation for why the Indian National Congress was unsuccessful in installing a developmental state is that, in addition to facing a mobilized business class set against the project, Party leaders also* demobilized *a massive and quite organized labor movement—thus reducing the state's leverage against the capitalist class.*

To readers familiar with Indian history, it might appear as somewhat mysterious that the simple fact of business opposition could have forced the state to retreat on its agenda, as described in Thesis 1. For it was also the case that, in the aftermath of the war, the subcontinent was rocked by the biggest labor upsurge in the first half of the century. Further, there was an enormously widespread sentiment across the labor movement and the Congress that business had prospered tremendously during the war—often by taking advantage of scarcities, sometimes by creating them—and therefore ought to submit to state regulation in the new dispensation. This being the case, the Congress leadership should have been able to take advantage of this sentiment to push through its agenda. Indeed, though this has been lost in the historiography of India, the sheer size and scope of the postwar labor upsurge did, for a period, intimidate the bourgeoisie enough for it to ask unions for a "truce," in exchange for which it acceded to a series of far-reaching concessions on economic matters.[95] So there was not only a social base for reigning in domestic capital, but it was sufficiently powerful for the latter to take note.

But instead of using this movement as a battering ram against the unified business class, the Indian National Congress chose to *split* the movement by creating a new union federation, and then *demobilized* it. This was premised on the Congress High Command's own antipathy to labor as an independent political force. Throughout its history, the organization had maintained a discreet distance from the growing work-ing-class movement in the cities. At best, the top leadership's attitude toward it was of an Olympian paternalism and, at worst, one of out-right suspicion and hostility. Elements in the Congress did call for a closer relationship with unions — mainly the Congress Socialists led by Jayprakash Narain — but their calls went unheeded and, indeed, were part of the reason why the Socialists bolted from the party in 1948. So instead of riding the crest of the union movement, the Congress High Command reacted to the escalation of class conflict in the postwar years by strengthening its alliance with *capital* and demobilizing *labor*. This was partly brought about by its basic antipathy to the movement; it was also occasioned, however, by its own confidence that, indeed, there was a basis for an alliance with domestic business around state-led indus-trialization. But as I argued in Thesis 1 and will show in detail in chap-ter 6, this was a fatal misreading of the situation, for business had no intention of cooperating. With the labor movement excluded from the political scene, the supporters of planning in the Congress found their hand greatly weakened relative to the forces lined up against the agenda. The Congress slid more deeply into a strategy of making con-cession after concession to business demands in the hope of placating Indian industrialists, a strategy that failed spectacularly. Thus the Indian planners attempted to appease the capitalist class, in a situation where they needed to usurp their autonomy from it.

LOCKED IN PLACE: THE REPRODUCTION OF THE STATE

The outcome of the initial critical years after Independence in India was the installation of a regime that was, as Peter Evans has correctly ob-served, in the middling range of developmental states. The arguments adduced in the preceding pages go some way toward explaining this outcome. What we have not yet understood, however, is why these in-stitutions *persisted*, despite their obvious failings. Why did political elites not reform the institutions in the appropriate direction, given that they were committed to fostering economic development? One answer, which is rarely made explicitly, is that institutions reproduce themselves through a kind of inertial dynamic — once in place, they generate a mo-mentum that makes it too costly to remove them, or perhaps clouds the availability of alternatives. But while it is true that institutional change has costs, so does the reproduction of *useless* institutions. That the lat-ter nonetheless remain in place must be seen as a choice state managers make *between* two costs, and hence not part of an inertial process. Nor is it plausible to suggest that the dust thrown up by existing institutions — perhaps in the form of roles and expectations that sustain them normatively — obscures the availability of alternatives. This may be valid for some institutions, but it is not convincing in the case of those overseeing economic planning. There are clear benchmarks for failure and success in this field, against which planners constantly weigh their own performance, and which therefore make failure something that is difficult to miss. Further, the variety of institutions in the world is something that is visible, and even studied, by all bureaucracies. A kind of menu of options is constantly available.

A more plausible alternative is the idea that states remain in place as an outcome of power relations. Once institutions are in place, agents coalesce around them, as the reproduction of the former becomes a condition for the welfare of the latter. And this may be a condition that obtains within the state as well as without. I suggest that the Indian experience be understood along these lines, but with a twist. The analysis thus far has operated at two levels: one is the structural level, at which I have investigated the relation between accumulation models and capitalist class interests vis-à-vis the state; the second is the institutional level, which has to do with the internal structure of the state. I have tried to show that the process of institution building was heavily affected by the orientation of the capitalist class and that this orientation, in turn, was conditioned by the accumulation strategy each country adopted. To be complete, the analysis of the state's immutability, once in place, ought also to operate at both levels, not simply the institutional.

By the 1960s state managers knew that the institutions of planning were not functioning as originally intended. There could have been two routes to reform, each resting at a different level: the first option would have been to change the orientation of the business class, making it more amenable to discipline. The most obvious route to this would be changing their investment strategy, from domestically based to export-oriented. Failing this, the second option would be to overhaul the state itself, so that the economic apparatus would be up to the task of monitoring and disciplining capital, even within an ISI strategy.

I show that both strategies were tried, and both failed. Starting in the early 1960s the Indian state installed a series of export-promotion measures to encourage firms to ease pressures on the external sector and induce greater efficiency. But it met with little success, for two basic reasons: first, without an entree into world markets, of the sort the Koreans received from Japan, Indian firms were hesitant to take the plunge; indeed, the foreign investment that did come into the country often *forbade* local partners from exporting their products. These investments were typically made by American and British multinationals, which differed in this respect from the Japanese firms that went into Korea—whereas the latter were interested in using their host country (Korea) as a springboard for exports, Western multinational corporations (MNCs) were mainly interested in their host country's internal market. The lack of easy access to foreign markets was made all the more significant as long as domestic markets continued to offer easy profits. Second, the fractured and uncoordinated nature of the state itself made its efforts to subsidize exports quite ineffective, and hence made the credibility of its overall export promotion program suffer. Credits and subsidies were neither effectively coordinated with existing taxes and surcharges that exporting firms paid nor were they effectively disbursed. This compounded the problem of the firms' own resistance to exporting.

A second route would have been to initiate reform at the level of the state itself, to make the planning apparatus more capable of disciplining capital. Now, even had such reforms been successful, it is highly unlikely that they would have resulted in an industrial policy as successful as that in Korea, since Indian firms would still have had more incentive than Korean firms to ignore policy signals. But it was a moot issue. Once the window for reforms opened, the legacy of past failure once again meshed with the dilemma of the current juncture. The central outcome of the struggles of 1947–51 had been the installation of a Planning Commission that had little power to implement its own plans. As a secular trend, the weakness of the planning agencies served to gradually erode their legitimacy within the state. The Planning Commission came to be identified with ineffectual red tape and bureaucratic hurdles, rather than with policy success. This gave its rivals within the state greater power to block any moves to increase its control over plan implementation; the agenda for reform was thus tilted *away* from giving planners greater power over capital, and *toward* granting capital greater freedom from the state.

There was thus little chance that a call would come from within the bureaucracy and political elites to give the planning agencies greater power. Rather, the call that was issued was to radically reduce the scope of planning itself, a tacit recognition of the ineffectiveness of the whole enterprise. The only remaining chance for a turn to a Korea-style state apparatus came with the installation of the new prime minister Indira Gandhi in 1966. But unlike Park Chung-Hee in Korea, Gandhi was in no position to overhaul the state apparatus: having little organizational base within her party and with few political allies, Gandhi turned, instead, to stabilizing her base within and without the state. And one of the conditions of this was sidelining the Planning Commission to the periphery of the economic state apparatus.

The end result was that, as India entered the 1970s, the "reform" impulse had spent itself, and the institutional structures of the state were even more enfeebled. Although the state continued to implement industrial policy and churn out five-year plans, its capacity to implement them was even weaker than in the preceding decade. The state had become locked in place.

PART II

Installing the State

CHAPTER 3

The Origins of the Developmental State in Korea

INTRODUCTION

This chapter serves two functions: first, it provides the foil to the argument that is offered about the Indian case by showing that the state-building agenda in Korea was supported by an alliance between state managers and the capitalist class, and that this alliance itself was made rational by the adoption of an export-led model of development; second, it offers a new explanation of the origins of the developmental state in Korea, one that diverges from the reigning consensus. In particular, it shows that the turn to ELI was not foisted onto the bourgeoisie by a dominant state but, rather, was opted for by leading industrialists themselves; the reason they opted for it, furthermore, was that they had an unprecedented opening into the most lucrative market in the world — the United States — thanks to an alliance that was struck with Japanese corporations, which essentially handed over their sales networks to the Koreans.

Two features of the Korean experience appear to make it worth serious study: first, until its drastic dismantlement starting in the late 1980s, the state had an uncommon capacity to exert influence over its business class, and hence avoid the fate of many developing countries, where state subsidies and protection became a trough at which businesses come to feed. How did a regime with such power consolidate itself? Second, this ability to discipline capital has developed in tandem with exceptional success in export markets of advanced countries. This, too, sets Korea apart from most of the developing world. What makes it especially interesting is that its export-led strategy came as a switch from a pure import-substitution policy that had dominated in the 1950s. The commitment to export-led industrialization thus involved modification of an established strategy of ISI, something other countries also tried but with little success. Both these phenomena — the developmental state and the turn to exports — were born virtually simultaneously. It is no surprise, then, that explanations of Korea's economic success tend to treat them together.

The view that has emerged in the literature, and which has received the assent of a growing number of commentators, is that both these phenomena — the Korean state's ability to discipline its capitalist class and the turn to ELI—were a symptom of the state's more general *dominance over* that class. The most popular version of this argument is that the Korean state after 1961 was able to achieve a position of dominance over its business class through a series of reforms: these included measures that increased the institutional coherence of the state—such as the creation of a nodal agency in the Economic Planning Board (EPB)—but centered most crucially on the usurpation of control over finance. Through the nationalization of banks in 1961 and the careful regulation of capital markets, the Korean state was able to bring its business class to heel; having achieved its position of dominance, the new regime launched its export drive and closely monitored capital's adherence to it. Both the ability to extract performance from business as well as the turn to ELI are thus presented as artifacts of the more general dominance of the state over capitalists. The developing consensus is thus *statist* in substance: industrial policy was successful because of the unique power the state had to override the proclivities of its own capitalist class, and it was this power that set Korea apart from other developing states.

The argument I develop in this chapter is, most broadly, in agreement with much of the new consensus. I agree that the Korean state was able to discipline its local firms to a remarkable extent; I also agree that the institutional basis of this capacity lay in the reforms of the state that were carried out after the coup of 1961, such as the creation of the EPB and the nationalization of banks; I also agree, finally, that this power was in large measure what accounted for the divergence in outcomes between industrial policy in Korea and that in other developing countries.

Yet I shall also urge that, in their zeal to overturn the neoclassical picture, the statists go too far. Specifically, I part company with them on the assertion that the Korean state was sufficiently autonomous from its capitalist class that it could simply impose a new development strategy—like export-led development—with little regard for how firms would react. My argument turns on a distinction between coercing particular *firms* and coercing large swathes of the entire class. Statists argue that the Korean regime's power extended to both domains; I will urge, instead, that while power over individual firms, or even groups of firms, was exercised with tremendous success, there is no reason to believe that the state's power over the entire capitalist class was any more developed in Korea than in other states. This is not to deny that the state wielded considerable power over domestic business; but all capitalist states have such power to varying degrees. The statists do not present any compelling reason to believe that such power was qualitatively greater in Korea than elsewhere.

Perhaps the most serious consequence of the statist exaggeration is the misunderstandings it generates about the origins of the developmen-

tal state in Korea: because the Park regime is assumed to have dominated its capitalists, the question of how it got them to switch to an ELI
strategy is not regarded as especially difficult. But once the thesis of
general dominance is rejected, the transition becomes more puzzling. I
shall show that, in fact, the transition occurred not because of the
state's unquestioned power over local capitalists but rather because of
the latter's own enthusiasm for it. And this enthusiasm, extremely rare
in developing countries, was made possible by a development that statists tend to overlook entirely but which was central to the story — the
emergence of an alliance of Korean and Japanese firms, which gave the
former group access to export markets that would otherwise have been
inaccessible.

It bears repeating that this critique of the prevailing wisdom does not
question the fact that the state did enjoy great success in disciplining
local firms — indeed that is a premise of this book. The argument here
simply urges that the limits to the scope of this power be realized more
clearly. Instead of a dominant state imposing a new development strategy on domestic business, and then punishing the ones that do not perform up to standard, I propose a state with more limited power. It was
a state that launched ELI in alliance with domestic business, not over it.
Further, it was the peculiar nature of ELI that gave the state the leverage
and the space to exercise its disciplinary functions. In other words, *pace*
the statists, it was not that the Koreans first built a developmental state,
which then herded local capitalists onto the new accumulation strategy.
The causal arrow, in fact, ran the other way — it was the launching of
ELI that provided the basis for building a developmental state.

In what follows, the statist argument is first presented in more detail.
I then show that, despite its insights, this school fails to make its case
for the state's inordinate power over capitalists. In particular, the two
sources typically alluded to — the legacy of colonialism and the usurpation of control over finance — cannot bear the burden that is placed on
them. The chapter then turns to an alternative account of the origins of
the developmental state in Korea and its relation to ELI.

THE TWO VARIETIES OF STATISM

The emerging consensus on the state in Korea during the quarter-cen-
tury after the coming of the Park regime in 1961 is aptly summarized in
one of the earlier analyses of the Korean experience, by Leroy Jones and
Il Sakong. The authors note that the heavy role of government in the
Korean developmental experience has led some to render it "Korea,
Inc." in a direct parallel to "Japan, Inc." But, they suggest,

> There is . . . one decisive difference between the two countries. In Korea, *the dominant partner is unequivocally the government*, whereas, in Japan, the reverse may be closer to the truth. . . . [In Korea], *the government's wishes are tantamount to commands*, and business dare not take them lightly.[1]

This position is echoed in an authoritative study contemporaneous with Jones and Sakong, which also takes the position that, in "Korea Inc., "it is the government that is the Chairman of the Board, with business holding a few of the directorships."[2] The proposition has tended to be maintained through the years by various students of the Korean experience. For example, a more recent book by Byung-Nak Song adverts to the "Korea, Inc." metaphor, which to him denotes a regime in which the state "was the primary decision maker," whose suggested economic targets were "taken by businessmen as equivalent to compulsory orders."[3] Then again, in one of the most detailed studies of the Korean case, Eun Mee Kim concludes that, while the power of the state has declined in recent years, the state-capital relation in the 1960s was one of "state dominance,"[4] that is, capital operated under the command of the state. We will encounter this strand of argument in more detail in a later section. But let us note for now that this position can be labeled *statist* at its core: in the relation between the state and business, it is the former that is said to be dominant.[5]

Of course, business must always operate in a policy environment that is nominally set by government. In this sense, "discipline" is imposed by the latter through a variety of ways—through tax policy, labor law, exchange rate policy, and so on. Industrial policy, however, presents a particular problem for governments because, unlike fiscal and monetary policy, it involves a more or less direct intervention in firm-level decisions regarding production and distribution. Instead of manipulating the environment in which all firms function while leaving actual investment decisions to owners, the state, through industrial policy, targets particular firms or sectors to influence decisions at the micro level. The mechanisms of this influence are often quite coercive: in Korea, firms that did not "go along" with state directives might find that their requests for credit were refused[6] or that they began to experience abrupt cutoffs in power supply[7] or that their tax returns were subjected to especially close scrutiny.[8] Any account of the developmental state must therefore explain how states acquire the power and autonomy to intervene in this, the most fiercely guarded prerogative of business.

Within the broader statist school, there are two positions regarding the roots of the developmental state. One is a distinctly minority view, which explains Korean developmentalism as a gift of its history, while the other, majority camp, sees it as the product of a more or less sharp break with the past. Both, however, agree on the fact of the state's domination over Korean capital.

THE CONTINUITY THESIS

This first variant of the statist school is, as observed above, a minority view. For proponents of this position, the unique capacity of Korean planners to enforce compliance was a happy legacy of the colonial and immediate post-colonial period. According to this argument, Korea as it emerged from the war of 1950–53 was bequeathed a state and a class structure that combined to provide a uniquely enabling set of conditions for industrial policy. The pillars of this legacy were the initiation of land reform, on the one hand, and the inheritance of a strong, bureaucratically efficient state structure, on the other. The former was critical in removing a class that proved to be an obstacle to rapid industrialization elsewhere both politically and economically, while the latter provided the state with the wherewithal to intervene effectively in the economy. In other words, land reform was crucial in enhancing state *autonomy*, whereas the bureaucratic inheritance was critical in boosting state *capacity*. Add to this the basic precondition that Korea was — by Third World standards — relatively developed industrially, with a foothold in light manufacturing and extractive industries, and one has a situation ripe for the advent of a developmental state.[9]

This argument has recently been subjected to effective critique by Stephan Haggard, Chung-in Moon, and David Kang, so I shall not dwell on it at great length.[10] But its basic weakness is that while it is plausible that the historical legacy of colonial rule and the war would *allow* a developmental state to emerge, it is by no means clear why they should *produce* one. Proponents of this strand of argument seem to rely on the premise that reforms and institutions of the sort they adduce are necessary for the emergence of a developmental state, and therefore, in demonstrating their presence in the Korean case, an explanation has been provided for why such a state did emerge. But even if we grant that such institutions were necessary for a successful interventionist state, it does not by any means follow that they were sufficient for it.

The history of Korea in the decade after the war bears out these doubts. Consider first the issue of the state. Here, the continuity thesis overstates the beneficial legacy of colonialism. It is true that the Japanese bequeathed a fairly developed bureaucratic structure to the Koreans; it is also true, however, that Syngman Rhee worked assiduously to mold this structure to his purpose, undermining its purported efficiency and solidity, and rendering it riven with the clientelistic ties that scuttled the chances of successful development policy.[11] Just as important is another aspect of the state which the continuity thesis tends to ignore, and that is the issue of intra-state coordination. Even if the bureaucratic legacy had been as propitious as this thesis claims, it would have run into the crosscurrents generated by the fact that, under Rhee, there was, in fact, no center of economic policy. Authority over such policy was shared along two axes: the U.S. representatives in Seoul and Rhee's policy regime, on the one hand; and, within the Rhee regime, between the various economic policy-making bodies, chiefly the Finance Ministry, the Korean Central Bank, the Monetary Board, and the legislature.[12] This parceling out of authority was a powerful obstacle to coherent policy, because not only was there no clear center of authority but powerful forces arranged themselves behind the various bodies, and the bodies themselves, owing to their different responsibilities, brought correspondingly different orientations to policy debates. Minimally this produced a deadlocked regime; maximally it generated genuine animus between the bodies. For example, a matter as simple as the annual budget was the product of wrangling between the Monetary Board (which was the arm of the United States), the Finance Ministry (Rhee's pagoda), and the legislature (dominated by the erstwhile landlords and old elites).[13]

This set of circumstances was further compromised by the nature of the state's relation to Korean business, which was thoroughly clientelistic. Rhee had no real base in Korean society — political or economic — and hence used the purse strings of government to buy the loyalty of domestic elites, particularly the business class.[14] The latter, in turn, happily conformed to the neoclassical economist's picture of avaricious, rent-seeking agents, geared steadfastly to profits from the manipulation of markets, and largely unconcerned with strategic investment in productive activities.[15] Note that this was not driven by an "exhausted" import-substitution regime in which businesses, having no outlets for their products, resorted instead to draining the public exchequer. Korea in the 1950s had just initiated ISI, and there were still ample opportunities for developing markets. The reason business resorted to rent-seeking activities was largely because it *could*; the easy access to state managers, the steady flow of U.S. aid, and the utter absence of any long-term strategy on Rhee's part made such short-termism an appealing alternative to the arduous and costly path of investment-led profits.

With a state apparatus of the kind just described, and the link to business that encouraged rent seeking instead of productive investment, it is difficult to see how the subsequent success of the Korean regime can be viewed as a continuation of the Rhee era. Nor can the 1950s be seen as a decade in which the basic prerequisites for success were present and all that was lacking was a regime sufficiently committed to development. On the contrary, conditions of the Rhee period were such as to actively prevent the emergence of a developmental state. What made the Park era different from that of his predecessor was not just Park's more determined passion for development. It was the fact that Park adroitly restructured the state itself to excise the institutional blocks to effective policy and, further, went about changing the state's relation to capital. Without such restructuring, there is no reason to believe that Korea in 1959 would have been any different than the Korea of 1969 or 1979. Indeed, American advisers present in Seoul in the late 1950s had just about entirely written off the country as a hopeless basket case.[16] Hence the emergence of a developmental state was not a product of history, in the sense that this variant of statism argues; it required, instead, an exogenous event, and this was the coup of 1961.

THE DISCONTINUITY THESIS

The argument for a continuity between the Rhee and the Park eras, in fact, has few takers. Far more common is the view that the military coup that put Park Chung Hee into power in mid-1961 was the critical event that endowed Korea with a developmental state. On coming to power, Park, it is argued, immediately set about rectifying the chief obstacle to effective industrial policy, namely, the patterns of corruption and institutional incoherence within the state. A second move was to rein in the kind of profiteering that businessmen had resorted to during the previous regime, which did not hold much promise for future economic development. This latter measure was launched with a flamboyant rounding up of the biggest industrialists, who were threatened with imprisonment and then released on their promise that they would hitch their wagons to the developmental project of the state. Oddly, despite the hint of a "pact" or compromise this episode conveys, it occupies an ambiguous position in the statist approach. Although the event is mentioned in almost all the accounts, its importance as an indicator of compromise is downplayed against the coercive power of the state over Korean capital. We shall examine the issue in more detail shortly, but for now the point to note is that this second variant of statism, while affirming the general dominance of the Korean state over capital, attributes it not to a historical legacy but to the changes wrought by the new Park regime. Once the dominance of the state was secured, its developmental ambitions were realized through the launching of the ELI policy and its ability to discipline its industrial class — thus was born Korean exceptionalism.

This account has much to recommend it. Park did indeed undertake reforms that were crucial to the subsequent success of the Korean state in extracting performance from its capitalist class. The revamping of the economic policy institutions, in particular, was of central importance in enabling the state to monitor, coordinate, and guide domestic capital. In this respect, this second variant of statism is superior to the first. Where I part company with it is on the matter of whether the reforms in question were capable of securing a *general* dominance of the state over the business community, so that the state could impose its own agenda on the class, regardless of the latter's own perception of its interests.

The main theoretical pillar on which the claim of dominance rests is the state's control of finance. Once Korean banks were nationalized, the argument goes, the state also secured its power over the business class. The burden of this section is to argue that the case made for the state's putative power fails to convince. There is no reason to think that control of banks gives the state sufficient power to unilaterally set the agenda, in the form of a particular accumulation model. Capitalists have a countervailing power of their own, through their control over final investment. Statists provide no argument as to how the state can be immune to this power, even if it does enjoy financial hegemony. But this does not demand that we reject altogether the importance of the state's control of this crucial resource. Instead, it suggests that we simply reformulate the scope of the power that it confers: while it does not enable the state to coercively impose new conditions onto the entire class—like an export-oriented development strategy—it does give the state an effective stick to wield against particular firms within the class once the strategy is in place.

This theoretical difference is of some significance: it not only provides a different analysis of the dynamics, and the limits, of the developmental state, it also calls for a closer look at the origins of the regime. I shall argue that, in assuming that the state was simply dominant over capital, and hence launched the new developmental regime and export-led industrialization on its own, statists overlook what is perhaps the critical factor that allowed for the policy change—the emerging alliance between Korean and Japanese capital. It was this alliance that made the sudden shift to ELI possible; further, it was the peculiar features of ELI that gave the state the leverage to discipline its capitalist class. It was not the case, then, that the turn to ELI and the ability to discipline domestic firms were both symptoms of the state's general power over capital. To the contrary, ELI emerged in large measure as an accommodation to the emerging orientation of local business groups, and it was ELI, in turn, that gave the state its newfound power to extract performance. Let us now turn to the facts of the case, and the statist arguments pertaining to them.

The Syngman Rhee regime fell in the fall of 1960, in the wake of new elections that were blatantly rigged by the incumbent. Rhee's ouster was followed by the ascent to power of Chang Myon, a development that turned out to be a short interregnum separating the Rhee era from that of Park Chung Hee. Chang Myon was able to hold power for scarcely nine months before being replaced by Park and his military junta through a relatively bloodless coup.[17] Although the Chang Myon interregnum was not given much attention in the initial studies of the Korean "miracle," the more recent analyses have shown that, despite the tenuous hold he had on power, Chang, in fact, attempted in his short tenure many of the same kinds of reforms that Park initiated more successfully in later years. In particular, Chang put on the table two measures that were to be carried forward with great success by the later junta: first, he maneuvered to give greater power and resources to the nascent planning agency, the Economic Development Council, which Rhee had placed in the Ministry of Reconstruction, thus signaling a more serious commitment to long-term planning;[18] second, Chang initiated the famous move against the biggest profiteers of the Rhee era, a move that has come to be known as the "illicit accumulation of wealth" episode. This measure was explicitly aimed at some of the biggest industrialists in Korea, who were known to have made fortunes through the black market and the manipulation of prices more generally.[19] Given his short tenure, Chang was unable to make much headway with either of these moves, but they were important in establishing a momentum for further reform, first, in signaling that Korean leaders were making initiatives for bureaucratic reform and, second, in immediately putting business on alert that changes in state-capital relations were on the anvil.

With the onset of the Park regime in May 1961, a genuine transformation of the Korean regime was set into motion, and that, too, was along the lines established by Chang.[20] First, the restructuring of the economic institutions of the state was completed and, in fact, taken further. Park immediately set about purging the bureaucracy of its most obviously corrupt denizens with an extensive review of the state apparatus; upward of forty thousand upper- and middle-ranking bureaucrats were screened in the initial months of power, and nearly two thousand were dismissed on charges of corruption.[21] It is impossible to imagine, of course, that corruption within the Korean state was confined to a scant two thousand miscreants, but the move was nevertheless of some importance: it sent a clear signal that graft, to the extent it was to continue, would not go unnoticed. The later trajectory of Korean development suggests that what was behind the "purge" was, in fact, not a commitment to eliminate corruption but to confine it strategically so that it would serve the political ends of the regime, without interfering with its economic strategy.[22]

Along with the effort to restore some coherence to bureaucratic functioning, Park launched his well-known initiative to curb the dispersal of effective authority between the institutions responsible for economic policy. Soon after the coup, a new Economic Planning Board was announced, which quickly became the apex body for economic policy and planning.[23] The new body took charge of statistical operations (previously housed in the Ministry of Home Affairs), the all-important budgetary operations (previously the provenance of the Finance Ministry), and overall plan coordinating authority (previously in the Ministry of Reconstruction). This effort to create a "super-ministry" reflected a critical element of continuity between the Chang and the Park regimes; the small group of planners in the Economic Development Council, which had been effectively sidelined by the Finance Ministry under Rhee, and had been newly empowered under Chang, found a ready audience for its ideas in the person of Park.[24] On the issue of monetary policy, the autonomy of the Monetary Board—which had been the main conduit for direct U.S. control over economic policy—was curtailed, making it a virtual arm of the Finance Ministry, and banks were brought under state control, so that their annual budgets as well as their top management became subject to approval by the Finance Ministry.[25]

The importance of these reforms lay not simply in the nominal restoration of bureaucratic efficiency but in their resolution of the institutional blocks to effective planning. The creation of the EPB and its promotion to the unquestioned nodal agency for industrial policy greatly reduced the conflicts between the state economic institutions; further, in vesting the EPB with powers of plan design as well as implementation, Park altered the balance of material power between state agencies, so that capacity of other ministries scuttling the planning process was also weakened. The control over the banking system that was established soon after served, in coming years, as a central mechanism to influence the flow of credit to industry, and hence to increase compliance with industrial policy. The overall effect, therefore, was to increase the capacity of the state to plan effectively.

With the restructuring of the state economic agencies proceeding on one side, Park also moved swiftly against the domestic industrial class. Immediately on achieving power, the military junta vowed to carry through Chang Myon's measures against the "illicit accumulators," threatening arrest and even expropriation.[26] In a well-publicized display of force, the junta rounded up and arrested many of the leading industrialists in the country as evidence of its resolve to eradicate the corrupt practices of the Rhee era. The strategy was not a punitive one, however. On arresting the businessmen, Park quickly called a meeting with leading representatives of the group and settled on a bargain: instead of a direct expropriation of their properties, the businessmen would face a series of fines, which, in turn, would be paid by investing the money in new enterprises. At one stroke, Park thus demonstrated that the junta held no brief against private property, while at the same time maintaining its dominance over the propertied class.

Some commentators have taken the release of the "illicit accumulators" as recognition by Park that the proper orientation toward the big industrialists was one of accommodation, not domination.[27] But the theorists of state dominance veer away from any such conclusion. Eun Mee Kim allows that the need to strike a bargain with industrialists after the initial arrests in 1961 could be taken as a sign that Park and the military junta "were forced to negotiate with the chaebol due to the latter's enormous influence" but advises that any such conclusion ought to be stoutly resisted: "the state was *clearly the dominant partner*, with capital under its control and with an expanded and reformed economic bureaucracy."[28] Karl Fields also agrees that the turn in 1961 was brought on with threats of imprisonment, reform of the bureaucracy, and, in particular, control over finance: "From this *position of dominance* and institutional capacity, the Park regime *engineered* Korea's export-oriented industrialization with the private Chaebol as the chosen instruments to carry out this strategy."[29] Ha-Joon Chang, in his otherwise excellent article on Korean industrial policy, repeats the importance of state control over finance, adding that, after these reforms, the business community were like "criminals on parole on condition that they 'serve the nation through enterprise' and, economically, a paper tiger *with little power to make investment decisions*—the ultimate capitalist prerogative."[30]

In this analysis, the state not only initiates a new strategy of economic development but, in fact, imposes it on an enfeebled business class. The key to the Korean success story for statists, therefore, seems to lie in a kind of "bootstrapping" model of the state: it is not that the state achieves its institutional capacity and power through a modus vivendi reached with business; rather, it secures its aims largely by first setting its house in order, usurping control over a key resource (finance), and then herding industrialists onto the new path. The rise of the developmental state is thus *causally prior* to the launching of the new development model.

Now, I agree with the statists that the "illicit accumulators" incident was not the harbinger of a "pact" between the state and the Chaebol. But, *pace* the statist position, this is not because the dominance of the state made pacts unnecessary. It is because the pact occurred later, around 1964–65, when the export-led strategy was made the pillar of the Second Five-Year Plan. To hold the earlier incident as the occasion of the formation of a developmental coalition is thus an empirical mistake. But before the evidence for this argument can be presented, the statist position must be addressed more fully.

A Critique of the Statist Discontinuity Thesis

It is one thing to say that the state initiates a new set of policies for future growth; it is quite another to insist that it can successfully *impose* them on its business class, regardless of the latter's preferences. These are quite strong claims, and it is surprising that Kim, Fields, Chang, and others do not expend greater effort in defending them. The debate over Korea is, after all, appearing in the wake of the long and intense discussion of the rise of the welfare state in the West, where many of the same questions about the relative power of the state were raised. Just as it was legitimately asked how states could impose welfare policy on intransigent capitalist classes in the West, we may ask how it came to be that the Korean state acquired its putative dominance over capital. If Korea's new development strategy was launched by the state, with the business class having to adjust to this turn regardless of its own preferences, wherein lay the source of this power?

Partisans of this view agree that the Park regime did not simply inherit its dominance over capital, as we have seen. It was, they argue, generated by a new factor, namely, *state control over finance*. In bringing the banks under the direction of the Ministry of Finance, the new regime radically increased its power to dictate investment strategies to capital. If this argument can be sustained, then, of course, the origins and subsequent success of the developmental state are mysteries no longer. The turn in strategy in the early 1960s is matched with a corresponding institutional innovation, and the two are connected with a plausible mechanism.

The control over finance is supposed to have given the Korean state sufficient power over the domestic capitalist class to enable it to impose a new development strategy of export-led development. Ultimately, whether or not this argument stands is an empirical question; and, as the following section will show, a careful examination of the early years of the Park regime in fact does not support the contention that the switch to ELI occurred because the state decreed it, regardless of how leading capitalists reacted. The empirical record, in fact, points firmly in the other direction. Nevertheless, despite the empirical evidence, there is also an important theoretical matter at stake here. Even if it is discovered that the capitalist class was a willing participant in the switch to ELI, it could still be claimed that this willingness was, in a sense, historically redundant. It could be maintained that this fact does not touch the basic argument about the state, namely, that even if Korean business had not been willing to make the switch, the state, through its control over finance, could have compelled it to do so. Hence, before we move on to the actual events, it will be useful to look more closely at the argument that state control over finance turned the Chaebol into a "paper tiger."

Now, it is part of the basic structure of capitalist societies that states enjoy a monopoly over the means of coercion and legislation, which automatically gives them considerable power over economic elites. This power is common to all such states, including late developers trying to initiate a process of industrial transformation. Nevertheless, it is also true that states are typically hesitant to unilaterally impose new economic policies on business classes because of the latter's control over investment. The introduction of new policy packages is therefore usually preceded by lengthy consultations with business representatives, and their effects on the investment climate are closely monitored. The statist argument appears to be that the control over finance gave Korean planners sufficient autonomy from economic elites to be immune to such worries, and hence the ability to unilaterally impose a new development strategy on the business class. The claim is therefore not only about the Korean state's power over its business class, but it is also about its power *relative* to the power enjoyed by other states. Control over finance supposedly gave Korean state managers a power to override considerations that handicapped their counterparts in other countries.

This counterfactual is not purely imaginary. As I shall discuss in more detail in the following section, the 1960s were a period when several late-developing countries attempted to push their economies in the direction of a greater reliance on exports. And indeed India, as I will show in chapter 8, was one such case; but most of these attempts met with very limited success, and this includes the Indian case. The exceptions to this rule were the East Asian cases. In many developing countries in the 1960s, ISI strategies had exhausted their run, leading to several attempts at export-led growth. But as Robert Kaufman has pointed out, the turn to world markets always remained cautious and halting, "export-adequate" rather than "export-led," and a primary reason behind this was the resistance of domestic business.[31] Similarly, despite its call to "export or die," the Egyptian government in the 1970s found its own efforts frustrated, again largely because of the resistance from domestic capitalists.[32] Could control over credit and finance be the reason that the Korean state was able to cajole its business class into the new strategy, where others so often failed?

Undoubtedly control over finance considerably increases the state's power over the business class. But it is not clear how this power could be sufficient to render state managers indifferent to the latter's reactions to policy changes. Consider the likely scenario if the state tries to unilaterally impose a series of new regulations or a new accumulation strategy — like export-led development — on the domestic bourgeoisie. If there is a widespread sentiment among firms that the new policy will be harmful to their profits or their rates growth, the most probable reaction will be a cascading decline in business confidence, as firms become unsure of future returns. If this does happen, the tangible result will be an economic slowdown, and this, in turn, will mean a decline in the *demand* for finance, since firms will be slowing down the pace of investment. Now, if the demand for finance is itself in decline, it is difficult to see how the state's *control* over finance can be an effective weapon over the capitalist class. Trying to use finance as a lever in this situation will be, to use Keynes's memorable phrase, like pushing on a string.

This suggests that, even though its control over finance undoubtedly increased the state's power, there seems no reason to suppose that this was sufficient to render it immune to the *countervailing* power that capitalists exercise through their control over final investment. And if state managers did have reason to be sensitive to the effects of a decline in the tempo of investment, then the statist argument about the unique power conferred by financial hegemony loses warrant. In other words, while such control may indeed have increased the power of the Korean state vis-à-vis capital, there is no reason to suppose that it gave it a power qualitatively greater than that enjoyed by other states. It could, of course, have been that what set Park apart from leaders of other states was his willingness to bite the bullet and suffer a period of slow growth in exchange for a turn to ELI. In this sense, it could be that the Korean state imposed the new strategy on its business class — and happened to get lucky in short measure as it caught on. This could be true — it is an empirical question. But the point is that this does not salvage the statist case that the Korean state enjoyed a singular dominance over its business class. Even if the turn to ELI had been imposed in this fashion, it would have been because of Park's political will and not because of some unique capacity of the Korean state.

It should be noted that once the new strategy was settled on — in the sense that large sections of the business class had switched their investment patterns accordingly — then there is no doubt that the control over finance was an effective weapon for disciplining individual firms. So long as business confidence remained high, the threat of withholding credit from recalcitrant firms could serve as a very effective weapon. The targeted business would face a real opportunity cost as the restriction in credit hampered its rate of growth, or resulted in closure. For state elites, imposing such sanctions would not entail great risk since, given that business confidence was high, it could be expected that other firms would pick up the slack generated by the targeted firm being punished. Hence, against a background of a buoyant investment climate, a state with adequate institutional coherence and capacity could effectively impose discipline on particular firms.

The key to the origins of ELI in Korea would thus seem to lie in the means by which state managers were able to elicit a switch to the new strategy by the business class without triggering a downturn in the investment climate. With the export-orientation model in place, so long as the investment climate remained buoyant and the state had the appropriate institutions in place, it could successfully punish those firms that did not perform up to standard. In this framework, the analytical focus shifts from the premise of overall state dominance to the conditions that enabled the state to elicit—not command—the turn to ELI by firms. The next section provides an account of how this was accomplished.

To anticipate, the turn to ELI was not imposed on Korean capitalists but was arrived at consensually; indeed, there was even pressure from business to initiate it. And this enthusiasm was, in turn, engendered by the ties that were developing between Korean and Japanese firms, which provided the former group with access to export markets that virtually no other country—except Taiwan—enjoyed. It was this access to markets that induced them to have a go at ELI, and not the coercive power of the state. Because it has been assumed that the state dominated capital, most commentators have failed to give due importance to the Japan connection.

Once this strategy was in place, the basis was laid for the Korean state's success at disciplining domestic business. Ready access to export markets was important to open the possibility of success—but it could not ensure it as an ongoing affair. In order to survive in the extremely competitive markets of the West, Korean capitalists required the helping hand of the state. That Korean firms could not survive in export markets without state assistance, at least in the initial decades, was important in increasing the latter's leverage. A partnership with the state now became the precondition for the extraordinary rates of growth enjoyed by the Chaebol in the three decades after the onset of the Park regime. Since the partnership generated such lucrative yields, state managers could impose coercive measures on particular firms without any great fear that they would trigger a downturn in business confidence.

Thus, on this argument, there is a close connection between ELI and the developmental state, just as there is in the statist literature. But whereas the latter version makes the developmental state causally prior to ELI, I argue it was the latter that was critical to the success of the former.

THE ORIGINS OF THE DEVELOPMENTAL STATE

This section is devoted to proving three basic points: first, that there is no reason to believe that Park had any intention of simply imposing his will on domestic business; second, that the turn to ELI was consonant with the emerging orientation of this class, which was generated, in turn, by its growing ties with Japanese firms; and third, that the new strategy was an important condition for the success of the state in disciplining capital, because now cooperating with the state was in the firms' interest. The empirical arguments can be enumerated briefly:

1. The Park regime, despite its initial rounding up of the biggest industrialists, was loathe to alienate them. Indeed, after the highly publicized arrests of the "illicit accumulators," they were quickly released and much of their "punishment" forgiven. Thus, far from being a "senior partner," the regime quickly recognized that it had to work within the constraints of business pressure.

2. The newly formed Park regime did not immediately launch an ELI strategy. In fact, its initial move, as represented by the First Five-Year Plan, was toward a firm continuation if ISI, with exports playing a decidedly minor role. It was only the onset of an economic crisis that compelled the regime back to the drawing board.

3. Once the crisis was under way, three factors combined to sway Park of the merit of an ELI strategy. The first was the initial success in exports experienced in the First Five-Year Plan; the second was U.S. pressure to generate more foreign exchange, which was bolstered by the decreasing quantity of aid the United States was willing to give. The third was the signal from Korean capital that exports were very much on its own agenda.

4. This willingness on the part of Korean capital needs to be explained. Since other efforts at ELI have foundered on the rocks of business resistance, it is this factor that sets the Korean case apart. I argue that what lay behind it was a growing alliance of Korean firms with Japanese capital, which afforded the former group access to markets that would otherwise have been inaccessible. Grasping at this opportunity, Korean business became a willing ally in the new strategy. The crucial component to actualize it was a normalization of relations with Japan, which both countries committed to by late 1963 but which became a juridical reality only in 1965.

5. Only after this class-level partnership showed promise was the state-capital partnership cemented in a series of measures committing the country to

an ELI path. Once this strategy was in place, agreed to by capital, the state was able to exercise its vaunted disciplinary powers without fear of provoking a class-wide reaction against them.

The First Phase of the Park Regime

As soon as the small group of army officers, led by Park Chung Hee and his brother-in-law, Kim Jong Pil, came to power, reform of the state economic apparatus and the initiation of an ambitious planning effort were placed at the top of the agenda. The measures enacted to remove the institutional pathologies and conflicts within the state, and to create a superordinate authority for the conception and implementation of economic plans, have been discussed above. In this regard, the argument presented here is in agreement with the statist consensus. But, *pace* the statist school, the striking fact is that Park and his colleagues had no intention of initiating a switch to an ELI strategy in Korea. Their goals on the assumption of power were far more modest and their vision narrower. Plans were to be established but not along the lines that ultimately came to be known as the Korean "model." It was only later, when this initial strategy failed and state managers were groping for a way out of the economic crisis, that an export-oriented path suggested itself as a viable alternative.

The immediate goal of the military junta was to find a stable social base for its survival. This involved policy along two dimensions: first, placating leading sections of business, and, second, finding a mass base for regime survival over the longer term, which in fact had to be created almost *ex nihilo*. Success on the first issue meant scaling back the threats that had been leveled at leading business houses. An immediate effect of the coup had been to bring business activity to a grinding halt, and business outlook was only further panicked by the decrees against the "illicit accumulators" of wealth.[33] Within days after the coup, top leaders arranged to meet with business leaders, already moving to persuade the latter to keep operations at a normal pace. Firms were assured that the anti-corruption drive would pose no threat to property, and that the junta "plans to deal generously with businessmen," asking only that they pay the fines levied on them.[34] Indeed, the junta made clear that it intended to draw a sharp distinction between official corruption in the bureaucracy — which would be dealt with harshly — and corruption among firms.

Despite these promises, U.S. observers were keenly aware that Korean capital was not convinced. Although there were signs of "greater confidence" within the business community early in the fall of 1961, the embassy staff was concerned about the group of top business houses

which, they had been told, had "not yet made up its mind to cooperate."[35] Worried about the possibility of a general downturn in the
investment climate, U.S. officials in Seoul busied themselves trying to
convince the regime, but especially Korean capital, of the need to cooperate. Ambassador Berger, in particular, was convinced by October—
five months after the coup—that the top business houses were on an
investment strike. He worked frantically on both parties, persuading
Park of the foolishness of levying even the fines that now remained to
be paid by the "illicit accumulators," while at the same time trying to
encourage "a more far-sighted view among business leaders."[36] Berger
did not have to work especially hard to convince Park. Of the thirty-
odd businessmen accused, only sixteen were placed under detention
and, within weeks, all but three were released.[37] By the fall of 1961
leading businessmen had already negotiated a reduction of the fines remaining to be paid, as U.S. officials were urging. In fact, it was clear by
mid-1962 that most of the accused would not even pay the bulk of the
fines they owed.[38]

This retreat from the initial threats to business did not, however, signal that the Chaebol would now rule the roost in economic policy. The
regime's intention was simply to avoid a concerted investment slowdown, not to elevate leading firms to a dominant position in the formulation of policy. The policy-orientation of the regime, as instituted in the
First Five-Year Plan launched in late 1961, was far more clearly tilted
toward small business and farmers. Thus the regime forgave all rural
debt that it deemed had arisen from usury, promised a scheme to mobilize savings for farmers and small businesses, and offered several other
clearly populist measures.[39] Further, the Plan was firmly set within the
ISI tradition: exports were encouraged, but their place within the framework of the plan was strictly secondary to the import substitution effort. And the exports most encouraged were not those produced by the
Chaebol but by smaller producers—the key sectors being fishing, farm-
ing, and mining.[40] The strategy was to use the plan to placate big business but mainly to win over masses of farmers and small businesses.
Exports were to be used to finance import substitution schemes, and not
as the center of the strategy itself.[41]

All this was partly occasioned by the fact that the state planning apparatus, though formally transformed by the advent of the Economic
Planning Board, was still subordinated to political expedience. Although the EPB held formal power over the formulation and implementation of the plan, the officers from the military junta in fact dominated
the planning. The role of the EPB was more in the way of "fill[ing] in
the details within the guidelines that they had been given" by the military.[42] With the civilian technocrats largely sidelined in the planning

process, the immediate need to create a social base for the regime found expression in the character of the plan.[43]

If it had proceeded as intended, there is little reason to think that the Korean developmental experience would have been substantially different from that of many other late-industrializing countries that relied on ISI. But within two years the First Five-Year Plan had to be abandoned, the initial targets forsworn, and a drastically revised plan offered in its stead. The economic crisis that precipitated this turn was itself caused by the junta's policies, particularly its monetary policies. Its scheme of mobilizing increased savings backfired miserably, triggering instead a massive withdrawal of currency from circulation, the evaporation of funds for industrial finance, and a balance of payments crisis.[44] Business investment again began to plummet, with reports coming in that higher production costs were "forcing many businesses to cut down, or even suspend, production."[45] Conceding that the plan was a failure, the regime officially proclaimed its annulment in late 1963, barely two years after it was launched. For the remainder of its original term, a revised plan was offered instead, with more modest targets. But the damage was done: even the new plan was not taken very seriously by economic actors, and decisions pertaining to investment and trade were carried out on bases unconnected with the document.[46]

The facts about the first two years of the Park regime thus run directly counter to the qualities the statists attribute to it. Far from dominating their business class, the new junta, as well as its U.S. advisers, operated in full cognizance of its economic and political muscle. And while they did not raise it to a superordinate position within the new strategy, they had to devise the strategy so that overt opposition from business would not be likely. Further, the failure of the first plan revealed the glaring weaknesses of the new institutions of the state itself. The EPB, despite having formal power, was nevertheless of little importance in the actual policy process; plan targets were of little operational significance; and policy makers were forced to admit that business investment decisions were being made on bases having little to do with the frame of the plan.

The Emergence of a New Development Strategy

At this point two shifts occurred that were crucial for the subsequent success of the Korean state in industrial policy. The first pertained to the state economic apparatus and the second to economic strategy. One of the positive fallouts of the plan debacle was that those elements within the junta who were associated with it suffered an enormous loss of prestige. Even before the full severity of the crisis was felt, Park forced an admission of failure from the military planners and extracted from them a series of resignations.[47] The demise of this group within the junta was balanced by a corresponding elevation of the status of civilian planners housed in the EPB. It was thus at this juncture, and not in 1961 when the institution was created, that the formal power of the EPB was actuated in a meaningful way. Its position was strengthened by a second factor in late 1963, which was the formal inauguration of the Park regime through an election that managed to hide its irregularities just well enough to ward off major crisis. With the military interregnum officially over and a new term of office sanctioned by law, Park was free to concentrate fully on the economic situation.

The second change was in strategy. Around this time the idea of a policy shift away from an ISI-centered strategy to one hinging on exports started to congeal. Although incentives to raise exports had been in place since 1960, talk of making exports the center of economic plans did not emerge until the early months of 1964; it was announced only in the middle of that year, and became embodied in the planning process in 1965.[48] By 1965 the centrality of exports was announced publicly, and in 1966 the Second Five-Year Plan — which put this shift into operation — was launched. Of the two changes — one within the state and the other in policy — the first is readily understood. At one stroke, the ouster of the military "planners" reduced potential rivals to Park and also gave him a scapegoat for the first plan's failure.

In the literature on Korea, the shift in strategy to export-orientation is also presented as an obvious move, for three reasons. First, despite the overall failure of the first plan, policy makers noticed that exports had been a conspicuous bright spot. While the rest of the economy stagnated, exports continued to grow, thanks partly to the incentives that had been put into place as far back as 1958, but also because of the military procurement the United States was initiating for its Vietnam operations.[49] The happy performance by the export sector would have attracted attention on its own, but it was further highlighted by the second factor, namely, Korea's growing balance of payments crisis, alluded to earlier. An increased emphasis on trade was the natural way to ease the pressure. Third, the United States was in the process of cutting back its aid commitments to Korea; thus the cushion that the inflow of U.S. monies had provided would not be available much longer. To cap matters, the American advisers and funding agencies were all applying direct pressure to increase the emphasis on exports, even to the extent of withholding aid disbursements, until Park agreed to a devaluation in mid-1964.[50] The switch to exports thus appears as understandable as the revamped planning apparatus.

There is no doubt that the increased emphasis on exports was occasioned, in part, by the early signs of success, American pressure, and the precarious situation in the external sector. But what is noteworthy about the Korean case is that, within a matter of a year or so, the regime's shift to exports went beyond anything the American advisers had envisioned. They had been pushing the planners to adopt what could be called an export-*promotion* strategy; in fact, they had been advising this very strategy in many developing countries at this time, as Congress was forcing a shift in aid disbursements from grants to loans for almost all recipients. Thus American strategy in Korea was of a piece with its injunctions to its clients throughout the developing world. But, instead, Korea ushered in what has become known as an export-*led* strategy.[51] While export-promotion policies were common throughout the developing world at this juncture, with uneven success, export-led strategies were much more uncommon. The latter not only made exports the pillar of economic planning—unlike the former, where exports were simply grafted on to existing policy—it had the additional feature of making export performance a condition for access to state subsidies for firms, as noted earlier in the chapter.

The difference is crucial for our purposes. Since export-promotion strategies are basically grafted on to existing programs, they do not require a drastic transformation of investment strategies by local firms. They are often used instead as a means of utilizing excess capacity and hence reaping economies of scale through accessing foreign markets; in other words, they are used as an outlet. Implementing such programs does not, therefore, require a great deal of power on the part of the state vis-à-vis local capital.[52] To put an export-led strategy into place, however, as Korea did, is not so simple. Commentators have noted that, in the Korean case, exports were not simply encouraged and subsidized but were made the fulcrum on which industrial planning rested. Further, the performance by firms on this front was made a condition for access to state largesse.[53] That the Park regime went so far as to enact such policies should not, therefore, be seen as a simple extension of the export-promotion measures being pushed by the United States. The implications ELI carried for local capital were of a different order, demanding far more from the firms. Firms were now being asked not only to sell in distant markets, of which they had little experience and knowledge, and which were often closed to them, but failure to do so was punished in a variety of ways.

Given this difference between the two strategies, the advent of export-led industrialization would be remarkable anywhere. But in a developing country, with poorly developed capital markets, infrastructure, and exporting experience, it is even more extraordinary. Commentators have tended not only to overlook the importance of the distinction be-

tween the two, but they have also underplayed how, after their maturation under the carapace of a protectionist state, Korean firms in the
early 1960s were no more immune to the deleterious effects of ISI than
their counterparts elsewhere had been: they were known as uncompeti-
tive, their products of poor quality, and their own supply chains unreliable. Further, many Korean firms were operating with obsolete and
decrepit machinery, so that their prices hovered above other Asian competitors in export markets. Cotton textiles, for example, were experiencing difficulties in U.S. markets because of high prices.[54] That the Park
regime had the confidence to enact a shift from ISI to ELI, despite these
rather typical weaknesses of local producers, demands attention. It cannot simply be seen as an extension of the export-promotion measures
that the Americans were encouraging and that had been in place since
the late 1950s.[55] We have seen that there is no warrant to assume that
the state simply foisted the new strategy onto a reluctant business class,
since Park and his junta were visibly concerned to maintain the goodwill of the class. Further, even had they been willing to make a go of it, I
have argued that control over finance could not have given them the
power that statists think it did. How a state that acknowledged its sensitivity to business pressure nevertheless moved so far in the direction of
ELI is the subject of the next section.

The Importance of Japan

The basic reason the Korean state ventured to initiate an export-led
strategy was that Korean capital had garnered for itself a unique window to foreign markets, through entering into an alliance with Japanese
capital. In other words, the reason why access to subsidies and credit
was made conditional on a *reasonable performance* in export markets
was that firms had a *reasonable* chance of *success* in these markets. It is
noteworthy that the changes that were wrought on Korean capitalists
starting in 1964–65 elicited very little opposition. Even if the state were
the dominant partner that statists claim it was, it is difficult to imagine
that firms would accept such drastic changes without even a murmur of
protest, if the state's command were the only force pushing toward ELI.
As this section will demonstrate, the absence of opposition is explained
by the budding links being forged with the former colonial power. Japanese firms were willing not only to facilitate the entrance of their Korean partners into the highly competitive U.S. market but also to provide critical credit and inputs for success. This demand-side opening
was the essential precondition for the success of the supply-side incentives that the Korean state doled out, and it was the factor that allowed
export promotion to slide into export-led growth. This, in turn, gave

the state the wherewithal to demand performance, without invoking a backlash from local capital.

Japanese capital did not enter into its alliance with Korean capital out of any altruistic sentiments. By the late 1950s Japan's economy was well into its "high-growth" phase, and one of the pillars of this phase was its flood of light-manufacturing exports into the developed world. The massive increase in investment had turned a labor-surplus economy into one with tight labor markets, and hence rising wages. This increase in labor costs was, in turn, threatening to endanger the competitiveness of its exports; added to this, however, was a rising tide of protectionist sentiments in Western, particularly American, markets against the Japanese competition. Faced with constraints emanating from both the supply side as well as the demand side, planning circles in Japan struck on a now well-known strategy: the relocation of its labor-intensive light-manufacturing industries to neighboring countries with lower wages, and a concomitant movement into heavy and electronic industries at home.[56] Japanese capital thus began entering Korea through direct investment and joint ventures; it also entered, however, in the form of trading companies, which played a central role in the Korean success story. These trading companies established links with Korean aspirants to the lucrative export markets of the United States, and provided them with essential inputs as well as the benefit of their sales and marketing networks. In turn, they were able to deliver the Korean firms as customers for capital goods to Japanese producers.

Students of the Korean case have often overlooked the importance of the Japanese as conduits to American export markets.[57] But, given the sad condition of most Korean firms, as evidenced in the steady stream of complaints against their exports, the connection is of paramount importance. Korean firms simply did not have the experience and knowledge of foreign markets to jump to an export-led strategy. Most of the literature has focused on the measures enacted by the state on the supply side of the export effort; but, as Sanjay Lall and Robert Castley have pointed out, this overlooks the fact that a crucial barrier to success in export promotion strategies is the costs associated with marketing and sales.[58] This is especially true in the case of products where brand recognition and quality play an important role, like synthetics, shoes, and the like—which formed the core of the Korean strategy in its initial stages. In markets for these goods, not only is quality of central importance but also the fact that the initiative lies in the hands of the importer in the target country, not the exporter. Links to these importers, their trust, and their satisfaction reigns supreme for export success.[59] Provision of cheap credit and other subsidies can do little to alleviate this side of the export dilemma.

In this set of circumstances, the entry of the Japanese into Korea offered local firms a rare opportunity for export success. The key lay in
ensuring that the Japanese would enter the country on conditions favorable to the growth of Korean capital—with assurances of technological
cooperation, access to markets, assistance in marketing, provision of
inputs and credit, and so on. For this, the state's intervention as an ally
of Korean capital would be crucial. But, in turn, this would give the
state the crucial leverage to discipline its domestic capital—the secret of
the developmental state. Let us now turn to the sequence of events.

Despite the years that stretched between Korean de-colonization and
the fall of Synghman Rhee, Korea and Japan still had not established
normal diplomatic relations. Taking a hard line against Japan in the
form of a demand of reparations had been a political staple of Rhee,
despite his knowing that the political tensions stood in the way of possible economic gains from the normalization of relations. Hence, despite
several attempts, the two governments had not been able to reach a
compromise settlement by the time of the 1961 coup.

Yet capital based in Japan—both Japanese and expatriate Korean—
showed an immense interest in setting up operations in Korea. In late
1960 a Japanese-Korean Trade Association mission to Seoul was planned
to establish economic ties, but it had to be called off because of the
Korean government's worries about its political repercussions.[60] Interestingly, this mission did not elicit much enthusiasm from Korean firms,
but only because they were disappointed that it was not composed of
the top Japanese businesses.[61] This was remedied by the middle of 1961,
after which the top Japanese industrialists started coming to Korea in a
steady stream.

One of the first to come was Yasuhei Yukawa, president of the Toyo
Chemical Engineering and Construction Company, and the director of
the Japan-Korean Trade Association. Yukawa had been one of Park
Chung Hee's instructors at the Japanese Military Academy, and thus
immediately was given an audience with the new leader. Yukawa proposed a project that in many ways was emblematic of the relation that
was to develop between the two countries' industries: he would set up
operations in Korea to produce electrical equipment, auto parts, canned
goods, and beer, 20 percent percent of which would be for the local
market and 80 percent percent for export. To this endeavor Yukawa
would bring Japanese technology and parts, while utilizing the idle capacity of Korean factories and, of course, Korean labor. Park agreed to
this with alacrity, with the proviso that the initiation of operations
would have to wait until normalization of relations between the two
countries.[62]

This initial success emboldened many other top Japanese firms and trading companies to follow suit. By early 1962 a Korean beachhead was established by Nissan, Hitachi, Neiyata, Marubeni Iida, and Mitsubishi.[63] The inimitable Yukawa soon followed with a mission of twenty leading Japanese firms to discuss future operations in Korea, which included Hitachi, Japan Cement, Fuji Electric, and Nichio Fisheries.[64] This was followed by a mission in September 1962 headed by Koshiro Uemura, the vice-chair of the Federation of Economic Organizations, and another in December headed by Toyoroku Ando, the president of the Onoda Cement Company. The Ando mission was noteworthy in that it consisted of thirty-two of the top firms and trading companies in Japan, much to the delight of Korean capital.[65] The activity was not restricted to exploratory missions: in 1962 thirteen Japanese firms had set up operations in Korea, despite the absence of normal relations between the two countries;[66] one year later thirty firms had opened offices in Korea, and agreements had been reached with local firms for the production of fertilizer, textiles, machinery, and transportation equipment.[67]

The textile industry presents a good example of this sort of collaboration. In mid-1962 firms in this sector were already facing a problem of overcapacity, which made a search for export markets something of an imperative.[68] But while the industry as well as the Park regime made the expansion of exports central to their plans, they were not at all optimistic about their chances in the competitive U.S. market; thus, when the first attempt to expand exports was launched in 1962 with the formation of the Korean Textile Trading Company, it was aimed at non–U.S. markets, since firms were convinced that they had gone about as far as they could there.[69]

The arrival of the Japanese in the early months of the new regime offered a means around this dilemma. In early 1962 Yukawa arranged for the formation of a Korean Bonded Goods Processing Association as a counterpart to his company, the object being the importation of cotton goods from Japan in bond, to be processed and then exported from Korea.[70] Toward the middle of 1962 this arrangement had become more generalized, with Korean firms exporting blouses, slacks, raincoats, and Aloha shirts by processing Japanese cotton goods which they had imported in bond from Japanese partners.[71] By late 1964 the strategy of using Japanese inputs for Korean exports was so firmly in place that the Korean government was lobbying the Japanese to allow Korean firms to import such inputs without having to open letters of credit.[72]

Of particular importance here is the benefits garnered by producers of synthetic fibers. On the one hand, Japanese firms used bonded processing arrangements with Korean partners for the manufacture and export of synthetic fibers;[73] on the other hand, they helped finance and build new plants for the further production of synthetics. Among the first such plants was the one announced by the Heung Han Chemical Fiber Company in 1964, a rayon plant built with the help of Japanese capital.[74] In the decade that followed "Japanese investment increased quickly and involved six cases out of eight cases of total investment in the synthetic textile industry."[75] The synthetics industry was not yet the most important segment of Korean textile exports, which was still dominated by apparel.[76] But the launching of the partnerships and joint ventures was strategically important, in that it offered the promise of moving up the ladder into more sophisticated products as well as escaping the protectionist barriers that ordinary cotton textiles were starting to face in the United States.[77]

Ties such as the ones being forged in the textile industry offered Korean manufacturers the opportunity to succeed in the competitive American market, a prospect that had hitherto seemed remote at best. And as Japanese firms continued to enter Korea—establishing branch offices, making tie-ups with local capital, arranging finance, and finding customers for Japanese capital goods producers—the idea of basing future policy on exports increasingly became not only palatable but also desirable for domestic firms. The years between 1960 and 1965 were thus of foundational significance for Korea and its state, in that the developments just described laid the basis for an entirely new growth model. The crisis of the First Five-Year Plan in 1963, particularly the balance of payments problems, inclined the junta toward an export drive; it could even have driven it to install an ELI model of growth. This path could not, however, have been sustained without the underlying alliance that Korean firms had forged with Japanese capital.[78]

This was the structural basis for future export success. For the success to be realized, however, normalization of relations between the two countries was required.[79] Korean business was, in fact, the prime mover among social groups lobbying for a rapprochement with Japan. One of the first Korean industrialists to pressure Park in this direction was Yi Pyon Chol, the founder of Samsung and one of the most notorious "illicit accumulators." Chol had close ties to Iue Toshio, the chairman of Sanyo, and was eager to establish a working relationship with the latter in the production of electronic goods, which, in fact, he later did.[80] Chol and other members of the "illicit accumulators" group formed the Korean Businessmen's Association soon after their release from prison, and this group, which had as its members the major industrialists in the country, turned out to be the primary fount of pressure for the normalization of relations with Japan, explicitly for the purpose of riding the latter's coattails into export markets.[81] A counterpart to this group in Japan was soon established in the form of the Japan–ROK Economic

Co-operation Organization; this group became part of the larger "Korea lobby," which had as its members the fifteen top firms in the country, as well as top politicians.[82]

The industrial groups did not confine their tactics to advocacy alone. The members of the "Korea lobby" in Japan provided the preponderance of funds for the ruling Liberal Democratic Party. More immediately, since much of the resistance to normalization came from Korea, the U.S. Central Intelligence Agency issued a report in 1966 which found that, in the years between 1961 and 1965, that is, the years between Park's ascent to power and the signing of the Normalization Treaty, Japanese firms paid for two-thirds of the budget of Park's Democratic Republican Party (DRP), with six firms alone contributing an estimated $66 million.[83] This was balanced by the well-known nexus between the DRP and Korean industrialists, in which the latter, especially the members of the KBA, were the chief source of funds for the former.

The ratification of the Normalization Treaty in mid-1965 realized the hopes of the Park government as well as Korean capitalists. Japanese enterprises quickly established Korea as a base for their exports to the United States. Systematic data are hard to come by, but a 1974 survey by the Economic Planning Board showed that 86 percent percent of Japanese firms in Korea produced mainly for export.[84] Of course, it is well known that foreign direct investment (FDI) accounted for a small portion of total foreign capital coming into Korea. But it is noteworthy that in key sectors the proportion was much higher: in the early 1970s, 20 percent percent of the total foreign capital in textiles was in the form of FDI, while in electronics it was 30 percent percent, and both these sectors were central to the export strategy.[85] Foreign firms, most of which were Japanese, dominated or accounted for a preponderant share in several key exports;[86] by 1974, 31 percent of all exports from Korea were made by foreign firms.[87] Further, the Japanese most commonly entered through joint ventures: of all Japanese direct investment in Korea between 1962 and 1974, 52 percent was with less than majority ownership, in contrast to the U.S. projects there, only 27 percent of which were with minority stakes.[88] Joint ventures were especially pronounced in textiles, electronics, machinery, metals, and chemical industries.[89] This facilitated the transfer of technological know-how, marketing skills, managerial techniques, and so on.

While the advantages that Korean capital garnered through alliances in Japanese direct investment were important, the more significant services were probably acquired from the Japanese trading companies in the form of marketing outlets and finance. As suggested earlier, the demand side of the export effort is frequently overlooked in the literature on the Korean miracle. Japanese trading companies were critical to the Koreans because of the array of marketing and sales networks they provided in the lucrative U.S. market: as Robert Castley observes, when they established deals with their new Korean partners, the trading companies "frequently brought their customers with them."[90] And in doing so, they provided the means to overcome one of the most obstinate hurdles for late industrializers trying to break into what Gary Gereffi has called "buyer-driven commodity chains."[91] But in addition to the easy access to markets, trading companies were also crucial in ensuring easy and steady access to credit from Japanese banks for their Korean clients, which was absolutely essential for a development strategy that hinged on the use of foreign commercial loans. It is often emphasized that the Korean state played a critical role in backing Korean capital's procurement of foreign capital, and this, of course, is true; but what is frequently overlooked is that the state often entered the picture after initial links between the concerned parties had been made, and this prior liaison was itself greased by the trading companies.[92] For firms trying to break into distant export markets, these two services — delivering up established customers and ensuring a steady flow of credit — were of paramount importance.

With these supports in place, Korean firms rapidly established themselves in the lucrative American market. By 1966 trade patterns between Korea, Japan, and the United States had switched almost completely. Whereas in the early 1960s Japan had been the major destination of Korean exports and the United States the major source of imports, this pattern was reversed within one year of the treaty (table 3.1). The American market, in fact, became the main destination for, and accounted for the bulk of the growth in, the "big three" of Korea's exports in the 1960s, namely, textiles, clothing, and plywood — all of which were being vacated by Japanese firms (table 3.2). As the Japanese moved out of these niches, the Koreans moved in. The ties made with Japanese multinationals were thus of pivotal importance in the launching of the new development strategy. Soon after Park came to power, efforts by both local as well as Japanese capitalists were under way to ease the latter's entrance into the Korean economy. At the center of the alliance lay the use of Korea as a launching pad for exports into advanced capitalist markets, the United States being the most important. The Japanese brought in technology, marketing networks, and finance, and the Koreans supplied cheap labor, a market for Japanese capital goods, and a means of bypassing U.S. trade restrictions against Japan. These potential gains in turn motivated the most powerful business groups in both countries to push for the normalization of diplomatic relations between the two countries. The commitment to ELI — as op-

TABLE 3.1
Main Sources and Destinations of Korea's Trade (%)

	Exports		Imports	
	Japan	United States	Japan	United States
1960–62	49	17	23	48
1965	26	35	39	37
1967	26	43	45	31
1968	22	52	43	31
1969	21	50	41	29

Source: Robert Castley, "Korea's Export Growth: An Alternative View," *Canadian Journal of Development Studies* 18, no. 2 (1997): 195 (table 5).

posed to simple export-*promotion*—was made possible by, and was largely a response to, these developments.

ELI and the Developmental State

A central theme of this book is that the turn to ELI and the rise of the developmental state were closely connected. We are now ready to flesh out this connection. The onset of ELI, which had been secured not *over* the preferences of local capital but in *congruence* with them, gave the state the leverage it needed to exercise its vaunted disciplinary powers. Even with the arrival of the Japanese—indeed, in some respects because of it—local firms had little hope of succeeding without the guiding hand of the state. With regard to Japanese capital, state support was needed along two dimensions: first, to ensure that these more powerful companies enter into partnerships on terms favorable to local producers so that the former not overwhelm the latter; and, second, to act as guaran-

TABLE 3.2
Japanese and Korean Shares of U.S. market, 1966 and 1971 (%)

	From Japan 1966	From Korea 1966	From Japan 1971	From Korea 1971
Clothing/Textiles	36	3	22	13
Clothing	20	2	13	14
Plywood	37	17	21	37
Footwear	26	3	12	4
Other manufactures	21	7	17	18

Source: Castley, *Korea's Economic Miracle*, p. 98, table 2.14.

tor in the efforts of local firms to obtain foreign loans and credits. Despite the Japanese intention to enter into partnerships with local producers, this would be difficult to cement without adequate assurances from the state on the possibility of default.

These services were balanced with the state's role in ensuring success in export markets. Korean manufacturers, though eager to expand into the highly lucrative U.S. market, immediately found themselves struggling. American importers were suspicious of the ability of Korean manufacturers to meet "international standards of efficiency," as an industrial mission from the United States related to Korean officials in 1962.[93] These doubts were entirely reasonable, as U.S. importers routinely found themselves having to file complaints against Korean exporting firms for delivering shoddy products.[94] The frustrations of their customers were paralleled by the suspicions of their new partners, the Japanese, who bluntly announced that, at this stage, "Korean firms cannot be trusted to deliver goods to the specifications ordered."[95] Local exporters were thus faced with the prospect of being shut out of markets, despite the extraordinary opportunity provided by the arrival of the Japanese. It took the state's intervention, a *disciplinary* one, to alleviate the situation: in 1964 the Ministry of Commerce and Industry instituted a series of quality-control measures on exports, as a way of raising the confidence of both the Japanese and the Americans.[96]

Measures such as these, and the institutions to support them, were not only tolerated by the Korean capitalist class but were necessary for its own success in the export strategy—a strategy it had shown a willingness to embrace. The promulgation of quality-control measures, for example, made sense not only for the new regime but also for the exporting firms themselves. Hence we observe that, as the turn toward exports solidified, instruments to help push firms toward greater efficiency and quality were installed, particularly those instruments that allowed planners to directly monitor and affect firms' investment decisions. The first step was the formation of the Korean Traders Association in 1965, which consolidated export manufacturers into one group; the group met regularly with planners to set export targets and then report back on performance.[97] Monitoring of exports was made routine starting in early 1966 with the Monthly Export Promotion Meetings, at which planners were able to keep tabs on the success of export targets, either through reports from individual industrialists or, more commonly, through reports by groups like the Traders Association.[98]

The establishment of the Korean Traders Association, and its use as a disciplinary device, quickly became a more generalized model. Korean firms were increasingly amalgamated into sectoral associations. These associations, in which membership was compulsory, were often staffed by government-appointed officers and assigned to relevant ministries.[99]

In all such arrangements, associations had representational monopoly over their constituents, and hence the power not only to lobby on their behalf but to collect information from their members and then to suggest targets based on this information; hence they could be held accountable for the fulfillment of these targets (Amsden and Hikino 1994). But, equally importantly, trade representatives also had the right to report on problems created by inept or unresponsive government officials, who, in turn, were expected to respond directly to the plaintiffs — indeed, in the Monthly Export Promotion Meetings, they were expected to respond, on the spot, to the President himself.[100] In this way, while the new arrangement served as a device to monitor firms and hold them accountable, it also retained its legitimacy with firms as it provided them with a forum to foist accountability onto state functionaries.

What ELI did, therefore, was to provide Park with an accumulation model that at once brought "on board" significant segments of the business class, while at the same time providing him with the leverage to demand. in return, a given standard of performance. With the enormous U.S. market offering unparalleled opportunities for expansion, firms, on the one hand, had to rely on state support to succeed against the more established and efficient international producers; on the other hand, those companies that did not "go along" faced a real opportunity cost if support were withdrawn, since other aspirants would happily step in and take their place. So long as the strategy remained a workable one, offering unique avenues for growth while also demanding close coordination and the need for high performance, the alliance between the state and capitalists could be reproduced. Capitalists would reap enormous profits, while abiding by the state's occasional use of coercion against laggard firms. The turn to ELI thus provided state managers with the space to build a developmental state, because the incentive structure ELI generated made it rational for firms to have such a state.

REPRISE

This account provides the empirical counterpart to the theoretical critique of statism. The nub of the criticism was that there is no reason to accept the proposition that the Korean state engineered a switch to ELI, impervious to the preferences of its bourgeoisie. The chief mechanism that is adduced to give warrant to the claim — control over finance — does not appear capable of doing the job. On the other hand, once the consent of a significant segment of the class is secured, control over finance is capable of disciplining individual firms. On this argument, if the state manages to hammer out an accumulation strategy with its business class, the exercise of developmental functions is a possibility, so long as business confidence persists — that is, so long as sufficient numbers of firms remain convinced of the strategy.

The preceding account is intended to show that the new strategy that did emerge in Korea—export-led industrialization—was just such a "pact" between the state and its bourgeoisie. It was not foisted onto business by the new regime; to the contrary, it was pushed by business itself. A consideration of the circumstance in which it arose reveals just why so many other countries failed to make such a switch, or even more modest switches: Korea was favored with the happy accident of falling within the ambit of Japanese capital's emerging accumulation strategy, in which declining industries were off-loaded to Korea, where they then set up shop to re-export; further, Japanese trading companies acted as intermediaries to the United States, helping to secure markets that otherwise might have been inaccessible. In return, they were able to have their Korean clients act as purchasers of capital goods to Japanese companies. A triangular pattern of trade thus emerged with Korea exporting light-manufactured goods to the United States while importing capital goods from Japan. As in the statist version, ELI and the developmental state are closely linked in my account. But whereas, in the former, it is the developmental state that engineers a turn to ELI, and is hence causally prior to it, in my analysis ELI provides the crucial leverage to the state to exercise its developmental functions. The causal arrow thus runs in the other direction.

Of course, that ELI gave the state an opening to expand its developmental capacity was no guarantee that the latter would, in fact, do so. Korean firms' alliance with their Japanese counterparts did not in itself produce developmental success—there was still ample room for failure. That it resulted in success is in no small part an achievement of Park and his regime, which was assiduously geared toward ensuring that ELI served as a bridge to genuine domestic development. The emphasis in the literature on the importance of state building, the effective coordination of policy agencies, the extraordinary zeal with which policy objectives were pursued—all this is fully justified. The opportunities offered by potential export markets would not have fructified without the presence of a state that was up to the task for which it became famous. The aim of this chapter has not been to deny the importance of this function; instead, it has been to suggest that an appreciation of the state's ability to foster development need not blind us to the constraints under which it operated, and under which it was born.

A Look Ahead

One of the main questions posed in this book has to do with the origins of the developmental state: why were some (very few) countries able to install such states, while others were not? The answer most typically provided points to the putative dominance of the state over the domestic capitalist class in the successful cases: because of the state's dominance over capitalists, political leaders committed to a developmental agenda were able to launch a project of industrial transformation once they got their house in order. I have called this a "bootstrapping" model of the developmental state, because, in it, the eventual outcome is primarily dependent on reforms and changes *within* the state as a precondition to successful developmental outcomes. The issue of capitalist preferences is not given the same weight in the explanations, and, in many cases, these preferences are explicitly announced as being of little explanatory value, since the state's dominance turned them into "paper tigers" anyway.

The burden of this chapter has been to question this model and offer in its stead a different one, one in which the state is presented as being constrained by the interests of the capitalist class. It bears repeating that I have not questioned the *fact* of state power but only its *scope*. Planners, particularly when they control finance, can certainly coerce particular firms or small groups of firms — here I agree with the statists. But it is not clear that this power extends to being able to coercively impose conditions against which the entire class — or preponderant sections of it — might be united. In particular, I have raised doubts about the ability of the state to unilaterally impose a development model on the local business class, regardless of its preferences; the mechanisms that statists claim give the state this power do not appear to withstand scrutiny. If the argument is to hold water, I must also then provide a new account of how Korea was able to launch ELI, if the state could not just impose it on business. I have done so by pointing to the arrival of the Japanese, which was the impetus that made local firms eager to participate in the new model — unlike in other countries around the world *in the same period*, in which firms consistently rejected an outward orientation in favor of sticking with local markets.

The criticism of the statist model so far has been confined to facts internal to the Korean case. In the next three chapters, these facts will be bolstered by a close look at the Indian case. I present India as a case in which a strategy to build a regime of disciplinary planning was put on the political agenda but, unlike in Korea, was rejected by the local business class. I then show that the business class, on rejecting the plan, launched a powerful offensive against it, which had the effect of scuttling the state-building agenda at the very outset. India thus figures in the story as a positive instance of the prediction made in this chapter at a theoretical level — that once capitalist development has progressed to a certain stage, states cannot simply impose a new order on capitalists regardless of what the latter think of it.[101]

The point made in this chapter and in the three that follow is this:

adequate state capacity is certainly a necessary condition if industrial policy is to be successful; but building this capacity requires, it would seem, an antecedent alliance with the targets of industrial policy, namely, the business class or leading segments of it. In other words, the critical conflicts for building state capacity occur not *within* the state but *between* the state and social actors. Once this is shown, part 3 explores the consequences of the divergent trajectories of state building: in chapter 7 I show how the two state structures — Korean and Indian — were different once they were in place, and how these structures generated very different degrees of state capacity, which in turn made for very a different *quality* of state intervention in the two cases. This is followed in chapter 8 by an examination of how the quality of state intervention in India itself generated obstacles to appropriate state reform, and in fact turned the direction of the reform away from the possibility of a Korea-like state.

CHAPTER 4

Precursors to Planning in India:
The Myth of the Developmental Bourgeoisie

INTRODUCTION

It is the argument of this book that the critical factor that blocked the building of a successful developmental state in India was the widespread and organized resistance of the business class. This assertion flies in the face of what is the dominant — indeed, virtually the unanimous — view among students of Indian economic history. The received wisdom is that business was not only amenable to capitalist planning but that, indeed, it took the initiative in actually *proposing* it. This chapter takes the first step toward showing that the conventional understanding of this aspect of Indian economic history is deeply flawed. It does so descriptively but also advances a more structural argument; in other words, I hope to show not only *that* the business class was opposed to the kind of disciplinary planning necessary for a developmental state but also that there were *structural reasons* for this opposition. This additional dimension is important, for, without it, not only does the analysis remain incomplete but it also leaves open the possibility that, in opposing a developmental state, the business class did not understand its own interests. Hence, had the INC leadership been more adroit in its negotiations or more careful in its public rhetoric, it could have brought capital on board, showing it that such a state was in its own interest. Along with the historical record, I hope also to correct this second view, by showing that it was *rational* for business to attack the planning agenda.

The main anchor for arguments pointing to the enthusiasm of Indian capitalists for industrial planning is a document that has come to be known as the "Bombay Plan." Released in two parts in 1944 and 1945, this was a plea, signed by five of the leading industrialists in the country, for a reliance on economic planning in the future development of India. Moreover, the document actually presented the outline of what such a plan might look like, proposing a set of policies which would, it argued, double national income over the course of fifteen years. In coming just two years before India achieved full independence from the British, the Bombay Plan does present compelling prima facie evidence that the leading lights among industrialists were ready, even eager, to build a developmental state. The failure to build such a state after 1947, then, is even more easily attributable to the failings of the state managers themselves.

If this canonical version of the Indian capitalist class were true, it would present a rather bizarre historical story. As I show in chapter 6, Indian capitalists unanimously and strenuously fought against a disciplinary planning regime in the immediate aftermath of Independence in 1947. That being the case, we would be forced to conclude—if the canonical understanding were true—that the class conducted a complete *volte face* within a two-year period, between 1945 and 1947. That would certainly be possible, but it surely appears somewhat implausible. The issue is of some importance, since we are centrally concerned with the nature of capitalist preferences and the impact of these preferences on state building. A close examination of those preferences, therefore, must occupy our attention.

The central task of this chapter is to offer an argument that makes Indian capital's apparent endorsement of disciplinary planning in the final years of colonialism consistent with its unyielding opposition to it immediately after. Given that this is intended mainly as a contribution to historiography, this chapter may not be of deep interest to non-specialists. Those readers whose main interest is in the actual conflicts around post-colonial state building, or in the comparative dimension, can simply read the chapter summary provided below and move on to chapter 5. They will not lose much analytically, since the structural arguments summarized in chapter 2's "four theses" relate primarily to chapters 5 and 6.

1. *The release of the Bombay Plan was not motivated by a genuine desire on the part of Indian business to launch a developmental state.* Rather, it was a maneuver by the more canny members of the class to maintain legitimacy in the face of the most massive popular upsurge in India during the century. It was a response to what has come to be known as the "Quit India" movement in 1942–43, which, while ostensibly aimed against the British, was also perceived as a real threat by Indian industrialists. The Bombay Plan was, in fact, an effort to blunt the calls for *socialist* planning by radical sections of the movement, by preempting them with a call for *capitalist* planning.

2. *Indian capitalists were, in fact, quite opposed to the idea of giving the state any real measure of power to control or channel the flow of investment.* The first evidence of this came in 1939, when the INC first attempted to hammer out an agenda for industrial planning through consultations with the business class. The Congress formed a body called the National Planning Committee, composed of businessmen and Congress "experts," which was given the task of devising a broad economic plan for future Indian development. But disagreements over the

nature and scope of state intervention in the economy immediately emerged, and played an important part in the demise of the body. This early episode was not, in retrospect, given due importance by the INC as a harbinger of things to come, but it was by the businessmen involved. The second bit of evidence came after the publication of the Bombay Plan in 1945. The plan document itself met with an icy reception from capital as a whole, despite the fact that its most prominent representatives had written the document. Further indications came later that year, when the colonial state released a *Statement of Government Industrial Policy* for India *based explicitly on consultations with the authors of the Bombay Plan, and on the document itself* — the *Statement* was roundly condemned by business circles for its (tepid) proposals of state intervention in the economy. Interestingly, the signatories to the Bombay Plan were quick to realize that they had overstepped their bounds, so instead of launching a campaign within the business class to rally others to their side, they meekly faded into the background. In sum, from around 1945 on, there was no significant segment within the Indian capitalist class that was amenable to disciplinary planning.

3. *This opposition to any real measure of power over private capital was generated by structural factors.* Was the business class opposed to disciplinary planning itself or, rather, was it dissatisfied with the particular policy mixes in which it was embedded? If the latter, then possibly had state managers proposed a different package of policies, a developmental pact could have been hammered out. I will argue that the opposition to disciplinary planning was to the idea itself, not to any particular policy mix. Two mechanisms were especially responsible for this: one a contingent fact about the Indian economic situation, and the other more deeply "hard-wired" into the development strategy being proposed. The contingent fact was that the same massive social movement that drove Indian businessmen to publish the Bombay Plan in 1944–45 also triggered an apparently significant flight of British capital from India. Hence, by the time the war ended and the Congress was on the verge of taking power, large swathes of the local market were being vacated by colonial capital. It was at this moment that the second volume of the Bombay Plan was released and postwar planning efforts initiated. But precisely because there was such scope for Indian business to extend its entry into the local market, most industrialists reasonably saw no reason to give the state new powers to restrict their field of operation. In other words, the proposals for giving the state greater *control* over the flow of private investment came precisely at the moment when capital wanted the greatest *freedom* over investment decisions.

This somewhat conjunctural set of factors was reinforced in later years by the deeper structural incentive structure generated by an ISI strategy. As argued in chapters 2 and 3, the Korean ELI strategy generated incentives for business to allow the state its disciplinary powers, but it was in the nature of ISI to make it rational for capitalists to agree to the windfalls that came from state protection and subsidization while opposing the demands from the state to reciprocate by meeting performance standards. Thus, because of these two mechanisms, Indian capital was opposed to the very idea of disciplinary planning, not just to the particular package in which it was delivered. The depth of this opposition will not become apparent until chapter 6, but the evidence mobilized in the present chapter should go a considerable distance toward establishing that the attitude of Indian business was structurally driven.

THE BACKDROP TO THE BOMBAY PLAN

It is no exaggeration to say that the Bombay Plan has come to occupy something of a mythic position in Indian historiography. There is scarcely a study of postwar Indian economic history that does not point to it as an indicator of the developmental and nationalist aspiration of the domestic capitalist class.[1] And virtually all commentators also agree that there is a direct line of continuity from the Bombay Plan of 1944–45 to the First Five-Year Plan in 1950. For example, one of the leading economic historians of India, Rajat Ray, takes the Bombay Plan as a sign that, by the time of the war, "the [capitalist] class *as a whole* was seriously committed to planning";[2] he concludes that "India's post-Independence socialist [*sic*] regime had its roots in the economic concepts which had developed in the late thirties and early forties. . . . The leading industrialists of India had come to subscribe to these conceptions during the second world war, and even before that."[3] In one of the most well-known books on industrial policy in India, Sharad Marathe points to the Bombay Plan as a precursor of postwar planning and suggests it was evidence that "even before India attained independence, there was almost universal acceptance of a very important regulatory role for the state which must not only prescribe the pattern but also *control the process of industrial change.*"[4]

Since my argument goes directly against this view, and since this view is so well entrenched in studies of planning in India, it is necessary to investigate the events of the time in some detail. The real impulse behind the publication of the Bombay Plan came from two directions: first, from the perception on the part of leading Indian industrialists that, with the coming of Independence, there would most likely be some kind of economic planning in India. This was made clear as early as

1939, when the INC organized a National Planning Committee (NPC) to put together the broad contours of an economic plan for Indian development. Given that planning was on the Congress agenda as early as 1939, it was imperative for capital to influence the direction it would take, and publishing the plan was seen as a way of shaping the terms of future debate. Second, and most immediately, it was prompted by the explosion of a massive social movement in 1942–43, which, business feared, carried the danger of snowballing from a movement against colonial rule into a movement against private property. The plan was an attempt to maintain the legitimacy of the business class by promoting the image that it, too, was committed to the project of social justice, while carefully redirecting the discussion of planning away from any talk of *socialist* planning.

The Rise and Fall of the National Planning Committee

In 1935, the colonial government in India passed the Government of India Act, which, among other things, allowed that while the central government would remain under the control of London, administration in the Indian provinces could come under popularly elected ministries.[5] While significant sections of the INC, mainly the Left, argued that the organization ought not to participate in the elections which the Act now allowed — for it clearly seemed a move to bring Indians into provincial office while keeping real power in Delhi — the Congress High Command decided in favor of running for office.[6] The campaign for office in 1937 was a spectacular success — the INC won landslide victories across the country, coming into power in all the major provinces: the United Provinces, Bihar, Orissa, Bombay, Madras, the Central Provinces, the Northwest Frontier Provinces, and Assam.[7]

This was the backdrop to the formation of the National Planning Committee in 1939.[8] Appointed in 1938 with Nehru as chairman, and given the task of devising a framework for future economic planning, the NPC was a fourteen-member body consisting almost entirely of businessmen and "experts" — an early indication of the incipient state's vision for future policy.[9] Although the NPC was to last less than two years, its tenure proved to be an experience of considerable significance for the actors involved, especially the industrialists. The body soon began to fracture on the issues that were to become the key fault lines between the state and capital in later years.[10] In particular, it became clear that there was a considerable divergence between Congress "experts" and the representatives of Indian business on the proper role of the state in industrial development.

All the members agreed that the future economy, whatever else it might include, would have a significant presence of the private sector. Further, they agreed that private capital would be the beneficiary of considerable support from the state in the form of subsidies, finance, cheap inputs, and protection. The disagreements arose on the degree of state control over the industry as a whole — either through outright ownership or through regulation. There seems to have been little controversy over the issue of defense industries and public utilities; almost all participants agreed that these would be owned and run by the state.[11] The differences arose in the industries that remained. Some of the "expert" contingent was of the opinion that the "key industries" for national development — mainly the capital goods industries — ought to be state-owned,[12] leaving mainly the consumer industries to private capital. This was not an altogether radical measure at the time, for most items produced in the "key" sectors were imported, and hence there was no significant domestic presence in them. Nevertheless, business representatives clearly found it unacceptable.

The debate thus became polarized around state *ownership* versus state *control* over industry, and it carried over into the various subcommittees assigned the task of devising sectoral plans. On most such subcommittees, businessmen found themselves in frequent disagreement with the Congress economists over the scope of state ownership and regulation.[13] As it happened, the more radical measures proposed by the Congress economists, even if endorsed by the particular subcommittee, were effectively tempered by the larger body. Thus suggestions made by the Public Finance Subcommittee that all key industries should be state-owned — and not simply state-controlled — was found unacceptable by the NPC as a whole.[14] Even in individual cases like the Engineering and Transport Industry, the suggestion of state ownership was shot down by the larger body, in favor of state control.[15] There did not seem any imminent danger, therefore, that the far Left within the Congress would dictate future policy. But it was clear that a significant current within the Congress brooked little patience for a powerful private sector.

The industrialists' alarm at the developments was sufficient to make the future of the NPC uncertain. In 1940 the Congress ministries in the provinces resigned their office, protesting the British decision to unilaterally include India in the war effort, without consulting Indian leaders. Within days of Indian entry into the war, Nehru and the other leaders were in prison after courting arrest. With the Congress governments now out of office, the NPC was almost completely dependent on the financial patronage of the industrialists who had been recruited to it. Given the disagreements that had emerged, it was not surprising that these funds soon started to dry up.[16] Even Nehru's release from prison in late 1941 did nothing to reverse this trend. By early 1942 funds from business had just about come to a complete halt, and the NPC went into hibernation. The first encounter with the idea of industrial planning for India had come to an end.

The experience of the NPC carried two lessons for industrialists, one positive and another negative. On the positive side, it was made clear that whatever the scope of private capital might be in the future, it would enjoy the protection and support of the Indian state for its growth. Even in the "key industries" category, despite its regulation by the state, private capital was promised cheap credit and protection from international competition.[17] And considering how the Congress ministries were actually implementing policy at the time, these promises must have carried a ring of authenticity. Throughout the provinces, the party urged its governments to make purchases from Indian (as opposed to British or other European) enterprises to whatever extent possible. In August 1939 V. B. Patel personally intervened to prevent a British firm from obtaining a license for setting up an electrification scheme in Gujarat; in Madras a fledgling cement company was granted a license for the exploitation of a mine quarry after Patel's intervention;[18] and in Orissa, the government gave the Birlas extremely generous terms on which they could open a paper mill which they had long sought.[19] Further, while the Congress ministries showed some sympathy for labor in their early months of rule, this quickly began to erode within a year, so that by 1939 the provinces' labor policy carried a distinctly pro-business flavor.[20]

Thus, as far as the Congress Party's own inclinations were concerned, the prospects for the business class seemed bright. But this is where the negative lesson of the NPC intruded. For while actual policy seemed very favorable to business interests and input, all the talk about "planning" was heavily imbued with statist and populist rhetoric. So long as the traditional leadership remained in control, the rhetoric would most likely remain just that; if events took a turn for the worse, however — for example, if the Congress Left made inroads into the High Command — the rhetoric might find its way into policy. The business enthusiasm for "planning" was, in this fashion, tempered by a concern about the vulnerability of the INC to these radical elements. In the years that immediately followed, this fear was to play a critical role in the decision to publish what came to be known as the Bombay Plan.

The Quit India Movement

The experience of the NPC was one of the central backdrops to the publication of the Bombay Plan. The second was the onset of what came to be known as the "Quit India" movement in the fall of 1942.

This was a campaign launched by the Indian National Congress in early August 1942, as a protest against the unilateral inclusion of India in the war effort. But Gandhi and the Congress High Command did not simply ask that the nationalist leadership be included in the relevant decision making—they called, instead, for the granting of full independence, in exchange for which India would voluntarily join the Allied forces.[21] The colonial state responded by immediately arresting the entire Congress leadership, as a preventive strike against the movement before it could gain momentum. But once the gauntlet was thrown, the country exploded in a mass upheaval that took even the Congress leadership by surprise.[22]

Research on the specifics of the Quit India movement is still thin, as are most aspects of the war period having to do with matters other than elite negotiations. Nevertheless, what is clear is that this was an uprising more massive and more threatening than anything since the Sepoy Rebellion of 1857.[23] The Congress leadership was scarcely in prison before a movement took to the streets, exceeding anything they had expected. For the first few days after the leaders were arrested, what occurred was mainly an urban and working-class phenomenon: Bombay was rocked by strikes and disturbances from August 9 to 14; Calcutta witnessed a series of strikes from August 10 to 17; Delhi was the scene of violent clashes through the same week; and strikes erupted in Kanpur, Lucknow, and Nagpur. Together these cities accounted for the preponderance of the Indian working class, Madras being the only region of any weight missing. After the first two weeks or so, however, working-class participation in the movement took a distinctly secondary place to a rural upsurge, as peasant groups under Congress command, as well as those under cognate organizations, embarked on an ambitious campaign of land seizures, agitations, and clashes with authorities that lasted until the end of the year.[24]

For most of the duration of the movement, its actual unfolding was almost entirely out of the hands of the Congress High Command. Indeed, the signal aspect of Quit India was that it was the first movement entirely out of the control of the Congress right wing: Gandhi had initiated a movement over which he had no control, and it was now careening "beyond any confines that Gandhi may have envisaged" for it.[25] Not only was the High Command not in charge, it did not even appear to have had time to prepare a program for the movement, at least not anything beyond the barest outlines.[26] More worrisome still was that the few Congress leaders who actually escaped imprisonment, and who were, in fact, leading the movement, were those who had gone underground when the authorities cracked down, and were decidedly on the Left—most prominently the young firebrands of the Congress Socialist Party like Jayprakash Narayan and Aruna Asaf Ali.[27]

How did Indian industrialists react to this upsurge? Interestingly, London seemed convinced at first that the movement had the backing of the Indian business class, owing to the latter's increasingly close ties to the Congress, and some of this has carried down as part of the mythology of the movement as an expression of "national" solidarity.[28] But there is not much evidence to support this view. Indeed, such evidence as we do have points firmly in the other direction—to the extent that business was aiding the movement, it was either under duress and on pain of retaliation by radical elements or in conditions where it did not interfere with profits.

Thus G. D. Birla's brother, B. M. Birla, was found complaining bitterly that he and his brothers were "being systematically blackmailed by the sponsors of the present movement," with threats of forcibly closing down their mills; he admitted that "G. D. Birla was rather a willing victim" of such maneuvers because of his proximity to the High Command, but he insisted that " the other Birlas were victims of circumstances."[29] From Bihar the governor reported that while Indian business there did take an interest in the movement, he found little evidence of active assistance; to the contrary, "my previous association with various Indian Trade delegations left me deeply impressed with the belief that business supremacy was, in their minds, more important than political freedom; and that the latter was only a means to an end."[30] Even the emblematic case of business support to the movement fell apart upon investigation: whereas it had been reported that a ten-week closure in the Ahmedabad mills had been an overt sign of support to the movement, a local merchant admitted that the closure was motivated by two factors: first, a warning by V. B. Patel that, in case of a Japanese invasion, "the accumulated profits of the mill-owners in the shape of money would have no value" and, second, and more important, on the calculation that whatever losses were incurred by the closure would be quickly made up by the resulting rise in prices that issued from decreased supplies in the market.[31]

It is true that members of the business class could not afford to come out openly against the movement, in light of the severe repression activists met with from the colonial state; to condemn the movement at this stage would have been seen as an open tilt toward the British. Hence public announcements about Quit India by the most prominent business organs were at best equivocal, calling blandly for social peace, and beseeching both sides to negotiate.[32] But, in private, fears grew that the upsurge against colonial rule bore the potential of transmuting into a call against the rule of capital.

An appropriate characterization of the overall attitude of Indian business is available in the report submitted by the governor of the United Provinces. Until recently, he wrote, Indian business had thought that

"Japan and the Axis would win [and] wanted to save their property; they definitely had a Vichy mentality. If our position on the various fronts continues to improve, they will be more inclined to drop this attitude."[33] So capital was not an active agent in the Quit India movement, in the sense suspected by colonial authorities. Its attitude, instead, was guided by more mundanely pragmatic considerations of protecting its investments and insuring a steady stream of profits. While it did fear a Japanese invasion and was anxious to avoid the animosity of the new aspirant to power, and while it was loathe to oppose the movement actively—both because of its ties to the INC and because it stood to benefit if the movement goaded the state into action on the military front—this did not translate into support for Quit India. Instead, capital tried to hedge its bets by doing what it could to assuage both sides of the conflict—whoever won, the main concern was that business, literally, continue as usual. Vichy indeed.

THE BOMBAY PLAN

The Quit India movement was the second element in the backdrop to the making of the Bombay Plan—the experience with the NPC being the first. The NPC experience had shown the Indian capitalist class that, whatever else the INC might do, it would almost certainly install a regime of capitalist planning after the attainment of Independence. Further, it was also clear that while the Congress leadership itself held no brief against private property, a powerful core among its "experts" was deeply suspicious of it. Given the right conditions, these more left-leaning elements could exercise real power within the organization. And the Quit India movement carried the threat of creating this very set of conditions. With each day the Left within the Independence movement was becoming stronger and more vocal in its demands. Even with Gandhi and the Right back in charge eventually, the growing strength of mass pressure could force them to take cognizance of popular demands and interests. In such circumstances, the intellectual biases of the Congress "experts" could become a political and economic reality.

These considerations seem to have had a direct bearing on the decision taken by the leading lights of Indian business to formulate a proposal on the need for a planned economy for postwar India. The Quit India movement had scarcely started when a terrified Lala Shri Ram, the Delhi textile magnate, wrote to Purshotamdas Thakurdas, expressing wonderment that the authorities were blaming him and G. D. Birla for instigating strikes in their Delhi mills. "We are doing our best to run the mills," he wrote, but he complained that "there is such strong feeling amongst the workers that the like of it I have never seen before. They are even losing the great regard that they had for my person;"[34] a week later again he declared that he had "completely failed" as far as his mill was concerned, "as all my reasoning, coaxing, cajoling, and threats have gone in vain." And as with most Hindu businessmen of the time, he reached instinctively for God and Gandhi — "God forbid, if the Mahatma started the [sic] fast and died, then I dreaded [sic] to think what would happen to not only Government property but to our lives and property."[35] Thakurdas agreed that "an unparalleled tragedy is being enacted in India" and decried the "demoralization and chaos" engendered by Quit India: "To think that you and Ghanshyamdas [Birla] have been responsible for the strikes in your mills would only indicate bankruptcy of commonsense on the part of those who believe it."[36] Both Shri Ram and Thakurdas, along with Birla, met repeatedly with British officials through August, trying their best to allay the latter's suspicions as to their role in the movement, as well as to coax them into taking a softer line against the Congress High Command.[37] Shri Ram summed up their fears nicely:

> I am afraid that this sabotage may any day start of private property also. Once the Goondas[38] know this trick, any Government . . . will find it difficult to control it. *Today Mahatma Gandhi may be able to stop it, but later on it may go out of their hands also.*[39]

Thus it was not just increasing radicalism that Indian business feared but its potential to break free of Congress control. In such an eventuality it was certain that the brunt of the new radicalism would have to be borne by the business community, in particular, and propertied classes more generally. A view toward the longer term advised that business, if it was to survive and prosper under the new dispensation, needed to take the initiative. It would have to shed its image of backroom maneuvering and profit mongering, and take center stage as a servant of the same aspirations that guided the broader movement. Of course, central to these aspirations was the idea of combining economic growth with distributive justice — the idea of planning.

By the late fall of 1942, as the initial fury of Quit India settled into a longer war of attrition being waged in the countryside, Tata and Birla took the initiative in setting up a committee of trusted fellow industrialists and economists to work on a proposal for long-term planning in postwar India.[40] The committee consisted of six of the most prominent industrialists in the country — G. D. Birla, J.R.D. Tata, Lala Shri Ram, Purshotamdas Thakurdas, Kasturbhai Lalbhai, and A. D. Shroff — as well as two well-known "experts," John Mathai and Ardishir Dalal, both employed as directors in the Tata business empire.

The group met for the first time in early December in Bombay, where it was decided that John Mathai would take on the task of actually drafting the document, and the working expenses of research and office work would be shared so that Tata paid for half and the others, combined, would pay for the other half.[41] Mathai had come prepared with a note that offered a limpid summary of the motivations of the committee, and what it hoped to achieve. It is reasonable to assume, the note began, that on termination of the war, a national government would come to power in the country, which would be "entirely responsible to an elected legislature." This responsibility will make the government open to the most pressing demands of the day, chief among which will be the demand for the eradication of poverty and the development of an economic policy suitable to such an end. And herein lay the rub:

> It must be expected that when a popular government are [sic] confronted by a loud and insistent demand for remedial action, *they will be tempted to adopt measures which find strong popular support without adequate consideration of their ultimate effect on the country.* For this reason it is of great importance that a well-considered and impartial scheme of economic development should be prepared in advance by those who can claim the requisite knowledge and experience. Such a scheme will provide a steadying influence upon government and upon public opinion by focusing thought on the more essential elements of the problem and by suggesting practical ways of meeting them.[42]

Mathai's note brings into relief the immediate issue on the minds of the committee, namely, preempting the growing influence of popular demands on the INC. Economic policy in the context of the postwar scenario would, of course, he observed, have to take cognizance of the circumstances in which it was functioning; chief among the changes of the time was most likely to be a distinct shift to the left:

> Among these changes, there is probably none which is likely to have a more direct bearing on economic organization in India *than the reaction which has been in evidence against the capitalist system.* . . . The inevitability of a change in the direction of a socialist economy even in a country like India must now be recognized *and leaders of industry would well be advised to take this into account and be prepared to make such adjustments as may meet all reasonable demands before the socialist movement assumes the form of a full-fledged revolution.*[43]

And now came the key:

> The most effective way in which extreme demands in the future may be obviated is for industrialists to take thought while there is yet time as to the best way of incorporating[44] whatever is sound and feasible in the socialist move-

ment. One of the principle tasks of the committee will therefore be to examine *how far socialist demands can be accommodated without capitalism surrendering its essential features.*[45]

This note has been quoted at length because it reveals clearly the impulse that underlay the Bombay Plan, and because virtually all the historiography of Indian planning has ignored this. The Bombay Plan was not a clarion call by a nationalistic bourgeoisie to its peers, exhorting them to join in the forward march of national progress; it was a document designed to forestall future socialist attacks on business by opening the way for *capitalist* planning. It was therefore fundamentally a defensive maneuver, designed to accomplish two tasks: first, to concede the legitimacy of subaltern demands for distributive justice and to make appropriate distributive outcomes part of the plan design; and second, and more important, once such features were declared part of the planning effort, to strenuously focus attention on the possibility of a capitalist economy meeting such demands. If handled correctly, the document held great promise: on the one hand, it would de-fang the Left, which appeared to be growing in strength every day; on the other, by being the first public unveiling of a genuine plan for postwar India, it would *set the terms* for future debate.

The document itself was published in two parts, each appearing almost exactly one year apart. The first part, a small booklet of scarcely fifty pages, was released in January 1944 at a press conference at Tata's house, and immediately became the focus of enormous attention. With the modest title of *A Brief Memorandum Outlining a Plan of Economic Development for India*, the document not only became the talk of policy circles, but it seems to have taken the relevant actors rather by surprise. The press greeted it with immediate enthusiasm, as did the business community.[46] It is not difficult to understand the universal enthusiasm elicited by the document; it seems to have been carefully designed to avoid controversy. Specifics about the degree of control, the scope of state power, the role of labor—all the points that had so divided the National Planning Committee—were studiously avoided. Instead, the document confined itself to a broad discussion of the magnitudes of expenditure that would most likely be necessary for a rapid growth of per capita income. It was more a forecast of fiscal magnitudes than a blueprint for planning.

The document proceeded as follows: first, it acknowledged the crushing poverty of the mass of Indians; second, it pointed out that only rapid economic development could alleviate this condition; third, it urged that this was impossible without concerted public action; having established the need for state action, the document adduced a set of conjectures regarding the scale of public expenditure on agriculture and industry that would achieve the desired result: a doubling of per capita income in fifteen years.[47] The plan immediately became the focus of national attention, generating an enormous debate within business circles as well as in the government.[48] Business for the most part hailed the document and rallied to its support; immediately after its publication, Birla had reached out to the Federation of Indian Chambers of Commerce and Industry, asking that it publicly endorse the document, a request the Federation readily complied with.[49] In keeping with the spirit of the plan, the statement of the Federation, too, kept only to generalities, applauding the idea of planning, expressing the hope that it would be in keeping with the democratic aspirations of the masses of Indians and reconcile the sundry interests of the community.[50] Indeed, most discussion of the document confined itself to generalities. When it did broach specifics, it was rare to find any piece that ventured beyond the confines set by the planners themselves, namely, the issue of finance and the realism of the targets.[51] In any case, the fact is that the Bombay Plan became the focus of the entire Indian press[52] and intelligentsia[53] — business as well as general — all of which applauded the effort of the Bombay planners.

Early signs thus indicated that the Bombay Plan was having the desired effect. All this was made easier by the fact that the plan document left out any concrete discussion of the instruments that would bring such plans into effect, the role of the private sector, the degree and modalities of state intervention, ways and means, taxation, and son on. These were left for the second volume, which was to follow one year later. For now, Birla and his colleagues simply wanted to show that the leading lights of Indian business had fallen into step with the nationalist movement's call for a planned strategy of development.

THE CAPITALIST CLASS AND THE DEMISE OF THE BOMBAY PLAN

The chief objective of the Bombay Plan had been to frame the terms of debate for future Indian development. This was occasioned most immediately by the onset of the Quit India movement, which sent tremors throughout the Indian business class. An additional incentive was the developing political scenario: even if independence was not to be in the immediate future (which, of course, it did turn out to be), it was clear by 1944 that the postwar situation would bring with it a significant degree of indigenous involvement in the Indian government. Further, the economic and political power of Indian business was such that any future policy negotiations would have to include it as a central player. For state managers — whether Indian or British — this meant that future policy would have to be sensitive to the interests and views of Indian businessmen. For the business class itself, it meant that the prudential strategy was to push itself into policy circles right now, while future plans were still fluid.

This involved complex maneuvering. Since some kind of state intervention in the future was a virtual certainty, it was imperative that its scope be defined carefully, and that the mass movement not be allowed to thrust it toward socialism. In turn, this demanded that capitalists not let themselves be isolated politically as the enemies of guided development — they had to remain within the ambit of the broad movement. But as we have seen, powerful representatives of the class *were* opposed to a strong state planning apparatus, especially if it involved labor. The task of the Bombay Plan was thus to preempt the mass movement, on the one hand, and, on the other, to carefully coalesce the broader business class around capitalist planning. The former would keep capital from becoming isolated, and the latter would then enable it to shape policy more effectively.

This section explores the degree to which the gambit was a success. The year that followed was the occasion of two developments that serve as indicators of how far the Bombay planners were able to go in creating a consensus around capitalist planning. One development was the attempt by the colonial state to craft a new industrial policy based explicitly on the Bombay Plan; the second was the publication of the second part of the plan in early 1945, which spelled out the actual instruments that would most likely have to be used.

As an attempt to capture the attention of the state, the Bombay Plan worked quite well. The British authorities were already at work fashioning postwar development plans, and any such plans would have to involve Indian business; the publication of the plan document gave the authorities an ideal vehicle to bring a leading segment of local capitalists into the process, which would only increase the chances of success. However, as a catalyst for bringing the wider class to the idea of capitalist planning, the efforts of Birla et al. were largely a failure. The prospects of a powerful state were still too unpalatable. But, more important, the changes wrought during the war opened new vistas for the expansion of business into sectors that had been controlled by British capital. The imposition of regulations and conditions by the state was not likely to be tolerated when such opportunities beckoned. Hence the reaction by the broader class to the new industrial policy statement and to the second part of the Bombay Plan was largely negative.

The Terms of Future State Policy

The onset of the war, and then the Quit India movement, created considerable dilemmas for the colonial state in India. It was clear that the end of the war would occasion the need for a controlled transformation of the economy back to civilian production. But this could not mean a return to the prewar status quo; the war itself had demanded great sacrifice from the Indian population, which would not countenance the continued disregard for its welfare on the part of the state. This was evidenced most dramatically in the Quit India uprising and the galloping popularity of the INC. The postwar colonial state would have to take clear and concerted measures to improve the material welfare of its subjects if it was to forestall the rapid slide toward social upheaval.[54] Initiatives toward this were already under way in the form of a number of Postwar Reconstruction Committees set up by the Viceroy, which were handed the task of designing policy for the coming dispensation.[55] But the effort remained perfunctory at best, and at the time of the Bombay Plan's publication it was clear that little headway had been made.[56]

The publication of the Bombay Plan jolted the state into action.[57] The initial reaction of the colonial state authorities to the Plan ranged from incredulous to dismissive. The Finance Department of the Government of India prepared a detailed note arguing that the financial targets required by the plan were not at all realistic, calling into question the whole set of calculations it offered.[58] Although this did offer some satisfaction to embarrassed state managers and governing circles, and it did elicit spirited ripostes from the planners, especially Birla,[59] it was really quite beside the point. The planners could hardly be expected to have drawn up a document with genuinely operational magnitudes, ready to be launched; the shrill reaction by the colonial bureaucracy seems to have been an artifact of its embarrassment at having its three years of "Reconstruction Planning" upstaged by a little document hurriedly drawn up by a group of Indian businessmen. And this was not lost on the higher authorities. While the government did issue its criticism of specifics, it also realized that the industrialists had managed a public-relations coup.[60]

Once the state managers recovered from their embarrassment, they realized that the Bombay Plan offered an important opportunity for carrying through their own designs. Whatever the postwar orientation might be, it would have to include the Indian business class as a central player, for it was by now much too powerful to be ignored.[61] And here was a segment of the Indian capitalist class that was not only amenable to postwar planning but clamoring for it. For the colonial state, this was an opportunity to kill two birds: on the one hand, to re-launch its efforts toward the *material* task of postwar conversion and development; on the other, to accomplish the *ideological* end of increasing its local legitimacy, through bringing on board the most prominent section of the Indian capitalist class.

Hence the Viceroy made the logical move: in a matter of weeks, he initiated a process that brought the planners closer to the state and its preparations for the postwar dispensation. In April 1944 a high-powered delegation of bureaucrats, headed by the finance member of the Viceroy's Council Jeremy Raisman and supply member Ramaswami Mudaliar, met with the planners (absent Birla) to elicit further clarification regarding their attitude to future plans.[62] Except for a perfunctory nod to the need for more careful consideration of the finance question, the meeting concentrated on the planners' attitudes to the future shape of plans more generally. And from this, several points emerged which revealed to the state representatives that there was real potential to bring the planners on board for future policy. It was decided that economic policy would become the provenance of the central government, as against the provinces, with whom the power currently resided; within the government, the primary responsibility for policy would rest with an autonomous planning body; the state, in order to implement plans, would be vested with power to intervene in the industrial sector;[63] and, finally, there would have to be some attention to distributional issues, though there was no hint of the radical proposals for codetermination that had, from the industrialists' viewpoint, marred the meetings of the NPC five years earlier.[64]

The meeting served to provide each side with an appraisal of what the other sought, as well as what to expect. The state now perceived that if it was to undertake schemes of long-term development after the war, it had in the private sector a powerful set of allies it could harness to the cause. This was of no small significance, given the hostility that Indian capital had evinced to any encroachment on what it perceived as its domain. Thakurdas and his fellow planners, on the other hand, could take solace in the fact that while they would still have to contend with a state that wielded considerable control over matters of investment, decisions on the scope of its actual ownership were put into abeyance for the time being, and major matters of policy regarding these issues would be decided on technical grounds. This, too, was significant: state control was on its way to being subordinated to matters of economic detail, not to social justice or democratic participation. Further, labor was now a part of distribution, not of production. This was a marked improvement over the radical proposals that so enticed the Congress Left and its experts.

The colonial state now had a powerful segment of the Indian business class hitched to its wagon, and not a moment too soon. The war was clearly entering its last stages, and industry, aware of the changes in economic policy that would surely follow after the war, was clamoring for a clarification of what was to come, and pointing to the interminable time being taken by the Reconstruction Committees. A statement of postwar policy was clearly in order, if for no other reason than to assuage the concerns of capital. The results of the meeting with Birla, Thakurdas, and the others had provided the basis for a policy statement, which state managers hoped would garner the assent of the wider class. What remained was to set the state machinery into motion so that the new policy could be made public.

During the next year, as the colonial state was occupied in producing the new policy statement, it worked closely with the Bombay planners. Wavell created a new Planning Department in the Viceroy's Council, and placed at its head Ardishir Dalal, one of the signatories to the Bombay Plan.[65] Dalal, in turn, established a committee to oversee industrial policy, and placed on it all the rest of the Bombay Plan signatories.[66] Members of the team were present in most internal discussions on future policy. And flanking them were a number of Indian officials, many of whom were friends or colleagues of the Indian industrialists.

The central point that soon emerged in policy discussions within the state was that, regardless of the particulars of the postwar scenario, industrial policy would have to rely on a host of controls over investment, prices, trade, and the like.[67] Administrators in the economic bureaucracy were concerned that business would not be likely to accept such restrictions on its freedom.[68] But they had Dalal on board; they had obtained the assent of Birla et al. in the April meeting; and they were assured by the Indian members of the Viceroy's Council that, given the backing of the plan signatories, such measures would have a good chance of being accepted by business.[69] And, in fact, Indian members of the Council went to some length to maintain links with plan signatories, urging them to lobby within the business class for the acceptance of the policy statement when it emerged.[70] Economic bureaucrats therefore had some reason to be optimistic that a regime of state-led development could be sold to the business class.

In sum, the publication of the Bombay Plan became the occasion for the colonial state to attempt an alliance with the leading members of Indian business, and to forge a postwar policy for which these men would form the link with the wider class. The basic contours for the new dispensation were decided on through a meeting with them, one of their members was put in charge of the planning department in the Viceroy's council, signatories to the plan were put on the central policy committee, and they were all kept in "the loop" as progress on the new policy was made. Hence the state was clearly making all efforts to fashion a policy that would be *acceptable* to Indian business. All indications were that one of the central aims of the Bombay Plan — to set the frame for future policy — had been a success.

In the first part of 1945 two events served as a test for the success of the second prong of the Bombay planners' strategy, which was to bring the wider class around to the idea of planning under a strong supervisory state. The first was the publication of part 2 of the Bombay Plan in January, and the second was the release of the *Statement of Government Industrial Policy* in April by the state, on which the Planning Department, under Ardishir Dalal, had worked for a year.

The Bombay Plan and the Indian Capitalist Class

As mentioned above, the release of part 2 of the Bombay Plan came almost exactly one year after part 1. Whereas the first part had only introduced the idea of capitalist planning and had given a rough estimate of the likely fiscal magnitudes, the second part hazarded a series of proposals on the institutional mechanisms necessary for implementing the plan. Most analyses have failed to make a distinction between the two parts of the Bombay Plan, confining their attention to the happy acceptance of part 1 by the business class. This has the unfortunate effect of obscuring a critical fact that the publication of part 2, and the announcement of the *Statement of Government Industrial Policy* revealed: capitalist preferences were indeed for planning, but not for *state-led* or *disciplinary* planning.

The second installment of the Bombay Plan was a different creature entirely from the first. Where the former went on airily about the large expenditures that planned developed would require, the latter got down to the nuts and bolts of actual implementation and administration. On this score, it could not avoid endorsing a heavy dose of state power over industrial activity. First, the document did allow for state ownership of some key industries. To be sure, state *control* of industry was strenuously recommended over state *ownership*, in keeping with the basic objective of making planning compatible with private property.[71] But once the issue of control was conceded, its institutional specifications could not be ignored. In a remarkable passage, the list of powers that would have to be granted to the state tumbled forth: the right to license investment projects, to control prices, allocate foreign exchange, set wages, control trade, and so on.[72] This was followed, perhaps in anticipation of the likely reaction from other industrialists, with a quick reminder that all such controls would presume a "national government responsible to the people" and that they would not betoken a slow slide toward socialism.[73] But the fact remained that the Bombay Plan had gone from recommending state assistance to industry (in part 1) to enumerating, and apparently endorsing, its legitimate powers over industry (in part 2) — from the state as nanny to the state as disciplinarian.[74]

Hot on the heels of part 2 of the Bombay Plan came the *Industrial Policy Statement* from the government, released in April 1945. The *Statement* was the fruit of one year's labor by the Planning Department under Ardishir Dalal, one of the original signatories to the Bombay Plan.[75] In keeping with the state's strategy of riding on the wave created by Birla and his colleagues, the *Statement* stuck very close to the agreements reached in discussions with the planners and was, in fact, entirely congruent with part 2 of the Bombay Plan. Its core proposals amounted to the following:[76]

1. There should be legislation that brings key industries out of the domain of provincial control and makes them subject to central authority. The *Statement* went on to list twenty such sectors, chiefly comprised of heavy industry.[77]

2. The object of legislation pertaining to industry after the war would be to expedite the rapid development of Indian industrial potential, coupled with a "high and stable level of employment."[78]

3. Toward this end, government would resort to the use of tariffs and various other measures to offer protection to industry; it would also offer such assistance as may be necessary for a path of balanced development. Among the measures used would be loans; the guarantee of a minimum dividend for venture projects (in exchange for government representation on management); financing R&D; the procurement of capital goods from abroad; and so on.[79]

4. To ensure coordination in investment, the government would exert control over the flow of investment through a licensing policy. This would avoid an undue geographical concentration of investment — which had characterized industrial development thus far — and also offer a solution for the propensity of private capital to flow into sectors that promised the quickest returns. The latter led to over-investment in particular sectors, leaving other crucial areas unattended.[80]

5. In addition to licensing, the government would also use other controls to guide investment, for "in a planned economy it is impossible to do without controls." Such controls would include the control over capital issues, and indirect controls such as taxation measures to avert excessive profits (only in monopolisitic industries — in industry with normal competition, profit would be unregulated), minimum wage laws, quality control, and training programs.[81]

This structure adhered to two basic parameters: first, it did not, in any of its proposals, venture beyond the agreements reached in the April 1944 meeting between the Bombay planners and the government delegation. The crux of that consensus had been around three points: the need to bring industrial policy under central control, the necessity for some degree of control over the economy by the state, and the need for some distributive measures by the state. Left out of the *Statement* was any reference to labor as a partner in production or as having a right to a share in profits, one of the main points of conflict in the NPC committees. Second, and related to the first point, the statement was very careful to make clear that, to the extent that the state did assume ownership or take direct control over enterprise, it would be confined to limits set by private capital itself. Three considerations were listed that would guide action in this regard: first, ordinance factories, public utilities, and railroads were already owned by government, and this would continue; second, basic industries "*may* be nationalized" but *only* "provided that adequate private capital is not forthcoming *and* it is regarded in the national interest to promote such industries";[82] third, industries that rely heavily on state funds (industries "in which the tax element is much more predominating than the profit element") may be taken over if necessary.[83] This, too, was in keeping with the Bombay planners' aspirations, and marked a victory over the line adopted in the NPC committees, where state ownership had been regarded with much more favor.

Despite this careful attempt to avoid the mistakes of the NPC, both the Bombay Plan document as well as the industrial policy statement met with a hostile reaction from wider sections of the capitalist class. The release of the documents had been followed by an assiduous propaganda campaign in their favor by Birla's *Eastern Economist*[84] and by the government itself, which deployed the Planning Department in various public forums to assure the business community that the proposals held no brief against profits or private property.[85] Nonetheless, business representatives immediately reacted against the bare mention of state ownership — even in key industries where private capital was not forthcoming — and to the powers of control and regulation that the two documents afforded the state.[86] In their stead, business organizations pressed for the fullest possible *decontrol* of prices and investment, in a broadside against the "undue interference and restrictions imposed . . . on trade and industries."[87] In all, the response elicited by both documents was mainly hostile.

What is perhaps most surprising is that, when faced with this response, the signatories to the Bombay Plan beat a quick retreat. Instead of propagandizing more strenuously in favor of their plan, and the Industrial Policy Statement that was based on it, they either remained silent or (in the case of Birla) actually joined the anti-state bandwagon. John Mathai, who had been the main author of both parts of the Bombay Plan, immediately concluded that "the Second Bombay Plan had not been taken seriously by Indian businessmen."[88] Since the Bombay Plan was the basis for the Industrial Policy Statement, the rejection of the former sealed the fate of the latter. Hence, even though the Bombay planners were in favor of the government's *Statement*,[89] they retreated into what one newspaper called a "loaded silence."[90]

Why did Indian business oppose the two documents so strenuously? One of the most important proximate mechanisms, and most frequently mentioned at the time, was their apprehension that the proposed controls would be in the hands of a foreign and colonial government, which would then use it to favor British business.[91] There is certainly some truth to this, but it should be qualified. By the onset of the war, the colonial state in India was, as I have mentioned before, aware of the fact that Indian business would have to be accommodated in any postwar arrangement. Indeed, one recent study has concluded that, in terms of its direct influence on policy, British business in India was already falling behind relative to its Indian counterparts.[92] Nothing in the sources I have examined contradicts this verdict — the state in India, despite its colonial status, was, if anything, more sensitive to Indian than to British business by the end of the war. Of course, this is quite compatible with the misgivings of the Indian capitalists with regard to the future use of policy instruments. But the sympathetic orientation of the state should not have gone entirely unnoticed. And it certainly remains a mystery as to why the Bombay planners, who were brought directly into the state, did not propagandize more strenuously within the business class in favor of their agenda.

A more serious problem with the view that the rejection of the two documents by the business class issued mainly from its distrust of the colonial state is this: if such were the case, then the change in government in 1946–47 should also have generated a corresponding change in attitudes toward state intervention. However, as I shall show in great detail in chapter 6, the onset of Independence in fact *heightened* the opposition to a strong planning apparatus. Any explanation for why industrialists rejected an interventionist state in 1945 must also be able to explain why that rejection persisted into the years of Independence. On this reasoning, and in anticipation of the evidence to be adduced in chapter 6, suspicions generated by the colonial character of the state cannot have been the underlying reason — though it might have added to more basic worries. The following section offers another mechanism as candidate.

The Roots of Business Opposition

The event that most immediately had precipitated the efforts of Birla, Thakurdas, and the others to draft the Bombay Plan had been the Quit India movement in late 1942. This same event also set into motion — or accelerated — another process, which was the increasing departure of British business from the Indian subcontinent. Unfortunately there are no reliable statistical measures of the exact dimensions of the withdrawal process; the most careful study of the issue has observed that British capital started leaving after 1931, and that this process "grew in volume during and after the Second World War, particularly in the [period] following the Quit India campaign in August 1942."[93] The best estimate seems to be that around 13.5 billion rupees (Rs 1,350 crores) — slightly less than 1 billion pounds sterling — worth of British capital was shipped out between August 1942 and July 1948.[94] This did not always take the form of the outright folding up of undertakings; it was sometimes just the liquidation of equity holdings or their transfer to Indian hands.[95] Nonetheless, it did translate into a shift of dominance from British to Indian capital.[96]

While the onset of the Quit India movement opened up an opportunity for Indian businessmen to take over British firms and their markets, its ebbing by 1943 also settled their fears about the possibility of a leftward lurch. By 1945 the Old Guard in the Congress was firmly and visibly in control of the party machinery again, at least in comparison to the state of affairs three years earlier. Hence the need for concessions was not as pressing as it had been at the time. Capitalists were no longer as concerned about the prospects of political isolation, since Gandhi and the Old Guard of Patel, Rajendra Prasad, and others would assuredly steer the Congress organization, and hence the Independence movement, away from its radical elements.

The situation as it presented itself to Indian business at the end of the war in early 1945 was therefore bursting with opportunities. That any future policy would have to center around considerable state support to industry was already settled; also likely was the decision to set up an elaborate system of tariff protections for local industry in the new economic policy — and, indeed, this was to be a centerpiece of future policy. In a context where many existing markets were being vacated by the withdrawal of colonial capital, the prospect of state regulation and control would only have appeared as a massive hindrance to the expansion of businesses into new and bountiful lines.

Hence the most plausible explanation for the cold reception given to the second part of the Bombay Plan and the Industrial Policy Statement is that by 1945 Indian business saw no need for concessions to the Left, while at the same time anticipating enormous opportunities opening up as it took over lines hitherto dominated by British firms. This was reinforced by the difference in the nature of the first and second parts of the plan. The first part had emphasized the subsidization that would have to come from the state in favor of domestic capital. This dimension of planning, of course, would have garnered support from capital, as indeed it continued to do in the years to come. But the second part of the plan, released in 1945, bared the teeth that would have to be given to the planning apparatus if subsidization were to be complemented by the disciplining of capital. It was one thing to agree to be the beneficiaries of public largesse; but handing over to the state powers of the kind proposed in part 2 of the plan — that was something else altogether, especially in the changed circumstances of 1945. Capitalists did not see the need to offer such concessions, not with the mass upsurge now in abatement, and lines of business opening up with the flight of British capital. This also explains why the Bombay planners themselves retreated so quickly. It is not clear if their views regarding the necessity of some degree of control had veered to a contrary position. Mathai seemed to think that most of them still supported the Industrial Policy Statement;[97] however, it is clear that by 1945–46 G. D. Birla himself was going over to the other side, railing against the consequences of controls and government regulation of industry, and demanding greater freedom for private enterprise.[98] This was to be a position from which he never wavered for any great length of time from this point on.

The roots of business opposition to the prospect of state-led planning, even in an utterly diluted form as in the *Statement*, thus appear to have been structural in nature. Whereas such intervention in Korea could be regarded as a condition for garnering high profits — because of the nature of ELI as an investment model — in Indian conditions there was ample opportunity for profits *without* state discipline. Markets would be protected from international competition; many lines opening up were those in which Indian industry already had a toe-hold, so the state's logistical support — as in export markets — was not necessary; the need for closely coordinated investment was not as dire, since the absence of competition made it possible to accept a slower emergence of backward and forward linkages. So state managers simply did not have the leverage to demand performance that their Korean counterparts did. Of course, state *assistance* was seen as very important by business, and it never stopped clamoring for it. Where it drew the line was on the issue of such assistance coming with *conditions* in tow. For the state, this posed a dilemma; since its own agenda was a developmental one and, in particular, one that was based on ISI, it was also committed, willy-nilly, to providing assistance to industry. Given the business opposition to regulations, however, whatever discipline was going to be imposed on the class within this strategy would have to be accomplished over its resistance — unlike in Korea, where business had an interest in a disciplinary state.

The opposition to discipline has been missed by most historical studies of the Indian capitalist class and the planning regime.[99] This lacuna in the literature is, it appears, one of the by-products of the bizarre convention in Indian historiography to never venture beyond 1947. Since the bitter opposition to disciplinary planning really came to the fore after that date, the myth of the developmental bourgeoisie still persists.[100] And until it is replaced with a more nuanced analysis of business preferences, the trajectory of state building in India cannot but remain a mystery. The chief purpose of this chapter has been to contribute to exploding that myth. In the next two chapters, we examine the vicissitudes of state building in India in the face of the stiff resistance from domestic capitalists.

CHAPTER 5

The Demobilization of the Labor Movement

INTRODUCTION

The previous chapter called for a reassessment of the view that, by the final years of colonial rule, leading segments of the Indian bourgeoisie had come to see the virtues of state-led development. I argued that the emblematic statement of this putative support for planning, the Bombay Plan, was not the crystallization of a class-wide sentiment welcoming active industrial policy; it was, instead, an attempt by a leading segment of the class to co-opt what seemed in 1942–43 to be a rapidly growing socialist tendency within the nationalist movement, by fitting the concept of planning into a capitalist framework. By 1945 it became clear that while this had caught the fancy of the state, it did not impress the wider business class. Indeed, by that time Birla himself seems to have cooled to the idea. Underlying this class-wide animosity to disciplinary planning, I argued, was a structural factor: by the end of the War, British business was being displaced in the subcontinent by its Indian counterpart, and the latter was in no mood to have its freedom curtailed by granting the state powers over the flow of investment. The upshot of this was that if the state was to assume such powers, they would have to be *usurped*.

The problem with this situation was that while capitalist opposition to a strong planning apparatus was growing, the strategy of the Indian National Congress was *eroding* its very capacity to install it. The end of the war brought with it a massive upsurge in the labor movement, led again mainly by Congress Socialists and the Communist Party of India. It was a mass upsurge that had put planning on the immediate agenda in 1942; the escalation of conflict in 1945 once again gave a boost to the Left. The difference, however, was that whereas the Quit India movement had taken off when the Congress leadership was in prison, the new wave of strikes came with the leadership poised to take state power. It was therefore in a position to react, and in early 1947 it took steps to demobilize and bring under its control the intolerably aggressive unions. The two most important such measures were the enactment of labor laws that drastically undermined collective bargaining and made unions dependent on state patronage, and the engineering of a split in the union movement, with the Congress launching its own pet union federation.

This episode is of some considerable importance to make sense of the final political settlement in the critical initial years after Independence. The demobilization of labor was carried out partly out of the Congress High Command's own suspiciousness toward independent labor action, but also to curry favor with business. Its effect, however, was to reduce even further the ability of state managers to withstand business pressure. In recent years consensus has grown among students of the state that the latter's ability to bargain with economic elites is increased when accompanied by popular mobilization and mass pressure.[1] This was particularly germane in the Indian case, for although almost all the Congress leaders agreed on the need for "planning," the advocates of disciplinary planning tended to be Left-leaning, and with closer connections to labor. The demobilization of the labor movement decreased the strength of this section of the leadership directly, by eroding its mass base and hence reducing its leverage within the party; it also thereby increased the power of the more right-wing elements, who, with the business class, saw planning as a process in which the state was at the service of firms. In the language of state theory, the demobilization of labor had the effect of reducing the autonomy of the state, which then made installing the apparatus for disciplinary planning that much more difficult.

It is important to include this episode in the analysis of state building, because the student of Indian history will rightly wonder how the capitalist class was able to impose its demands on a party that was at the helm of a massive social movement. Unless we attend to the shifting balance of power among social forces, the explanation of the ultimate outcome cannot but appear as overly deterministic—a resuscitation of some sort of instrumentalist view of the capitalist state, in which the only social force influencing policy is the capitalist class. But it is also important, as suggested in chapter 2, because it allows us to spin some tentative counterfactuals about what might have been, even with bourgeois recalcitrance unchanged, had the INC chosen not to so marginalize labor from the political scene.

This chapter focuses on three issues. First, it examines the basic framework of the relation between Congress and the labor movement in the years leading up to Independence. I argue that this relation was always uneasy, with much of the Congress leadership unwilling to go beyond a benign paternalism in their attitude toward workers and their organizations. This was witnessed more sharply in the decision taken in 1936 to deny labor leaders functional representation within the Congress High Command; as a result, labor always remained at the margins of the organization. This was, of course, a setback for the sympathizers of the labor movement in the short run. But it also meant that the movement always developed at arms' length from the party's leadership, and, once it exploded after 1945, the latter's distance from it—their lack of experience with it—induced a greater suspicion of it.

The consequences of this relation between the INC and labor are examined in the rest of the chapter. The second issue we take up is the upsurge in the labor movement after 1945, where it is shown that the end of the war witnessed the biggest explosion of strikes and union activity in the country's history. In reaction to the steady erosion of real wages on one side and the rampant profiteering by businesses on the other, workers' organizations in virtually all sectors of industry took to the streets in the period stretching from 1945 to 1947.

Third, we examine the Congress reaction to this development. It consisted of two related components: first, steps were taken to curtail the independence of the unions, with legislation that made the state, and not unions, the arbiter of industrial conflict. Second, the movement itself was split, with the creation of a new federation sponsored by the Congress, and explicitly committed to industrial peace. Once in place, Congress leaders and activists across the country applied pressure of varying intensity on workers to join the Congress unions, as a means of undermining the other, more independent and Left-leaning ones. This was capped at the end of 1947 by calling an Industrial Truce Conference, which brought together labor leaders, business leaders, and state managers, to agree to an end to industrial conflict. With the labor movement now weakened and split, the outcome was largely as desired: 1948 and 1949 saw an impressive reduction, if not total end, of strike activity. By the end of 1949 labor no longer posed an immediate threat to profits or industrial peace.[2]

The labor movement switched to lower gears just as negotiations between the state and capital on the instruments for industrial policy entered their critical phase, in 1949. The result was that as Indian business intensified its pressure on the state, the latter's own immediate autonomy from it was declining, as unions settled into the new dispensation. Within the party, the exodus of the Congress Socialists, a development that was a reaction to the High Command's rightward swing, compounded the loss of the mass base. Hence, just as business tightened the screws, the mass base as well as the organizational base for resistance was at its weakest. This dynamic is examined in the next chapter.

CONGRESS AND THE POPULAR CLASSES

The Indian National Congress had its origins in the late nineteenth century as something of an elite pressure group. Comprised mainly of the educated middle class—mostly lawyers—and the wealthy, it maintained in its early years a studied distance from popular mobilization and mass organization. This changed rather dramatically with the arrival of M. K. Gandhi in the second decade of the twentieth century, who thrust the Congress into mass activity on a scale hitherto unimaginable. Under Gandhi the INC rapidly grew into an organization at the helm of a genuine mass movement, and could point to a massive base of support. By the 1930s, through its leadership of several popular mobilizations, the INC could legitimately lay claim to being the single, most powerful representative of national aspirations in the subcontinent. This was not, of course, without its complications, the most serious of which was Gandhi's own rather idiosyncratic view of popular mobilization and his role in it. Further, at the core of the INC's leadership was a strong conservative current, never entirely comfortable with the radicalism of popular movements and ever fearful of the danger of such efforts exploding into class warfare. So long as Gandhi held sway in the party, however, this strand of the leadership — represented in the 1930s by figures like Rajendra Prasad, G. B. Pant, and, most important, V. B. Patel — could rely on his own particular brand of elite paternalism to hold such possibilities at bay. This was in large measure the basis of Gandhi's undisputed stature in the INC — on the one hand, his singular capacity to mobilize the masses, especially in rural India, which earned the respect of the Left; on the other hand, his staunch defense of property and wealth, which earned the trust of the Right.

As the INC grew into a genuine mass organization, its leadership, not surprisingly, came increasingly to reflect this new development. As India emerged from the Great Depression, a younger generation of leaders inspired by the movements of the time gravitated toward the Congress, and brought with them their own views and agendas. Of these, none was more important than the young Jawaharlal Nehru, the U.K.-trained barrister and son of Motilal Nehru, himself one of the older generation of leaders in the INC. Nehru came to the Congress inspired, like the rest of the leadership, by the idea of Indian independence, but he was also influenced deeply by a kind of vague fabian socialism. He quickly rose to prominence within the leadership, not only because of his impressive lineage but also because of his sharp strategic sense and considerable oratory skills. Indeed, by the mid-1930s Nehru was second only to Gandhi in his mass reach. Along with Nehru, however, there also grew at the fringes of the Congress leadership a layer of young organizers — Jayprakash Narayan (known as J. P.), Ashok Mehta, and Narendra Deva — who readily identified themselves as socialists and were more clearly influenced by Marxian ideas; partly because of their ideological commitments, these leaders were also more assiduous in giving their mass work an organizational form and permanence.

These new entrants into the ranks of the Congress leadership grew increasingly restive in the 1930s, calling for a greater incorporation of popular demands into the organization's platform. An early acknowledgment of these concerns appeared in 1931, at the annual meeting of the Congress in Karachi. The struggle for freedom, the Congress declared, was not just a juridical matter; it must also attend to the social and economic uplifting of the masses of Indians: "in order to end the exploitation of the masses, political freedom must include real economic freedom of the starving millions."[3] Along with the explicit nod to popular economic interests, the Karachi meeting also produced the first programmatic commitment to state economic control from the Congress, as it declared that in independent India, "the state shall own or control key industries and services, mineral resources, railways, shipping, and other means of public transport,"[4] embedded in a larger economic program.[5] This resolution reflected the Janus face the Congress maintained with regard to popular demands. On the one hand, it bore the imprint of the Civil Disobedience movement that had begun in 1930 and raged through 1931, a great upheaval in the wake of the Great Depression; on the other, with regard to its vision of the future dispensation, the resolution went only so far as to commit itself to an *etatism* of sorts. And this reflected the continuing hold on the leadership by the Congress Right.

Despite the statist coloring, the Karachi resolution was significant in that it became the touchstone for the Left in its advocacy of economic planning, and hence was regarded by Nehru, Jayprakash Narayan and the Left as a victory of sorts. But while the Congress had now made an explicit recognition of popular economic interests and demands, and was capable of leading genuine mass campaigns, the Left was painfully aware that the party still had no organizational links to popular classes. It still remained an elite organization, with leaders committed to egalitarian politics, to be sure, but still at a remove from mass organizations. It remained a party whose contact with popular classes was sporadic and disjointed, lasting typically as long as the leadership cared to carry any particular agitation.

By the mid-thirties the Left was busy making moves to rectify this state of affairs. In 1934 Narayan, Narendra Deva, Ashok Mehta, and others formed the Congress Socialist Party (CSP) as a caucus inside the INC, as an explicit challenge to the Right within the leadership.[6] The CSP recognized that the Congress was still the dominant presence on the Indian scene and hence intended to remain as a tendency within the broader current, at least for the immediate future. But it also feared that the party was lagging in its efforts to incorporate popular classes into its fold and hence was missing out on the chance not only to throw the British out at an early date but also to take battle to the Indian elites. So long as Gandhi was alive, the Left had no real chance of ever displacing the Right warhorses from the leadership;[7] they could, however, change the organizational environment within which they functioned. Hereafter, it was the CSP that was most active on all fronts relating to mass work, especially trade unions and peasant organizations, in a direct effort to bring popular pressure directly into the INC.

The culmination of Left efforts came in 1936, within and outside the Congress. Outside the INC, in April, Socialist and broader Left initiatives resulted in the formation of the All-India Kisan Sabha, the first national peasant organization committed to a radical agrarian agenda; around the same time, Nehru launched an effort to turn the Indian States Peoples' Conference — hitherto simply an elite organization functioning in the Princely States — into a mass body, moving beyond petition-signing campaigns and incorporating an agrarian agenda similar to that of the Kisan Sabha. Both these developments signaled a maturation of popular movements, on the one hand, and the increasing links being forged by one section of the INC with these movements, on the other.

Within the Congress, the two meetings that year in April and December found Nehru at the helm as president, and at the height of his infatuation with socialism. Decrying the "growing divorce between our organization and the masses," and calling on the Congress to "build up our organization with its mass affiliations as well as work among the masses," Nehru unveiled an ambitious agenda to forge permanent links with popular organizations, and to bring into the INC concrete forums for the representation of these interests. Such measures amounted to turning the INC into a genuine anti-imperialist "joint popular front"; Nehru argued that the pressing need now was to build up organizations of workers and peasants and then to establish links with them on a permanent basis, toward which a first step could be "corporate membership" of trade unions and peasant organizations in the INC.[8] In other words, workers and peasants were to have functional representation within the Congress.

The idea of functional representation of subaltern classes in the Congress was, in the end, defeated, thanks to an adroit campaign waged by the Right.[9] And from this point on, Nehru's enthusiasm for turning the INC into a genuine mass organization waned steadily, until it transmuted into a paternalistic statism scarcely distinguishable from the views of the Right.[10] But the events of 1936 remain extremely significant for our concerns. Despite the tactical defeat the Left suffered, the fact remained that popular organization was now far in advance of where it had been in the beginning of the decade; further, the Congress now had an articulate and committed Left presence in its leadership in the form of the CSP; more important still, this element of the leadership, unlike much of the Right, had direct and powerful links with the mass movement and mass organizations. From this point on, despite the grip of the Right on the highest echelons of the Congress hierarchy, there was a genuine challenge to its vision of the Independence movement and of what an independent India would look like. Ironically, from the standpoint of the Indian elites, the success of the Right in forestalling the entry of popular classes into the Congress in an organized form was to prove to be a double-edged sword. For while the Congress itself could still continue to be of service to elite interests, the movements now bore the danger of developing independently of the Congress and careening out of control. And this, in turn, could, in the future, force the Congress to bargain with movements that may have remained subdued had they been kept in the Congress fold. This was to become a real concern, as we shall see, in the latter part of World War II and immediately after it.

The Postwar Labor Upsurge

For some, the war had been an opportunity for enormous windfall gains in income. Industry and merchants groups benefited tremendously, as enormous deficits, and hence inflation, financed their operations in India.[11] The steady rise in prices afforded splendid opportunities for local business to reap profits, while a thriving black market for goods under controlled distribution gave a boost to merchant groups who were able to corner those items in short supply.[12] On the other hand, wages, though increasing in money terms, failed to keep up with the price rise and hence declined in real terms. Throughout the war years and in the immediate aftermath, Indian labor suffered a declining real wage, which did not stabilize to prewar levels until 1950.[13] In 1945–47 the real wage hovered at between 80 percent and 90 percent of its prewar level. This should be considered while keeping in mind that the 1939 wage levels were hardly adequate to begin with.[14]

As conditions for workers failed to improve appreciably after the war, unions and organizers took to the streets in wave after wave of strikes. The Indian labor movement was led at this time by two labor federations—the All-India Trade Union Congress (AITUC) and the Indian Federation of Labor (IFL). AITUC was the oldest of the labor organizations in India, founded in 1920, and had a strong base in the industrial centers. In the first two decades of its history AITUC had had a strong Congress presence in its leadership: its very first president was the Congressman Lala Lajpat Rai, and in the years that followed AITUC worked closely with the INC. The proximity of the two organizations peaked in the later 1930s, when the former even passed a resolution in favor of joining the latter.[15] But as we saw in the previous chapter, this was precisely the time when, despite Nehru's efforts, the INC struck down any moves to have functional representation of labor within the organization. The direct links Congress had with labor remained limited to Gandhi's HMSS, a kind of volunteer service for labor which, while it took part in labor actions, never really assumed the role of a full union. Hence AITUC continued as an independent body.

The IFL was a younger body, founded in 1941 as a breakaway faction from AITUC. It was led by followers of M. N. Roy, one of the founders of the Indian Communist movement and renowned for his debate with Lenin in the Second Congress of the Communist International. Roy led his colleagues out of AITUC in 1941 over the issue of nonparticipation in the war, arguing against the position of the Congress to abstain until Britain conceded more favorable terms for Indian self-rule; he founded the Radical Democratic Party (one step in his rapid move away from communism), and the IFL was its offshoot. Meanwhile, as the Congress leaders were imprisoned with the launching of the Quit India movement, the Communist Party, which had always had a significant, though not dominant, presence in AITUC, now found itself at the helm of the organization.[16]

Hence, when the Congress leaders emerged from prison after the war and took the reins of government in September 1946, they found themselves confronted by two labor organizations; moreover, both organizations were out of their control and both were led by leftist parties, and hence both opposed the continuing upward redistribution of income due to inflation and business malfeasance. As a result, starting in late 1945, the strike activity level and labor actions in India exploded. The new militant mood within the Indian working class was, of course, dangerous in itself, but now it was even more so because it was being harnessed by a political grouping which the Congress neither controlled nor trusted. This was a legacy of the decision taken in 1936 to deny labor functional representation in the INC, which we examined in the previous section.

Employers, for their part, responded with a steady stream of pleas to the public and the new government to take measures to quell the labor unrest. Significantly — and the importance of this point will emerge particularly sharply in the next chapter — while business complained unrelentingly about the strike wave, one searches in vain for public calls emanating from this class for economic concessions to labor. Instead, the typical tactic was to point to the strikes and demands as signs of labor's narrow self-interest,[17] the proper response to which was to remind labor of the need for sacrifice in order to build the nation.[18]

By early 1947 it was clear that no end was in sight to the industrial conflict. By the spring of that year Nehru began to float the idea that a conference was needed in order to bring the two sides together to reach an agreement—a truce—so that production could return to normal levels.[19] Both labor and capital saw this as a welcome opportunity to break the impasse, and hence arrangements were quickly made for the affair. India achieved its independence on August 15, 1947, and four months to the day after that the Tripartite Conference was held to end the class hostilities.

A "RESPONSIBLE" LABOR MOVEMENT

The upsurge in the labor movement in the immediate aftermath of the war was, in a certain sense, a boon for the Congress. In forcing Indian business to the bargaining table, it also strengthened the hand of the Congress Left, in the persons of the Congress Socialists, Nehru, and Congress labor leaders like G. L. Nanda, Khandubhai Desai, Hariharnath Shastri, and V. V. Giri. This wing of the party was now in the position of pushing through the very policies business had recoiled against in the early days of the National Planning Committee. On the other hand, it also raised important dilemmas. The labor movement was not a creature of the Congress; it was led by the All-India Trade Union Congress, an autonomous federation whose leadership, to be sure, did include Congress members but also extended far beyond it— to socialists, independents, and, most disturbingly, the Communist Party of India. This was the legacy of the decision in the mid-thirties not to allow functional representation in organizations of the popular classes: the organizations grew in spite of the ambivalence the Congress had toward them, and they grew through a leadership cadre not chosen by Congress and hence free of its control.

The considerable independence of AITUC would have been seen as a threat to the High Command even in the best of days. In the years following the war the threat was palpable and quite immediate—until labor could be persuaded or induced into peace, it would be impossible to initiate the process of recovery. This worry was reinforced by the continued warnings being issued by business and its organs to the effect that labor's intransigence was the single, most important impediment to national reconstruction.[20] The worries induced by business pressure were compounded by the fact that so long as labor remained under the guidance of an independent and recalcitrant leadership, it would be extremely difficult to win over the Congress Right led by Patel—and if Patel could not be brought into the game, it would be next to impossible to placate Indian business. After Gandhi, it was Patel that the business class looked to for succor, and when it came to the arduous negotiations on matters of planning, the conduit to the latter would have to be the Gujarati strongman. For much of the Congress Left, therefore, it seemed that if their ambition of a labor-inclusive industrial regime was to become a reality, a necessary step was to bring labor under heel. This was to be done in a two-step process: first, by attenuating the ability of "irresponsible" labor leaders to use the strike weapon with wanton abandon; and, second, by reining in the very independence of the labor movement itself.

Of course, this was not the only conceivable alternative. A large section of the Left and the Communists were pushing the INC to embrace the labor movement and to continue pushing from below to force through the compromise sought by unions. Business, they argued, would not willingly concede the rights and powers that labor sought. Any negotiations would have to be backed by strength. The Congress Socialists were, in fact, actively organizing in this direction. With a strong base in the public services, railways, the textile industry, and the coal industry in Bihar, the Socialists continued throughout 1946–47 to organize labor actions throughout the country. In this they were, of course, joined by unions under Communist leadership, such as Tramway workers in Calcutta, the post and telegraph workers, as well as workers in the textile industry. Perhaps most surprising was the emergence of a Gandhian Left within the Congress, in the persons of J. C. Kumarappa, Shankarrao Deo, and even Khandubhai Desai, which began to launch an increasingly vocal attack on Indian business.[21] In so doing it was quietly and discreetly going against the positions which Gandhi himself was taking at the same time, and in the same forum. Throughout the immediate postwar period, Gandhi maintained a steadfast opposition to independent action by labor organizations, with a stance that insisted, in fact, on compulsory arbitration as the most legitimate means of resolving disputes.[22] Indeed, an examination of Gandhi's magazine, *The Harijan*, in the last three years of his life (1945–47) fails to offer up a single instance of a strike that Gandhi regarded as just. Thus the Gandhians, in their defense of the various actions by labor, were striking out a path quite distinct from that of their leader.[23]

Despite this contrarian strain within the Congress, the mood of the leadership was firmly set against the possibility of an independent labor movement. India was about to wrest independence after a decades-long struggle, and, as far as the High Command was concerned, the task of reconstruction and nation building could not be trusted to the whims of an undisciplined working class. Early intimations of the attitude of Congress were displayed in August 1946, when the All-India Congress

Committee passed a resolution that was highly critical of continuing strike activity, and attributed it in part to the influence of "certain individuals" who were out to "exploit the ignorance of the workers" for their own ends. The resolution decried the "total absence of a well-defined national plan" to deal with labor issues and urged that steps in this direction be taken.[24] Toward this end, in early 1947, while still heading up an interim government and shortly before Liaquat Ali Khan's budget, the cabinet proposed and passed its key legislation on labor issues, the object of which was to provide a framework for labor-capital relations in independent India.

Labor Legislation

It is fair to say that the legislation of early 1947 embodied the contradictory aims that the INC had taken on. On the one hand, it put into place many of the mechanisms the party had been promising through the past decades. Trade unions were recognized as a legitimate vehicle to be used by labor in the pursuit of its interests; the legitimacy of strikes as a means of negotiation was similarly acknowledged, as was the importance of collective bargaining, at least in theory; at the plant level, the Industrial Disputes Act provided for the formation of works committees to smooth the day-to-day friction and to generate a culture of mutuality between employers and workers. In all this, the point was to strengthen the capacity of labor, on the one hand, while also creating the institutions for a congenial regime of industrial relations.

But while the new government gave to the labor movement with one hand, it took away with the other. Unions were recognized as the sole representative of labor's interests, and employers were enjoined to bargain with them on relevant issues; but the power of the unions to compel such bargaining was severely curtailed, as was the prospect of genuine collective bargaining. With regard to the former, the power of the unions was limited by two components of the labor legislation. First, while unions were given legal sanction, there was little in the way of actual protection against employer coercion. The legislation governing this — the Trade Union Act of 1928 — only provided for protection against criminal conspiracy proceedings. In 1947 amendments to this Act were proposed that would also provide for protection against unfair labor practices, in a manner fashioned after the Wagner Act in the United States. Although the Assembly approved these amendments, the Act never came into effect since the cabinet had not given the amended Act the necessary notification. Unions were thus left largely unprotected against employer malfeasance.

A second, more important means of weakening union power was the law relating to industrial conflict, which was contained in the Industrial Disputes Act of 1947. First, unions could resort to a strike or a lockout only after providing notification of at least fourteen days. But, more important, in the case of public utilities, the government was given the power to compel the parties to resort to an arbitrator if it saw fit. This immediately foisted compulsory arbitration onto workers in the postal service, the railroads, and the power industry. But the Act also gave state governments the power to declare *any* industry a public utility for a period of six months; this meant that compulsory arbitration could now be extended to virtually all sectors of industry. The combined effect of these two aspects of labor law was this: when faced with an intransigent management, labor was forced to contemplate a strike only if it provided a two-week notice to the appropriate government. But the moment it got whiff of any such impending action, the government could simply intervene and refer the dispute to an arbitrator—labor thus had the *right* to strike but very little *ability* to do so. Without this ability, and without the amendments in the Trade Union Act protecting unions against unfair labor practices, labor had little ability to compel employers to bargain in good faith.

With unions largely without the power to insist that employers bargain in good faith, the prospects for genuine collective bargaining rapidly receded. If the likely outcome of an industrial dispute were its referral to an arbitrator, employers would automatically have the upper hand if they could drag out the proceedings interminably. And, indeed, they have such power.[25] While the law provided for compulsory arbitration, it did nothing to ensure rapid delivery of a verdict. Management was left with the ability to drag out the proceedings for months, even years.[26] This meant that under the new dispensation, collective bargaining held little value to employers, as their recalcitrance was only likely to deliver the parties to a conciliator or arbitrator, and, in such a case, the whole matter would turn on which of the parties would give in first. And management, with immeasurably greater resources at its command, was, of course, always the favored party.

In so curtailing the scope and power of unions, the INC did not leave the fortunes of Indian workers entirely to the winds. Instead, those matters which are normally the objects of deliberation between labor and capital—conditions of employment, promotion, wage scales, safety, leave and holidays, discipline, and the like—were now covered by a new legislation, most prominently the Industrial Employment (Standing Orders) Act and the Factories Act. Together, these defined the conditions of employment to which employers with establishments above a specified size now had to adhere. Nominally, these orders and conditions were to be drafted through consultation with unions so as to in-

sert a semblance of mutuality into what would otherwise seem a blatantly authoritarian series of measures; but the authority rested firmly
with the state.

There was a point to all this. As stated earlier, the Congress leadership was not aiming for the despotism of capital but for wresting initiative away from labor and placing it with the state instead. Labor could
not be trusted with the power to articulate and fight for its own interests, not so much because the party was anti-labor but because the latter was, in the eyes of Congress, not yet mature enough to take a sufficiently balanced view of the situation. Its demands would thus have to
be tempered by the hand of the state, and the measures just described
were a means to this end.

Dividing Labor

The new labor legislation was passed over the loud objections and denunciations of the bulk of the Indian labor leadership. Inside the Legislative Assembly and outside, leaders of AITUC and the IFL loudly objected to the measures restricting the scope of the strike weapon and
collective bargaining.[27] N. M. Joshi, the veteran AITUC leader and perhaps the leading liberal in the labor movement, led the charge against
the new legislation and was joined by Maniben Kara and S. Guruswami. The three veteran unionists objected to the clauses described in
the previous section on the predictable grounds that they effectively
stripped labor of any means to force employers to the bargaining table.
But Joshi also pointed out that the policy was courting a greater danger:
if labor disputes were settled through arbitration as a matter of course,
and if the arbitration machinery were incapable of delivering timely and
effective decisions — as indeed it appeared — then the government was
courting the danger of delegitimizing the very institutions of labor policy.[28] With unions already weakened, this erosion of the state's authority
in labor relations would just about rule out the possibility of industrial
peace. To this, Guruswami added that in the absence of adequate measures the proposed works committees, too, would be of little use; as
presently constituted, they tended to be used as vehicles for undermining unions rather than as complements to them.[29] The Industrial Disputes Bill, which contained the provision for the committees, provided
no protection against such an eventuality.[30] What Guruswami, Kara,
and Joshi all pointed to was the internally contradictory character of
the legislation Congress issued on labor matters: not only was it rife
with measures that hobbled unions, but these measures undermined
even the ones that were friendly toward labor and reflected the long-
promised steps toward social democracy.

In this matter, however, labor did not present a united front. Crucially, those unionists who were also in the front ranks of the Congress leadership, particularly those who held ministerial office, put their weight behind the legislation. Hence, both within the Assembly and without, the proposed labor legislation was championed by Gulzarilal Nanda, the Labor Minister Jagjivan Ram, N. V. Gadgil, Hariharnath Shastri, Mohanlal Saksena, and others; indeed, the only Congress labor leader who did not openly support compulsory arbitration and the curb on strikes was V. V. Giri. For the vast majority of Congress members, the concerns of labor could not be held dear over the "national interest," and the latter came increasingly to be identified with the imperatives of smooth industrial production. The switchover from nationalist movement to nationalist government thus brought with it a corresponding shift in the attitude toward labor. Whereas in previous years it had been a force to be harnessed, it now became a threat that had to be controlled.

Having decided on their labor legislation despite the objections of some of the most powerful and respected unionists, the Congress High Command could not but follow their actions to their ominous conclusion. Having defeated the legislative opposition, they now faced the possibility of noncompliance within the labor movement. The debates in the Assembly and the loud campaign outside it immediately made it clear that unions as presently constituted could not be relied on to uphold the order that the Congress was trying so hard to create. As the largest and most militant federation, AITUC presented the biggest danger. The initial Congress strategy was to try to take over the leadership of AITUC, which was numerically dominated by the Communists. Recall that the Congress did not have a union of its own. Its labor leaders were active in either the AITUC itself or in Gandhi's HMSS. In a bid to bolster the presence of Congress in the AITUC, in November 1946 the HMSS asked all *its* supporters to join AITUC. But this was resisted by its most powerful affiliate, the Ahmedabad Textile Association, which blandly reported that it was not its policy to join national federations. Initial attempts to control labor by taking over AITUC had thus come to naught.

By the middle of 1947 the High Command moved more resolutely to hitch labor more tightly to Congress's wagon. The labor leaders and the HMSS called a conference in May, three months after the Industrial Disputes Act was passed, to launch a new national labor federation, one explicitly committed to the party's labor policy. In his letter of invitation to the meeting, Gulzarilal Nanda made it plain:

The stand taken by [AITUC] in reference to the principle and procedure of arbitration . . . has been strongly disapproved [*sic*] by many prominent trade unionists. It is felt that it will militate against the best and most vital interests of the country . . . if at this stage a central organization of labour is not formed in harmony with the ideas and resolutions of the Indian National Congress.[31]

The idea had wide support within the party, from the Right as well as much of the Left (with the exception of the Socialists).[32] The Old Guard like Patel and G. B. Pant were present at the meeting, the Ahmedabad Textile Association abandoned its objection to joining a national federation, and even a prominent Socialist, Hariharnath Shastri, hopped onboard. The new federation was called the Indian National Trade Union Congress (INTUC) and was fashioned to be the arm of the party, disclaimers notwithstanding. The constitution of the new Union Federation had the usual odes to social justice, full employment, living wages, and the like; but the meat lay elsewhere, in the part that was, in effect, its leitmotif: "Every affiliated organization shall offer to submit to arbitration every industrial dispute in which a settlement is not reached by negotiation and shall not sanction or support a strike unless avenues of a settlement have been exhausted, and a majority of its members vote by ballot in favor of strike."[33] Having concluded that they could not wrest control of AITUC away from the Communists, the Congress High Command thus set about creating a new union, effectively splitting the labor movement.

Understandably the leadership of the AITUC regarded the exit of the Congress members from the organization as a catastrophe. When Congressmen attributed their departure to the iron grip that Communists had on the organization, N. M Joshi objected vigorously, insisting that while the Communist Party of India (CPI) did have a substantial presence in the leadership, there had been no experience of sectarianism or underhandedness from their side. He pointed out that only five of the twelve office bearers of the organization were Communists, that all the office bearers had been elected unanimously, and that all decisions taken since 1938 had also been unanimous[34]. Within a year of his issuing this statement, the CPI did, in fact, initiate a sharp swing to the Left under the leadership of B. T. Ranadive, adopting the very sectarianism of which it was being accused. But in mid-1947 Joshi's argument was largely valid. AITUC was not yet in the grip of the CPI, and it did function in a more or less democratic fashion. If anything, it was the departure of the Congressmen that hastened its slide into sectarian wilderness.

By mid-1947 the High Command was, in its own view, closer to the objective that had animated its strategy ever since the installment of the interim government in September 1946: industrial peace. It had passed labor law that granted it the power to intervene in any industrial dispute as well as radically curtailing labor's use of the strike weapon. Matters that were usually settled through collective bargaining were now dealt with through detailed regulations within labor law, and the daily, micro-level affairs that arose outside the purview of these regulations would be settled by works committees. To reduce the threat of noncompliance, it had inaugurated a new labor federation, INTUC, which was sworn to uphold Congress policy in industrial matters. Indeed, under the aegis of a largely friendly government and bureaucracy, INTUC grew by leaps and bounds, soon becoming the largest union federation in the country.

The Significance of Demobilization

With the formation of INTUC and the split in the labor movement, the threat of strikes and direct action rapidly receded from the industrial scene. In late 1947 the Congress called an "industrial truce" conference, with leading representatives from labor, industry, and the government present, to reach some kind of accord. With INTUC now accounting for a large proportion of the unions in the country, a truce was announced, with labor agreeing to quell the rank and file and to attempt to revive industrial production.[35] The truce worked—strikes quickly dropped down to prewar levels, and labor soon ceased to be a threat.[36]

The de-escalation of industrial conflict certainly made employers happier. It also had the effect, however, of drastically weakening the position of the pro-planning forces within the INC. A commitment to "planning" was just about ubiquitous in the Congress Party; but it was the Congress Left that was committed to some kind of *disciplinary* planning, with a strong state apparatus and a concern to hold firms accountable for the largesse they received from the state. Within the High Command, it was the conservative, older generation—Patel, Rajendra Prasad, C. Rajagopalachari, and others—who exercised the most influence. As discussed above, the power of the Left was, understandably, directly proportional to the strength of the mass movement. With labor now demobilized, the position of these proponents of a strong planning apparatus was gravely weakened.

The Congress leadership appears not to have seen this as a problem. From the outset, labor had been seen by much of the leadership as a nuisance, as an agent that kept interfering in the links so carefully being forged with representatives of the business class. The assumption seems to have been that, since Birla, Tata, and others had announced a commitment to planning, all that was needed now was to hammer out the details. Both sides agreed that, whatever else these details contained, they would not include power devolving to labor. This being the case, the Congress leaders appear to have been confident that the path was now open to instituting the apparatus for capitalist planning.

As I shall show in the next chapter, events were to prove this assumption quite wrong. The Indian capitalist class certainly did desire something called "planning," but it had nothing at all to do with *disciplinary* planning; on the other hand, much of the Congress leadership visualized state-led development in just this way—if they were to dole out public revenues to firms, the latter would have to be held accountable for what they did with them. This difference in conceptualization would prove to be critical, the point on which the entire conflict of the next four years would turn. Congress leaders realized that both sides—the state and capital—were in agreement on ISI; what they did not realize was that this very agreement also generated a further incentive for firms to resist the component of ISI that state managers prized, namely, the regulation of private investment.

The demobilization of labor removed from the scene the agent that could have been pivotal in giving the state more leverage against the business class. As I admitted in chapter 2, this is a somewhat conjectural thesis. But it does have support from other studies of state-society relations, in the developed countries as well as in LDCs. Several scholars have argued that the ability of state managers to push through legislation that business opposes is greatly increased in the presence of mobilized mass movements.[37] It is a reasonable hypothesis that the best chance Indian state managers had to install the necessary state agencies for disciplinary planning would have come through a greater reliance on the labor movement, since, as the next chapter will show, capitalists were implacably opposed to it. In forcing labor off the stage, Nehru and the advocates of state-led development only increased the power of their opponents.

CHAPTER 6

The Business Offensive and the Retreat of the State

INTRODUCTION

The previous two chapters have shown that the momentum of events in the years after the war was not in a direction favorable to disciplinary planning. The business class gave a very cool reception to the second volume of the Bombay Plan in 1945, as well as to the publication of the industrial policy statement four months later. The signatories to the Bombay Plan, in turn, did not respond by taking the battle for state-led industrialization to their colleagues but, instead, meekly faded into the background. This, I argued, provides strong reason to believe that not only did the Bombay Plan not represent the sentiment of the business class generally but, by 1945, it may not even have been an accurate indication of the signatories' attitudes themselves. All this was to show that there was no "pact" around disciplinary planning in the offing for Indian state managers after the war. If such a state was to be built, it would almost certainly meet with resistance from capital.

The policy of splitting and then demobilizing labor, examined in the preceding chapter, served only to make the chances of installing the desired state apparatus even more remote. If business was in no mood to support a disciplinary state, removing the pressure the labor movement was exerting would only strengthen the hand of the former, and hence reduce the state's autonomy.

This chapter now brings into focus the actual struggle around the key instruments of industrial policy in the years immediately after Independence. The basic thrust of the argument is that, while the new state managers had on the anvil a fairly ambitious agenda for installing the instruments for disciplinary planning, this agenda was derailed by a massive and coordinated offensive by the business class. I show this by examining in some detail the conflicts surrounding two events: the setting up of the Planning Commission in 1950, which was the center for all economic planning in the years that followed, and the enactment of the Industries (Development and Regulation) Act (IDRA), first proposed in 1949 and finally passed in 1951, which was the key legislation on the power of the government to implement industrial policy. These two instruments are widely recognized as central to the whole industrial policy regime. Together they formed the hinges on which the two critical dimensions of state capacity turned, as discussed in chapter 2: the Planning Commission was to be the mechanism that secured internal state cohesiveness, while the Industries Act provided the institutions for the state's "embeddedness" in the industrial sector. The fate of the Planning Commission and the IDRA thus largely governed the overall quality of the developmental state.

The course of this chapter's progression is somewhat more complicated than in the preceding chapters. I therefore summarize its main claims.

1. *From the outset, state managers tried to tailor industrial policy so as to be able to achieve two objectives: elicit the support of the capitalist class, while also having the capacity to discipline members of that class.* Toward the first objective, Congress leaders explicitly rejected the demands the Left was making for large-scale nationalization of industry and, as shown in the previous chapter, for the devolution of significant power to unions. In addition, they continued in their commitment to put a number of mechanisms in place to foster the growth of private industry, like the erection of tariff walls, the provision of cheap credit, imports, and so on, which have been at the heart of import-substituting industrialization. But in order to achieve the second objective, they also proposed legislation, in the Industrial (Development and Control) Bill,[1] that would grant the state considerable power to regulate the flow of private investment in exchange for its high profits and would punish firms found to be delinquent.

2. *The dilemma this posed was that the very provisions designed to elicit the support of private capital also made it rational for it to resist the instruments of discipline.* The incentive structure, as described in chapter 2, was this: the largesse ISI bestowed, and the conditions generated by it, made it not only rational, but also possible, for firms to resist the attempts to install a disciplinary state. ISI made it easy for firms to amass huge profits without having to worry about their competitive strength. This being the case, they had little direct incentive to submit to discipline, unlike their counterparts in Korea. The domestic capitalist class, therefore, launched a massive offensive against the proposals for disciplinary planning, the focus of which was the Industrial (Development and Control) Bill. In fact, business called for a complete revocation of the bill from the Constituent Assembly. In its stead, it proposed a bill that would leave industrial regulation to industry associations, manned by representatives chosen by the concerned industry, and granted the power to prescribe the occasion for, and nature of, state regulation. Regulation by the state was to be replaced by industry's self-regulation.

3. *The capitalist class, however, was itself handicapped by two factors: first, it could only launch an attack on the disciplinary aspects of planning, not planning itself; second, its own proposals—for industrial self-regulation—failed because of the experience with trade associations after the war.* The attack on disciplinary planning would have been most effective if it could have been on the very idea of state intervention. But there was a powerful consensus within the business class in favor of some kind of organized state assistance to industry, which was, of course, the heart of ISI. In the language of the time, this went under the rubric of "planning." Business was therefore in the delicate position of demanding that the national community grant it favors, while insisting that the instruments proposed to ensure reciprocity be abandoned. For this to be palatable, capital would have to propose an alternative set of instruments; but the ones it did propose—regulation by industry associations—lost all legitimacy through the concrete experience with such arrangements after the war. This made it difficult for business to push back entirely the initial thrust for state-led industrial policy.

4. *As a result, the legislation for industrial policy was passed after all, and a planning commission was installed; but both were severely compromised by the state's concern to appease capitalists.* The new Planning Commission (PC) was put into place, but instead of giving it the kind of powers required for industrial planning, it was made a largely advisory body; that is, instead of restructuring the state around the needs of industrial planning, the institutions of planning were made to accommodate themselves to the existing structure of the state. The immediate mechanism behind this was a revolt by state managers to the idea of a new institution that would have power over them; but this revolt was itself made possible by the atmosphere of tentativeness among supporters of planning, who were in full retreat against the business offensive. Similarly the Industrial (Development and Control) Bill was also passed (under a slightly different name), since business could offer no realistic alternative. But by the time the bill finally came out of committee deliberations, its punitive and disciplinary components were drastically watered down, making it very dependent for success on the willing cooperation of business. Thus, even though the key instruments for industrial policy were *formally* installed, their actual *power* was radically compromised.

The Commitment to Import-Substitution

In chapter 4, it was argued that the Bombay Plan had failed to elicit the support of the domestic capitalist class. This was evidenced most directly in the reception given to the second volume of the plan but also in the hostility evinced toward the industrial policy statement of 1945, which had used the plan as a template. Superficially it may seem that the opposition was driven by a concern that such powers of intervention and regulation, in the hands of a colonial state, would only be used to the detriment of local capital. This may indeed have been a genuine concern; had it been the sole or even overriding concern, however, then the animus toward state intervention should have dissipated in the years following Independence. I argued in chapter 4 that, indeed, even by 1945, there were deeper reasons behind the opposition to activist industrial policy; these centered mainly around the opportunities made available by the departure of British firms and by the Indian takeovers of many of the firms that remained. With new avenues for corporate expansion opening up, the last thing Indian businesses wanted was for the state to dictate the pace, and even the extent, of the new ventures.

We now come to the other, and more fundamental, reason for domestic capital's opposition to disciplinary planning. The basic, structuring fact about the Indian development model up to the mid-1980s was the persistence of import substitution. It was observed in chapter 4 that the commitment to protecting domestic industry from world competition and heaping public resources on it was already a staple of the INC program by the later 1930s, and figured prominently in the deliberations, and conclusions, of the National Planning Committee.[2] The concern to shelter and nurture industry also occupied center stage in the proposals of the Bombay Plan,[3] and was carried over into the preparations for postwar reconstruction by the colonial state in its final years, as evidenced in its internal memorandums[4] and the industrial policy statement of 1945.[5] Through all the complex negotiations and permutations of the war years, the one principle that remained unquestioned was the state's obligation to assist private capital.

This principle was continued steadfastly in the years immediately following the war. Once it was clear that independence was imminent, Nehru again set about putting committees in place to draw up an agenda for capitalist planning. The National Planning Committee was revived just long enough to publish its reports, many of which had gone into cold storage when the committee had collapsed with the outbreak of war.[6] As the INC was asked to form an interim government in the fall of 1946, which was to ease the transition to full independence in August 1947, Nehru immediately constituted an Advisory Planning Board (APB) to draw up the broad framework for plans under the new dispensation.[7] The board worked at a frenzied pace to produce a report by mid-1947, which enunciated a set of policies that were broadly consistent with the momentum established in the previous years.[8] At the heart of these policies, again, was the idea of state assistance to industry—

financial, technical, and logistical — as the core of a program of national development. And central to this assistance was the protection given to local firms from foreign capital.[9]

The examples of such policy statements in the early years of independence could be multiplied. Just two years after the report of the Advisory Planning Board, a Fiscal Commission was appointed that again repeated the same commitments in its report, which were carried over into the First Five-Year Plan, and so on.[10] The point is that, from the very earliest discussions of Indian industrial planning, the domestic capitalist class was given every assurance that the new state would be singularly committed to using public monies as a means of accelerating the development of private industry. This was, of course, directly in the state's interest, both for its legitimacy as well as for purposes of revenue maximization. Fostering industrial development was regarded as an essential component of "nation building," and shepherding that development at the fastest possible pace would only facilitate other activities that state managers deemed important.

The members of the Indian capitalist class thus knew that, whatever else may come, there would be a private sector in the development strategy and that this sector would be the beneficiary of considerable state assistance. What was not yet settled was the *scope* of the private sector, and the *terms* on which it would receive its largesse. This being the case, it was now in the interest of the bourgeoisie to ensure that the scope would be the maximum that was consistent with steady profitability and that the terms would be as favorable as possible. Operationally this meant two things: first, that the public sector should be restricted to those areas where private capital was not already established and, more important, not forthcoming; the flip-side to this was that it would ensure the maximum possible scope for private capital and, more importantly, keep the initiative for its expansion in its own hands. Second, it meant fighting against the idea that, in return for giving firms resources, the state had the right to police private capital in any way. The state could *urge* discipline, but it could not usurp the right to *enforce* discipline.

This set of incentives was made possible by the conditions of ISI and stood in contrast to the incentive structure generated by the export-led strategy that Korea adopted. The basic argument for the different incentive structures generated by the two accumulation models has been developed in chapter 2, and I will not rehash it again here. But briefly, in the Korean case, the opening provided by the Japanese would have been in danger of going to waste if Korean firms did not drastically ratchet their performance level upward. Firms therefore had a direct interest in accepting state discipline, so long as this discipline was essential for their succeeding in export markets. This enabled Park to embark on his state-building enterprise without any real opposition by the capitalist class; it enabled him to impose the very set of regulations and conditions that Indian capitalists would fight against in their country. In India, because there was no direct threat of being exposed to world-class competition, the connection between profitability and performance was severed, and local business had no reason to accept the imposition of discipline. How it fought back the agenda of disciplinary planning is a subject to which we now turn.[11]

JETTISONING NATIONALIZATION

The first issue to be settled was the scope of the private sector in independent India. Was it to be a residual that was left over after the maximal expansion of state enterprises? Or was the principle to be that private firms ought to be the driving force behind industrialization, with the public sector taking up the less profitable areas, those in which capitalists showed little or no interest? A small but vocal contingent in the INC was pushing for the former principle; as we shall see, however, this section lost ground and was marginalized almost immediately, and the final decision was much closer to the second of the two principles.

The Left's Final Gasp

The previous chapter focused on the massive labor upsurge in the two years after the war and the attempts by the Congress High Command to quell it in the first part of 1947. We now turn to the complement to these efforts, namely, the initiation of steps to formulate a framework for future industrial planning in India. In late 1947 the Congress leadership appointed a committee to draw up a draft for the party's economic policy. Reflecting the mood of the time, the committee that was put together to draft the document was chaired by Nehru and dominated by the Left and Gandhians.[12] It met four times between December 10 and January 25, and released its report in late January 1948. In many ways its recommendations were utterly conventional and in keeping with the program the INC had been committed to for two decades; it called for land reform, fair wages, labor rights, economic planning, and the like. But it also endorsed granting considerable concessions to labor — like a program of profit-sharing and works committees — and boldly recommended a progressive socialization of industry.[13]

The *Report of the Economic Committee* was, in theory, to be a framework for the future economic policy of the government. Taken at face value, it seemed to be a positive response to the mass upsurge in the postwar years. But, in fact, the document represented the swan song, not the rise to prominence, of the Left within the party. The labor movement was already split by the formation of the INTUC by the Congress, and its demobilization was under way. Further, changes in the Congress organization in the past year had severely weakened the links between its mass base and its leadership.[14] This had the effect of increasing the independence of the Congress cabinet from the party's hold, which meant, in turn, that the actual force wielded by the *Report of the Economic Committee* would be questionable. With the mass movement in abeyance, and the hold of the party over its government greatly weakened, the means for translating the recommendations into policy were becoming thin. And in a few weeks, with the departure of the Socialists, the situation would become more dire still.

None of this prevented the business class from responding to the document with alacrity as soon as it was released. Within days after it was announced, prominent businessmen and the major industry associations all issued loud denunciations of the *Report*.[15] Industry warned that not only would the recommendations of the committee depress business confidence even further but that Nehru and his colleagues had journeyed far beyond anything suggested in the past. Of particular concern was the encouragement the *Report* gave to the progressive socialization of industry, which, the critics rightly pointed out, was not only new but also went against the daily assurances the Congress leaders had been giving ever since Independence. It is not clear whether business actually feared the threat of nationalization or whether it simply took up the issue as a way to intensify pressure on the new government to scale back planning more broadly. In any case, the attacks on the *Report* continued through the spring of 1948.

During this time, in March 1948, the Congress Socialists finally made good on their own threats and exited from the INC to form the Socialist Party.[16] Their departure had the immediate effect of removing a source of conflict inside the Congress Party. But an added consequence was that it drastically diluted the political base within the party for the votaries of state-led development. Since the 1930s the Congress Socialists had been one of the most persistent forces within the INC pressing for an economic policy that rested not only on strategic industrial planning but on the kind of planning that disciplined capital. Although still a relatively small group, the Socialists nonetheless boasted a very committed phalanx of cadre at the grass roots, and, with the exception of Nehru, the Congress had few leaders with the mass appeal of men like Jayprakash Narayan and Ashok Mehta. On the other hand, Nehru had little organizational strength or acumen; this rested firmly in the hands of Patel, through two main mechanisms: Patel was the main fund-raiser for the party and was also in charge of assigning party nominations for candidates in elections.[17]

With the exit of the Socialists, the dismantling of the *mass base* for disciplinary planning *outside* the INC — with the demobilization of labor — was now compounded by a weakened *political base* for disciplinary planning *within* the INC. Even with the labor movement derailed, the presence of the Left in the party had given planners a bedrock of cadre and organizational resources to fight for their agenda; the exit of the Socialists now fatally reduced even this leverage. On the other hand, the continuing mobilization by business meant that the class pressure *against* a strong state gained in relative strength and found an easier expression within the INC through the ready conduit of Patel and the Right. In the coming months Nehru was thus to find himself in a hopeless position in the battle to install the institutions of planning — growing increasingly frustrated with a capitalist class that showed no signs of reducing its intransigence and a party leadership that was either unwilling or incapable of pushing through its own stated policies.

The Retreat from Nationalization

With the template for future economic policy released by the Congress Economic Programme Committee in late January, the next step was for its translation into policy by the new government. As a first step toward the passing of legislation, in early April 1948 — scarcely two months after the Economic Programme Committee released its recommendations — the state issued its own *Industrial Policy Statement* (*IPS*), which laid down the broad contours for all future industrial policy.[18] This statement did, in fact, constitute the framework for Indian industrial legislation for the better part of forty years after its passing. It was not, however, a piece of legislation per se; it was not passed as an act of Parliament but was merely an enunciation by the government of the likely path its future policy would take. The actual legislation for industrial policy would be submitted to Parliament one year later in 1949, and we shall come to that presently. It is useful to examine the two matters separately, because each was significant for different reasons: the *IPS* marked the final rejection of nationalization as a programmatic commitment, whereas the Industrial Development and Control Bill became the flash point for the battle over state regulation of private industry.

The most noteworthy aspect of the *IPS* was how it quietly but firmly moved to dilute what were, from the standpoint of capital, the most objectionable elements in the recommendations of the Congress Economic Programme Committee.[19] The main purpose of the *IPS* was to demarcate the proper domain for the private and public sectors in industry. It thus divided industry into three areas: that which was reserved for the state, a second in which existing private firms would be allowed to expand but where new undertakings would be the primary responsibility of the state, and a third which would be left to private capital but subject to state regulation. Significantly, in the first category—industries that were to be exclusively state-owned—only three were listed: defense, railways, and atomic energy.[20] Of these, the first two were already state concerns and the third did not exist. The second category was more heavily populated but focused mainly on capital goods and infrastructure.[21] But here, too, the *IPS* carefully maintained that private firms would be allowed to set up new concerns if the state considered it feasible.[22] In other words, if business made a convincing case, it would be allowed to expand into these fields as well.

The threat of nationalization thus receded far into the background with the *IPS*. It was not officially forsaken: the official policy was to let existing industries in the second category expand for the next ten years, after which the matter would "be reviewed" by the government.[23] Technically this left open the *possibility* of socialization. But the entire thrust of the *IPS* was away from state ownership and toward state regulation; further, the statement was issued in the context of the state's steady retreat from its radical pronouncements and continual assurances from ministers and party leaders that business had nothing to fear from the threat. The more astute business leaders thus realized that the "ten-year" clause was more a nod to the waning Left and a recognition of the need for a populist image, rather than a real statement of intention. In a speech delivered soon after the IPS was released, G. D. Birla complimented it as a "step in the right direction," which "should remove the nervousness of investors."[24] The trade organ *Commerce and Industry* even recognized the IPS as a "partial and somewhat fundamental reversal of some of the points contained in the Congress Economic Policy Report."[25] The retreat away from nationalization continued over the next months, with assurances coming from Nehru, Patel, and the relevant ministers.[26] "Take it from me," Patel announced publicly in late 1949, "if anyone talks of nationalization, it is only for the sake of leadership."[27]

With nationalization no longer a *programmatic* threat, the proposed contours of Indian industrial policy were not very different from most other late industrializers: a mixed economy with state regulation of industry. Further, those industries where the state proposed to take the lead were the very ones in which private capital had shown hesitancy or sheer inability to invest. The matter was amply recognized by *Capital*, one of the leading organs of the business community, on the release of the IPS:[28]

> Those branches of industrial activity which the state reserves exclusively are, for the most part, spheres from which new private enterprise has long since withdrawn. Those industries in which the state reserves new enterprise to itself, but has decided to let existing undertakings develop for a further period of ten years, call for the employment of capital on a scale which, in the present depressed condition of the market, it would be very difficult to mobilize through unaided private effort.

The IPS was thus a very different creature from the *Report of the Economic Committee*. With it now in place as the official policy of the Indian government, Nehru made it clear that, in the equation between the Congress Party and the Congress government, the initiative was to rest squarely with the latter.[29] It should not, then, be a surprise that the *IPS* bore a closer resemblance in spirit and word to its predecessor, the *Statement of Government Industrial Policy* of 1945.[30] Like the *Statement* of 1945, the *IPS* went to some pains to assure private capital that property was not in danger;[31] that nationalization would be driven by technical, and not programmatic, considerations; and that the state's role would primarily be that of a regulator. Here, too, the *IPS* moved to establish a friendlier face to business: it declared the government's intention to set up a Central Advisory Council for Industry in order to institutionalize business input into the formulation and implementation of industrial policy. Thus, while the future direction of industrial development was still to be guided by the state, the *IPS* suggested that it would be with the continued input of Indian industry.

With socialization of industry now off the agenda, the operative issue became the nature and the degree of regulation that the state would exercise over capital. While the latter was largely satisfied that the *IPS* had rolled back one of the most objectionable elements of the Economic Committee's *Report*, the matter could hardly rest there. In the next section we examine the battle over the key legislative instrument that was to frame Indian industrial policy for the next forty years, the Industries (Development and Regulation) Act. The IDRA marked the final step in the translation of the Congress program into policy. And it also precipitated the final conflagration between capital and the state in the institutionalization of the post-Independence planning apparatus.

The battle over the IDRA was also important for another reason: the reaction of the business class to its provisions was so shrill that it had an indirect effect on the second key instrument for industrial policy, namely, the proposed Planning Commission. While initial designs for the PC tended to endorse a fairly powerful institution, the state managers' main concern by the time of its institutionalization was to avoid, at all costs, a further downturn in the investment climate. A strong PC was therefore considered something of a risk. This, then, provided an opening for forces within the state to take the offensive against the PC, in order to protect their own power in the state structure. Under the combined impact of the business attack and the revolt of the political class, the final form given to the Commission was extremely weak in the end.

DISCIPLINARY PLANNING AND THE BUSINESS OFFENSIVE

If industrial planning was to be anything other than notional, investment decisions could not be left to the predilections of private capital alone. The idea that investment would have to be monitored and regulated had been a staple of the Congress program since the 1930s, figuring prominently in every major set of reports and recommendations over the past two decades. Private capital, too, appeared to have given its assent to the idea on several occasions, the most conspicuous of which was the second volume of the Bombay Plan, but other occasions included almost all the government committees on which representatives of business had sat since the end of the war.[32] What is more, the use of a licensing procedure to channel industrial investment had been on the anvil since at least the initial meetings of the NPC in 1937–38 and had been reiterated in the new planning committees after the war.[33] For the new government, then, there was reason to believe that the passage of the act institutionalizing this ought to be a simple matter.

But, as we have seen in the last two chapters, this was a serious misreading of the situation. As the war was coming to an end, with large swathes of British business evacuating from India, on the one hand, and a massive reserve of sterling balances building up in England, on the other, Indian business was in no mood to have the heavy hand of the state on its shoulder as it set out on its wave of expansion. The cold reception given to the second volume of the Bombay Plan was the first indication of this orientation. Now, as the Congress government submitted its new bill for passage in the Assembly, the full realization would come.

The Industries Bill

Within two months of the release of the *IPS*, bureaucrats in the Industry Ministry set about preparing a draft of a bill to govern industrial policy.[34] The motivation behind the bill was twofold: first, to take the power over industrial policy away from the provincial governments (which, under the British, had sole power); and, second, to devise a mechanism whereby the power now vested in the central government could be used to keep investment congruent with economic plans. Not surprisingly, the main such mechanism was to be industrial licensing.[35] Channeling capital flows by the use of such a procedure has not been uncommon in the developing world; indeed, although attention has focused on the Korean use of credit to regulate industry, licensing was used in South Korea to a considerable extent,[36] though I have not seen any detailed study of its dynamics in that case.[37] In India industry tended to be more consistently self-financed than its Korean counterparts at the outset of industrialization. To the extent that external financing was sought, this was secured more from the "curb" market — indigenous bankers and moneylenders — than from the banking system. Hence control through the hold over finance could not be an effective instrument of control on its own.[38] It would have to rely, at least initially, on another mechanism, and licensing was a natural candidate.

Work proceeded for the rest of 1948 and early 1949, and in March 1949 the bill was submitted to the Constituent Assembly for approval as the Industries (Development and Control) Bill.[39] The bill mandated that every new industrial establishment above a certain size, as well as every substantial expansion of an industrial establishment above the minimum size, would require a license; it gave the state considerable power to direct firms in their operations and investment; and it made the contravention of the state's directions in these matters illegal and punishable by law.[40] Significantly the state's punitive use of power was extended not only to cases of gross mismanagement but also to cases in which industrialists were found to be undertaking practices that might "reduce [the firms'] production capacity or economic value"; in other words, it gave the state the power to punish if firms were willfully ignoring issues of efficiency.[41] The bill was therefore explicitly geared toward the use of coercion where necessary.

However, the bill also mandated that the state establish a Central Advisory Council for Industry (CACI), as declared in the *IPS*, which would include representatives of industry, and that consultation with this Council be mandatory on any occasion where the state deemed it appropriate to revoke a license or take over the management of a recalcitrant firm.[42] Nevertheless, the ultimate executive authority remained with the state, not with the Advisory Council; the status of the latter would remain advisory. The main thrust of the bill was thus to endow the state with enormous power over the direction and use of investment, albeit through consultation with industry through the Advisory Council.

The bill was not, it seems, simply dropped onto the nation as a complete surprise. The Central Advisory Council for Industry had already been constituted and had met in early 1949, where a draft was presented to leading industrialists, who, in turn, had given it their approval.[43] As usual, this liaison group was the signatories to the Bombay Plan — G. D. Birla, A. D. Shroff, and Lala Shri Ram, as well as an "outsider," H. P. Mody.[44] Here, as in the past, the state tried in its preparations to gain the allegiance of a lead segment of the business class to ease its acceptance by the class as a whole. But here again, as in the case of the industrial policy statement of 1945, the rest of the class refused to yield, and the "liaison" beat a hasty retreat.

Business reaction to the bill immediately after it was released was shrill and unyielding. The only part that was endorsed was the intention of taking industrial policy away from the state governments and vesting it in the center;[45] the rest of the operative sections were attacked almost without exception. The key issue was the declaration that future private investment would have to be approved, guided, and monitored by the state. Industrialists immediately warned that for the state to arrogate to itself this power was simply unacceptable, as it would not only restrict the scope of entrepreneurial initiative but would also grant too much power to state bureaucrats over firms.[46] As soon as the bill was submitted to the Constituent Assembly, it was roundly attacked by the business press as well as through the direct lobbying of industrialists. The immediate aim of the attack was to stall the passing of the bill, so that industry associations could have more time to formulate alternative legislation or at least so they could bring about acceptable modifications in the ultimate result.[47] The ubiquity and ferocity of the attack was sufficient to produce the desired result: when the bill was introduced in the Constituent Assembly in late March 1949, it was quickly handed over to a Select Committee to be reviewed and resubmitted for consideration during the next session.

With passage of the bill postponed and its details under review by the Select Committee, business pressure was now brought to bear in earnest. It is important to note just how united the opposition was. Throughout 1949 and 1950 the various organs of the business community not only lobbied government to remove the bill, but a perusal of their papers reveals a concerted and organized effort. The more prominent organizations — the Federation of Indian Chambers of Commerce and Industry (FICCI), the Indian Merchants Chamber (IMC), the Bengal Chamber of Commerce, the Associated Chambers of Commerce (ASSOCHAM), and the Madras Chamber of Commerce — regularly exchanged drafts, solicited comments, and conferred on strategy to influence government.[48] For their part, state managers strained to convey to capital that they were willing to modify the bill drastically, subject to the condition that it ought not to appear that government was "yielding to outside pressure."[49] Indeed, the Select Committee itself worked quietly through the spring to assure business representatives that it was open to all manner of suggestions as to how to modify its contents.[50] But the stance taken by the most prominent industry associations and many industrialists did not offer much comfort. Many of the most well-known and powerful industrialists began a campaign that, far from seeking to modify the bill, simply called for it to be scrapped outright.[51] No amount of tinkering could make acceptable a piece of legislation that was, as B. M. Birla complained, "fundamentally objectionable."[52]

Soon after the bill was submitted to the Select Committee, FICCI called for a meeting in which it could express its concerns regarding the legislation. The Committee, of course, was only too happy to agree; but to its surprise, the FICCI delegates took this occasion to make the demand for the bill's withdrawal from the Constituent Assembly, pronouncing it unacceptable. This simply stunned the Industry Minister S. P. Mookerjee, who protested that it was pointless for FICCI to have asked for the meeting "only to say that they were against the Bill in toto."[53] He reminded the Federation delegates that although it was not possible to withdraw the bill altogether, the Committee was prepared to "modify the bill even beyond recognition, as long as the title and the preamble remained intact."[54] The business delegates were only too happy to take this opening, and they immediately presented Mookerjee with an alternative. They suggested a new bill, which would resemble the first only in that it, too, would provide for central, as opposed to provincial, control over industrial policy and that the Central Advisory Council for Industry would be retained. But here the resemblance would stop. The Federation demanded that all authority to license, and the disciplinary power that came with it, be withdrawn. Instead, industrial policy would be carried out through the formation of industrial committees in each industry. Each industrial committee would be staffed primarily with businessmen from that sector. And whatever regulation the government contemplated would issue through consultation between the CACI and these industrial boards.[55] The upshot was that while the state would still have the power to regulate in some fashion, this power would be on a case-by-case basis and would have to pass through two filters: the assent of the Central Advisory Council and that of the sectoral industrial committees, both of which would be dominated by representatives who would be nominated by business.[56] With this the two sides retreated, with the promise that further dialogue would continue.

This initial proposal by FICCI is significant, for it encapsulated what

Indian capital regarded as the acceptable form of industrial policy: one in which *regulation of industry* would basically be *industry's self-regulation*. In truth, business groups realized that *some* kind of regulatory apparatus would be foisted on their activities. The demands for withdrawing the bill altogether were, in part, strategic — they were intended to put the state on the defensive, as indeed they had. Having played the maximalist card, space could now be pried open to make more realistic demands. As Lala Shri Ram, erstwhile signatory to the Bombay Plan, wrote to his colleagues in the Federation: "at this stage, the Government will not withdraw the Bill in toto. It is, therefore, advisable to get such changes made as may *take the stink out of [it].*"[57] The core elements of such changes were visible in the initial proposal that FICCI delegates made to the Select Committee described above, namely, that the scope of state controls would be reduced and a series of business-dominated filters would be put in place to vet any disciplinary state actions.

The Congress government and the Select Committee, for their part, continued to hope that some kind of modus vivendi could be reached with the business community. But six weeks after the Select Committee's initial meeting with them, FICCI officials sent the promised memorandum to Mookerjee — and it was, if anything, even more unaccommodating than their initial demands. The Federation reiterated its call for the evisceration of all clauses dealing with licensing power.[58] The scope of the bill, furthermore, was now to be drastically reduced to just six industries.[59] Even here, the terms on which they were regulated were to be altered: the Federation now demanded that the provision for a Central Advisory Council be rescinded.[60] In its stead, the Federation suggested a Central Industries Development Board, which would be dominated by industrialists whom the government would nominate but with the Federation's approval.[61] The difference between the two institutions seems to have been twofold: first, the latter body would be formed with a greater presence of, and control by, industry; second, executive powers would be vested in this board, not in the state.[62]

The sum total of these demands amounted to this: state power to regulate and control industry would now be confined to six industries; this power would not include the right to restrict the inter-sectoral flows of capital;[63] regulation of sunk capital (in the six scheduled industries), such as it was, would be carried out through consultation with an industry-dominated central board; regulation would be administered by this board, in tandem with industry-dominated sectoral committees. The state's power to influence industry, on this view, was to be confined to instances in which industry itself called for the state to intervene. These demands were in keeping with the basic elements in capital's strategy to "take the stink out of" state regulation: narrow down its scope to the greatest extent possible and ensure that any cases of disciplinary intervention pass through filters that require the approval of capital.[64]

Capital Turns the Screws

Direct lobbying with the concerned agencies, as FICCI was undertaking, was one natural means of exerting pressure to bring about the desired changes. This was accompanied by two other strategies, both meeting with some success. First, and perhaps most important, some of the biggest industrialists were, quite vocally, slowing down their investment in new undertakings; in other words, they were launching what appeared to be an investment strike. And, second, businessmen were using their personal connections with members of the Congress High Command to plead for policy changes. Put differently, the bourgeoisie brought to bear both its structural power in the political economy, as well as the situational advantage of many of its members, in order to pressure the state to change its course.[65]

The domestic economy in the aftermath of Independence was already suffering from enormous strains, partly because of the postwar shortages many countries experienced, added to which was the economic fallout of the partition between India and Pakistan, which disrupted production in the northwest and the east.[66] In this context, starting in the early months of 1947, many of the largest industrial houses began a slowdown in new investments, a move they themselves often brought to the attention of state managers as a show of their dissatisfaction with policy developments.[67] Through the next three years, slowdowns were confirmed in textiles, engineering, transportation, shipping, and sundry other industries.[68] How much of this was purely a consequence of an investment strike, as against a combined effect of the strike with the dislocations of the postwar settlement, is impossible to disentangle. But *that* there was a strike appears indisputable—industrialists made this much clear themselves, as they announced their unwillingness to invest until government changed its "unsound and retrograde" policies.[69] Hence, just days after the Industries Bill was presented, the Secretary to the Madras Chamber of Commerce could be seen writing to Sir Percival Griffiths of the India–Burma Association in London:

> Who in their senses would invest money in India and risk the meddling of an untutored bureaucracy? *The best help you can give us is to arrange for all British Industrialists who might be planning to invest money now to hold back.* . . . If Government can be made to realize that this Bill is another se-

rious blow to the confidence of the foreign investor, we may confidently look forward to some improvements.[70]

The withdrawal of new investment was complemented by the provision of fairly transparent directions as to what it would take to restore business confidence — the evisceration of the Industries Bill. "If passed in the present form," FICCI warned in a memorandum to the Finance Ministry, the bill "will negative [sic] all that has been done in recent months to revive the confidence of private enterprise";[71] lesser organizations followed suit, as in the case of the United Provinces Chamber of Commerce sternly warning the Industry Ministry that the bill would surely "shake the gradually returning confidence of the investing public."[72] Memorandums by business organs to the various economic ministries from these months are peppered with advice on how to repair business confidence — *their* confidence.[73]

As the slowdown continued, the priorities of the Congress High Command could not remain unaffected — discussions increasingly came to be dominated by the matter of the recession and how to reverse it.[74] Starting soon after the announcement of its very first Budget in early 1947, the new government began to beat a reluctant, but palpable, retreat under the weight of the business offensive.[75] This meant a step back from many policies that had been proposed as a response to the mass pressure of the final, tumultuous days of the Independence movement; internally it meant a change in the balance of power in the party away from the most vocal proponents of a strong, disciplinary developmental state. In thinly coded language, the conservative wing of the Congress High Command began a campaign against a blind commitment to "social objectives," counseling, instead, a turn to "flexibility" and "pragmatism."[76] The barometer for the soundness of Congress governance thus slowly shifted, from a fidelity to its decades-old platform to its ability to restore and revive the investment climate.

Nowhere were the effects of these constraints more apparent than in the frustration of the new Prime Minister, Jawaharlal Nehru. Ever since the late 1930s, when the National Planning Committee had first been convened, Nehru had been aware that, if capitalist planning were to become a reality, a modus vivendi would have to be reached with the Indian bourgeoisie.[77] And throughout the months since Independence, Nehru had, in fact, quietly gone along with Congress turning away from its populist tilt, its demobilization of labor and peasant organizations, and its attempts to gain the confidence of local capital — indeed, in many instances, he had championed such measures. Privately Nehru made no secret of his awareness that "our monied people are on strike and trying to bring pressure on government."[78] Publicly he appealed to business representatives time and again, sometimes threatening, sometimes pleading—all to no avail.[79] But now, two years after Independence, with the critical piece of legislation for capitalist planning under attack and the investment strike showing no sign of abatement, Nehru began to realize that his elusive modus vivendi may be out of reach. "We have very largely tried," he wrote to a colleague, "to meet their [i.e., industrialists] viewpoint in our general policy and in our efforts to win them over," but "they have shown little appreciation of this and want more and more, and meanwhile condemn government action frequently."[80] To the cabinet, he pleaded that an investigation ought to be launched into the large number of plant closings that had been witnessed in recent weeks; and in a passage reminiscent of postwar Marxist theorizing on the state, he complained that Indian capital was unwilling to countenance a state independent of its control:

> [Our] policy, thus far, has been on the whole favorable to the employer classes and Government have in most matters accepted their advice. *It is true that Government do not function just as agents of these classes and perhaps a certain independence on the part of Government in regard to its policy is not found agreeable by the bigger industrialists and financial interests concerned.* One is driven to the conclusion that there is a certain attempt being made . . . to create difficulties for the Government so as to induce it to change its policy.[81]

With the entire Congress High Command now concerned to placate capital, Nehru's appeal did not carry much weight. The cabinet quickly diverted Nehru's appeal to a committee, which, in turn, narrowed its focus to the details of a small number of particular mills, ignoring the larger issue Nehru was raising.[82]

Nehru's growling impatience with the capitalist class may have found some purchase within the High Command but for two factors. First, as already mentioned, the departure of the Left and the demobilization of labor weakened his own bargaining position within the party; but the second factor was the looming figure of V. B. Patel, Deputy Prime Minister, who had very close ties to some of the most powerful business houses and was Nehru's chief antagonist in the cabinet. Patel's close ties to the business class made him a magnet for direct lobbying. Through the summer of 1949 G. D. Birla sent a steady stream of letters to him, many while Birla was on a trip to England, warning of the dire times to come and exhorting Patel to put his weight behind the business initiative. Soon after the Industries Bill was presented to the Assembly, Birla dispatched a missive to Patel highlighting the objectionable parts of the draft.[83] This was followed by a barrage of letters from England, cautioning against an aggressive expansion of new public sector undertakings while also reporting on the worries that British and American capital evinced about the "investment climate" in India.[84]

For his part, Patel promised to do what he could on the matters that concerned Birla.[85] But, significantly, the Patel camp also urged Birla to mobilize the business community to end its investment slowdown. Patel's secretary, V. Shankar, complained that while "I can understand industrialists and businessmen withholding investments because they are not sure of the projects," he could see "no justification for giving way to panic . . . merely because somebody happens to 'sneeze' somewhere else."[86] Industrialists had to realize that their own credibility was crucial if the partisans of disciplinary planning and regulation were to be defeated; the winds were definitely shifting toward capital in the Cabinet, but it was crucial that the other side not be given any more ammunition: "if we can secure some evidence of the bona fides of businessmen in one sphere of activity, I am sure we will have broken the ice."[87]

But the Right had little to be concerned about. With labor split and demobilized and the Socialists out of the Congress, the partisans of disciplinary planning were with little mass or organizational base. Patel stood like a rock against almost all the measures that business found objectionable. That most of the Select Committee members deliberating on the bill were also Congress members made this especially significant, since it was universally acknowledged that Patel was the paramount power within the organization. Nehru had greater leverage with the mass base of the party — the very base that had steadily been demobilized and sidelined over the past three years.[88]

Hence, by the end of 1949, just two years following the end of British rule, the direction in which the Indian political economy was heading was distressingly uncertain. From the standpoint of Congress, the measures proposed in the Industries (Development and Control) Bill were not all that controversial; they more or less followed the ideas that had been "in the air" since the war — an industrial strategy based on import-substitution, with a heavy dose of state regulation. The party had good reason to think that there was some measure of support for such a strategy within the capitalist class, since licensing and state regulation had been proposed in the Bombay Plan document itself, authored by the leading lights of Indian industry. Opposition to regulation on the release of the industrial policy statement of 1945 had been couched by industrialists in the language of anti-colonialism, implying that, under the control of an independent, sovereign government, such measures would be acceptable.[89] But the first two years of Independence shattered this complacency. The reactions to the Industries Bill made it clear that the disciplinary components of the new strategy — the measures that were intended to allow the state to impose performance standards on firms — were not acceptable to industrialists. To punctuate their opposition, business groups not only launched a massive lobbying campaign but also undertook a "go-slow" strategy toward new investments, and made no secret of the reasons why. We now examine the institutional resolution to this dilemma.

THE INSTITUTIONAL OUTCOME (1): THE PLANNING COMMISSION

The most immediate and dramatic effect of the Indian bourgeoisie's campaign was a shift in the regime's immediate priorities: from installing the instruments necessary for disciplinary planning to undertaking measures that would revitalize the investment climate. This did not require turning away from state intervention per se; it did prompt, however, a concern to refashion the instruments of industrial policy so that they would be more in line with capitalist preferences. Policy proposals increasingly came to be assessed on the basis of the effects they would have on business confidence, even if this carried in train long-lasting consequences. This turn toward immediate exigencies had a drastic impact on the installation of developmental policy instruments. The two key elements in the new apparatus — a Planning Commission and the Industries Bill — were both, in their final design, fashioned to accommodate business demands as much as possible.

But this change was not simply imposed by Indian capitalists on a unified political elite. In fact, the investment slowdown created an opening for elements within the state, worried about being subordinated to the new Planning Commission, to ally with business around opposing a disciplinary policy apparatus. Under the protection of Patel, denizens of the Congress High Command were now able to present their partisan worries in a more universal garb, pointing to the possibly disastrous economic consequences of a powerful planning regime. We have already seen, in the preceding section, that Patel was very sympathetic to the concerns business houses voiced about the powers being vested in the state by the Industries Bill and the more general industrial strategy. With the debate around the PC now on the agenda, Patel was able to parlay his power within the party into a diminution of the new body's mandate; this retreat was then accentuated in the final form taken by the other critical instrument for industrial policy, the Industries Bill, which emerged from the Select Committee in 1951.

The Consensus around State Intervention

Through all the sound and fury over state control of industry, nationalization, labor rights, trade policy, and so on, the basic idea of state intervention in the economy was never questioned in postwar India. Indeed, throughout the months in which the attack on economic legislation was conducted, firms clamored incessantly for the state to step up its assistance to them in a variety of ways. There was no question, therefore, of a demand for free markets. All the controversy was about the nature, not the fact, of state intervention.

As we have seen, capitalists in the Indian economy after the war had to contend with the state's vision of future economic development, which was some distance from their own preferences. But they also had to contend with the fact that they had emerged from the war in less than healthy condition. There was the inevitable wear and tear to which firms had been subjected in the war, with the enormous demands that had been placed on them.[90] But there was also the fact that industry now found itself in a situation where recovery from these strains seemed arduous. In the years after the war, capital goods in the form of plant and machinery were extremely scarce; not only did India not have any capital goods industry to speak of, but imports from the developed world were not on the near horizon, as European powers embarked on the reconstruction of their own economies and because the United States did not regard South Asia as a pivotal region.[91] The problem with plant and machinery was mirrored by the problems with raw materials and intermediate goods, especially since, after Partition, much of the Indian cotton and raw Jute supply was now in Pakistan.[92] In both these cases, businesses constantly called for the assistance of the state in securing the requisite import of goods.

While the state was called on for securing inputs, many firms also turned to it for increasing throughput. Slumping demand after the war was sharply felt by several industries, especially heavy industry such as coal, steel, and chemicals, which called on the state to keep demand buoyant as well as to procure replacement capital.[93] More generally, state action was regarded as central to the expansion of the Indian market, which even the government's sharpest critics recognized was too narrow for sustained accumulation.[94] State intervention was thus required for the expansion of Indian production and consumption in an integrated manner.[95]

This was the dilemma for the business class in India: it did not want, and therefore could not demand, an economy run on the principle of laissez faire. State support and access to public funds in the form of subsidies, credit, and state procurement were absolutely essential to its future development. It could not, therefore, attack the commitment to "planning" per se. Indeed, the most prominent organs of the class heartily endorsed the principles when presented in their most abstract form in party pronouncements and reports.[96] Further still, given that business itself was calling for state assistance and involvement, it was imperative that this assistance be carried out in an organized fashion, rather than through a haphazard aggregation of individual projects. Hence, in early 1950, the Federation of Indian Chambers of Commerce and Industry could be seen releasing a frustrated critique of the utterly uncoordinated nature of the government's immediate development efforts since the war. The Federation openly called for a more concerted coordination of industrial policy.[97]

So there was no doubt that state intervention was called for nor that capital would support a move to secure internal coherence for the state, through some kind of coordinating body. But, for the leading segments of the capitalist class, the purpose of this body was not to be a disciplinarian; it was to be more akin to a doting nanny, ever present to dole out assistance on demand but hesitant to use its power except when requested.

The Rise of the Planning Commission

Throughout the twenty-odd years since the formation of the National Planning Committee, the Congress had not wavered in its commitment to the idea of capitalist planning. But beyond a fidelity to the broad idea, the concrete questions of institutional form and powers were not seriously debated. A perusal of the relevant documents reveals that the major concern in the early years of debate was with wresting control over industrial legislation away from the provinces. And in this, both business and the INC were united.[98] Beyond this, the organization spoke with different voices about what planning would entail.

Despite this lack of consensus, influential voices in the organizations' leadership and brain trust advocated a planning apparatus with strong powers of enforcement. Chief among these was K. T. Shah, who was the moving force behind the work of the National Planning Committee in 1937–40 and was also central to the work of the Advisory Planning Board in 1946–47. In the deliberations of the APB, it was Shah who took the lead in preparing detailed memorandums on the necessary apparatus for planning;[99] in the board's *Report*, the sections on the "machinery of planning" were almost entirely lifted from a draft he had prepared.[100] Most of the recommendations on a planning apparatus focused on broad and entirely unobjectionable issues; but, in a significant passage, Shah averred that, although many of the Planning Commission's powers would be advisory, when it came to the allocation of resources it should be "empowered to give final decisions, subject only to an appeal to Government."[101] Thus planners would have effective power over what was perhaps the fundamental issue in industrial policy, namely, the allocation of scarce resources.

It is difficult to assess whether Shah's voice was in a majority position, but it was not without support. Throughout the early years of Independence, the main proponents of planning seem simply to have assumed that the new body would have strong powers of enforcement as well as formulation. Shah's own political fortunes declined soon after 1947, but the baton for carrying on the work of putting together a Planning Commission fell to G. L. Nanda and, to a lesser extent, Shankarrao Deo, both Gandhians and both in favor of a strong Planning Commission. As work on the establishment of the new body began in earnest in late 1949–early 1950, it was Nanda and Deo who took the initiative, thus guaranteeing that the drive for a strong commission was kept alive.

The immediate question that arose in the Congress deliberations was the relation that the PC would enjoy with the ministries. Would it be a purely advisory body, leaving the acceptance and implementation of its plans to the ministries, or would it have strong powers of enforcement as well? Nanda believed openly that a Planning Commission without the latter kind of powers would be of little use. In a memo urging the High Command of his view, he warned that "a Plan is not a body of recommendations of a reporting committee which may be accepted or rejected in part. . . . The part which will be rejected may be found by the Planning Commission to dislocate the entire creation, rendering the Commission incapable of taking responsibility."[102] Throughout the first half of 1950 he continued to push for the conferral of strong powers of enforcement onto the new body, convinced that without them it would rapidly lose relevance.[103] What this amounted to was a call for the PC to be a true nodal agency, with power not only to impose discipline on firms but also to control the policy process—as with the Economic Planning Board (EPB) in Korea. But there were two problems with this. First, the specter of a coercive planning body was seen as a threat to the recovery of business confidence; second, the proposal would require not simply the creation of a new institutional body—the PC—but also the *usurpation* by this body of many of the powers and prerogatives of existing ministries. This opened the possibility of resistance within the political elite itself.

In the years since Independence, industrial policy had been under way in its disjointed and haphazard manner, as mentioned above. While there was a nominal coordination provided by a small body within the cabinet known as the Economic Committee, this was a very informal affair, with no real apportionment of power or responsibility, and no permanent staff.[104] Under this system, ministries had launched projects, budgets had been passed under particular assumptions, and import and export licenses had been handed out. There appears to have been a fear, in this context, that a restructuring of the state apparatus would cause undue disruption to the recovery that these projects and proposals were attempting.[105] The installation of a strong PC would mean the arrival of a new authority, with its own preferences and mandate, on top of the existing economic policy apparatus; it would require the setting up of new lines of authority and new channels of communication; and, crucially, it carried the specter, for business, of having to establish a whole new set of ties to a new set of state managers, whose chief responsibility would be to monitor the investment behavior of firms. This likely scenario came to be seen as too risky. In Congress Working Committee discussions, the tide shifted strongly against the appearance of a body armed with strong powers of coercion in the economic field, specifically because of fears that it would be unacceptable to capital.[106]

Hence, when Nanda submitted his proposal to the Congress Working Committee for the PC to be a true nodal agency, he found himself unable to carry the day, and the matter was referred to the cabinet to be worked out.[107] Of course, this was the worst possible turn of events for Nanda and his supporters. The cabinet was the arena where the concerns of the capitalist class were given the greatest succor, far more than in the Congress Party organs, which were more directly accountable to their mass base. The cabinet was also the body in which members stood to lose the most if ministerial power was reapportioned toward the new PC. With individual ministers and top bureaucrats now having a direct incentive to scuttle the proposal for a powerful planning apparatus, they found a welcome justification in the economic climate.

The final announcement of the PC's installation was issued in March 1950. As anticipated, its powers fell far short of what the supporters of disciplinary planning had hoped for; as one commentator observed, "the objectives of the Commission appear to have been formulated with the clear purpose of doing minimum injury to . . . business confidence."[108] Its enumerated powers were basically advisory, with real power left to the ministries.[109] The PC's prerogative was confined to devising comprehensive plans and "[making] recommendations to the cabinet," with the further stipulation that, in framing its recommendations, "the Commission will act in close understanding and consultation with the Ministries." But "recommendations" and "consultations" had no binding power.[110] They would depend, instead, on the degree to which the Commission could either mobilize powerful coalitions behind its recommendations or persuade the parties involved of the merits of its decisions.

The proponents of a strong planning apparatus apparently harbored the hope that, despite this initial restriction of the Commission's powers, the situation might be improved in the near future.[111] But events in the next months worked only to further entrench the opposition to its promotion. As a perceptive commentator noted, by mid-April it was clear that Patel had decided against the Nanda line, adding his weight to the resistance in the cabinet. And, the commentator wryly noted, "since he [Patel] has taken up the cudgels, it is not difficult to prophesy [*sic*] who will have to make room for whom."[112] Patel took to the offensive at the meeting of the Congress Planning Committee in April, demanding that the proper approach to planning ought to be guided by a "practical," not "ideological," perspective—a line of argument that clearly was a coded attack on Nanda and his colleagues.[113]

But the final thrust against the PC came in the summer of 1950 when, in a controversial move, the erstwhile Finance Minister John Mathai submitted an angry resignation from the cabinet. In a series of public appearances, Mathai announced that a central factor motivating his resignation was the move under way to install the PC as a "super-cabinet," running roughshod over what was properly ministerial prerogative.[114] His resignation immediately put Nehru on the defensive, forcing him to reiterate time and again over the next months that the PC would not be allowed to encroach on ministerial powers, that it was there to *help*, and not sideline, ministries. In the days surrounding Mathai's resignation, Patel wrote angrily to Nehru that the fledgling PC was already demanding inclusion in matters that ought to be beyond its authority. A conciliatory Nehru quickly assured Patel that the PC was "anxious not to do anything which comes in the way of any ministry."[115] From the start, therefore, the PC was forced to accommodate itself to the principle of ministerial autonomy from its authority. Even after Mathai's resignation, as Nehru's biographer reports, several key ministers "had no liking for the Planning Commission and failed to cooperate with it and facilitate its working."[116] The Commission was therefore dependent to a large extent on Nehru's periodic pleas to ministries that they cooperate with it in policy implementation.[117]

At the end of the day, then, the appointment of the Planning Commission did not signal a restructuring of the state apparatus in order to facilitate economic planning, as originally hoped. To the contrary, the PC had to accommodate *itself* to the existing structure of the state—the PC was simply added to the existing setup as another of its component parts. Of course, this was accompanied with much ballyhoo about its promise in coordinating policy and streamlining projects, but the coordination was to depend solely on its ability to mobilize state agencies behind its views.[118] Meanwhile, the actual centers for administering and implementing industrial projects were left exactly where they were: budgeting remained with Finance, trade with Commerce, and so forth; what is more, the jurisdiction over industries was even more scattered: for example, power over the textile and jute industries was strongly guarded by the Commerce Ministry because of their importance as exports, while the steel and machine tools industries were under the Industry Ministry, the coal industry was the prerogative of the supply industry, and so on. A direct corollary to this was that the PC had no power to demand compliance by the other ministries in transmitting information, abiding by plan targets, or monitoring firms. I will address the pathologies of this system in detail in the next chapter.

The appointment of the Planning Commission capped the decades-old movement toward industrial planning in the Indian political economy. Where it had once been seen as the centerpiece of the new Indian state, the harbinger of its strategic restructuring, it now stood reduced to a toothless referee, dependent for its power on the patronage of sympathetic ministers.[119] Business pressure alone did not directly cause the slide from the initial vision to the eventual outcome. The resistance of bureaucrats and ministers threatened by the new body was also responsible. But the resonance that the ministers' arguments held within the Congress government and the broader environment was dramatically increased because of the antecedent offensive that business launched against disciplinary planning. On the other hand, had Nehru and his supporters not demobilized the labor movement so swiftly and sidelined the party Left, which was the main political and organizational base for planning, the need to rely on purely voluntary support from business for the restructuring of the state would have been less pressing.

THE INSTITUTIONAL OUTCOME (2): THE FILTERS ON DISCIPLINE

The curtailment of the Planning Commission's powers was of considerable significance, for, unlike the Economic Planning Board in Korea, it would not now wield much institutionalized power within the state over other policy agencies. Despite its formal appearance, the PC was not to be anything like a genuine "nodal agency." As we shall see in the next chapter, this was to be a major factor behind the fragmentation of the policy apparatus and the resulting lack of selectivity for which Indian industrial planning became famous.[120] But while the matter of the PC was critical for the internal coherence of the state apparatus, still unclear was the nature of the powers the state as a whole would wield over firms. That was a matter that the Industries Bill was meant to settle.

The Difficulty of Industrial Self-Regulation

Capitalist strategy, as explained above, had been to reduce the scope of the Industries Bill and ensure that the workings of the disciplinary apparatus come under the control of business groups to the extent possible. The key to this was the place that sectoral committees and the central advisory body (whether a board or a council) would occupy and whether these groups would be able to act as genuine class-friendly filters for business. In the initial version of the Industries Bill, the broad direction had definitely been toward a strong disciplinary regime, with sweeping punitive powers accorded to the state not only to steer the course of private investment but also to monitor its use;[121] further, although there was provision for a Central Advisory Council for Industry, its function was not made sufficiently clear to allay industrialists' fears. Hence capitalists demanded that the bill be changed to hand over effective power to sectoral committees or boards so that regulation would effectively be sectoral self-regulation.[122]

One fundamental weakness in this demand made its success exceedingly remote. If regulation were to be the self-regulation of capital, it would have to come through some kind of cartels or trade associations that would assume responsibility to organize production, quality, and so on. But the experience with such organizations in India since the war had greatly reduced their credibility. In the immediate aftermath of Independence, the onset of rampant inflation had forced the government to impose price controls on a number of key commodities. From the outset, business organizations objected to controls.[123] But, more important, key trade associations entered into negotiations with the state, promising to hold the line on prices if formal governmental control was abandoned.

These agreements were a resounding failure. Most conspicuous was the debacle of decontrol in textiles and sugar. In textiles, the state announced the decontrol measure in January 1948, giving the industry the power to set its own prices. In addition, a business-dominated Textile Advisory Board was appointed to advise government regarding textile policy.[124] Regulation was thus left to the industry itself, and policy was to be formulated on the advice of industry representatives — an arrangement very similar to what business representatives were to propose to state managers two years later in their negotiations over the Industries (Control and Regulation) Bill. But the arrangement failed miserably. Prices shot up "to fantastic heights"[125] within weeks, amid mounting evidence of rampant profiteering by the mill owners. On July 30, just six months after allowing decontrol, the government was forced to reimpose control on textile prices and distribution. After this experience, state managers were far more circumspect about allowing mill owners to regulate industry conditions. Throughout 1949 and 1950 textile mill owners found themselves unable to push through their demands for greater freedom, as their own legitimacy was so drastically reduced.[126]

The textile mill owners' association was famous for being unable to control its members.[127] An organization that was tighter and more ambitious in its agenda for internal control was the Indian Sugar Syndicate, which was given exclusive rights of representation for the sugar industry in 1940.[128] Further, this organization not only had the power to negotiate for the industry but was also given the right to distribute investment licenses and hence control the addition of new capacity, as well as setting industry prices. After 1947, while promising to hold the line on prices, the syndicate nonetheless persisted in pushing prices up in order to take advantage of postwar shortages. As with textiles, the government stripped the organization of these powers in 1949 and took over the control of prices itself.[129]

The experience with textiles and sugar greatly reduced the legitimacy of the demands the business class made on industrial policy legislation. State managers were open to negotiating on just about every aspect of the bill, as we have seen. The problem was that, after three years of making one concession after another, handing over regulatory powers to industry — after the aforementioned experience — would have brought the state to the limit of its own legitimacy with the broad population. Some kind of state control, therefore, was necessary.

The Final Settlement

With industrial self-regulation losing legitimacy, what remained was the possibility of some state-led regulatory apparatus. For the state, the final legislation for industrial policy — the Industries Bill — was conditioned by two forces: first, the recognition that capitalist demands for control over the administration of industrial regulation could not be accommodated, in light of the experience with industrial self-regulation; and, second, that, despite this, the contours of the new regime would have to be brought closer to the preferences of business groups. The bill had originally been introduced in the spring of 1949; in early 1950 the Select Committee submitted a revised version, which was also rejected in the Constituent Assembly and sent back to a new committee. As 1950 came to an end, two years had passed since the original legislation had been introduced, and time became a factor. The Planning Commission was now in place, Independence was three years old, and the promise of a new, state-led industrial policy regime awaited the passing of the enabling legislation.

Business demands around the bill had centered around two goals: first, to radically reduce the scope of industrial regulation, particularly licensing policy; and, second, to put buffers into place that minimally would oblige state planners to garner the consent of industrialists before exercising their coercive or disciplinary power over industry. Initially it appeared that the Select Committee would concede both demands, as the version of the Bill that came out in early 1950 greatly reduced the number of sectors to be open to state regulation and also provided for the independent Industries Board that the FICCI had demanded.[130] In the penultimate version, however, passed in late 1951, the number of target industries was increased;[131] but this version also went quite some distance toward meeting capital's second demand, that is, to put filters in place that would blunt the state's use of disciplinary instruments.

The key feature of the bill embodying business-dominated filters was the provision for bodies called Development Councils (DCs). These councils were to be sectoral bodies that would be the connection between the planning apparatus and targeted lines in industry. As demanded by the business community, they were to be dominated by industrial representatives and technical staff[132] and would serve to collect information, assist in the distribution of inputs, relay standards of efficiency to firms, and, most important, have considerable say over when and if the state could move punitively against an undertaking.[133] In more contemporary language, the DCs were to be the site of the state's "embeddedness" in the industrial sector.[134] But complementing, and bolstering, the role of the DCs was another body, the Central Advisory Council for Industries, which also was to act as a buffer between the state and the industrial sector. Whereas the Development Councils were to serve as liaisons to particular lines, the Central Advisory Council was to be a more inclusive organ, serving as a sounding board for the class of industrialists more broadly. Further, unlike the DCs, it allowed for the presence of a wider range of interests, including labor and consumer groups.[135]

Together, the DCs and the CACI were designed to act, to the extent possible, with the consent of business representatives whenever the state moved against a particular firm. Congress ministers described this function explicitly as a "brake" to be placed on the state's use of coercion over firms.[136] Here is how the Industry Minister H. K. Mahtab presented it to critics in the Constituent Assembly:

"The introduction of the Development Councils is the most important feature of the Bill. These Councils will keep in close touch with the industries, and try to help them in all possible ways. Issue of directions will come in only when the Development Councils will [sic] fail in their method of persuasion. . . . There is [also] provision for a Central Advisory Council representing all industries. . . . It has been made obligatory that whenever any direction is to be issued or control is to be exercised on management, the Advisory Council has to be consulted."[137]

Hence, while the state was not willing to simply hand over regulatory control to industrial associations, planners did craft legislation so as to "carry along" the business community to the extent that they could. Targets would be set through consultation with the DCs and communicated to firms through them, and, when any particular undertaking needed to be coerced or disciplined, the state would move only after consulting with this body as well as with the CACI.

But crucially, in their efforts to dilute any mention of coercion, Congress legislators avoided turning the DCs into genuine corporatist bodies. Industry representatives serving in the councils were to be there on a voluntary basis, as "experts" performing a service, not as actual representatives of their sectors.[138] Of course, since they were present as nominal advisers, the industrialists had nothing but their own judgments and instincts as the basis on which they would recommend targets and productivity levels to planners; this was of central importance, for if their own judgments were to be the basis for their recommendations, then, since they had no real mechanism of accountability to "their" sectors, firms in those sectors would have good reason to regard these targets as arbitrary, and hence lacking legitimacy. For it to be otherwise would have required organizing sectors themselves into organizations or associations, giving these bodies legal rights of representation, and having industry representatives present in more than just an advisory and voluntary capacity.

As we shall see in the next chapter, this is largely how Korean sectoral councils functioned, in contrast to their Indian counterparts. In Korea and Taiwan, industry was organized into sectoral associations, which were then given formal powers to represent "their" firms to state managers. The latter, in turn, were able to hold the associations accountable for collecting information and organizing the effective implementation of industrial policy.[139] In an important sense, the trade and sectoral associations were an extension of the state planning apparatus, accountable to it as much as to their own members. In fact, it was not unusual for their presidents to be retired bureaucrats or even to be appointed directly by planners.[140] In their capacity as virtual extensions of the planning agencies, the sectoral associations functioned to drastically reduce the transaction of costs monitoring economic actors, as well as that of transmitting relevant signals to the latter.

Indian planners recognized the limited value of the DCs if they could not act as corporatist bodies. But the High Command was extremely sensitive to domestic capital's aversion toward any hint that the state was curtailing its freedom. Hence, in early meetings of the Planning Commission, D. R. Gadgil, one of India's most prominent policy experts, argued strenuously that, if the DC's were to be the site for setting targets and negotiating with firms, they would be of little use unless each sector "was organized effectively under a representative body [that] could control its members."[141] But instead, he continued, the whole planning apparatus was being crippled by the state's fear of disturbing the "status quo" in economic organization.[142] To this, a candid reply was offered by none other than Nehru himself, who admitted that, under the crisis conditions of the period, "there was a need for caution to avoid a major breakdown."[143] Thus, while both planners and politicians were aware of the wide spectrum of institutional choices available, and of the likely effectiveness of alternative instruments, they felt constrained to choose the one most likely to restore business confidence. In the next chapter we shall examine in detail how this was to limit the planners' ability to actually use DCs as a means of crafting industrial policy.

PART III

Reproducing the State

CHAPTER 7

State Structure and Industrial Policy

INTRODUCTION

The previous three chapters have focused on the "critical juncture" of 1947–51, the period in which the basic institutions of Indian industrial planning were installed. The main conclusion that emerges from the study of those years is that, contrary to the received wisdom concerning the Indian political economy, there was no real consensus around industrial planning on the morrow of Independence; in particular, the business class was virtually unanimous in rejecting the idea that the state ought to be vested with the power to regulate or control the flow of private investment. This did not generate a resistance to "planning" per se — to this, representatives of the class continued to give lip service. But "planning" to these groups represented something quite different from disciplinary planning. To them, the term denoted the duty of the state to provide whatever assistance private enterprise was demanding; further, this assistance was to be provided under the guiding hand of agencies which, they insisted, industrialists themselves ought to administer.

Not only was the understanding of state-supported development different, but the business offensive also managed to substantially influence the final shape of the policy apparatus. The Planning Commission as well as the IDRA turned out to be quite unlike their original design, and this was explicitly intended to make them more palatable to industrialists. This was a dramatically different outcome than that in Korea, where the Park regime was able to install a genuine nodal agency in the EPB, and where the counterparts to the Indian Development Councils were structured so they could realistically expect to bargain with business associations and exert some influence over them. Underlying this different outcome was the fact that, unlike the Indian National Congress, the new regime in Korea had been able to ally with its capitalist class around a development model that made a disciplinary state desirable to both sides.

This chapter begins the next stage of the analysis. Having examined how the state institutions were put into place, and why they took the form they did, we now move on to examine their consequences over time for industrial policy. Thus the task of this chapter is to reveal the causal link between state structure and the quality of industrial policy. In drawing out these links, I shall show that the overall weakness of industrial policy was generated by a lack of capacity in the two tasks that are central to a developmental state: the capacity to impose discipline on state agencies around a coherent project and the capacity to discipline private capital into abiding by that project. If successful, this argument confirms the thesis, which has been developed by the statist literature on developmental states, and which I accept, that adequate state capacity is a crucial pivot on which industrial policy turns; it also, however, confirms my qualification of that thesis by showing the enduring consequences of the "critical juncture," in which it emerged that the installation of a state with adequate capacity was itself mediated by its relation to the domestic business class.

This chapter is also intended to contribute to the statist side of the literature on another dimension, namely, the issue of what comprises a cohesive state. In the most well-known recent work on developmental states, Peter Evans has placed primary emphasis on a well-oiled bureaucracy as the key to state cohesion.[1] While this does seem to me an absolutely essential precondition, the analysis of India provided below calls for a modification of the thesis. Both India and Korea began their development programs with robust bureaucracies; if anything, India inherited an administrative apparatus that was more bureaucratically sound than that in Korea. Yet, as I will show, the Indian state was far from cohesive in its functioning. Indeed, Evans himself has noted the absence of "selectiveness" as one of the main pathologies of Indian development policy.[2] Why, despite having a properly "Weberian" bureaucracy, was the Indian state unable to muster coherence?

The reason is that a bureaucratic tradition, although necessary, is not sufficient to achieve coherence. State functionaries who are guided by the duties of their station certainly will be less likely to be guided by strategies for personal gain. In this respect, they add to the state's cohesiveness as a corporate body. But the breakdown of cohesiveness need not occur at the level of the individual state functionary; instead, it can take place at the level of the bureaus that house the functionaries. State agencies are often assigned tasks that genuinely conflict, as when Finance Ministries are enjoined to maintain monetary stability while Planning Boards are expected to initiate rapid development policies, which will often create monetary *in*stability. Bureaucratic rule-following cannot be expected to generate coherence in such cases, *because the "rules" themselves are in tension.* It is not that officials in the Finance Ministry are overstepping their authority when they argue against large development projects; making such arguments is *part* of the ministry's responsibility. Coherence in such cases depends on there being some agency that is given the authority to settle disputes and turf battles as they arise. As we will see, the Korean state was equipped with just such an agency; in India, however, although the PC was ostensibly supposed to provide such a service, it was never given the authority to carry it out. Development policy in the latter was therefore handicapped, since each ministry functioned as an "imperium in imperio," whereas in Korea ministries were disciplined by the nodal agency.[3]

The chapter is divided into three parts. In the first part I examine the Korean state apparatus, focusing on the mechanisms that secured its internal cohesiveness and those that established its links with private firms. I also present evidence showing that the policy apparatus in Korea was not, as some commentators have argued, committed to minimizing administrative density, red tape, and discretionary control. Indeed, on this dimension, it rivaled the Indian state. The difference, it will emerge, lay in the other two dimensions, namely, the state's cohesiveness and its "embeddedness."

The second part of the chapter shifts the focus to India. I show how the institutional structure of the state was such as to make it extremely difficult for planners to influence the actions of other state agencies as well as the actions of firms. But I also argue that the same structure, in addition to reducing the ability of the Planning Commission to impose discipline, also generated *incentives* for ministries *not* to abide by announced polices. This attention to state structure will also enable us to show that the lack of selectiveness, which Evans correctly identifies as a handicap in the Indian case, was generated by institutional mechanisms, not by simple bad judgment or overambition.

In the third part I provide empirical evidence showing that the state structure was such as to enable large domestic firms to ignore or undermine the state's planning efforts. On the two dimensions of industrial policy — controlling the direction of investment and then ensuring its productive use — the state was probably more successful with the first than the second. But in both realms, at least as far as the private sector was concerned, the overall verdict must be one of relative failure.[4] The larger and more powerful business houses were not only able to ignore plan signals but were even successful in turning the planning apparatus to their own use, thus unsettling the entire process.

This chapter is devoted to showing how state capacity — or its absence — matters. In the next chapter we shall examine the reasons why state managers were unable to reform the state in a developmental direction even when it became clear that the institutions in use were failing.

STATE STRUCTURE AND INDUSTRIAL POLICY IN KOREA

The basic argument I am attempting to develop is that at the heart of industrial policy in capitalist economies is the state's capacity to impose discipline internally and on firms, and it was the lack of such capacity that underlay failure in the Indian case. The relevant mechanism is thus the structure of the state, particularly its planning apparatus. The pathologies of this apparatus were manifold; they will be better appreciated, however, if they are set against the qualities of the Korean state institutions. This will enable a discussion of not only *what* Korean planners were able to do but *why* they were able to do it, whereas their Indian counterparts were not.

The Institutional Basis for Disciplinary Planning

An enduring myth of the Korean case is that it was successful because industrial planning was implemented through a policy apparatus that was relatively free of administrative red tape and the discretionary autonomy of bureaucrats, that firms had direct and easy access to policy managers, and that rules were transparent and non-discretionary.[5] This is then contrasted to the "license-permit raj" of India, where the proliferation of controls and discretionary autonomy is understandably considered the culprit behind policy failure.

In fact, this picture of the Korean experience is off the mark. The planning regime from the 1960s to the 1980s was laden with controls, rules, and discretionary autonomy that do not appear any less dense than its Indian counterpart. Like India, Korea also relied heavily on a system of industrial licensing to control the private investment of capital.[6] Firms had to obtain a license to start new operations, as well as to expand existing capacity, just as in India.[7] Formally firms had a maze of administrative hurdles to cross before they were allowed to set up operations. In the mid-1980s anyone wishing to start a new industrial plant had to solicit as many as 310 approvals and process as many as 312 documents before permission was granted;[8] in 1987 the Korean Federation of Industries complained that it took 530 days and 62 steps to establish a new undertaking.[9] It was not just that new undertakings had to cross a plethora of hurdles before setting up. The markets they functioned in were also heavily regulated. As late as 1986 the prices of 110 commodities — which included capital as well as consumer goods — were set administratively.[10]

Discretionary controls were the most crucial component on the external front as well. It is true that short-term credit for exports was often given on a non-discretionary basis. But Yeonmi Ahn has argued that this accounted for only a small portion of all total credit allocation—60 billion won out of 828 billion in 1970, or 7.2 percent.[11] Long-term credit (with a maturity of more than three years) still remained discretionary. This has been given more force by Dani Rodrik, who has confirmed that the Korean experience was one that relied on a highly selective and discretionary regime of export incentives.[12]

What set the Korean political economy apart, then, was not that it abjured the kind of elaborate controls that seem to have bedeviled other countries. The difference lay in the nature of the state that implemented them, and in its relation with private capital. Unlike in many other countries, where the bureaucracy was left to its own to implement rules—often without clear directions from political authorities and without solid backing for their enforcement—the red tape in Korea was used as a means of increasing the state's leverage over targeted firms, who were allowed easier access and faster entry, if they abided by the conditions attached. For this, three conditions were essential, which were often lacking in other countries—*first*, clear lines of authority within the state, which allowed a clear enunciation of priorities; *second*, smooth and steady flows of information between state agencies to facilitate monitoring; and, *third*, institutionalized channels of communication with private firms, not only to obtain their input but also to clarify the state's objectives and the consequences of noncompliance. I shall now outline how Park established such a state and how it had the effect of generating discipline, and then show how it was precisely these qualities the Indian state lacked.

AUTHORITY WITHIN THE STATE

As is well known, one particular agency occupied the heart of the Korean economic apparatus in its period of "high planning" (1961–mid-1980s). Although this is usually assumed to have been the Economic Planning Board, which was set up in 1961, this is probably not accurate. The true heart of the state was, until his death in 1979, Park's own residence and office, *the Blue House*. Of course, the EPB was the administrative core of industrial planning, but its authority was always overshadowed by Park's own power, which he did not hesitate to use against the EPB when necessary. Thus, when the Heavy and Chemical Industrialization (HCI) drive was launched in the early 1970s, Park shunted the EPB to the sideline because of its opposition to the policy, and he created the HCI Promotion Committee (HCIPC), which was now entrusted to oversee all economic decision making.[13] The important point is that Park ensured that there was always *some* nodal agency invested with the power to oversee and implement policy.

In the first two decades of development, this agency was the EPB. Not only was the EPB the fount of the formation of industrial policy, it also enjoyed supreme control over the annual budgetary process and allocation of credit. This meant that the same agency responsible for annual planning also devised the annual budget, without having to obtain parliamentary permission or the agreement of the Finance Ministry.[14] In fact, the Finance Ministry had no power to override the decisions of the EPB.[15] The nodal agency also had supreme power over the allocation of credit[16] as well as foreign aid.[17] Ministries were made responsible to implement the decisions of the EPB, had to submit their spending estimates to the board for approval, and also had to report regularly on project implementation.[18] The result was that the various strands of industrial policy were effectively coordinated because it was the task of one agency, namely, the EPB, to render them consistent and then to enforce them. The key, it should be noted, was not that all relevant tasks were the sole provenance of the EPB—that would most likely have been beyond the ability of any bureaucratic agency. The critical factor was that the various units working in the overall field were compelled to submit to the board's authority, and to conform to its overall direction of priorities. It was thus a question of power.

INTER-AGENCY CHANNELS OF INFORMATION

If any agency is to enforce compliance on others, an efficient system of monitoring and information gathering must be in place. There were two major aspects to the flow of information in the Korean case: first, it was made certain that the various state economic agencies and the EPB were in steady communication, so that the board could ably monitor progress on policies and, in turn, was in a better position to prod compliance or to make policy adjustments in light of incoming reports; second, the moving force behind industrial policy, Park Chung-Hee, established his own independent access to information so that he could bypass normal bureaucratic channels when necessary.

In order to translate medium-term (five-year) plans into actual policy, they were broken down into annual plans, embodied in the annual fiscal budget, which was the bailiwick of the EPB. The board supervised the allocation of funds to various ministries for their projects, which were also subject to its approval. During the course of the year ministries reported their ongoing expenditures and allocations to the Finance Ministry every month, which, in turn, submitted the information to the EPB for scrutiny.[19] Project evaluation was handled by the ministries and reported, also on a monthly basis, to the Office of Planning Coordination within the EPB.[20] These evaluations were then consolidated into quarterly reports and submitted to the president's office for his perusal. In addition to this formal inter-ministerial communication, there were the well-known, often informal weekly and monthly meetings to monitor the progress of policy implementation. Perhaps, however, the key institutional vehicle was the monthly export promotion meeting, in which industry representatives, bureaucrats, and Park himself monitored the firms' progress on export targets.[21]

As well as being present at many of the inter-bureaucratic meetings, Park also established independent channels of information. The most important of these was probably the Planning and Control Office (PCO) located in each ministry. The PCO started as an experiment within the EPB in July 1961, with the task of reporting to Park on the progress of policy implementation,[22] but soon a cell was established in every ministry and had to report quarterly to the Office of Planning Coordination, which was located *not* in the EPB but in the president's office.[23] Park did not rely on such institutional channels alone; he also took a direct interest in many key projects, bypassing established avenues and insisting that relevant agents report directly to him.[24]

The picture that emerges from this examination of the state is that the organizational setup was molded and re-molded to be adequate to the task of fostering development. State institutions were compelled to surrender their autonomy to the directives of a nodal agency, and so overwhelming was the drive for coherence that the nodal agency (the EPB) was itself subject to the supervision of Park himself. This is more than just bureaucratic rule-following. This is not merely a bevy of punctilious clerks pushing files from one agency to another, driven by the logic of rationalization; instead, exemplified here is the formal logic of rule-driven action subordinated to the attainment of particular *ends*, and the rules themselves negotiated in light of these ends.[25] Indeed, the recourse to discretionary allocation of rents was a significant step away from narrow Weberian rule-following. What made it work, and what made the entire arrangement work, was the clear enunciation of desired ends by powerful authorities, and the accountability of the agencies to these authorities were the ends not attained. To round out this analysis, we turn now to the final component of the developmental apparatus, the channels of information and authority between the state and firms.

THE STATE AND PRIVATE FIRMS

One of the most important vehicles for state-capital communication has already been cited above in the discussion of the monthly export promotion meetings. This was but one in a network of institutionalized ties between bureaucrats and firms that the Korean state used with such success and that scholars like Peter Evans have highlighted in their work. For our purposes, two aspects of this nexus deserve special attention. First, firms and associations of firms that met with state officials

often did so as agents to carry out development policy. Hence the forums in which discussion took place were goal-oriented events, in which
firms conveyed to state managers progress on projects and the inputs
required for further improvement—they were not just "talking shops."
The structure of the forums reflected this orientation. The firms and
associations that were called to participate were not just random "business leaders" but those actors who would be relevant to carrying out
the task at hand. Hence, in formal settings such as export promotion
meetings, policy makers met with the Korean Trade Association, which
was organized as an amalgamation of sectoral groups;[26] on matters pertaining to electronics policy, negotiations were with the Electronics Industry Association of Korea;[27] for policy on the automobile industry, the
intermediary was the Korean Automobile Industry Association,[28] and so
on.

Second, and following from the first point, the discussions with relevant economic actors were not simply a means of gathering information
about their needs and their views; they were, and this is just as important, a way of imparting to them the nature of activities they were expected to carry out and the consequences that would follow in the event
of noncompliance. This was the "disciplinary" aspect of "embeddedness" that some scholars shunt aside. Again, the structure of the associations reflects the aims. Mark Clifford reports that early on in Park's
tenure he forced virtually all businesses of any consequence in Korea to
join sectoral business associations, which soon numbered more than
two hundred, almost all of them granted a representational monopoly
over their constituents.[29] Once formed, each sectoral organization was
assigned to a ministry; further—and this is crucial—in many cases the
governing staff and their officers were either bureaucrats whom Park
assigned or retired military officers.[30] This was a direct consequence of
state managers' goal of using information not only to assist business
firms in *their* aims but also to monitor them in order to asses the extent
to which they were abiding by the *agreements* previously reached with
the state.

In order for the state's demands on firms to be regarded as legitimate,
it was essential that firms, too, be able to expect proper action from the
state. A state that simply barked out orders to industrialists, setting
targets and performance standards, without due regard to how realistic
those demands were, or to its own role in providing coordination and
key inputs, would soon face a loss of confidence from business. It is of
some importance, therefore, that the ministerial meeting with business
associations also served as a forum in which the latter could express
their concern about inadequacies in the state apparatus. Gilbert Brown
reports that in the monthly export promotion meetings firms were en-

couraged to report on the quality of state assistance, and the relevant officials were expected to "respond before the President to criticisms of past government performance."[31] This shows the functional interdependence between the state's cohesiveness and its "embeddedness" — one reason why industrialists could repose confidence in the meetings as forums for negotiations was that the functionaries were themselves being carefully monitored by planning authorities, and by Park himself. It is hard to imagine the same sensitivity to firms' criticisms if ministries had not been tightly integrated around the development project, and accountable for its progress.

Although the use of a quasi-corporatist setup through the formation of these sectoral organizations was important, it may be imprudent to make too much of it. I suspect that an equally valuable means of ensuring compliance was through direct negotiation and communication with leaders of firms. As is well known, a few enormous conglomerates known as the Chaebols dominated the Korean industrial structure and accounted for a large proportion of the Korean economy (see table 7.1). These organizations were not only large, they were agglomerations of highly diverse undertakings under the head of a single president or family.[32] This meant that so long as the state kept the Chaebols harnessed to its development project and maintained steady lines of information with them, the transaction costs of influencing the flow of investment throughout the economy remained relatively low — since, at least in manufacturing, the Chaebols *were* the economy. Since each group was highly diversified and collected information on all its activities, state managers, in bargaining with the small number of Chaebols, were able to gather knowledge of, and influence investment in, several sectors at once.[33]

What could have been a highly bureaucratic, over-regulated, and labyrinthine state — with all the controls and red tape mentioned earlier — was made into a more nimble, adaptive, and disciplinary institution because of the constant flow of information in both directions. But it is crucial to keep in focus that the access to information was backed up by the clear enunciation of goals by the political leadership and its willingness to enforce compliance. As I argue in the next section, one of the most important differences between India and Korea lay in just this dimension: in Korea, bureaucrats had the clear backing of political authorities not only to monitor performance but also to punish; indeed, Park and his junta monitored the bureaucracy itself, in order to keep it in line with development goals. In India, however, the entire operation was left to the bureaucracy — there was no direct involvement by either the Planning Commission or political leaders.

Thus the dynamic was as follows: in the mid-1960s Park adopted a development model — export-led industrialization — once it became clear

TABLE 7.1
Chaebol Share in National Manufacturing Sales (%)

	1978	1980	1981
Top 5 Chaebol	15.7	16.9	22.6
Top 10	21.1	22.8	30.2
Top 20	29.3	31.4	36.6
Top 30	34.1	36.0	40.7

Source: Jung-en Woo, Race to the Swift, p. 171.

that significant sections of the domestic capitalist class were in favor of it. Once the model was adopted, state structures were realigned to ensure success in the strategy. The two linchpins of this reorganization were the channels of information within the state, and those between the state and firms, which were used to draw up an accurate assessment of the latter's needs and capabilities regarding the overall development model. On the basis of this information, "bargains" were struck with firms with regard to production targets and input requirements. The state provided key inputs and assistance; but it also used the same channels to monitor the firms to ensure that they kept *their* end of the bargain. This is why they were not only structured into sectoral organizations but were also attached to relevant ministries and frequently staffed with trusted officials; this reduced the cost of state monitoring, which, in turn, increased the reliability of disciplinary mechanisms. So long as the general strategy was working and firms continued to be eager to invest in conformity with the overall accumulation model, enforcing discipline was relatively unproblematic since business confidence was not impaired by it. And so long as this discipline was enforced effectively, the accumulation model, in turn, enabled firms to continue to reap high rewards.

STATE STRUCTURE AND INDUSTRIAL POLICY IN INDIA

With the basic dynamic of the Korean policy regime in hand, let us turn to the Indian case. The period under scrutiny in this chapter is that of the first three five-year plans. This was the time when the policy regime was still largely insulated from the intense sectional pressures of the 1970s and 1980s; it was also a time when the degree of corruption was of manageable proportions. Lastly, it was the period when industrial planning lay at the core of the entire policy regime, unlike in the 1970s and 1980s, when it was subordinated to the Gandhi family's personal ambitions. This period therefore provides a better setting to examine the effects of the state structure itself on the policy process, as against later years when the effects of the state institutions were overlain by the other factors just mentioned.

Starting in 1951 India launched the first of its five-year plans, which was followed smoothly by a second and third in 1955 and 1960, respectively. These first three plan periods are considered a discrete period — a honeymoon period, in a sense, for planning — after which, it is thought, the apparatus steadily fell into desuetude and hence disrepair.[34] After the third plan, there was a lull of three years in which the future of the PC was uncertain; the fourth plan was never launched seriously, and the fifth — in the mid-1970s — was delayed for another three years and, in the end, was largely a public relations exercise.[35] By the early 1980s the turn to liberalization had started to set in, making a return to serious industrial policy increasingly unlikely. Hence the first three five-year plans were of a seriousness that was unmatched in later years.

In Korea, after the ascension of Park Chung Hee, the state apparatus was restructured around the goals of state-led industrial policy, as explained in the preceding section. Underlying this restructuring was an alliance between state managers and leading segments of the Korean capitalist class around a path of export-led development. The two components were reproduced through their mutually reinforcing effects: the need for state assistance in export markets brought firms to the state's doorstep, which gave the latter the leverage to demand performance; further, it was in the interest of firms to submit to discipline, since this was a critical condition for their continuing survival in those markets. Conversely, the continuing success of the strategy gave state managers the legitimacy and autonomy to continue to restructure state agencies as circumstances demanded.

In the Indian case, the adoption of import-substituting industrialization meant, most crucially, that local firms did not have an incentive — of the kind their Korean counterparts did — to continually upgrade performance and productivity. Their insulation from international competition made it possible to sunder the link between productivity and profit making. Instead of depending on competitive success, profits could now flow from catering to domestic, protected markets over which firms enjoyed monopolistic or oligopolistic power. The critical difference between the two cases, then, was that the onus for extracting performance from domestic firms fell more heavily and more one-sidedly on the Indian state than it did on the Korean state. Firms in India had much less reason to be party to disciplinary planning than did those in Korea. Hence there was an even higher premium on building adequate state structures in the former, in order to communicate with, monitor, and discipline private capital.

TABLE 7.2
Market Concentration in Select Industries, circa 1965

Name of Sector	No. of Products in Sector	No. (and %) of Products of Which Top Four Firms Control More Than 75% of Output
Automobile and Allied Products	102	101 (0.99%)
Drugs and Pharmaceuticals	97	96 (0.99%)
Insecticides, Plastics, and Chemicals	114	113 (0.99%)
Alkalis and Allied Chemicals	20	18 (0.90%)
Acids, Fertilizers, and Other Chemicals	132	130 (0.99%)
Tools	66	65 (0.98%)
Light Mechanical Engineering	93	89 (0.96%)
Industrial Machinery	71	70 (0.99%)
Alcohol and Organic Chemicals	27	25 (93%)
Metallurgical Industries	71	67 (94%)
Rubber Manufactures	75	74 (99%)
Mineral Industries	52	43 (83%)
Heavy Chemical Engineering	15	13 (87%)
Electrical Engineering	39	33 (85%)
Paper Industries	14	11 (78%)

Source: Sudipto Mundle, "Growth, Disparity, and Capital Reorganization in Indian Economy," *Economic and Political Weekly*, Annual Number (March 1981): table 1.

Aspects of the Indian industrial structure were such as to make the task of disciplining possible, at least in principle. Although some scholars worry that monitoring firms in ISI might be beyond the ken of most states,[36] it needs to be emphasized that this should not be overdrawn. Most centrally, the ability to monitor should be directly proportional to the degree of concentration in the manufacturing sector of an economy. And, in this respect, Indian industry was, if anything, more concentrated than that in Korea for most of the relevant period. Table 7.2 shows the four-firm concentration of some key industries during the mid-1960s, which was the key period in Indian industrial planning. As the table shows, most of the key industries were completely dominated by four or fewer firms, making the industrial structure extremely concentrated. Just as important was another aspect of concentration, namely, the extent to which particular industrial *groups* dominated the manufacturing sector. In Korea the groups known as the Chaebols accounted for a preponderant part of industrial activity. In India, too, a small number of business groups controlled large swathes of the economy; the share of the top twenty business houses in the sales of the organized private manufacturing sector was 61 percent in 1972 and 87 percent in 1981.[37] The extreme concentration in manufacturing meant that, at least in principle, state managers ought to have been able to monitor and exert pressure on relevant actors — either through intervention at the sectoral level or through direct pressure on business houses, which controlled most of the production in the private sector. And this capacity would only have been strengthened if mechanisms central to the Korean and Taiwanese experience had been adverted to, such as the amalgamation of firms into sectoral associations, in order to economize on transaction and monitoring costs.

In the previous chapter we saw that the effort to enact legislation and to install institutions adequate to this task was, to a considerable extent, rolled back by the capitalist class in a de facto alliance with state managers. We now turn to examining the effects of the planning apparatus that was, in fact, put in place.

The State and Private Firms

The final version of the IDRA had granted the state the power to steer investment through the allocation of investment licenses, a mechanism also used in Korea. While the need to secure a license was to act as a constraint on the free movement of capital, it was also recognized, at least in principle, that this negative form of control would have to be balanced by regular consultation with industry at the sectoral and aggregate levels.[38] This would serve two functions; first, it would provide the state with a means to assess the investment sentiment and opportunities when setting development targets; second, it would keep state managers abreast of the progress of investment in the various sectors and undertakings. The chief mechanism for this task was to be the establishment of numerous Development Councils (DCs) at the sector and industry levels, and a Central Advisory Council for Industry for overall planning.[39]

The linchpin in this strategy was the Development Councils. In theory, the DCs were to be the link between the state and industrialists, the means for producing and reproducing the consensual participation of private capital in the policy process.[40] As in Korea, each DC would represent an industrial sector, or cluster of sectors, and would include owners from that sector, along with an official from the relevant ministry. The DCs would then assist the state in gathering information, setting targets, assessing the needs of units in that sector, calculating technology requirements, and also, and most crucial, in targeting firms that were laggards and would therefore have to be induced to improve performance. Hence the disciplinary component of industrial policy in any given sector would be carried out with the approval of, and in alliance with, representatives of that sector.[41] The DCs were thus an ingenious means of ensuring that action against a firm would not be taken as a sign of a wider assault on the class and would therefore not hurt business confidence.

The proposal had two weaknesses, which appear to have been responsible for its ineffectuality. First, despite their being the link between the state and private capital, the DCs were advisory bodies whose members were to be nominated by the state because of their expertise in the area—they were not corporatist organizations in which members could bargain with the state as official representatives of the sector.[42] This meant that targets and investment strategies arrived at on the basis of their advice would not be regarded as morally binding on firms. This was critical; if firms in that sector did not consider the targets binding, they were also not likely to regard the discipline meted out on the basis of those targets as legitimate. And since the DCs were a part of an apparatus that was, inter alia, committed in theory to disciplinary planning, firms would regard them as partaking of that same inquisitorial and punitive strategy.[43] In addition, representatives on the councils were themselves reluctant to divulge their investment plans, since other members were current or potential competitors who might use that information against them.[44]

Given this first weakness in the makeup of the Development Councils—that they were purely advisory institutions, even though the policies made through their support were to be binding—their future was made even more uncertain by the second weakness, namely, that participation in them by nominated representatives was voluntary. This meant that, in addition to their structural weaknesses, "their effectiveness would depend almost entirely on the attitudes of the owners of the industries for which they were constituted."[45] Since the members were reluctant to divulge critical information, and since firms in the sector they represented were unlikely to look kindly on their usurpation of authority, it was no surprise that the industry owners' attitudes were indeed lukewarm. Thus DC members used the councils more as sites where they could express grievances around policy—of a minor character—and push for greater largesse to their particular firms, since more weighty mattes were off the board.[46]

The problem went even deeper. All the changes in the IDRA had been made to reconcile the need for disciplinary planning with the perceived need to garner the consent of the capitalist class. The DCs and the Central Advisory Council for Industry (which I shall turn to shortly) were set up as filters, so that all policies would be made through the participation of, and negotiation with, industry representatives; "embedding" the policy institutions in this fashion was supposed to be an assurance to industry that state power would not be abused or used capriciously.[47] For example, any decision to punish firms that were lagging in their performance or reneging on bargains with planners was to proceed only on the report of the relevant Development Council; and, before actually proceeding against the targeted firm, the decision was, in turn, to be vetted by the Central Advisory Council.[48] Consulting with these bodies was to be mandatory for the state. But there was a limit to this process, in that the ultimate power to *mete out* discipline remained in the hands of, and at the ultimate discretion of, the state. Consultation with the CACI was mandatory, but the latter's advice was not binding.

For industrialists, the whole strategy unraveled on this issue. No amount of "consulting" would erase the obnoxious fact that it was part of a process that hinged on the use of state power to coerce firms. This immediately made the consultative bodies themselves an object of suspicion, as already noted. But it raised a further problem: if they were to function simply as advisory and informational bodies, why the need for new institutions at all? This was the natural objection business associations could now make: if the government only wanted to be in regular contact with industry and gather information, why not use existing business organizations, which already had their secretariats organized around this task? As the Bengal Chamber of Commerce pointed out to the Planning Commission, the DCs would simply duplicate the work the Chamber of Commerce was already doing and were therefore unnecessary.[49]

So the irony was that, in attempting to make the planning regime acceptable to domestic capital, state managers had become so tentative that they were proposing institutions more or less identical to *existing* institutions evolved by the *class* itself. Capitalists already found these institutions unacceptable because of their place within a disciplinary planning regime; now they could legitimately be shown to be *redundant*, further weakening their legitimacy. This directly paralleled the end game within the state: the new Planning Commission, instead of transforming the state around the needs of planning, had been instituted so as to leave the overall structure of the state undisturbed.[50] So, too, with the new policy instruments to negotiate with the capitalist class.

Herein lay the critical difference with the Korean case: in Korea the state had not hesitated to create new institutions, new forums for organizing the capitalist class as the state negotiated with its representatives. State structures and business organizations were molded around the task to which they were committed; in India, on the other hand, the *task itself* was made to accommodate to existing structures, both within the state and the capitalist class. This was not an unconscious process;

for example, members of the Planning Commission knew that negotiations and bargains with industry would be of little value unless firms could be held accountable, either directly or through a body that "could control its members."[51] But in the crisis conditions, created partly by the business offensive, state managers were reluctant to attack the status quo; as Nehru said in reply to the charge that the Congress was timid in the face of capitalist intransigence, under the crisis conditions, "there was a need for caution to avoid a major breakdown."[52]

Given the weaknesses in the Development Councils — that they were seen as part of an illegitimately punitive regime and were also redundant — it was no surprise that progress on their institutionalization was slow. After being announced in the IDRA in late 1951, the first three were set up in 1952, another in 1953, and four more in 1954.[53] By 1955 the momentum for creating new DCs was already slowing down, and the Industry Ministry announced that the government had decided to proceed slowly in the appointment of new ones.[54]

While Development Councils suffered from industrialists' lack of interest, the Central Advisory Council faced the liability of being essentially useless. Established as an overarching body to air business views and advise state managers on policy, the body was simply far too large to be effective. Meetings usually consisted of dozens of businessmen and bureaucrats, each simply making a prepared speech on sundry, often unrelated, topics that were of little use in actual policy.[55] Advice on policy could hardly be helpful unless given on the basis of a concrete sectoral or firm level, which was what the DCs were intended to provide. The CACI was supposed to function more as a class-wide organization for vetting proposals coming from the DCs and the ministries in order to build consensus around the policy in question. But since the DCs never got off the ground, the CACI rapidly degenerated into a "talking shop." As industrialist B. M. Birla characterized it, aside from "passing certain resolutions or debating some theoretical points," the CACI "is not able to achieve any great result."[56] Meetings of the CACI rarely numbered more than two a year, and the body soon became one of the many irrelevant semi-annual gatherings of officials and industrialists for which India is famous.[57]

Industry's initial lack of interest in these bodies was bad enough; the effects of this disinterest were amplified, moreover, by the dynamic in which it was occurring. For while the Development Councils were little more than topics of debate, the First Five-Year Plan was off and running — without them. The first plan was launched within months of the formation of the Planning Commission; in fact, it was launched before the IDRA was even passed in late 1951.[58] As a coherent and coordinated investment strategy, this first plan was not especially impressive.

Because of its hurried instigation, it was basically an ensemble of investment projects initiated by individual ministries, the chief concern of which was to reverse the economic downturn of the first three years of independence. No real attempt was made to fashion it into a coherent and internally consistent investment strategy.[59] This had an important institutional consequence, namely, that ministerial links with private firms — which were to be the basis for launching individual projects — had nothing to do with the instruments to be installed through the IDRA. Institutionally the first plan bypassed the policy instruments that were supposed to undergird planning.[60]

This meant that the institutional momentum established in the first plan was for ministries to work out their own ties and liaisons with firms on an ad hoc basis, rather than through a centralized, officially mandated agency like the DC. Now, the DCs, as indicated above, were already suffering from the suspicion and lack of interest of industrialists. That investment projects were now being launched without the participation of the DCs compounded the problem of slow progress with the more pressing concern of their increasing *irrelevance*. Bureaucrats were not likely to wait around for the appropriate Development Council to form in order to establish ties with private firms. And as they went about using their own resources to make the necessary links, the process of setting up the councils became a mundane bureaucratic assignment rather than a pressing institutional necessity. As time wore on and the fate of the DCs was left to the slow grind of bureaucratic procedure, an institutional network of ties between the state and firms was forming, which made the very need for DCs less pressing for both parties.

Hence the momentum the first plan established — partly as an outcome of the government's hesitation to push harder for the passage of the IDRA — was for the bargaining process with firms to be dispersed across ministries and, more important, to be ad hoc and informal.[61] The initial suspicion on the part of business made the future of the DCs uncertain; but the resulting tardiness in forming them had the effect of reducing the bureaucracy's own interest in them. Not surprisingly, the second plan, which was the most ambitious of all the Indian plans, saw no appreciable institutional shift in the administering of industrial policy. The liaisons with firms remained informal and ad hoc. This established a permanent wedge between forums like the CACI, in which policy was debated and discussed among political leaders and industrialists, and those in which actual bargains were struck between state managers and firms — this in sharp contrast to Korea, where policy direction came out of the same channels in which bargains were struck. This difference was crucial, for it became increasingly clear in the Indian case that the policy announcements made in forums such as the CACI had no direct connection with the actual decisions on investment projects coming out of the ministries. As I shall show later in this chapter and in the next, a central effect of this disjunction was to discredit the planning process itself.

Autonomous Agencies, Dispersed Information

That the state's links to capitalists were informal and dispersed need not have been completely disastrous. Undoubtedly certain inevitable problems arose from it, chiefly that the bargaining process became far less transparent that it could have been, and far more open to bureaucratic caprice, on the one hand, and industrialists' abuse, on the other. But a sufficiently integrated state apparatus, with a smooth flow of information and inter-agency accountability, could have gone some distance toward mitigating some of these effects. Even though the administration of industrial policy and state-capital bargaining were dispersed, a structured pattern of reportage and communication could have enabled planners and top economic ministers to monitor, and therefore control, the workings of the system. In this section I examine how the dynamic of inter-agency relations overlaid the state-capitalist relations — and in such a way as to only exacerbate the deleterious consequences of the former.

For the state to effectively direct industrial policy and planning so that industrial transformation would not only be in the desired direction but would also be efficient, certain minimal conditions were required: some mechanism was necessary that would provide planners with a steady *supply* of information about the economy, that would give them the means to draw up plans and put them into operation by using such information, and that would hold other agencies and private firms *accountable*, respectively, for implementing and abiding by these plans. In the Korean case we have seen how the state was restructured to achieve just these ends. But in India the administrative momentum immediately after the 1947–51 interregnum went stoutly in the other direction.

The Planning Commission was the agency in charge of designing plans in India, similar to the Economic Planning Board in Korea. But unlike the EPB, the PC had no direct control over the critical instruments needed to implement a plan — the annual budget, the allocation of investment licenses, and the allocation of foreign exchange.[62] These remained the provenance of different ministries.[63] This was in keeping with the outcome of the struggle around the new state immediately after Independence, in which supporters of a strong planning apparatus were beaten back and forced simply to graft the PC onto the existing economic apparatus rather than restructuring the latter around the aims of industrial planning. This signified not just a division of *labor* between ministries but an actual independence of *jurisdiction*, and hence of *power*. The dispersal of authority was the fundamental structuring principal in Indian industrial policy, which meant that planners had no control over how other agencies interpreted and implemented policy. This led to a developmental dynamic very different from its Korean counterpart.

This was most plainly reflected in the inability of the PC to control the flow of information within the state, and to influence the operationalization of the plans. In theory, intervention on the part of the PC was to occur at two junctures: in the initial stage of formulating the plan, the state of the economy and of particular sectors was to be appraised by establishing various sectoral working groups that would submit reports to the PC;[64] then, on the basis of these reports, the PC would begin the process of setting targets for each sector for the next plan. Once the overall targets for the five years had been worked out in aggregate terms for each sector, these would be translated into annual plans and, within each annual plan, they would be set into operation as particular investment projects. These projects in the private sector would be realized through the granting of licenses to applicants who wished to invest in the desired direction of the project.[65] The funding for these projects would come from a portion of the annual budget known as the capital budget. Theoretically the economic ministries would submit projects each year to the Finance Ministry, which would then check to ensure that the projects were within the limits of the annual budget, and these would then be sent to the PC to be vetted, so as to ensure their conformity with the targets of the plan.[66] The five-year plan would thus structure the annual workings of industrial policy under the overall direction of the PC.

In practice, however, the planners were made marginal at all but the broadest level. The working groups that were supposed to transmit sectoral- and firm-level information to the PC at the stage when the plan was being formulated were, at best, a patchy affair. Planners found it difficult to elicit the effort they needed from ministries to gather and collate information, much less submit it to the PC. The PC would establish deadlines by which reports would have to be submitted, but the working groups would respond with excuses and apologies for being unable to comply.[67] Hence the plans came to be based on information gathered by outside statistical organizations or through the PC's own staff. Inevitably this meant that the gathering of information was basically a macro-level forecasting exercise, with sectoral targets based not on actual industry information but on *past* trends which were then projected into the future.[68]

This handicap at the plan *formulation* stage was compounded at the level of operationalization in annual plans. First, the machinery for establishing annual plans was not set up until toward the end of the second plan.[69] In other words, until the third plan, there was no institutionalized mechanism for the PC to have a hand in concretizing the five-year plan into annual budgetary provisions; until the third plan, this was simply left up to the Finance Ministry, though informal discussions were held with the PC. But even after that, once the procedure for annual budgets was put into place, the planners were often left out in the cold. Theoretically, once the ministries had submitted project proposals to the Finance Ministry to put the annual plan into operation, the proposals were to be vetted by the PC. In practice, however, the Finance Ministry often gave its final approval to the projects without consulting the PC at all.[70] Hence, at both stages of the planning process for industrial policy — the formative and the final — the planners' lack of authority in the overall process left them without the information necessary for effective plan formulation and operationalization.

If we examine the flow of information as an ongoing affair, the situation was equally dire. In Korea economic ministries were required to submit regular reports to the EPB on the progress of the plan; this was reinforced by the installation of special planning cells in each ministry, whose function was to report directly to Park on project implementation. Channels were thus established both within and independent of the bureaucracy. In the Indian case the ministries never established any uniform machinery for transmitting information to and from the PC. Some ministries established planning cells, others passed off the responsibility to a middle-level bureaucrat (on *top* of his daily responsibilities), and still others relegated it to a low-level section officer.[71] The institutional needs of planning were simply never allowed to significantly affect, much less transform, the state apparatus.

Worse yet, ministries jealously guarded whatever flow of information did occur. This was true vertically (between the ministry and the PC) as well as horizontally (between ministries). Thus any request for information or any positive suggestion by the PC to relevant sections of a ministry had to be funneled through the ministry's secretariat, which meant that it was passed back and forth between several uninterested bureaucrats before it saw the light of day.[72] Similarly, requests for information from one agency to another was subject to the same process. So if the Textile Commissioner in the Commerce Ministry wanted information from the Iron and Steel Controller in the Industry Ministry, he was subjected to the fact that "proposals made by these organizations on matters of importance . . . *are minutely processed at all levels in the secretariat of the ministry concerned*" before reaching their target, and then again before making it back to the initiating party.[73]

This structure of inter-ministerial relations made it difficult to establish an ongoing process for evaluating plans. Throughout the period under study (1947–70), no formal machinery existed to report on the progress of plan projects, and hence planners had no way to adjust plans to changing situations.[74] The Planning Commission was thus in the position of having to intervene and attempt to make adjustments *after* the onset of a crisis, instead of at the appearance of early warning signs.[75] The monthly and yearly progress of industrial projects, as well as their adjustment and monitoring, was left largely to the ministries.

Unlike its Korean counterpart, the internal structure of the Indian state was such that the needs of coherent industrial policy were never allowed to encroach on the principle of ministerial autonomy. This was not a problem of having an insufficiently Weberian, rule-following bureaucracy; at the core of the dilemma lay the question of authority and power. Even when high-level bureaucrats were able to pinpoint where the resistance was coming from or the source of a particular delay, they could do little about it. Consider the following observation made by the highest-ranking bureaucrat in the Industry Ministry, when asked why policies were not followed through:

> If a policy decision has to be taken in another Ministry at the ministerial level and . . . [it] is not taken, neither I nor my minister can really force them to do it quickly. We can only ask them, cajole them and prod them. Beyond that, I really do not know what we can do. . . . We can go on writing to them and reminding them. But, we have no administrative authority over these matters. We can only request or press them.[76]

This observation made by an official in the Industry Ministry could easily have been stated by a member of the PC as well. Each ministry was handed its tasks, and no other agency had the power or authority to demand performance. Hence each ministry was a state within a state.

State managers were aware of this dilemma. But the proposed solution to the problem dutifully observed the basic principle of autonomy. Since restructuring the state was not to be countenanced, the solution attempted was to form inter-ministerial committees of high-ranking bureaucrats to coordinate activities between the various agencies.[77] These committees, however, only reproduced in a smaller setting the basic problem afflicting the state apparatus — no one member of the committee could override the preferences of another or demand performance from another; further, as ad hoc affairs, their effectiveness was entirely dependent on the energy and initiative of their members to mobilize lower-level bureaucrats into discharging the required effort.[78] On the other hand, once formed, these committees were rarely dismantled. They merely added another node in the increasing complexity of the state apparatus—which, in the Indian case, meant another independent authority.[79]

Thus the Planning Commission had little authority to impose discipline on economic ministries, and the ministries themselves were bereft of a stable mechanism of coordination. It is important to recognize that the *dynamic* effect of this state of affairs was for ministries to *increase* their autonomy from the PC and from one another as time wore on. Consider that, for each ministry, the availability of informational and organizational *inputs* was largely unreliable, for the reasons outlined above—the recognition of ministerial autonomy and the absence of effective coordination; on the other hand, the pressure to show results, for project-related *output*, was ever-present because of the commitment to development. With the reliability of inputs in doubt, and the pressure to perform a virtual certainty, the rational response of each ministry was to *decrease its dependence* on outside agencies, and thus *increase its self-sufficiency*. Hence, by the 1960s, many ministries had developed their own technical cells, which often monitored not only their own sectors but other, related ones as well—this was done precisely because they found the existing central technical bodies unsatisfactory.[80] But as each ministry developed its independent capacity in this fashion, the central coordinating agencies like the PC and the development wing of the Industry Ministry came to be seen not only as unreliable but also as redundant;[81] this only reinforced the tendency to view their efforts at coordination as encroachment. The overall effect of this process, of course, was to further splinter the state apparatus, and to make coordination and discipline all the more unlikely.[82]

In sum, the Indian state's economic apparatus presents, in many ways, an inverted image of its Korean counterpart. At the core of the difference lay the fact that Indian planning authorities were never given the kind of institutional power the Koreans had to demand compliance and performance from other state agencies. Instead of restructuring the state apparatus around the needs of industrial policy and planning, the latter was grafted on top of the existing state structure, in recognition of ministerial autonomy. The result was a massive institutional weakness in the planning apparatus and the diminution of the planning authorities' capacity to implement policy. Further, the dynamic effect of this structure over time was to exacerbate the process of autonomization. The initial weakness in state capacity was not only reproduced, but the attempts of the ministries to adapt to these conditions had the ironic effect of deepening the weaknesses over time.

This goes toward substantiating the criticism made of the "embedded autonomy" approach to industrial policy. This approach, as developed by Peter Evans, Linda Weiss, and others, places greatest emphasis on the importance of a rule-following bureaucracy as critical for state cohesiveness.[83] While a properly Weberian bureaucracy is undoubtedly an important precondition for a cohesive state, the preceding account shows that it must be structured by the appropriate distribution of authority within the state apparatus. What is more, in the absence of this authority, not only is cohesiveness unlikely but any cohesiveness that *does* exist will quite possibly *erode* over time. The Indian case, as discussed above, serves as a notable example of this process. Not only was its inherited bureaucracy insufficient to lend coherence to industrial policy, but the structure within which it reproduced itself had the effect of blocking the effort at coordinated policy, on the one hand, while exacerbating the splintered structure of the state, on the other. A weak state thus only got weaker.

THE RATIONALITY OF NON-DISCIPLINARY INDUSTRIAL POLICY

So far we have examined in some detail how the structure of the economic state apparatus — a legacy of the critical juncture of 1947–51 — made for a weak capacity to intervene successfully in the industrial sector. There was no stable and visible mechanism for bargaining with firms and extracting information from them about investment plans and about the progress of existing projects. What India had instead was a bevy of ineffectual talking shops. Parallel to this was the stubbornly fractured state apparatus, which made it exceedingly difficult for planners to gather information needed to design and evaluate plans, and to ensure their faithful implementation. Up to this point, then, the two main objects of study have been the vertical and horizontal flows of information and authority embodied in planners' knowledge of the industrial sector, as well as their knowledge of, and control over, the economic bureaucracy. The conclusion was that, in contrast to the EPB in Korea, where planners could *demand* performance from other agencies, the Planning Commission in India was completely dependent on the *willingness* of the ministries and the bureaucracy to implement policy according to the design.

We must now examine the factors that militated against the willing implementation of industrial policy by the economic ministries. It may be true that the PC did not have the authority to push through and monitor its projects. Bur surely the bureaucrats in charge of implementing policy could have ensured their fidelity to broad plan design. And certainly the bureaucrats could have enforced discipline on firms to extract performance. If they did not, then, in keeping with the claims expressed in these chapters, this should be explained not as the consequence of corruption or some similar factor but as a product of state *structure*. To this I now turn.

First, I outline how the existing state structure made it *rational* for bureaucrats in the economic ministries to ignore all but the broadest plan priorities in the allocation of investment, and why it was *rational* for them not to discipline laggard firms. Then, in the last section, I adduce evidence showing how, given this policy regime, large firms were not only able to escape discipline but were, in fact, able to turn it to their advantage. Thus, whereas the preceding section showed how planners were crippled by the lack of state capacity, this section shows how, given the insufficient capacity, economic bureaucrats at lower levels of the state found it irrational to use what power they *did* have.

State Structure and the Calculus of Bureaucratic Decision-Making

The original design — or, perhaps more accurately, the fantasy — motivating the institutional setup of the PC and the IDRA had been for industrial policy to be governed by the two-way flow of information and direction between the state and firms. The intermediate mechanisms for this were to be the Development Councils, which would form sectoral targets in consultation with manufacturers, and the ministerial working groups, through which the agreed-on targets would percolate up to the Planning Commission; the PC would then design five-year and annual plans on the basis of this continual flow of information. Next, the information would be transmitted to licensing agencies as the basis on which industrial licenses would be granted to targeted firms, and these firms would then initiate the investment projects in ongoing consultation with the state through the DCs. But because of the resistance from firms and ministries, both intermediate mechanisms were crippled from the outset. The industrial policy process was now marked by a giant institutional and informational "gap" between the Planning Commission, which designed overall policy, and the agencies that implemented policy — the licensing committee in the Industry Ministry (which handed out investment licenses) and the ministries themselves.

This gap between the policy designers and their executive arm meant, operationally, that the execution of industrial policy was basically left to the bureaucracy. Let us now examine how this made non-disciplinary industrial policy a rational course of action for economic bureaucrats. This is most usefully done if we divide the policy process into two components: the allocation of investment licenses and the subsequent monitoring of their execution.

ALLOCATING LICENSES

The responsibility of putting plan targets into operation in the private sector lay with the industrial licensing committee, an inter-ministerial body located in the Industry Ministry. The licensing committee included representatives from the various economic ministries but, significantly, not the ministers themselves.[84] Based on the sectoral targets worked out in the PC's plan documents, the licensing committee was to invite applications from potential investors and, if the candidate met the requirements, allow the initiation of the projects.[85] Had there been proper communication between the PC and the ministries, this process could have run smoothly. But, as we have seen, the five-year plans were basically macro-level forecasting exercises, not the product of actual information from the relevant firms and sectors.[86] Furthermore, annual plans were not even a regular exercise until the early 1960s.[87] Thus, for much of the planning period, licensing authorities followed only the most general and vaguest guidelines in the disbursement of licenses.

This created a dilemma for licensing authorities: directives in the plan document were hazy at best and, more important, could not be taken as reliable forecasts of the direction of investment. On the other hand, *actual* applications for investment licenses would pile up at their door, as firms moved ahead on their own plans. And these applications would not uncommonly be for projects that exceeded the notional targets in the plans or would be for sectors that were deemed low priority, such as luxury consumer goods. In a setting where the state's basic mandate is to accelerate the investment process, it seemed irrational to licensors to deny these applications on the basis of a plan document of little value to them. It meant denying real investments in the hope that other, more desirable investors might make an appearance — but with no reliable knowledge of the actual chances of that happening.

The resolution of this dilemma, not surprisingly, was in favor of the actual pattern of investment demand, as opposed to the normative one embedded in the plan document.[88] But this had far-reaching consequences. First, it meant that licensing authorities began to develop a general distrust of, and disregard for, the work and advice of the PC. Instead, the licensors increasingly relied on their own ad hoc rules of thumb and prognoses for the disbursement of investment projects.[89] An important outcome of this was that they not only ignored the sectors that planning authorities deemed high priority, but they even went so far as to allow a substantial portion of the new investment licenses into lines explicitly banned in the plan document. Thus, for example, one study found that out of a random sample of approved licenses, about one-quarter were for products in which further investment had been altogether disallowed.[90]

If the *rationale* for granting licenses became increasingly uncongenial to a guided industrial policy, the *manner* in which they were issued exacerbated the situation. Again, because licensing authorities had no reliable knowledge of firms' investment plans, and no stable mechanism for eliciting such information from planners or from firms, they could not develop a careful *phasing* of the license approval process.[91] This was of some importance, because the sudden grant of a large number of licenses was likely to create supply bottlenecks as investors rushed to acquire the resources needed to initiate their projects. In an underdeveloped setting, this meant, in concrete terms, that there would be a rush on two scarce goods in particular — foreign exchange and raw materials.[92] But officials were loathe to deny applications as they appeared, precisely because they could not be certain that the prevailing level of business confidence and enthusiasm would be maintained over time. Further, denying applications when they did not have a clear set of guidelines — in the form of a detailed map of targets or through continual communication with higher authorities — was to leave themselves open to the charge of impeding new investments. This made it a safer bet to grant the licenses as they came in — without phasing them — and hope for the best.

But granting licenses in this manner virtually guaranteed that a substantial number would remain unimplemented. Firms would greet each new five-year plan with a rush of applications; the committee, having no clear set of priorities, and no means of phasing approvals, would grant a large number of licenses. This would, in turn, create a rush on foreign exchange and create other supply bottlenecks, which meant that many investment projects would be delayed or abandoned.[93] Lacking the policy apparatus to devise a proper prioritization or phasing of licenses, the committee could do little to remedy the situation. Instead, its response to the fact of unimplemented licenses was to resort to granting licenses for *more* than the targeted or desired capacity in each sector so as to allow for a quantum of unimplemented licenses.[94] Here again, even if the PC intervened, the committee ignored it, on the argument that the PC simply had no idea what it was talking about.[95] Of course, this only served to increase the uncertainty in the system and to drive actual policy further away from plan forecasts and dictates.

MONITORING AND DISCIPLINE

Two elements were central to the process through which licensing authorities made their allocation: first, in the absence of an effective state machinery for setting priorities and targets, the criteria they used were ad hoc and necessarily vague; second, the process itself generated uncertainty in terms of outcomes — the very opposite of what it was supposed to do. This created special problems in the second stage of the industrial policy process, which was the monitoring and disciplining of firms.

Even in the best of circumstances, imposing discipline on firms is a delicate task for a bureaucrat. It means a willful interruption of production and throughput, with potential costs not only locally but also on a larger scale. In Korea an important factor facilitating this process — apart from the larger development model and its incentive structure for firms — was the clear authority that Park and the Blue House lent to disciplinary functions. So when a bureaucrat came calling on a firm, he came with the unambiguous sanction of the highest authorities. This was a direct outcome of the smooth integration of state agencies. In India, on the other hand, the task of disciplining was left to the bureaucracy, in splendid isolation from the larger authorities. This made for an immediate disincentive to impose discipline, which was only reinforced by the institutional maladies analyzed in the previous section.

The task of monitoring was the responsibility of individual ministries, much as in Korea. But, unlike in Korea, the ministries themselves were not accountable to planners in any meaningful way. Bureaucrats therefore had a great deal of autonomy in their execution of industrial policy. But autonomy brings with it its own problems. We have seen that investment licenses were granted on an ad hoc basis, which created such strains on the system that a certain proportion would remain unimplemented. For the administrative ministries, what made this especially poignant was that the licenses were themselves granted on the advice of these ministries. As observed earlier, the licensing committee was an inter-ministerial body. Decisions on any project were made by the committee based on the advice transmitted to it by representatives of the ministry that had administrative authority over that sector.[96] It was the views of the ministries that prevailed in the committee.[97] These ministries were largely responsible for the strains caused by the licensing procedure.

Since the ad hoc and unsystematic granting of licenses caused various breakdowns in the industrial policy regime — the various bottlenecks — firms could point to any number of failings *within the system itself* as a cause of their poor performance and lack of progress in actualizing the licenses granted to them. Ministries charged with monitoring their performance were thus put in the awkward position of having to discipline firms for failures for which the ministries themselves may have been responsible. The natural response to this was a reluctance to punish laggards, since culpability might have to be shared. Hence bureaucrats tended to keep funneling resources in the direction of projects once they were launched, since highlighting their failure by punishing them would also bring the spotlight onto themselves. Increasingly the rule that came to dominate industrial policy at the ministerial level was that the allocation of resources should be "fair" rather than "selective."[98] In other words, if a firm has been granted a license, it would be unjustifiable to punish it — it would be unfair — since the state itself is implicated in the firm's failure.

Recall now that the Indian industrial sector was intensely concentrated, as illustrated in table 7.2. Given this level of concentration, it is hard to imagine that the authorities were unaware of the strategy of firms or that gathering this information was beyond their capacity. The framework developed here is intended to explain the non-implementation of discipline so that it is consistent with bureaucrats *knowing* of firm-level malfeasance. I have argued that, even had they known of the rent-seeking activities of Indian capitalists, their isolation from the centers of power and the structural problems of the economic apparatus made it irrational for bureaucrats to use coercive methods on the miscreants. This is important, for with the absence of corporatist structures, the only route available to bargain with firms was through the business houses. But the incentives bureaucrats faced made it very unlikely that the large business houses would be held accountable, despite the fact that their key location in the economy could have made it possible to exercise considerable influence through disciplining them.

Like other pathological dynamics analyzed in this chapter, this one, too, reinforced itself dynamically. Since it was in the interest of bureaucrats to obscure the fact that firm-level failure might be the result of state failure, they rarely punished firms.[99] But since punishment was hardly ever attempted, any disciplining that *might* occur could be charged with being arbitrary and punitive. This made the criteria of adherence to plans and efficiency norms essentially moot for the implementation of industrial policy. Instead, the governing criteria came to be current demand for licenses and the past practices of the licensing authorities as guides. From an offensive and pro-active policy regime, the state structure induced state managers to change direction toward a defensive and reactive regime.[100] Hence the rationality of non-disciplinary industrial policy was laid fully in place.

Industrial Policy and the Strategic Action of Firms

We have seen that the structure of the Indian state was such as to critically impair the capacity of the designated planning agencies to design policy and put it into operation; further, this structure had the perverse effect of generating incentives for bureaucrats in economic ministries not to discipline firms. Until this point, the firms themselves have been ephemeral, shadowy creatures in the analysis. It has been noted that they were suspicious of, and did not do much to participate in, the Development Committees. But beyond that, the focus has been on the state. This final section of the chapter now brings in capitalist firms as intentional actors, who were not simply objects of policy but were active players in the overall dynamic of industrial development. We will examine how, *given* the structure of the state economic apparatus, some firms were able not only to escape disciplinary planning but to turn it to their short-term advantage in the form of rent-seeking.

To recap, the basic difference between India and Korea in our analysis has been the different development models each country adopted. For India, the orientation to ISI has several important consequences, the most important being that it made it in the interest of private firms to demand state *assistance* but to refuse state *discipline*. The dilemma of this state of affairs was that while the adoption of ISI put the *onus* of disciplinary planning much more squarely on the state—as opposed to ELI, where firms had an incentive to cooperate in their discipline—the attack by the capitalist class compromised the *ability* of the state to impose discipline, by scuttling the state-building project.

The ability of the state to plan strategically was thus severely hand-icapped; on the other hand, *firms* could plan strategically about how to use the planning regime to extract the highest achievable revenues at the lowest risk and cost.[101] The initial decades after Independence held great promise for firms that had the gumption and the wherewithal to expand into new lines: protective barriers were laid in place, British firms had evacuated, and state largesse flowed in vast quantities to industry. It soon emerged that larger business houses devised strategies that were not only successful in securing scarce resources for their expansion plans but also enabled them to overturn the central aims of industrial planning.

Since the state apparatus was such that the imposition of discipline was highly unlikely, firms were not only free from pressure to invest efficiently but were even able to redirect resources granted for one project into other, low-priority projects that were more lucrative. As to the first issue—freedom from concerns of efficiency—once an investor secured a license, it provided him with a virtual monopoly in his sector.[102] On securing a license, the investor was therefore under no direct pressure to innovate, to introduce new techniques, or the like. But the licensing system had another advantage: since entry by new firms was forbidden once a certain capacity had been licensed, the holders of the license did not actually have to start operations immediately after obtaining permission. If, for example, profits were slow owing to a sectoral slump or a small market, they could simply wait for an upswing before actually starting production—without having to worry about new entrants.[103] This meant that firms could orient their acquisition of licenses not only toward current opportunities for profits but also toward future ones. It was therefore quite common for business houses to apply for installing new undertakings and then to leave the project in abeyance once the license was acquired. This practice, known as "preempting competition," became very common: around 50 percent of the licenses acquired by large business houses were used for this purpose.[104] Licenses were therefore used as insulation from current competition where operations were under way, as well as a means of holding new lines "open" until greater profit opportunities appeared.

But firms did not simply use licenses as a way to secure captured markets; they also used them to access scarce resources that could be clandestinely diverted to other projects.[105] This was the natural counterpart to the preemption of competition. It was made possible by the fact that such resources as foreign exchange, raw materials, and so forth, typically required a prior acquisition of an industrial license for the project in question; however, because of the fungability of many such resources, even if they were officially secured for a particular project they could often be diverted to other uses.

The overall result was that—given the incapacity of state managers, and the disinclination of bureaucrats, to impose discipline—business houses were able to "work the system" in such a fashion that price signals, and not plan signals, were often the basis on which investment flowed into sectors. In a painstaking study of 129 investment projects by large business houses, Aurobindo Ghosh found that lags and delays in the implementation of industrial licenses were more often the result of conscious choice than of unavoidable circumstances.[106] Implementation of the licenses was phased in accordance with the managers' perception of profit opportunities, not with the conditions laid out in the licensing agreement.

Hence firms adhered to the following overall strategy: as opportunities for profits opened up in particular sectors, they would flood the policy apparatus with applications for licenses that they would then quickly implement. If profits were very large, such that they found it rational to produce at more than the sanctioned capacity, they would divert resources acquired for other projects toward the high-profit ones, and would produce at the warranted capacity level, in excess of the sanctioned level.[107] Where profits were slow and markets either saturated or growing slowly, firms would preempt the entry of competitors by obtaining licenses, and then simply wait it out until conditions improved. This provided them with the flexibility to exploit opportunities in current markets, without the danger of losing markets to entrants in those areas where operations were kept in check.[108]

This ability to "work the system," however, was not open to all firms but was primarily a tool of the few large business houses that dominated the industrial sector. This, too, can be explained without resorting to "corruption" as an explanatory mechanism. The complex system of license applications and approvals naturally favored those firms with the resources to push through the paperwork expeditiously. Indeed, given the lack of monitoring and the small likelihood of discipline, it made sense for firms simply to flood the system with applications whenever a call for tenders was announced. Large houses typically filed *several* applications for the *same* project, from different divisions or firms under their umbrella.[109] This gave them an enormous advantage over smaller and medium-sized firms that were strapped for resources. Studies of the licensing system in the 1960s found that, in the period from 1956 to 1966, the top twenty business houses in the country were able to capture approval for 41 percent of the new licensed capacity in the industrial sector.[110]

From the standpoint of the bureaucrats making licensing decisions, it made good sense to give more licenses to large business groups. Since top state managers were left out of the picture in most such decisions, for the bureaucracy, along with the power to allocate licenses came the responsibility of accounting for the choices that were made. As noted earlier, the ministries and licensing authorities were given the task of being selective, but this was embedded in a larger project of accelerating the pace of development. This meant that there was constant pressure to "keep the line moving," to shorten the approval process so that projects could get under way.[111] This made bureaucrats look more favorably at established and large business houses as recipients of licenses, as they were seen as more likely to have the capacity to carry projects to fruition. A failed project in the hands of a well-known business house would be easier to justify than if it had been handed to an unknown firm. Here again, the structure of the policy apparatus intrudes: since the industrial policy regime was split, such that middle- and lower-level bureaucrats were handed the key responsibilities without support from higher authorities, the decisions most rational to them were the ones that were "safest" on paper.

Thus the large business houses were able to turn the system to their own ends, partly because the whole process favored well-endowed enterprises and partly because bureaucrats found it rational to rely on them. To smaller and medium-sized firms, however, the policy regime was a numbing maze of regulations and bureaucratic red tape. This contrasts interestingly with the Korean case: in both countries the industrial policy regime was characterized by a battery of administrative hurdles, red tape, and government controls; in both cases the system favored large over small and medium-sized firms. In Korea, however, the favors to the large firms were doled out consciously, with clear objectives, and with the ability to monitor and, if necessary, discipline. The favors, therefore, did not undermine the policy regime. On the contrary, so long as the underlying development model was secure, and firms found that submitting to discipline was a necessary condition to their own growth, the subsidies and favors — with monitoring and discipline imposed by the state — brought forth the desired response. In India, however, the favors to large firms were not embedded in a disciplinary regime; indeed, their acquisition was a symptom of the *failure* of the regime to monitor and to impose discipline. Hence, whereas in Korea a seemingly overregulated state could be justified by pointing to its enormous success in presiding over an industrial transformation, in India it was the critics of regulation that held the upper hand, as regulation only seemed to produce a maze of red tape suffocating most businessmen, on one side, while supporting bloated and inefficient business houses, on the other. In the next chapter I examine how the ineffectuality of the regime was itself partially responsible for making reforms of an appropriate sort unlikely.

CHAPTER 8

Locked in Place:
Explaining the Non-Occurrence of Reform

INTRODUCTION

The argument presented in chapters 4 through 7 can be broken down into two parts: chapters 4, 5, and 6 showed that although building a developmental state was very much on the agenda in India, the capitalist class launched an offensive that largely scuttled this project. The planning apparatus that was institutionalized in the 1947–51 period was simply grafted onto the existing state structures, rather than restructuring the latter around itself. The capitalist offensive, in turn, was explained by the interests generated by an ISI model of development, which made it possible for business to garner high profits and state largesse with no real need for innovation. Chapter 7 then showed the consequences of this apparatus for industrial policy, chiefly, that the structure of the state made disciplinary intervention extremely unlikely, even irrational. In tandem with the analysis of Korea in chapter 3, those chapters provide an answer to one of our central concerns, namely, why Korea was able to put developmental apparatuses in place, whereas India was not.

We now turn to the second question guiding the investigation: if the institutions of industrial planning were not up to the task, why were they not reformed in the appropriate fashion once their inadequacy became known to state managers? While the previous chapters have been aimed at explaining the *installation* of state institutions, this chapter seeks to understand their *immutability*. This is an indispensable part of opening up the "black box" of policy formation and its outcomes, especially where the explanation involves the reproduction of useless state agencies and seemingly perverse policies. The question this chapter seeks to answer is why did state managers not reform the economic state apparatus in the appropriate fashion if it was so clearly failing. We can discount the possibility that they simply did not know of the inadequacies of the system—if anyone understood this, it was the policy makers and bureaucrats.

This chapter offers an argument about the structural constraints on appropriate reform, both within and outside the state. First, I examine competing explanations for why reform might not have occurred. I then show how an economic crisis, largely brought on by the policy apparatus itself, put the issue of reform on the agenda. Once reform was on the agenda, it becomes possible to take up the question of *what* the term came to denote, and *why*. In the Indian case, reform in the mid-sixties came to mean liberalization, and not the recasting of the state apparatus in the direction of a disciplinary state. The bulk of the chapter is dedicated to explaining why this was so; why was reform taken to mean *less* intervention in markets, rather than *better* intervention?

There could have been two direct routes to appropriate reform, that is, reform toward a disciplinary state: the first could have been to change capitalist preferences toward exports, so that the capitalists' orientation toward discipline would come closer to their Korean counterparts and they would be willing to abide by a disciplinary state; a second route could have been a drive from within the state to revamp it, so that it could govern capitalist strategies better *within* an ISI regime. The third and fourth sections below — "The Attempt at Export Promotion" and "Agenda Setting and the Declining Legitimacy of the Planning Process" — are dedicated to showing why neither of these possibilities germinated in the period after the crisis. Despite an effort at export promotion in the 1960s, capitalists remained wedded to their preference for domestic markets. In the latter section I show how a drive to reform the planning apparatus could not have come from within the state, for two reasons: the planning dynamic itself strengthened the political power of capitalists against the planning regime, and the same dynamic also weakened the planners relative to their adversaries within the state. Hence, when the move to institute reforms finally came, they were resolutely in the direction of less, and not better, intervention, and this is examined in the fifth section below, "The Reform Episode of the Mid-Sixties."

EXISTING EXPLANATIONS FOR THE ABSENCE OF REFORM

Most analyses that have pointed to the maladies of the Indian developmental regime have tended to throw up their hands at the apparent irrationality of keeping in place, year after year, policy instruments that were manifestly sub-optimal.[1] But while the continuance of the policy regime may have been irrational in terms of its effect on the economy, it may have been quite rational in terms of the actual possibility of reform, and in terms of the interests and beliefs of the relevant players. This has led some to attribute the endurance of the policy instruments to the doctrinaire commitment of state managers and bureaucrats to "socialism,"[2] while others attribute it to the material interests of the bureaucracy, through corruption and the like.[3] Formally these explanations are superior to those that seem to take planners for idiots. And I have no doubt that ideological factors and the material interests of bureaucrats in controlling the levers of the economy were of some importance in the perpetuation of the regime. There are, however, reasons to think that an explanation which relies on structural constraints on state reform is preferable to those relying on ideology and interests.

Consider first the issue of ideology. Many analyses that point to ideology as the culprit make a crucial methodological error: they take as evidence the *public pronouncements* of top politicians and bureaucrats.[4] Of course, this makes it simple to attribute the continuance of a regime of ineffective controls to such things as "socialist ideology," since no politician is about to walk onto a podium and declare that his commitment to the regime stems from his venality, lack of political will, or, worse yet, the power of interest groups. In any case, the evidence adduced in previous chapters—especially chapters 4 through 6—should, I believe, disabuse readers of the idea that the Congress, even Nehru, were anti-capitalist in any sense of the word. The entire economic strategy of the Indian state was based on developing capitalism, albeit under the guiding hand of the state.

Now it could be that the ideological commitment was not to socialism but to a regulated capitalism, and that was what prevented appropriate reform. If this is to explain why India stuck with inadequate policy instruments, it also fails to convince. State-guided capitalism can be of various kinds: it can be the ineffective kind—as in India—but it can also be the kind reflected in highly successful developmental states. The fact of an ideological commitment to state-guided capitalism can explain why *free-market* solutions were not countenanced; it cannot explain why the state did not resort to other, more effective *forms of state intervention*. The ideology-based critique gets its punch by narrowing its class of counterfactuals to only one on each side: ineffective regulations, on the one hand, and the free market, on the other. If this is the range of options, then the ideological argument becomes more plausible, since it could be true that many top policy makers were ideologically opposed to free-market solutions.[5] However, if the range of alternatives is broadened to include developmental states, then ideology *cannot* have been what maintained the ineffectual policy instruments— since *effective* forms of state intervention and regulations were *perfectly compatible* with that ideology. Hence ideology-based arguments are credible only if one accepts their essentially neoliberal premise—that the only alternative to ineffective state intervention is the free market.

Let us turn to the possibility that state managers stuck with ineffective instruments of state intervention because the managers were corrupt and used their position as "gatekeepers" to milk the private sector. This is probably the most plausible of all the theories introduced thus far. What is more, it is undoubtedly true that such motives were widespread among state managers. But this, too, fails as an explanation for why appropriate state reforms were not carried out. The example of Korea — and even that of Japan — illustrate that corruption, as a personal motive, is perfectly compatible with effective state intervention. There is no reason why bureaucrats cannot accept bribes *and* hand over licenses only to the most efficient, or sufficiently efficient, producers.[6] The key is to discover analytically those institutional preconditions which make corruption spread cancerously, so that it swamps the ability to make developmental decisions, and those which constrain it to more benign forms.[7] And no doubt any such analysis will have to include in its purview the *structural constraints* on designing appropriate state institutions. If appropriate reform is blocked off structurally, then the likelihood that corruption will take its more destructive form increases radically, simply by default.

In sum, while ideology and corruption surely played some role in preventing appropriate reform, they cannot have been the moving forces. The remainder of the chapter offers an alternative analysis, one that points to structural factors, both within and outside the state, that made the turn to developmental reforms prohibitively difficult. Through this, I hope to show that the reason ineffective state institutions stayed in place was not because planners were ignorant, dogmatic, or simply corrupt but because they *could not* change them.

THE CRISIS OF 1957 AND THE SEARCH FOR SOLUTIONS

The realization that the development strategy and the planning system were in need of reform came in the late 1950s, with the onset of a massive foreign-exchange crisis. The crisis revealed two things: first, that the degree of state cohesion and coordination was far below what state managers had thought; and, second, that the economy's absorption of imports was outpacing its export performance, and if the pace of development was to be maintained, exports would have to be increased. In this fashion, the crisis of 1957 marks the point at which some of the critical shortcomings of the Indian development model became known to state managers as well as to the public. This makes a close study of these years of considerable analytical importance.

The crisis came looming on the horizon shortly after the launching of the Second Five-Year Plan in 1956 and was a direct consequence of the dynamics outlined in the previous chapter. As soon as the plan was launched, private firms flooded the economic ministries with applications for investment licenses, which the ministries were loath to turn down. The Planning Commission had not worked out any effective blueprint or priority list for projects,[8] largely a result of the commission's own isolation and lack of authority. Without any priority lists and effectively free of supervision, ministries and the licensing committee had to make decisions based on their own ad hoc criteria, which typically turned on a vague sense of the projects being "worthwhile."[9] This practice, it seems, was encouraged by T. T. Krishnamachari (known as TTK), the Commerce and Industry Minister at the time. Although there is no conclusive proof that he encouraged over-licensing as a willful snub to the Planning Commission, TTK had long held that the Commerce and Industry Ministry should have been the nodal agency for all industrial policy and had regarded the PC as an interloper.[10] It is quite likely, therefore, that the practice of over-licensing was carried out with his tacit approval.

The rush of investment licenses created a corresponding pressure on imports of capital goods as industrialists moved to put their undertakings into operation. This was exacerbated by a partial liberalization of the imports of consumer goods,[11] which TTK also allowed on a whim. This need not have been a terrible problem had the reserves and allocation of foreign exchange been effectively monitored. Then the sudden depletion brought about by increasing imports could have been noticed and appropriate rationing discussed. However, the events revealed that not only was there no centralized collation and no analysis of the foreign exchange situation but the machinery to monitor its level and allocation was not even in place.[12] The results were a mirror image of what happened in the licensing committee. B. K. Nehru, who was an officer in the Finance Ministry, reports the following:

> Foreign exchange could, at least in theory, still not be spent without the concurrence of the Ministry of Finance, but as that Ministry did not know how much exchange it had to spend, *all it could do was decide whether, in its wise judgment, it regarded the project as important enough to sanction.* As virtually everything that came up was important and desirable, the natural result was the issue of sanctions beyond the unknown but obviously limited availability of foreign exchange.[13]

Planners did not have the power to formulate and advise priorities; the licensing committee could only use vague criteria of "project desirability" to issue licenses; the Finance Ministry, also lacking the basic machinery for monitoring foreign exchange, used similarly vague and ineffectual criteria, and hence ended up running down its reserves. Underlying all this was the principle of ministerial autonomy: the reason the requisite machinery was not in place was because planners had no means of ensuring the restructuring of state institutions around the needs of planning.

Restructuring in any given ministry therefore occurred at the whim of the incumbent minister; the flip-side was that powerful ministers could go on ignoring the advice of their colleagues, which would make the machinery that *was* in place essentially useless, and hence liable to fall into desuetude. Here, too, the foreign exchange machinery is a good example. B. K. Nehru reports that in the early 1950s there was a system of monitoring exchange reserves that he had helped to establish. But this fell into disrepair, as TTK, who was in charge of trade policy, chose to disregard it completely in making his allocations. By the time of the crisis of 1957, it had not been used in years.[14]

The immediate result of the crisis of 1957 was a drastic scaling down of plan targets, especially in the public sector, to a few 'core' projects, which Nehru and his cabinet tried its best to push through.[15] In nominal terms they were rather successful, but in real terms the cutback was drastic: in 1958 the plan outlay was reduced by 20 percent, climbing to 80 percent in real terms by 1961.[16] Politically recriminations flew across ministries and in Parliament. Each economic minister accused the other of sabotage,[17] but all admitted that no one had had any idea of what actually had been going on. As Nehru admitted in Parliament, "different ministries went on ordering things without anybody knowing the entire picture for some time."[18] As the second plan faded into the third, the problems did not get any better: over-licensing continued unabated, and imports continued to run ahead of the country's capacity to pay. Within a few months of the third plan's launching, all the capacity recommended for the private sector in many industries had already been licensed,[19] amounting in the aggregate to about half the total foreign-exchange allocations for the entire five years of the plan.[20] From this point on, India limped from one payments crisis to another throughout the 1960s.

The onset of this continual crisis made two points abundantly clear: first, that the planning apparatus was woefully inadequate; and, second, that the solution to the problems in the external sector would have to include a greater emphasis on exports.[21] As India entered the 1960s, it joined the increasing number of countries that recognized the importance of exports even within an overall commitment to ISI. Export promotion was now included as an integral part of the planning process.[22] It is sheer myth, as I suggested in chapter 3, that the long endurance of ISI in developing countries owed its existence to state managers' dogmatic prejudice against exports. A closer look at the Indian case may further our understanding of the real reasons for its continuation.

More important, an examination of the events that followed the crisis of 1957 promises to uncover what the constraints were on initiating appropriate reform of the state apparatus. Recall that there were two possible roads to reform: one that went the Korean way, through a change in the development model from ISI to ELI, and a second that maintained ISI but revamped the state apparatus to make it capable of performing the disciplinary tasks that were initially out of reach. The crisis put both routes on the *historical*, if not the *immediate*, agenda. In other words, the types of reform were not articulated exactly in the manner laid out here; there is no evidence that state managers, for example, were considering an outright switch of development models. But then again, neither did the Koreans, until the possibility was recognized after the initial successes and the appearance of the Japanese. What India in the early sixties had in common with the Koreans was the desire to increase exports and reform the state—whether or not this issued in an overhauling of the development strategy depended on the initial results and the power of the concerned agents. To say that reform was on the "historical agenda" is simply to say that state managers were now pointed in a direction where, with sufficient progress, their ambitions could have eventually been concretized in a policy apparatus that was genuinely developmental. As we shall see, the nature of the constraints within and outside the state worked to keep both routes to reform off the immediate policy agenda.

The Attempt at Export Promotion

The weakness of the Indian policy apparatus had its origins in the refusal of the bourgeoisie to countenance being subject to state discipline. It was this refusal that prompted the offensive against the state-building efforts in 1947–51 and that also created the opening for a section of the state managers to claim autonomy from the Planning Commission. Since firms did not have an interest in being disciplined, they not only fought off the attempts to build a state suited to that task but, once the actual apparatus was in place, the biggest firms were able to bend its policies to their own needs. This only reinforced the interests of the most powerful sections of the Indian capitalist class against a disciplinary state.

One route to reform was by changing the preferences of the capitalist class or at least of significant sections of it. A development strategy that relied on exports of manufactured goods — as in Korea — was the most obvious mechanism for accomplishing this. As more and more firms became oriented toward world markets, their preference ordering would come to approximate that of the Korean exporters, and hence would become more open to a strong disciplinary state.[23] This is what Indian state managers tried to initiate, starting in 1958–59 — almost exactly the time when Korean efforts at export promotion began. But the results turned out to be very different from those witnessed in Korea. There were three basic constraints on the export-promotion strategy: firms' own preference for domestic markets, the role of multinational corporations (MNCs), and the nature of the export-promotion schemes.

The Preference for the Domestic Market

A basic problem with all attempts to foster exports within an ISI model has been the preference on the part of firms for the domestic market. This is not surprising — the very essence of ISI is to funnel the flow of capital into targeted sectors by increasing their profitability. Its effect, however, is to orient firms away from export activities and toward the exploitation of domestic profit opportunities. Once this preference is established, it has the dynamic effect of eroding the export capacity of domestic firms over time, as the guarantee of domestic profits reduces the pressure to innovate. This is the basic dilemma of ISI.

Indian firms were no exception to this. Studies have shown that, on average, domestic prices for potentially exportable products were consistently above world prices, and consistent with that was the profitability of the former over the latter.[24] Indian firms therefore had no reason to initiate sustained efforts to break into foreign markets and develop exporting capacity. The most natural result of this preference was the long-term decline in efficiency and marketing skills. Atrophy in the latter domain was particularly harmful, since, as I argued in chapter 3, facility in marketing and sales skills is especially important in the export of light-manufacturing products, which is where developing countries invariably begin their exporting strategy. But even in the case of capital goods, brand reputation and quality are of central importance for export success. In India, firms with a lock on local markets made little effort to maintain these capacities.[25]

The result was that, insofar as exports figured in firm strategy, they tended to be used mainly as a means of exploiting excess capacity in periods of local recession.[26] Exports were seen as a means of riding out rough weather in the home market, rather than as the core of the firms' investment strategy. That strategy continued to be dominated by local conditions. Thus, over time, Indian firms came to resemble their counterparts in other developing countries, which found themselves unable and unwilling to have a go at export markets on their own.

The Strategy of Multinational Corporations in India

Indian firms did not have the capacity to expand into export markets on their own, once their level of productivity became shaped by the luxury of local monopolies. Korean firms, too, had been in this situation in the early 1960s; as discussed in chapter 3, the helping hand of Japanese corporations was a critical component of the circumstances that allowed them to break through. While moving out of light-manufacturing markets and into high-technology ones, Japanese firms gave the Koreans easy access to the niches that were being vacated. It was this development that underlay the Korean capitalists' enthusiasm for exports. Was such an option not open for Indian capitalists?

The strategy of MNCs in India was such that there was no real possibility of their playing the kind of role that Japanese firms did for the Koreans in providing access to export markets. In fact, their strategy pointed sharply in the opposite direction. In Korea the Japanese entered into key export industries like textiles, electronics, chemical and allied products, machinery, and so on, in joint ventures, and most of the investment coming in was oriented toward exports. In India MNCs entered in two forms: through establishing wholly controlled branches and through joint ventures of varying degrees. By the mid-1960s the former group accounted for about 45 percent of the total Foreign Direct Investment (FDI) in India. Almost all this investment (90 percent) was in plantations and petroleum.[27] Joint ventures — through holding majority shares or minority participation or purely technical collaborations — accounted for about 55 percent of FDI. Unlike the MNC branch operations, the joint ventures were mostly in manufacturing, and that, too, with concentrations in high-technology industries (table 8.1). The bulk of joint ventures between Indian firms and MNCs were thus in the manufacturing sector, which, in principle, held open the possibility of the latter shepherding their Indian partners into export markets. However, this is where the difference with the Korean case comes into sharp relief. Unlike in Korea, where Japanese corporations set up shop mostly to export, the corporations coming into India exported very little of their production. Table 8.2 shows the place of exports in the three types of joint ventures. This reveals the fundamental difference between MNC strategy in Korea and in India: firms coming into India did so exclusively to exploit the local market, not to use it as a base for exports. Not surprisingly, the national base of MNCs in the two cases was very different; in Korea it was Japan that accounted for most of the foreign

TABLE 8.1
Sectoral Spread of Joint Ventures, circa 1965

Industry	Number of Collaborations
Plantations and Extractive	11
Manufacturing, of which	1006
Food, Beverages, and Tobacco	12
Textiles	59
Transport Equipment	115
Machinery and Machine Tools	250
Metals	107
Electrical Goods and Machinery	162
Chemical and Allied Products	177
Miscellaneous	124
Services	34
Total	1051

Source: Reserve Bank of India. *Foreign Collaboration in Indian Industry: Survey Report* (Bombay: Reserve Bank of India, 1968).

investment, whereas in India it was England and the United States. A classification of joint ventures in India by country is provided in table 8.3. Thus, whereas Korea was the target of Japanese multinationals, India was the destination of British and American MNCs, which had no intention of using India as a base for exports. To make matters worse, a large number of the collaborations came with explicit *restrictions* on the right to export. Of the 1,051 collaboration agreements studied by the *Foreign Collaboration Survey* in 1968, 455 (43 percent) came with export restrictions.[28] Similarly, a survey of 270 agreements by the Dutt Committee in 1969 found that 65 percent had export restrictions imposed by the foreign partner.[29] Not only were foreign firms coming into

TABLE 8.2
Exports as Percentage of Total Production in Manufacturing Sector Collaboration Agreements

Type of Collaboration	1960–61	1961–62	1962–63	1963–64
Majority Partnership	1.9	1.9	2.0	2.4
Minority Partnership	3.9	3.9	3.0	3.2
Technical Agreements	4.4	3.8	3.1	3.2

Source: Reserve Bank of India, *Foreign Collaboration in Indian Industry*, pp. 24, 52, 73.

TABLE 8.3
Country of Origin of Collaboration Agreements, circa 1965

Country	Agreements
United Kingdom	420
United States	194
West Germany	149
Switzerland	66
Japan	51
France	35
Netherlands	24
Sweden	18
Others	94
Total	1,041

Source: Reserve Bank of India, *Foreign Collaboration in Indian Industry*, p. 102.

India for the domestic market, they were also taking steps to prevent or handicap the possibility of exporting the products produced through their partnerships.[30]

The orientation of foreign firms toward the Indian domestic market was of considerable importance. These firms mostly entered into collaborations in the very sectors that could have provided the base to enable India to break into new and more lucrative export markets. Not only were they not interested in this possibility, they went so far as to put obstacles in the way of their Indian partners who were initiating export efforts. Of course, not all joint ventures contained export restrictions; in theory, Indian firms could have made a go of it on their own. This remained highly unlikely, however, given the alternative of protected markets at home and their own lack of knowledge of the distant markets.

In sum, the strategy of foreign firms in India made them unlikely candidates to induce a change in the preferences of Indian firms. The domestic bias of the ISI model was only reinforced by their orientation. This points to an important dimension of the East Asian experience, which is often underplayed even by scholars who are aware of the importance of Japan's contribution: the role of sheer luck. It was nothing other than historical good fortune for Korea and Taiwan that they fell into Japan's regional strategy, which was based on finding new export bases for penetrating U.S. markets in some products while carefully managing a transition to becoming middleman in other markets.[31] Both dimensions of the strategy benefited Korea and Taiwan, though, of course, it could not have worked nearly as well had they not built the requisite state capacity to oversee a successful appropriation of technology, marketing skills, investment coordination, and so forth. India, and much of Latin America, seems not to have had this option. The switch to ELI would therefore have to be initiated from within, since there was no deus ex machina coming from without.

The State's Effort at Export Promotion

The nature of ISI was such that it inclined most firms away from export markets; the character of foreign investments in India made it impossible for local firms to get the helping hand of MNCs in switching to exports. This only left state export promotion programs as a possible candidate for inducing a change in capitalist preferences so that capitalists would orient themselves toward a greater emphasis on exporting.

The efforts to provide special assistance to firms in order to export began almost immediately after the crisis of 1957. Over the next decade and continuing thereafter, Indian policy managers set up a number of export promotion schemes designed to increase the relative profitability of exports while also providing some of the organizational infrastructure for success.[32] These included the provision of rebates on capital goods and other inputs, cheap credit, fiscal concessions, import entitlement schemes,[33] as well as the formation of an export promotion board[34] and individual export councils.[35] In addition, export obligations were imposed on particular projects and sectors, either on their entire production or on a certain percentage of it. These obligations tended to be directed toward producers of commodities that were deemed to have export potential, as well as toward firms who wished to produce items that were considered low priority for development plans.[36]

While these efforts were not a complete failure, they did not elicit anything approaching the desired response. An important source of the failure seems to have been the structure of the policy apparatus itself. We have seen in the previous chapter that one of the fundamental problems of the industrial policy regime was the parceling out of authority between ministries, with no clear nodal agency and hence no clear direction. This complexion of the state structure naturally had an effect on the export promotion schemes as well. Instead of a centralized and carefully coordinated system of administering the schemes, the method that was actually adopted was similar to the other aspects of industrial policy—they were handed over to the bureaucracy, which, since it lacked effective means of coordination, established myriad schemes that were overlapping, discontinuous, and administratively cumbersome.[37] This not only meant that firms willing to export were not provided with an efficient means of subsidy, it also frequently made for inconsistent decisions on policy implementation, and hence reduced the legitimacy of the measures. Exporters had to wade through a mass of administrative hurdles ranging across a number of agencies, which meant that they could be blocked at one of any number of nodes; this increased the likelihood of delays in compensation, which, in turn, made them reluctant to commit funds to export efforts.[38] The nature of the state machinery implementing export promotion thus reduced the chances of its success.

Furthermore, despite the announcement of sectoral export subsidies, producers appear to have remained firmly wedded to domestic markets. Unfortunately very few industry-level studies of Indian industry were conducted with this issue as a focus. But what little research there is supports this verdict. In one of the few existing analyses of firm strategy, C. P. Chandrashekhar argues that textile manufacturers in the 1960s continued to prefer producing for local markets, despite the announcement of generous export subsidies.[39] This is somewhat significant, since the export promotion program for textiles seems to have been one of the most generous of those put into place.[40] This was a source of some frustration to the bodies established for collecting marketing information for textile firms, who reported that, when they relayed product specifications to these firms, the latter were *not sufficiently keen to manufacture cloth according to the buyers' requirements.*[41]

Export promotion seems to have been less than successful in eliciting firms' enthusiasm. Also failing was the imposition of export *obligations* on them. Throughout the 1960s Government investigations discovered that the demand that particular firms export a certain percentage of their product in exchange for particular privileges was routinely ignored by the recipient. This was noted immediately after the schemes were launched[42] and continued into the publication of the Dutt Committee Report, which observed dryly that "conditions continue to be attached to licenses which are of no practical value."[43] Hence firms were able to use the export permission to secure scarce funds or inputs and divert them to more profitable activities, instead of using them to actually produce for export.

So the failure of export promotion schemes was partly owing to the chaotic character of their implementation and partly owing to the firms' own strategies, which were steadfastly committed to the domestic market. And, of course, each reinforced the other: the schemes' entanglement in the bureaucratic morass of the state made them unattractive to the potential exporters, who nonetheless did try to use them to get access to scarce resources; the firms' strategy, in turn, made bureaucrats front-load more paperwork and administrative hurdles as a means of screening applicants, all of whom came under suspicion as potential rent-seekers.

Let us take stock. The crisis of 1957 alerted state managers to the pressing need for reform, and in the 1960s efforts began in this direction. I have argued that, once the issue of reform was on the immediate agenda, two possible routes were open to a genuine developmental state: first, a change in the preferences of capitalists, from ISI to ELI or some combination of the two; and, second, a continuation of ISI but accompanied by a drive within the state to make the state more capable of successful intervention. This section examined the obstacles that lay in the way of capitalist preferences changing to some kind of export-orientation. There was a basic problem: with protected and assured local markets at hand, firms looked to exports mainly as an outlet for excess capacity, and thus they did not gear their investment strategies toward them. Given this fundamental preference, the change would have had to be induced, either through opportunities made available by other firms—as in Korea—or through effective subsidization by the state. The former was ruled out by the preferences of the foreign firms, which were overwhelmingly committed to the exploitation of local markets. In this sense there was a basic difference between MNC strategy in Korea and India. The latter option was made unlikely because of the nature of the state itself: the lack of proper coordination made it very difficult to implement export promotion in a consistent and efficient fashion, which served only to reinforce the firms' preexisting preference for domestic markets. These three factors—the preference for domestic markets, the orientation of the MNCs, and the quality of export promotion programs—combined to close off the first route to reform, namely, through a change in capitalist preferences. In the next section we turn to the possibility of initiatives *within* the state as a second possible route to reform.

AGENDA-SETTING AND THE DECLINING LEGITIMACY OF THE PLANNING PROCESS

Starting in the early 1960s, murmurs calling for an overhauling of the planning apparatus could be heard within the Indian state. First mooted during Nehru's final years, these calls reached a crescendo upon the ascension of Lal Bahadur Shastri in 1965 and continued into the initial years of Indira Gandhi's rule. Most analyses of this period have focused on the fleeting character of reform, which is, as I will attempt to show, not hard to understand. But what is not usually touched on is the issue of why "reform" in those years came to be understood as *reducing* state intervention, instead of *improving* it. There were certainly voices within the policy elite who tried to push this latter agenda; later scholars, however, have tended to take for granted the equation of reform with liberalization. This is, I submit, largely an artifact of the hold neo-classical economic assumptions have had over development studies in the 1970s and 1980s. It has frequently been assumed that, whatever else it may involve, a solution to inadequate planning instruments will have to center around the outright retreat of the state from the economy. The experience of the newly industrialized countries (NICs), however, should alert us to the possibility that reform could have been envisioned differently, as an effort to improve the *quality* of state intervention. This being the case, it immediately turns the absence of this issue from the agenda into a research question: why was the "reform" agenda crafted as it was, with liberalization as its mainstay? I shall address this question in this section.

The basic argument presented here is that the tilt of the reform agenda toward liberalization was a reflection of the balance of forces within the state and without, and that this was an outcome *generated endogenously by the planning process itself.* This involved two dimensions: first, the inadequacy of industrial policy gave legitimacy to the arguments in favor of reducing the scope of industrial planning; and, second, the formal position of the Planning Commission as the core of the planning process implicated it in every failure of that process — with the result that an already feeble PC found its legitimacy and its power declining even more. Thus the dynamic result of the planning process was to delegitimize the idea of disciplinary planning, while at the same time weakening its main agent.

The Increasing Power of Capitalists

In the previous chapter it was argued that the structure of the state economic apparatus was such as to make disciplinary planning very unlikely. Vertical links, which would have connected firms to state agencies and state agencies to the Planning Commission, were virtually absent, and horizontal flows of information between state agencies were just as tenuous. The result was that the implementation of industrial policy was basically left to the bureaucracy, which then devised its own ad hoc rules of thumb to grant resources to firms. This created a number of imbalances and strains in the system, but, precisely because the bureaucracy was implicated in these strains, it was chary of punishing firms that were not abiding by the terms of the licenses. This left the field open for large business houses to turn the policy system to its own advantage and use it to secure safe monopolies over lines with high immediate returns while preempting the entry of firms into other lines that could be of interest down the road. The immediate result of this arrangement was, as we have seen, the foreign exchange crisis of 1957. But, in the aftermath of the crisis, the reaction of state authorities only served to weaken the planning apparatus further.

One of the first adjustments the bureaucracy made — and it is not clear whether this was done with the top authorities' approval — was to ease the foreign exchange constraint by looking more favorably on investment proposals in which the domestic firm could arrange for its imported components through a foreign partner. The fact that capital goods and various other inputs would now come out of the equity, loans, and credits the partner provided would ease the domestic demand for foreign exchange.[44] But it also had the effect of increasing the independence of licensing decisions from plan directives, as such collaborations were often in the very sectors which industrial policy was committed to treating as low priority—sectors like luxury consumer goods, with high private but low social returns.[45] And, of course, as investment flowed into these areas, a demand was created for backward linkages, which only put further pressure on the bureaucracy to ignore plan directives, such as they were. The ability of firms to escape plan directives and not be punished was now compounded by the willing approval of projects in sectors which planners had wished to treat as low priority.

The reaction of licensing authorities to the foreign exchange gap only further eroded the authority of the Planning Commission, since the bureaucracy was now ignoring plans even more egregiously. The effects of the crisis on the budding public sector projects complemented this. The ability of the large business houses to capture a disproportionate share of the foreign exchange and attendant inputs entailed their scarcity for the other class of undertakings, which included public sector projects. Industrial projects in Indian plans were designed with a certain expectation of balance in the development of various sectors; the public sector, in particular, had been handed the large, high-overhead projects that could only be undertaken with initially heavy infusions of imported capital goods, and hence of foreign exchange.[46] The capture of the latter by large business houses had two effects.

First, it created immediate shortages for the public sector projects, lengthening their gestation and increasing project costs. Hardest hit were the new steel projects and the large fertilizer plants proposed in the second and third plans.[47] These projects were first put on the anvil in the second plan, but the shortages were such that they were still not complete by 1965, which was the end of the third plan period.[48] This was of critical importance, since these undertakings, and others like them, were supposed to be the foundation for other downstream industries, most of which were in the private sector.

The second effect, following from the first, was that even more pressure was put on the bureaucracy—and indeed, on top-level planners—to open up industry to private sector firms. The delays in public sector projects were met by accusations from big business and by some state managers claiming that the state needed to scale back its ambitions to control the commanding heights of the economy and place increasingly greater reliance on the private sector.[49] Indeed, given the constant imperative to increase production at any cost, state managers reacted by opening up more and more sectors of industry to private capital, sectors that had been reserved for public enterprises.[50] Of course, since these were the very sectors that private capital had historically been unwilling to enter into, opening them up also meant one of two things: allowing a greater presence of foreign capital as partners to domestic firms, who would supply capital goods and funds, or granting large amounts of public monies to domestic firms to ensure sufficient profits.

Concessions to domestic private capital were accompanied by a loss of leverage against foreign capital by the public sector. Public sector projects were taken up in fields in which India had no experience; these projects were therefore, of necessity, started up with the assistance of foreign firms, either directly or through intermediaries. The ambition was to hinge the collaboration on technology licensing agreements and the participation of Indian engineers so as to allow for a smooth transfer of know-how and the development of indigenous capability. But as delays mounted because of the foreign exchange shortage, pressure also accumulated to get the projects under way, with long-term objectives taking a backseat to immediate imperatives.[51] Under severe pressure to get operations in motion, key projects in fertilizers, petrochemicals, and steel were agreed to virtually on a turn-key basis, which allowed for only a minimal involvement of Indian technicians.[52] This had the medium-term effect of undermining one of the key rationales for the public sector, namely, its potential role as a portal to international technology.

In sum, the reaction of the economic bureaucracy to the new crisis situation was to ignore plan directives even more brazenly; the result with regard to the state-capital balance was to tilt the scales perceptibly toward the business class, both domestic and foreign. Private capital not only was allowed entrée into fields that were considered low priority — as long as it saved on immediate foreign exchange — but this had the medium-term effect of creating extra demand in lines allied with the low-priority ones, putting even more strain on bureaucrats to allow entry into these, lest the original investments go to waste. More still, the strangulation of several key public sector projects allowed business houses to point to the state sector as a bastion of inefficiency and a source of industrial bottlenecks. The pressure to disregard plan directives was now compounded by the demand that lines that were to have been reserved for the state enterprises now be opened to the private sector in order to relieve bottlenecks. The two dimensions of the process thus combined to accelerate the erosion of the legitimacy of industrial policy while simultaneously giving a boost to the power and authority of domestic and transnational capital.

The Waning Power of the Planning Commission

The crisis of 1957 and the shortages of the years that followed had the effect of delegitimizing the planning process. It also had the effect of weakening the position of the Planning Commission within the state apparatus. This is not surprising; it would have been remarkable had the PC been able to insulate itself from the loss in prestige that planning suffered. But some discussion is needed because, in theory, planners could have taken the crises of 1957 and what occurred after as an occasion to launch a campaign toward appropriate reform, on the correct premise that a deep source of the crises was the PC's lack of any real authority. Why, then, did they not do so?

Part of the reason was tactical: the PC had never really been accepted by most of the political elite in the country, particularly those in the economic ministries. As the decade of the 1960s began, these sections of the Congress went on the offensive against the PC, arguing that it was planning per se, and not its mode of implementation, that was behind the travails of the Indian economy, and that the only way out was to rely more heavily on the private sector.[53] This movement against the Planning Commission was launched just as Nehru was entering his final years, a period when he could not give it the support he had given previously. The attack thus occurred in a context in which the balance of power within the top leadership itself was changing.

Underlying this, however, was a deeper problem, which lay with the PC itself. To this point the narrative has focused on the PC's lack of any real authority and power in the planning process. Although it had the formal responsibility to devise plans, it did not have the power either to elicit the information necessary for effective plan design or to ensure its implementation. But the commission did not sit still as it watched its plan documents turn to dust. As the independence of the other ministries and the bureaucracy became clear, planners reacted by demanding some representation on the intra- and inter-ministerial committees that oversaw the implementation of policy. By the second plan in 1955, it came to pass that important committees — like the licensing committee — also included one representative of the Planning Commission.[54]

The problem, of course, was that the commission representatives were not a link between the ministries and the PC in any real sense. If the PC had had the kind of authority the EPB enjoyed in Korea, its functionaries on the committees could have been instrumental in facilitating the flow of information, as well as in imposing discipline on these bodies. However, in reality, it was the committees that came to dominate the commission representatives. The planners had no genuine authority to compel performance from ministry representatives — in the provision of information or compliance with plan documents — and often found that their advice was ignored;[55] worse still, they were often not even in a position to give advice, since some of the crucial bits of information were simply unknown, as in the case of the foreign exchange budget. This was the dynamic in the two most important inter-ministerial bodies in the planning apparatus, the industrial licensing committee and the foreign exchange committee. The licensing committee included representatives from the economic ministries and was chaired by an officer of the Industry Ministry; although a PC delegate was on the committee, his power to influence decisions was no greater than anyone else's. In fact, as one ex-chair of the committee told me, when planners did raise objections they were simply ignored.[56] Similarly, although decisions on the allocation of foreign exchange were ratified by an inter-ministerial committee that included PC representatives, the latter were brought in at the very final stage of discussions, when there was little chance of influencing the outcome.[57]

The participation of the PC in these agencies thus did little to increase its influence over the policy process; it did, however, *implicate* the commission in the decisions that *were* taken. Planners now found themselves in an unenviable position: they could not do much to ensure that other agencies maintained a fidelity to the plan design, but they could also not claim innocence from the outcomes of policy implementation since they were formally present on the relevant bodies.[58] The crisis of 1957 revealed the planners' dilemma in the sharpest terms possible: on the one hand, PC representatives had been present on all the relevant bodies; on the other, clearly the PC had not the faintest intimation of the impending crisis.[59]

This was the deeper problem facing the commission as Nehru was in his final years. As the planning process came under heavy criticism, and cabinet ministers began to call for a scaling back of state intervention, the PC found that it was in no position to launch a counteroffensive. Its formal participation in policy bodies amounted to a tactical debacle. While implementation of industrial policy had clearly been out of its control, ministries could legitimately claim that everything that happened was with the knowledge of the planners. Thus what could have been an opening to push through a restructuring of the state around the needs of planning turned into a fight for the PC's very survival. And with its chief patron, Nehru, about to exit the scene, it could only watch as the momentum against it grew. Its tactical weakness allowed other state agencies to take the offensive to its limit: not only had the planners not been able to prevent the strains and failures of the system, their presence actually, the charge went, exacerbated the problem. The commission's original mandate, critics said, had been purely advisory. By involving itself in executive functions, its first fault was in transgressing its legitimate authority; moreover, it played no constructive role in

the process. By the mid-1960s the PC was openly attacked as an interloper in the state economic apparatus — grasping, meddlesome, and,
above all, ineffectual. The solution proposed was to return the commission to its original pristine state — a purely advisory body.

THE REFORM EPISODE OF THE MID-SIXTIES

Jawaharlal Nehru died in late May 1964, and with his death the Planning Commission lost its main patron and benefactor. Next followed a
brief interregnum in which the post of prime minister was filled by Lal
Bahadur Shastri, who himself passed away suddenly in January 1966.
His death marked the ascension to power of Indira Gandhi, who, but
for the brief period of 1977–79, remained prime minister of India until
1984. The reform episode of the mid-sixties, lasting from 1964 to about
1969, thus straddled the Shastri years as well as the early part of Indira
Gandhi's reign. In the next section we examine how, in these years, the
PC lost whatever institutional power and prestige it had, abandoning
almost all control even over policy *formation*, much less implementation.

The Shastri Interregnum

Chapter 7 had shown that the Planning Commission had very little control over the policy *implementation* process. Nevertheless, it was not an
agency that was altogether without power. It still enjoyed some nominal
authority over policy *formation* (the poor quality notwithstanding),
chiefly through its design of the five-year plans but also in its efforts to
be included in devising the annual plans (from the early sixties); further,
it also participated nominally in the key policy committees, a fact of
much annoyance to the bureaucracy. As shown in the previous section,
the dynamics of the industrial planning regime had gravely weakened
the position of the Planning Commission. Nehru's death now provided
its foes with the perfect opening for institutionalizing their independence from it. That the incoming prime minister Shastri was increasingly skeptical himself about the PC's role and its ability to perform up
to standard only served to embolden its adversaries. Having been a
long-time minister under Nehru, Shastri carried into office the resentment and suspicions that most of the cabinet harbored toward planners,
seeing them as grasping and officious in their dealings with the state
policy agencies.[60]

In his brief span as prime minister, Shastri put in motion a series of
institutional measures that had the intention, and effect, of sidelining
the PC in the policy formation process and increasing its impotence in
policy implementation. The signal event was the establishment of the

Prime Minister's Secretariat (PMS), which now became an independent center of power for most matters of policy, including economic policy. The PMS was set up at least partly to enable Shastri to acquire more direct control over economic policy without having to bargain with the economists of the Planning Commission. This was a clear break from the Nehru years, when planners had been an important part of the process through which economic policy emerged.[61] In most relevant forums, if ministers or high-ranking bureaucrats wanted to press for a particular policy, representatives of the PC would be present to submit their own views in the deliberations. With the establishment of the PMS, ministers as well as businessmen had direct institutional access to the prime minister without having to deal with the presence of the planners. Conversely the PC was now cut off from the prime minister and, institutionally, set adrift.

The separation of the Planning Commission from the prime minister was aggravated by the clear orientation of the new PMS against the planners. Steering this and giving it direction was its chief, L. K. Jha, who now emerged as the most important bureaucrat in the policy apparatus. A high-ranking member of the elite Indian Administrative Service, Jha "had [the] bureaucrat's disdain for the 'non-professional' character of the Planning Commission,"[62] which he not only considered incompetent but also too powerful. In this, he clearly and accurately reflected the sentiment of most of the economic bureaucracy as well as the ministers. Balancing this disdain for the PC was a strong sentiment that authority over actual policy rightly belonged to the ministries and that planners should have no more than a purely advisory role. This sentiment, as Michael Brecher notes, gave expression to "a struggle between the professional civil service — which wants to restore the autonomy and the power of the Ministry secretariats, especially Finance — and the economists who hold sway in . . . the Planning Commission."[63] Jha's partiality toward ministerial autonomy was given concrete expression through his close ties with the secretariats of the economic ministries. Drawing on connections made though his long career, he adroitly maneuvered to exclude the PC from policy matters, hence "reestablishing the influence of the bureaucracy in the formulation of economic policy."[64] Shastri's ascension thus had the effect of institutionalizing the locus of power *away* from the PC and *into* the ministries.[65] Whereas the latter had exerted their power mainly at the stage of policy implementation, this was now balanced by a ratcheting upward of their independence in policy formation.

Added to the restructuring of inter-agency relations within the state was the changing complexion of relations between the state and capital. This occurred along two dimensions: relations with domestic capital and relations with foreign capital. Regarding the former, Shastri clearly expressed his wish to begin dismantling the regime of controls and regulations on industrial activity, as well as to have business included at the highest levels in policy formation. Toward this end he created a Business Advisory Council, consisting of prominent business representatives, and asked the PC to include them in important discussions relating to the impending fourth plan.[66] Just as important, however, were Shastri's overtures to international capital, mainly American. By 1965 the World Bank and the U.S. government had come around to the view that any additional loans to India would have to be contingent on its willingness to make two basic changes: opening up its economy to greater foreign investment, and the liberalization of internal controls. This melded easily into the pressures that were building up within the Indian government to roll back the regulatory apparatus. In negotiations with the Bank and the United States, Shastri made his willingness to liberalize clear as well as to allow U.S. corporations greater access, especially in the fertilizer and infrastructural sectors.[67]

Shastri died in January 1966, before he could set the liberalization process in motion. But in his eighteen months as prime minister, he had already made considerable headway in further marginalizing the PC. The momentum established in his tenure was firmly in the direction of markets as a solution to the problems of industrial policy, rather than a restructuring of the state in appropriate fashion. This momentum would continue into the early years of Indira Gandhi's rule.

The Ascension of Indira Gandhi

Two elements structured the reform process in the Shastri interregnum: the institutional marginalization of the PC and the commitment to roll back the scope of state intervention in industry. Indira Gandhi, in the initial years of her rule as prime minister, resolutely continued both aspects of reform. This appears to be at variance with the well-known populism and peculiar brand of "socialism" that Gandhi came to espouse in the 1970s, and in some ways it is; in her early years, however, Gandhi had no intention of lurching in the direction of the populist state capitalism that she eventually chose. Indeed, the turn back to intensified ISI came largely as a response to a failed attempt at greater liberalization in the early years of her rule. The eventual return to ISI, however, was not a return to the regime her father had constructed. One aspect of the "reform episode" remained in place and untouched: the further parceling out and fragmenting of the state economic apparatus, which Shastri had initiated and Gandhi consolidated. Through all the twists and turns of the later years, the Planning Commission would never again be an important factor in policy formation, and its demise put an end to the idea that industrial policy ought to be directed by a nodal agency.

THE MARGINALIZATION OF THE PLANNING COMMISSION

Gandhi's early years completed one component of the processes that Shastri had set in motion, namely, the further shifting of power from the PC to the ministries. We have seen in the previous section that the maladies of the planning process, and the commission's formal complicity in these difficulties, had gravely weakened its position in the state apparatus. This, in turn, had strengthened the position of its foes, which found expression in the maneuvers Shastri and Jha made to emphasize a greater reliance on markets and on ministerial autonomy. Once Gandhi came to power, she appointed a new deputy chairman of the PC, who now brought that impulse to the halls of the commission itself.[68] The new deputy chairman was D. R. Gadgil, who had long been a critic of the PC and was one of the most respected economists in India. Gadgil was strongly of the view that the commission ought to have nothing whatsoever to do with policy implementation, that getting enmeshed in administrative matters had been a major cause of its ineffectuality.[69] Once in office, he joined the movement to put power exclusively in the hands of the ministries.

Interestingly, while Gadgil's desire to make the PC a purely advisory body has become well known to students of Indian political economy, his reasoning has not been studied as closely. Gadgil's views were not those of a civil service mandarin — like Jha — who resented the commission's encroachment on his domain. They flowed from a clear realization of what was *politically* possible at the time. Soon after taking office in the fall of 1967, Gadgil gave public notice of the changes he wished to initiate within the PC, among which was a greater reliance on market forces and reducing the scope of state intervention. Note, however, the rationale for this change:

> Detailed planning of the production effort and investment can benefit the whole economy appropriately only if accompanied by meticulous price and distribution control. *If, because of a variety of circumstances, such a regulatory regime cannot be operated*, must not larger reliance be placed on market forces and competitiveness?[70]

Again, a few weeks later, Gadgil declared to a U.S. embassy officer that he was in favor of greater liberalization because successful state intervention "required much more administrative effort and sophistication than were available."[71] The decision to roll back state control and regulation was prompted by the realization that the Indian policy regime lacked the capacity to be effective;[72] also implicit in the decision was the realization that it would be politically impossible to build that capacity, given the alignment of forces. Hence, if the state could not be built up to be adequate to its task, then the *task* had to be scaled down to make it commensurate with the state's existing *capacity*. The Planning Commission had admitted defeat.[73]

So as Gandhi came to power and Gadgil became the new deputy chariman of the PC, the institution was now restructured to make it little more than a think tank for plan formation. Recall that in the years of the first three five-year plans ministries had resorted to establishing their own technical and planning cells, as a response to the unreliability of the planning apparatus — the anemic flows of information, lack of coordination, and so on.[74] Once in place, of course, these cells only furthered the slide into fragmentation that so plagued the planning regime. Under the new dispensation, this process was given official sanction: the Planning Commission was ordered to do no more than devise the broadest contours of each plan; the actual detailed planning, which translated the broad plan into actual projects, would be handled by newly created "planning cells" in each ministry. Many of the commission's own technical cells were dismantled, giving institutional expression to the idea that the PC ought to withdraw altogether from the field of plan implementation.[75]

A second mechanism through which the ministries' autonomy was strengthened was the decision to disallow members of the PC from attending meetings of committees that oversaw plan implementation.[76] Recall that the practice of commission representatives attending such meetings had evolved with the realization that a massive gulf separated plan formulation from plan implementation; planners had demanded that they be allowed to attend these meetings, in the hope that they might influence the decisions taken. This had been a source of great frustration to the ministries, and, in the circumstances of the reform period, it was no surprise that this practice was abolished.

This was not a purely political battle. Many in the bureaucracy seem to have sincerely believed that less "interference" by the commission would make for better industrial planning and policy. What seems to have gone almost entirely unnoticed was that while a decentralization of the operational side of planning may make some sense, it had little chance of succeeding unless there was some mechanism of *coordination*, and some measure of *accountability*. This was where the Korean state excelled, and, as we saw in the previous chapter, this was at the core of the Indian state's maladies. But if the ministries were not willing to countenance the authority of the Planning Commission, why would they agree to a new center of power?

Interestingly, it was a commission set up by the government to study the administrative apparatus and to recommend changes that came to this realization. In one of its reports on the state economic apparatus, the newly established Administrative Reforms Commission conceded that there was a real need for a "nodal agency" in industrial policy,[77] but then immediately warned that the chances of actually putting such a body into place were remote. If it were established, it would mean:

> the surrender to this agency of many functions hitherto performed, and perhaps jealously guarded, by [other] agencies, . . . [for] the concept of a nodal agency implies *some degree of discipline from this agency* over ministries handling individual sectors of industry. . . . In the past, proposals involving this kind of discipline have been successfully resisted by sectoral ministries.[78]

Note the language of the passage: clearly at least some sections of the bureaucracy realized that at stake here was not the quotidian task of paper pushing but the real relations of power within the state; they also recognized that at the heart of the matter was the capacity to impose discipline (their own term) by one agency over others, and that this had not only been resisted in the past but would also encounter resistance now. To show that this was no isolated realization, I quote another report that noted the need for a nodal agency and made a similar observation:

> A single agency for co-ordination will invariably mean some amount of control by this agency over other Ministries and this development is bound to be resisted. *The very concept of "co-ordinating agency" implies some degree of discipline.*[79]

The trade-off was clearly recognized: greater state capacity required a nodal agency with the power to impose discipline, but such a reform would mean the end of ministerial autonomy. This could not be countenanced, for the entire thrust of the period pushed resolutely in the direction of ministerial autonomy, which had found its most pointed expression in the marginalization of the PC. Thus the writing was on the wall, and Gadgil and other members accommodated themselves to the new dispensation.

THE GREATER AUTONOMY OF MARKETS

With the PC thrust even further into the outer reaches of policy circles, the second prong of the reform process was set into motion, namely, the greater reliance on autonomous market forces. This was to have two dimensions: internal liberalization, which meant fewer controls on private capital, and external liberalization, which meant a combination of devaluating the rupee and lifting import controls. There was a strong impulse for internal liberalization, both among state managers — as seen above — and within the capitalist class.[80] The problem was that, in an economy with a shortage of foreign exchange, internal liberalization easily translated into a drain on foreign reserves and, possibly, exchange crises. This worry about the external sector was even more relevant in the case of external liberalization, especially of imports. Until now, strict quantitative controls on imports had been the main mechanism through which the state had handled the problem, though with less than spectacular success. To reject such controls altogether, however, raised fears among state managers. They were therefore unenthusiastic about external liberalization. So, too, capitalists were not eager to let in a flood of imports, which would surely be one result of liberalization.[81]

Thus one of the main constraints on the prospects of *internal* liberalization was the danger it posed on the *external* front, which was only exacerbated by the independent fears about the latter. Relief on this front was therefore something of a condition for the success of internal as well as external liberalization. Unless there was a comfortable supply of foreign aid or private finance coming into India to cover the drain that would be caused by liberalization, the foreign exchange gap would squelch attempts to free up markets from controls.

The agencies pushing hardest for external liberalization were the World Bank and the administration of Lyndon Johnson in the United States.[82] Throughout the first half of the 1960s the World Bank had been relentless in its insistence on India giving greater entrée to foreign — particularly American — corporations in its development plans; the long lags in public sector projects, which were, as we saw in the previous section, at least partly caused by the maladies of the policy regime, lent a real urgency to these demands. Bank officials tirelessly pushed for a reduction in public sector programs, as well as a greater reliance on foreign capital to take up large projects.[83] By 1965 Lyndon Johnson, too, joined the fray, taking a personal interest in extracting compliance from India in return for U.S. aid.[84] The Bank and Johnson now worked in tandem to coax Indira Gandhi into accepting a broad package of liberalization policies, on both the internal as well as the external front.[85] Externally, India would agree to a devaluation of the rupee and to a liberalization of imports; internally, the regime of price and investment controls would be drastically rolled back, allowing a freer hand to business initiative.[86] In return, the United States would arrange for a steady flow of aid to ease the strains that the reforms would exert on India's foreign reserves.[87]

There was already considerable momentum domestically for internal liberalization; the doubts, as mentioned above, concerned opening up the external front. But an extraordinary circumstance of the mid-sixties pushed Gandhi into accepting the U.S. proposals: in 1965 and 1966 India experienced two of the worst droughts of the postwar era, making the nation almost entirely reliant on food aid from the Johnson administration in these years. Johnson himself recognized this as a perfect opportunity to force the policy changes that the World Bank and the United States had been clamoring for, and he demanded the acceptance of the reform package in return for food and promises of continued flows of financial aid.[88] In mid-1966 India accepted and set about putting the package in place.

The most conspicuous element in the reform package was a devaluation of the rupee in May 1966, along the lines the Bank recommended. This was accompanied by the announcement of a new agricultural strategy using the new high-yield seeds and technology being provided by Western firms, which formed the basis of the Green Revolution. As for industry, steps were immediately taken to roll back the licensing regime — by 1967 forty-two industries were freed from any licensing requirements, and all other existing industries were allowed to increase capacity by up to 25 percent beyond licensed capacity without government approval. This was accompanied by a loosening of controls on the prices and distribution of several industrial commodities.[89]

Thus the initial years of the Gandhi era continued, and rounded out, the momentum Shastri had established. The Planning Commission had fallen into disrepute by the early 1960s because of the failures in state economic policy, creating an opening for the ministries to increase their independence from it. This offensive found expression in the creation of the PMS, which immediately de-linked the PC from the prime minister. The drive to strengthen the practice of ministerial autonomy continued, by the further marginalization of the Planning Commission. And since ministers and high-level bureaucrats, asserting their independence, were driving this marginalization, there was little chance that the decline of the PC would be replaced by the rise of some other agency as a nodal point for industrial policy. On the other hand, the decline of the PC was coeval with the delegitimation of the planning process itself among bureaucrats, leading to calls for an increased reliance on markets — a call the new PC itself came to accept, since reforms in the direction of disciplinary planning were clearly not in the offing. This momentum was strengthened by the intervention of the World Bank and the United States, both of which pressed for liberalization and a greater opening to international capital.

Reprise

The liberalization episode of 1966–67 was the culmination of a dynamic that had been in place since the late 1950s. Starting in 1957 the Indian political economy had been teetering on the verge of crisis, largely brought on by the planners' inability to impose discipline, both within the state and on private capital. This made the need for reform blatantly clear to all concerned parties. In turn, the nature of the domestic political economy decisively shaped the structure of choices available to reformers. Reform in the direction of disciplinary planning could have come from two directions: a change in the preferences of the domestic bourgeoisie, so that it came to favor an ELI strategy—à la Korea—and hence have an interest in appropriate reform; or through initiatives from within the state itself. But the allure of safe domestic markets, coupled with the restrictions MNCs placed on exports from joint ventures, made a turn to exports unlikely. This left the second possibility, a drive from within the state, as the remaining option. But, in an ironic turn of events, the ministries were able to use the weakness of the PC as a weapon against it, arguing that the crises had occurred because of its excessive intervention and centralization, thus raising the cry to roll *back* the PC's power.

This explains why a turn to disciplinary planning was not on the reform agenda in the mid-sixties. It also helps to clarify why greater reliance on markets *was* on the agenda. There was no reason that a greater emphasis on market forces had to accompany the eclipse of the PC: state managers could simply have opted for a regime of controls, sans a central coordinating agency. But, again, the peculiar dynamic of the early sixties worked to put liberalization on the agenda as an answer to the problems of industrial policy. The maladies of the policy regime not only weakened the PC, but the methods the bureaucracy chose to deal with the crises after 1957 worked to delegitimize the idea of state-led industrialization while strengthening the hand of private capital—both national and international. Each crisis was greeted by a paralysis within the policy apparatus and the opening up of greater swathes of the economy to private capital, whether or not it corresponded to plan directives; each spurt of private investment diverted resources away from public sector projects, creating long lags in their completion, which in turn created bottlenecks, which then opened the door to accusations that state sector projects were too ambitious and needed to be rolled back in favor of private initiative. And where the efforts of domestic capital could not compensate for the failures in the state sector, foreign investment became the most obvious palliative. This dynamic, coupled with that described in the preceding paragraph, created a pincer movement on the idea of disciplinary planning, from both within and outside the state. The liberalization package marked its culmination, as Indira Gandhi agreed to take the first steps toward greater internal and external reliance on markets as a solution to the problems of Indian economic policy.

The package did not stay in place very long: by 1970 it was already being reversed, and the era of populist policy was about to begin. The turn to liberalization had depended crucially in the short term on the continuation, even acceleration, of the flow of aid from the World Bank and the United States. Without such aid the removal of controls held the danger of causing another foreign exchange crisis hot on the heels of the drought and the economic dislocations of the mid-sixties. In any event, the Johnson administration, for reasons that remain unclear, chose not to hold up its end of the bargain. The promised increase in aid did not materialize; in fact, aid from the United States and the World Bank—the main sources for India—after 1967 dropped off precipitously. From $695 million in 1961–62, it dropped to about $350 million in 1967–68, and was down to $24 million in 1968–69; this led to an overall cutback of aid from about $1 billion in 1961–62 to $318 million in 1968–69.[90] The drop in aid was calamitous for the liberalization plans. The United States had accounted for more than 60 percent of all aid coming into India during the Third Five-Year Plan, with the European Economic Community a distant second at 15 percent;[91] as American sources dried up, there was simply no other avenue available to make up the difference.

As a result the Indian state immediately had to re-impose the import controls that the package had targeted for removal by 1969–70. And as import controls were put back in place, they had to be complemented by internal price and distribution controls to offset the distortions they would invariably cause in the domestic price structure. The inability to pay for external liberalization thus also brought back, by necessity, the controls on the domestic economy. In 1970 the forty-two industries that had been freed from licensing were again placed under the purview of the state authorities. So long as foreign exchange remained a constraint, this regime of controls would remain in place. And the foreign exchange situation did not become comfortable again till the waning years of the next decade, that is, around 1977–78.[92]

In a very real sense, however, it was the late sixties that were the climacteric, and the events of 1970 the denouement. For despite the reversion to what came to be known as "socialism" under Gandhi in the seventies, the idea of disciplinary planning was dead forever by 1967. The Planning Commission was never to surface as a genuine co-ordinating agency of any kind, and ministerial autonomy was to be challenged only by the ever-increasing demands of obeisance coming from Gandhi and her family. As for the prospects of appropriate reforms, they were no longer even an issue—the Indian development apparatus had become firmly locked in place.

CHAPTER 9

Conclusion

THIS BOOK'S CONTRIBUTIONS to the political economy of development in India and Korea can be assimilated at three distinct levels: its reassessment of the historiography of the critical periods in the two countries, and particularly of the role of the respective capitalist classes; its offer of a more general framework that seeks to explain the structural mechanisms which influenced the actors choices, and which, I argue, may be generalized to other cases; and, finally, in the implicit counterfactual that there were options open to India *within* the broad carapace of ISI which it did not take, and which, had it taken them, might have produced better outcomes. In conclusion, I shall draw together these threads and offer some thoughts as to their broader implications.

BRINGING CAPITAL "BACK IN"

Empirically I have suggested that in the years critical to the consolidation of the Indian and Korean states, their respective capitalist classes played an absolutely pivotal role. Arguments about the importance of capitalist class interests, or of class power, are not difficult to come across in scholarship on other areas in the developing world; Latin American studies, in particular, have a strong tradition of focusing on the interplay of state and class in the development process. But in Asian studies, particularly in South Asian studies, the reigning assumptions have tended to regard capitalist class dynamics as, at best, of secondary importance in comparison to state dynamics.[1] Perhaps the most respectable reason for this neglect has been the feeling that local industrial groups in these regions were simply too small to count for much in political conflicts. And certainly it is true that Indian and Korean manufacturing sectors were smaller than their counterparts in South America. But how small is too small? If the evidence presented in this book manages to persuade, then the conclusion to be drawn is that the "minimal" necessary size of the industrial capitalist class, for it to be taken seriously as a political force, needs to be adjusted downward.

The importance of capitalist class interests and class power is most clearly brought out in the Indian case, as it is possible to chart the precise extent to which state managers' agendas had to be adjusted to accommodate them. Policy experts and high-level leaders in the INC had taken it for granted on assuming power that, if the state was going to assist local industry in its maturation, this would also require its wielding a significant dose of regulatory power. It bears repeating that after 1947, especially with the departure of the Congress Socialists, there was no question of doing away with private property; while there were individuals within the Congress leadership who bore animus toward private capital, almost all the High Command realized that the foreseeable future would be a capitalist future. The regulation of capital, therefore, was not motivated by an ambition to supplant the latter, though lip service may have been paid toward this end in order to placate the party rank and file. Discipline was seen instead as a natural accompaniment to the subsidization of industry, particularly in light of the war experience, when industrialists had made extraordinarily high profits through the black market and the manipulation of price controls. But as we saw in chapter 6, the wave of protest that business groups launched compelled the new regime to beat a quick retreat on key elements of the new policy apparatus. Short-term imperatives of restoring business confidence and repairing relations with capitalists rapidly came to overshadow the long-term agenda of transforming the political economy around the needs of effective industrial policy. The chapter focused on two elements—the Planning Commission and the institutional links to firms, namely, the Development Councils—but the list could have been extended. In the end state managers were able to install these instruments formally, but they clearly bore the imprint of the business attack—both were designed in a way that would minimize their offensiveness to industrialists, which meant, in effect, that their power to monitor, regulate, and bargain with firms was drastically reduced.

This episode of the initial years after Independence is of singular importance, not only for the subsequent evolution of the Indian political economy but also for our broader understanding of the nature and orientation of the Indian capitalist class. The most widely held perspective sees Indian capital as an enthusiast of state-led development, but saddled with a state that was both incompetent and grasping. In this view, which many nationalist historians and economists maintain, India at mid-century had the unusual fortune of harboring a capitalist class that included significant elements that were not only forward-looking but also willing to embrace capitalist planning—as witnessed in their participation in the National Planning Committee in the late 1930s and, most pointedly, in the publication of the Bombay Plan. Typically, after a summary discussion of the pre-Independence statements in support of state intervention, a straight line is drawn linking these to the *fact* of Indian planning. And once the premise is accepted that business groups were supportive of the industrial policy regime, then it also colors explanations for the latter's inability to push India toward industrial dynamism. Hence the evident weakness of the policy apparatus is explained by attributes of state actors: the factionalism of the INC, corruption, the endless maze of regulatory hurdles, and so on. This follows straightforwardly from the premise that, throughout, business groups were supportive of capitalist planning; if the weakness of the state apparatus cannot be attributed to their resistance, then its roots must lie in the character of state actors. In other words, the INC had a golden opportunity to initiate state-led development, insofar as providence delivered to state managers a capitalist class that was actually enthusiastic about planning—but the party frittered it away.

I believe that we must now reject this conception of the Indian capitalist class and its orientation at the time of Independence. The evidence presented in part 2, especially chapters 4 and 6, established several points. First, after 1947 there was a virtual consensus among capitalists that the state cannot have the power to regulate, monitor, and discipline firms; instead, its intervention was to be purely supportive, doling out subsidies and offering protection to emerging sectors. Second, the instruments to which business groups objected were *the very same ones* they had apparently *endorsed* in the years leading up to Independence. The most conspicuous example is the proposal for industrial licensing, which the FICCI and other associations demanded be dropped entirely in 1949, or at least scaled back massively. But in virtually every major document industrialists had endorsed in the preceding decade, they had given a nod to the need for licensing—including the Bombay Plan, the second volume of which explicitly endorsed its use in the future planning regime. This point is critical, for it makes it impossible to argue that, *before* 1947, industrialists had been in favor of industrial planning in principle but had rejected it *after* 1947 once its *policy instruments* were unveiled—for the instruments under consideration after Independence were the same as those preceding it. The traditional view regarding capital's enthusiasm for industrial planning cannot, therefore, be sustained.

The evidence for Indian capital's resistance to state regulation and discipline, which is at the heart of any industrial policy, is overwhelming. Why, then, has the mythology about their being in favor of it continued for so long?[2] There are, no doubt, ideological blinders that have obscured the view of some scholars, for the idea of a progressive and forward-looking industrial class has been a staple of nationalist ideology in the subcontinent. But there has also been a robust tradition of scholarship that has been skeptical of nationalist mythology and that, by now, ought to have established an alternative reading of the period. I believe that the main reason the old interpretation continues to hold sway is an institutional one: the unfortunate fact that more than five decades after 1947 there is still no real historiography of post-colonial India. Within India and without, historians of the subcontinent have simply not ventured beyond the events surrounding the departure of the British and the onset of Partition. And to the extent that they have, it is typically in the way of the perfunctory "epilogue," or "aftermath," to the real object of investigation, which is invariably confined to the colonial period.[3] Since the historiography of India simply does not venture beyond 1947, no real body of work focuses on the interregnum between the publication of the Bombay Plan in 1944–45 and the onset of planning in 1951. It becomes possible, for this reason, to infer that the stated support for industrial policy in the earlier years was sincere and continued to fuel the process after 1947 up to the time the policy apparatus was installed — the massive opposition mobilized during 1948–50 is simply rubbed out.

But the call to revise our understanding of Indian business is not based on the post-1947 conflicts alone. I argued in chapter 4 that historians of India have also misdiagnosed the significance of the precursors to planning, in particular the support that seemed to be evidenced in the Bombay Plan. This matter is significant in that, if my arguments about capitalist preferences in the post-colonial years is correct, it appears to throw up a puzzle: since the Bombay Plan of 1945 signaled an apparent enthusiasm for industrial policy — even of a disciplinary character — on the part of leading industrialists, there would seem to have been a rather dramatic volte-face in the span of merely two years, for the signatories to the Bombay Plan were among the most vociferous critics of the proposed planning regime after 1947. The evidence adduced in chapter 4 suggests that there was, in fact, no genuine reversal in the alignment of these industrialists' preferences. Their putative support for disciplinary planning had been quite thin from the start and was driven by a particular conjuncture. The impulse to offer up a declaration in support of planning was motivated, I suggest, not by a genuine enthusiasm for state-led development; rather, it was a tactical move on the part of the more politically canny Indian industrialists to shore up capitalist legitimacy in the wake of the Quit India movement. It was driven by the fear that the small but suddenly powerful Left would only increase its hold over the Independence movement in the waning years of colonial rule and stir up the escalating anti-capitalist sentiments. The Bombay Plan was an attempt to outflank the Left by inserting the issue of "planning" into a bourgeois framework. Hence, when the danger of a triumphant Left receded by 1945, also evident was a change in the public pronouncements of the signatories themselves, particularly Birla, who was by now issuing declarations against the heavy hand of the state — even as the second volume of the plan was released.

This depiction of the Indian capitalist class is revisionist, but I believe it is far more consistent with the evidence. Nevertheless, it is also true that much more research is needed on the early post-colonial years to achieve a fuller picture of how class dynamics interacted in the political economy. Most of our understanding of this period still depends on scholarship that is decades old by now, written more or less contemporaneously with the events and hence subject to all the flaws that weaken such work. The paucity of archival material for many aspects of Independent India is a formidable hurdle, but hardly insuperable. Certainly, if the arguments of this book are persuasive, it can no longer be maintained that the Indian capitalist class was simply not big or powerful enough to merit careful historical investigation.

Capital and the Developmental State

Thus it matters how capitalists react to the state-building project. This argument is meant to caution against the stronger statist claims, in which the state is regarded as so powerful an actor in developmental settings that it renders the preferences of other actors more or less irrelevant. But are the capitalist reactions themselves entirely a matter of historical accident, products of particular histories of the countries, local culture, and the like? Can we move beyond the mere insistence on the importance of class, to an account of the mechanisms — if there are any — that generate the contrasting reactions? I have suggested that what accounted for the contrasting orientations toward the developmental state was the underlying development model: import-substituting industrialization in India and export-led industrialization in Korea. In both cases, it was rational for capitalists to abide by an interventionist state. But in the former it made sense to reject the disciplinary components of the interventions, since the structure of ISI sundered the link between profitability and productivity; in the latter the state was able to leverage an acceptance of its disciplinary institutions, since Korean firms could not survive the highly competitive export markets unless the state assisted them in achieving high standards of efficiency and product quality.

This argument is not intended to imply that, once the choice of development models was made, the kind of state it would generate was a fait accompli. It is worth emphasizing here that what the development models affect directly is *capitalist preferences* with respect to state building; their impact on the *outcome* of the state-building project depends on the extent to which capitalists are then able to translate these preferences into state policy decisions. And there is no reason to assume that the latter process is unproblematic. Certainly, in the Indian case, industrialists were able to successfully steer the state away from those instruments that were deemed unacceptable. But, as argued in chapters 5 and 6, that was at least partly because the balance of forces in India after 1945 greatly strengthened their hand at the expense of the state—through, for example, the demobilization of the labor movement. In other circumstances it is possible to imagine a state that could override the objections of local firms to disciplinary planning.

To those familiar with the debates among state theorists during the past two decades, this should be a familiar argument, but it is worth rehearsing at some length. Development models play an important role in the arguments of the preceding chapters because they generate a determinate set of interests for capitalists in relation to the state. Pointing to the effects of the models clarifies that the reactions of the respective business classes to state building were not simply based on contingent facts about the particular policy mix, fiscal strategy, personalities, and so on, but were structurally generated. So, for example, as long as the INC remained committed to launching the country on a path of ISI, the Indian bourgeoisie could not but be expected to oppose disciplinary planning. But that does not guarantee that capitalists, in their opposition to the state-building agenda, would necessarily succeed. It only points to the fact that, if state managers were to install such a state, it would have to be over the resistance of domestic capital.

State theorists have expended a great deal of energy in recent years investigating the conditions under which political elites can push through legislation in spite of opposition from dominant classes. The main locus for these discussions, of course, has been the debate around the origins of the welfare state in the West, which, in many cases, was installed despite opposition from segments of capital. Formally the Indian political elite was in a situation not dissimilar to that faced by its counterparts in the West when confronted with opposition to installing welfare states. And the solution, I submit, would formally have had to be similar; in the language of state theory, the state would be required to secure sufficient autonomy from local capital to override the latter's objections and opposition. What are the sources of state autonomy? There are at least three conditions in which states may override resistance from local capitalists. First, capitalists may cavil at the disciplinary components of a developmental state but may simply be too weak to resist. A second possibility is that capitalists may be sufficient in strength to matter but may be blunted by a counterweight, the most obvious example being a mobilized labor movement. Third, states can gain leverage in some extraordinary circumstance, like war, during which firms may find their hand against the state weakened. As it happens, we have examples at hand that illustrate these hypothetical scenarios.

Taiwan is perhaps a case where the installation of a developmental state occurred in a setting where the bourgeoisie was simply too small and too weak for its preferences to matter, at least in the early years. When Chiang Kai-shek and the Kuomintang (KMT) established their authority on the island in the late 1940s, the local economy was still predominantly an agrarian one. Although there had been industrial development during the inter-war years under the Japanese, it had been of a kind that did not leave behind a robust group of domestic business groups. Under Japanese rule, local ownership and management of enterprises was extremely rare, either because of legal restrictions on Taiwanese ownership or because of the smothering power of the zaibatsu over local markets. Karl Fields reports that, in 1929, no less than 91 percent of local industry was under Japanese ownership.[4] The main avenue left open to aspiring Taiwanese entrepreneurs was to collaborate with the colonial power, and for a few families this brought some degree of success. But it also transmitted a crippling weakness: during the war mobilization in the 1930s the colonial government was easily able to force local firms to merge with Japanese ones, thus wiping out Taiwanese business groups in one stroke. By 1941 Japan could again boast almost total control over the island's industry, its measure now being 95 percent.[5]

The consequence of this state of affairs was that when Chiang Kai-shek and the KMT took over the island, there was very little of a local capitalist class to contend with. The advantage of the new political elite was further strengthened by the fact that the few industrialists who were around were tainted by their collaborationist past, giving them little legitimacy with the new regime or local population. Once in power, the regime did move quickly to initiate the growth of local private capital, but precisely because many of the new industrialists had little managerial or technical experience, they were unusually dependent on the state for their survival.[6] The initial decade of the regime was therefore marked by a multidimensional weakness of the Taiwanese capitalist class: structural, political, and managerial. If ever there was a case that fit the statist literature of recent years, Taiwan appears to be it.

At the other end of the spectrum, the installation of a planning regime in postwar France would seem to embody another possibility, that of the state overcoming business opposition by relying on a powerful labor movement. Business in the post-bellum years was not at all favorably inclined toward industrial planning. Indeed, the possibility was viewed with considerable hostility, as it was seen as the thin wedge of a "communist revolution and statist takeover of the economy."[7] The problem was that the balance of forces in postwar France was hardly one that favored the bourgeoisie. Structurally French capital lost some of its clout over policy because of a sharp slowdown of the economy after the onset of war, a slowdown that persisted into the early postwar years.[8] Even more debilitating for business was the enormous political damage wrought by its association with the Vichy regime. As with so many other countries in the period, French politics was shaken by the collaborationist face of its ruling class. Organizationally the handicaps imposed by the general climate were aggravated by another factor, namely, the dissolution of most of the traditional business associations after the war.[9] Weakened economically, morally, and organizationally, French capitalists thought prudence the better part of valor and "resigned themselves [to waiting] for a shift in the political climate".[10]

This loss of legitimacy and economic power for business was complemented, on the other side, by an enormous increase in both the prestige of the Left and its political power. Again, as in much of Europe, the prestige of the Communist Party was immeasurably bolstered by its leadership of the resistance against Nazi occupation.[11] So whereas business groups found their organizational and political power receding during the immediate postwar years, that of the Left and labor grew in massive proportions. Riding the crest of their surging popularity, the French Communist and Socialist parties received close to half the total votes in the elections of 1945 and 1946.[12] This surge in power for the Left did not last long, however; for example, the Communists left the coalition as early as 1947, and business began to regain its power over the policy process soon thereafter.[13] But in the critical years when they did have power, the Left was able to push through a series of key reforms that endowed the state with considerable disciplinary capacity, which remained in place even after the business recovery.

The central elements of these reforms were a series of nationalizations that brought the commanding heights of the economy under state control. Several basic industries — coal, gas, and electricity — were removed from private ownership; but, most important, the four main depositary institutions and insurance agencies were nationalized, bringing more than half the total bank credit in the economy under state control. Further, a National Planning Commission was created within the policy apparatus, as was a national agency for statistical analysis. Finally, a special institution, the Ecole Nationale de Administration (ENA), was set up to train senior civil servants in the art of economic management.[14] These changes endured even after the change in the ruling coalition after 1947 and set the institutional basis for economic planning under de Gaulle and his planning minister, Jean Monnet. Hence planners were able to use the small window of opportunity in 1945–47 to push through a transformation of the policy apparatus, capitalizing on the tilt in political power toward the Left.

Turning now to postwar Japan reveals a third route to dealing with the bourgeoisie. The installation of a developmental state in Taiwan was made easier by the fact that there was little potential of local resistance. On the other hand, it was no mean achievement, since the policy apparatus that the new administration inherited from Japanese colonialism was hardly suited to implementing industrial policy. The situation in postwar Japan — the country seen as being the trailblazer in forging a developmental state — presents another route to dealing with a domestic capitalist class, and it is worth discussing at some length. In this case, state managers had at hand a state apparatus already endowed with considerable capacity for developmental policies. This happy circumstance was, of course, a legacy of the wartime mobilization, which had radically transformed the domestic political economy. Postwar policy makers inherited not only a sturdy framework of economic control mechanisms but also the means to administer and monitor production and distribution.[15] Thus, for example, wartime controls over key industries — coal, steel, petroleum, power, and others — were carried over into the years of the Occupation and after.[16] During the war a large number of trade associations had been established as a means of industrial control and state-capital coordination; many of these were either directly continued into the postwar period or continued in a transmuted form through mergers.[17] Agencies charged with overseeing and coordinating wartime production were carried over into the following period, most famously in the merger of the Munitions Ministry and the Ministry of Commerce and Industry to form the new Ministry of International Trade and Industry (MITI) in 1949. Not unnaturally, this administrative momentum brought with it a substantial continuity in bureaucratic expertise and state cohesiveness, as key officials serving in the wartime ministries played leading roles in the new policy agencies.[18]

The consequence of this inheritance was that Japanese state managers, when they launched their own era of developmentalism, were spared much of the "heavy lifting" that was foisted onto their counterparts elsewhere. Unlike policy elites in India, Korea, Taiwan, and much of South America, who had to create many key state institutions ex nihilo, Japanese bureaucrats already had many of the administrative resources and policy instruments they needed. This was fortuitous for two reasons: first, Japanese capital in the postwar years was not at all sanguine about the prospects of a disciplinary planning apparatus; and, second, when they began to press for a turn to ELI in the mid-1950s, state managers could make credible promises to targeted firms that the latter would receive adequate support for their entrance into world markets — promises which, absent a supple developmental apparatus, would have rung hollow and hence would have failed to elicit the needed response from firms. I shall return to this second advantage in the next section. For now, let us examine the first consequence more closely.

Attempts to secure some degree of sectoral coordination among firms had been under way ever since the 1920s, as a response to the emergence of overcapacity and declining profits. But, in the interwar period, these moves were primarily initiated by prominent industrialists and trade associations, as a means for firms to voluntarily coordinate sectoral prices and production levels. Attempts at sectoral coordination, because they depended on voluntary compliance, proved to be of limited success; trade associations were simply not equipped with instruments necessary to enforce discipline, making it impossible to prevent defections from the parameters that had been agreed on.[19] Not surprisingly, by the early 1930s, domestic firms were calling on the state to help overcome this dilemma. State intervention was to serve two purposes: first, as a referee of sorts ensuring that firms complied with agreements regarding prices and production; and, second, as a mechanism to ensure the steady flow of needed inputs. Hence, even before Japan entered the war, an alliance of sorts was developing between the state and domestic capital around the need for market coordination and sectoral cooperation.[20]

While a kind of rapprochement did develop, it is important to note that it did not, in the 1930s, open a space for any kind of genuine industrial planning or, more important, for disciplinary planning. Japanese capitalists were open to the idea of state assistance but not to granting the state any substantial power to influence firm-level investment decisions.[21] Its role was to be limited to overseeing agreements reached by firms themselves, as against pressuring firms toward its own economic plans. The move in this more ambitious direction did not come until the war effort was substantially under way. Between 1942 and the end of the war state managers pushed through a series of legislations that transformed the political economy, allowing them substantial power over firms.[22]

During the war capitalists had tolerated the emerging panoply of controls and regulations, partly as a short-term concession and partly because wartime exigencies made them difficult to resist. After Japan's surrender, the hostility capitalists had to state disciplinary powers immediately rose to the surface, as calls were issued to dismantle the system of wartime controls. But here industrialists found themselves in the horns of a dilemma not dissimilar to that of their Indian counterparts, as described above in chapter 6. While Japanese firms were hostile to the idea of state-imposed economic guidance, they were not in a position to call for an opposition to state intervention itself. There were two basic reasons for this. First, firms themselves were faced with enormous shortages of every kind of input, from raw materials to capital goods to finance, making it necessary not only to rely on the state for assistance but also to turn to it once again as an instrument for coordinating price and production levels.[23] Second, the American Supreme Command for the Allied Powers (SCAP) was not only ideologically inclined toward a regulated economy but was also materially dependent on its instruments in the severe conditions of the early postwar years.

The consequence of this dilemma was that Japanese industrialists, like their Indian counterparts, pressed for a "business-coordinated" state intervention, as opposed to the drive for a state-led planning model.[24] In other words, as in India, the bourgeoisie was in favor of the regulation of economic activity so long as its parameters were defined, as an ongoing affair, by capitalists themselves through their organizations. The very fact that it was not desirable to demand an end to state intervention but to try instead to modulate its scope posed a dilemma for Japanese firms reminiscent of the one the Indians faced. The efforts to extend the power of the state to a level that would enable disciplinary planning were to be repelled; but this would have to be done while supporting the efforts to create a state machinery appropriate to the task of "business-coordinated" intervention. This handicapped the Japanese bourgeoisie in its attack on a disciplinary state in a way, for example, that U.S. capitalists simply were not when they successfully oversaw the dismantling of wartime controls in their own country.

But the legacy of wartime economic planning, and the attendant administrative capacity with which it endowed the state, made the Japanese scenario depart significantly from the Indian one. In India, industrialists were able to significantly repel the efforts to build state capacity appropriate to industrial planning. The institutional outcome was that the state was left bereft of some of the instruments that would have been key to enhancing its capacity as a developmental state. And the reason for this, of course, was that Indian political elites were in the position of having to create many of the needed agencies and institutions ex nihilo—there was no significant legacy of industrial planning or extensive state-led industrial coordination to build on.[25] In Japan, however, although capitalists were able to blunt the accretion of new state capacity to some degree, this did not leave state managers in the same weak position as their Indian cousins. For, in this case, the status quo ante was a state with a degree of capacity far ahead of anything in the subcontinent or in any other country that undertook developmentalism. This is not to say, by any means, that Japan emerged from the war a full-blown developmental state. There were significant changes that were made in the postwar years, contributing to its consolidation. But the fact remains that, in the face of stiff resistance from local capitalists, the inheritance of wartime institutions made for a much easier set of conditions than those faced by political elites attempting rapid industrialization in other regions.[26]

Thus, in examining the cases of Taiwan, France, and Japan, we see three routes to a developmental state, even if capitalists may be opposed to the prospect. In Taiwan, local industrialists were simply too weak to hazard concerted resistance to the new state; in France, political elites were able to ride the wave of a mobilized labor movement to overcome bourgeois opposition and restructure the domestic state structures; and in Japan, state managers were able to hold fast to state structures inherited from wartime economic planning and, later, to build on them for developmental ends. To return to the original point in this discussion, these examples lend credence to the conclusion that capitalist preferences, although critical, do not unilaterally dictate the outcome in state-building projects. Hence development models do not correspond to types of states (disciplinary/non-disciplinary) as a matter of necessity; they do not make politics irrelevant. Rather, in generating bourgeois preferences, these models serve to *set the terms on which politics are conducted*. As in many structural arguments, there is still considerable room for historical contingency. A developmental state may be installed — though it will be less likely — even if capitalists oppose it, as in the examples discussed above; on the other hand, despite bourgeois support, state managers may very well fail in the state-building project — owing to intra-elite rivalries, coalitional dilemmas, or the like. The importance of development models like ISI and ELI lies not in the fact that they singularly determine outcomes but in their ability to influence the likelihood of the outcomes by singularly affecting the disposition of a crucial actor.

THE ROUTES TO AND OBSTACLES AGAINST ELI

Development models are important because, by orienting capitalist preferences, they exercise a powerful, albeit not determinant, effect on the attempt to transform states in a developmental direction. But if ELI makes capitalists inclined to accept a developmental state, why did so few political elites in the postwar period adopt it as the governing model? What makes this particularly relevant is that the turn to greater exports was tried in a large number of countries in the 1960s and 1970s. Why, then, did only Northeast Asia emerge as the region in which ELI was consistently implemented? I argued that the answer to this puzzle lies in the particular circumstances of "late-late developers." First, in all the countries where export promotion was attempted, it was preceded by a period of import-substitution, which handed over large swathes of the domestic market to local firms. These countries, therefore, did not jump straight into exports but rather attempted to navigate a transition from ISI to ELI. But they then immediately encountered a problem: for most firms in these countries, the highly competitive export markets also presented a much higher risk. State managers quickly discovered that, *ceteris paribus*, local industrialists preferred the easy life of domestic markets to the rigors of external competition; instead of committing to ELI, firms opted instead to use external markets mainly as an outlet in times of excess capacity. Hence the way to effect the switch to the new model was, in the first instance, to reduce the risk foreign markets presented. And there were two obvious routes to achieve this: either by somehow altering the costs of entry themselves or by altering who *bore* the costs, that is, moving that responsibility from the firms to the state. The first method *lowers the level* of costs, while the second *socializes their payment*.

Most countries that have turned to export promotion in the twentieth century have relied on socialization of entry costs, through state subsidization. Relying on the state for this service, however, has been no simple task, for in the absence of a cohesive, rational policy apparatus, firms view the promise of subsidies as not being credible. Hence, as I argued in chapters 2 and 3, the response of firms to export promotion programs during the 1960s and 1970s was rarely more than lukewarm. Korea was unusual not only because of the presence of Japanese firms to offer a second means of reducing entry costs (on which more shortly) but also because the turn to ELI was more or less concurrent with a drastic overhaul of the state in a developmental direction. This immediately raised the credibility of planners' promises also to subsidize and coordinate the necessary investments. In most developing countries, including India, the efforts at export promotion were not accompanied by a transformation of the policy apparatus. The strategy remained dependent on the state structures that had been established in earlier years, typically those of concerted ISI.

In the Korean case, local firms were presented a unique opportunity by the entry of Japanese capital. The Japanese, in providing the Chaebol with their sales and marketing networks, reduced a critical entry barrier to U.S. markets. The Japanese were vacating these, as their own development strategy switched from light manufactures to heavy industry; they now positioned themselves as middlemen in the U.S. markets and as suppliers of capital goods to Korean exporting firms. I have argued that the alliance with their erstwhile colonial masters was central to orienting Korean capitalists toward exports and, by extension, to ELI. But while the alliance with the Japanese may have been critical in triggering an interest in exports, it is unlikely that this interest could have been *sustained* in the absence of a cohesive and rational developmental state. Entry into markets could be made easier through the acquisition of sales networks, but sustained success in them required actions for which state assistance was critical — acquisition of technology, inter-firm coordination, cheap finance, and so forth. Hence it was of considerable importance that Park's efforts to transform the state were more or less coeval with the arrival of the Japanese. So just as the Japanese could assure easier entry into American markets, Park, with his newly transformed state, could make credible promises to provide the coordination and assistance required for sustained success in those markets.

In India, when the turn to export promotion came in the wake of the 1957 foreign exchange crisis, there were no parallel mechanisms to reduce entry costs into export markets. In fact, as I showed in chapter 8, the MNCs setting up joint ventures, or technology partnerships, explicitly prohibited the export of goods produced by their Indian partners. Far from duplicating the strategy of the Japanese in Korea, British and U.S. firms in India actually precluded the use of their resources for exports. Hence Indian firms had little possibility of finding a parallel route to reducing the costs of entry into export markets. The effect was to perpetuate, and perhaps even reinforce, the preference for domestic markets. It is noteworthy that this characteristic of FDI in India was of a piece with the experience of many developing countries where U.S. and British firms were the chief source of foreign investment. Whereas Japanese firms integrated their Northeast Asian partners into an export strategy, their Western counterparts' primary interest in host countries was as potential markets for their goods, not as export platforms.[27] In any case, the contrast between India and Korea in this regard is conspicuous. If domestic capitalists were going to be persuaded to hazard an effort at export markets in a consistent fashion, it would not come from a reduction in their entry costs through strategic alliances with multinational firms.

If costs could not be reduced through strategic alliances with an external patron, then the other possible route to changing capitalist preferences was through their socialization by the state. The precondition for this was a transformation of the state apparatus, making it sufficiently cohesive and efficient to lend credibility to the government's promises of subsidizing entry into foreign markets. But this possibility was blocked by the power dynamics within the Indian state. The natural candidate to lead the project of state transformation would have been the Planning Commission, which had a direct interest in increasing state cohesiveness. But the maladies of the planning process brought about a decline in the commission's power within the state, increasing the relative power of the ministries. Hence, over time, the balance of power tipped irreversibly away from the supporters of state transformation, and toward those in favor of the principle of ministerial autonomy—the very opposite of what was required for reform.

As a result, when export promotion was launched, it was not accompanied by a reform of the state apparatus in a disciplinary direction. The implementation of incentives and subsidies in the program therefore suffered from the same weaknesses that afflicted the overall planning process—a chaotic structure, lack of coordination, endless and overlapping red tape, and the like. This was in stark contrast to the Korean case, where a restructuring of the state rapidly followed the turn to exports, which allowed for a far more efficient implementation of the program and hence gave a massive boost to the state's credibility with firms. Given this, Indian firms could not view as realistic the state's promise that their entry costs into export markets would be socialized. The preference for domestic sales therefore remained in place.

Had India been able to initiate a transformation of the state apparatus, could it have launched a successful turn to exports? Could there have been a purely "state-sponsored" road to export promotion, even without an external alliance of the kind the Chaebol established with Japanese firms? Here, too, Japan's experience is instructive, for it seems to offer a positive example of a state-sponsored turn to ELI. I submitted in the preceding section that the apparatus of wartime planning bequeathed a state that was, in critical respects, developmentalist in orientation. I also suggested that this inheritance played an important role in Japan's turn to an export-led strategy after the war. In the context of the present discussion, the significance of the Japanese experience should be clear. The turn to exports, which was being encouraged as early as 1949 by Joseph Dodge in his notorious economic adjustment plan, was taken up in earnest by the state in 1954, with the end of the Yoshida cabinet. This was in many ways the first case of postwar ELI among late developing countries, and, like the other successful cases, it relied critically on heavy state subsidization. The twist was that Japanese policy makers had at hand the kind of state structure that other countries—those that tried a turn to exports in later years—so sorely lacked. Thus, unlike the experience of so many other countries, where maladroit state apparatuses undermined planners' exhortations to firms to commit to export production, Japanese planners found themselves endowed with a state that made the turn to exports something firms could countenance. Even without an agent that could play the role of patron (the way the Japanese themselves were to do for Korean firms a decade later) the turn to ELI became a real possibility because the state, through its credible promises to socialize costs and coordinate investment, was able to forge an alliance with local firms. Does this suggest the possibility of a purely "Japanese road" to ELI, based solely on state subsidization, as against the "Korean road," which combined that strategy with one based on international firm-level alliances? Was the Korean alliance with Japanese firms, in a sense, redundant? Or, put differently, does this show that ELI was a distinct possibility for countries even without an external alliance?

The Japanese experience does give one reason to think that a "state-sponsored" road to ELI may have been possible more widely. But a closer look also suggests that, for any other country, success would probably have been less spectacular, perhaps even less certain. Two facts about Japan are relevant here. First, although the state did play an important role in the success of Japanese ELI, firms also had a bedrock of economic muscle to draw on, which eased the burden on the state. During the first decade or so of the strategy after 1954, Japanese exports consisted mainly of labor-intensive, light-manufacturing goods, like most developing countries.[28] But unlike most developing countries, Japanese producers had decades of experience in many of these lines, especially in textiles and clothing, where they had already been using best-practice techniques during the interwar years.[29] Advances in the production of clothing and textiles began to accelerate in the first decade of the twentieth century, so that, by the 1920s, local producers were able to compete effectively in world markets. Crucially the competitiveness came not just from low labor costs but through the adoption and diffusion of advanced technology. Hence, by 1935, Japan accounted for 57 percent of all textile imports into the United States. Further, as evidence that success was not based on low wages, we can point to the fact that, by the 1920s, Japanese goods were displacing Indian competitors not only in India's key export markets but in the Indian domestic market as well.[30] Hence, when the turn to export promotion came in the mid-1950s, Japan was building on decades of competitive strength (unlike most late developers), reducing the necessary scope of state subsidization and coordination.

Second, although Japan did not have a patron as directly involved in acquiring markets as it was itself to be for Korea a decade later, Japan was not altogether bereft of assistance. In sectors critical to subsequent export success—machine tools, steel, automobiles—Japanese producers were afforded life-sustaining markets by the United States through military contracts for the Korean and then the Vietnam wars. Indeed, the income from special military procurement remained a vital component of total export earnings through much of the 1950s, remaining as high as almost 25 percent in 1956.[31] The political links with the United States, in this sense, created an export market for local producers. The benefits flowing from this were manifold. First, local producers were able to increase their production runs dramatically, generating a huge increase in retained earnings; second, firms were assisted by the U.S. government in what John Dower describes as "the systematic acquisition of American commercial licenses and patents,"[32] which, again, was very visible in key sectors like machine tools;[33] and, third, the inflow of foreign exchange made it possible to pay for the incredibly rapid absorption of new technology. Even aside from the military connection, State Department officials worked assiduously during these years to pry open world markets for Japanese exports—not only in Europe and Southeast Asia but also in the United States. These efforts ranged from engineering Japan's ascension into GATT in 1955; to signing fourteen trilateral agreements with Asian and European governments, which gave them preferential access to U.S. markets in exchange for their granting concessions to Japanese imports;[34] to pressuring Congress and U.S. firms to accept greater Japanese penetration of their markets and, indeed, to establish tie-ups with Japanese producers.[35] This role of the United States was critical, in that it secured market access for Japanese producers who were already competitive in low-end lines like textiles, while it also provided technology, suppliers, and sales links to more nascent sectors, which would form the backbone of export success in later years.

These two facts—a level of competitiveness atypical for developing economies and the leverage provided by the U.S. connection—should recommend some caution about taking the Japanese case as an exemplar for a state-sponsored road to ELI, as distinct from the Korean road, which combined state sponsorship (socialization of entry costs) with a transnational alliance (lowering of entry costs). For if the preceding two paragraphs are more or less accurate, then the Japanese state had quite a bit of help in inducing firms toward ELI, help that other developing countries could not be expected to draw on. Very few, if any, had a comparable level of manufacturing competitiveness when they tried out export promotion in the postwar years, and very few had a sponsor such as the United States, even if this was less than the leverage Japan provided for the Koreans in later years. It is therefore not a simple matter to take Japan's experience as proof that the switch to ELI can be made solely under the aegis of an adroit state, since the state alone was not responsible for the switch. This is not to say that the absence of these conditions ruled out ELI for any other countries. It is only to suggest that, in these other cases, the turn to exports would have to be slower, more embattled, and build slowly on accumulated experience and state sponsorship, rather than the almost overnight turn accomplished by Korea and Japan.

OF POSSIBILITIES AND ROADS NOT TAKEN

The final possibility left to explore is that of India building a better developmental state even having adopted ISI during the 1950s. We have seen that one of the factors that increased the difficulty of shifting to ELI in the 1960s was the quality of the state apparatus that had been installed in the critical juncture of 1947–51. Could it have been otherwise? Could India have built a successful developmental state in those initial years if political leaders had crafted a better strategy? Of course, the easiest route to such a state would have been through the adoption of an export-led industrialization strategy itself in 1947. But as I have argued in this chapter and above in chapter 2, virtually *no* developing country in the immediate postwar era saw fit to embark on ELI. This was partly because, in all such countries, the industrial base was still exceedingly narrow, with a capitalist class that had very little experience in export markets, that was saddled with plants and equipment in need of repair after the war, and that was more eager to expand into hitherto untapped domestic markets. On the international scene, too, the 1950s were a period in which manufactured goods from developing countries faced tough tariff barriers in the more advanced countries, making those markets far less attractive. India was no exception to these tendencies; indeed, India was an exemplar of a concerted and ambitious program of ISI.

This means that, at least in its initial stages, Indian development policy had little chance of being anything other than an import-substituting policy. The realistic option was therefore to create an effective developmental state *within* ISI. In the preceding sections, and in chapter 5, I suggest, somewhat speculatively, that one possible route to a more effective developmental state could have been to ride the crest of the mobilized labor movement in the years after the war. In the language of state theory, the failure of the INC to install an effective planning apparatus was largely the result of its reduced autonomy from the business class after 1947, which was itself brought about by the class-wide mobilization. But it has been a staple of state theory over the last two decades that the state's autonomy to undertake measures unpopular with the business class is increased in the context of a mobilized labor movement. Hence the suggestion that, had state managers been willing to use the labor movement as leverage — rather than demobilizing it — it may have been possible to install a powerful developmental apparatus *despite* business opposition.

Certainly, even within ISI, a state with greater internal cohesiveness and monitoring capacity would have brought about more dexterous policy, even if it did not meet the level of that in Korea. Here, two routes lay open for the Indian political elite. One would have been to impose a stronger state apparatus on the domestic bourgeoisie and then to set about implementing an industrial policy that was basically the same as the one which has actually been followed, namely, a statist policy, skewed toward heavy industry, with labor politically and economically enfeebled. But this would have depended on a rapid marginalization of labor, once state managers had used their muscle to force a stronger state apparatus on local capital. The path to a political settlement in India would have therefore resembled somewhat the one in postwar France, as discussed above, where state managers were able to foist a planning regime on local capital, riding the wave of a massive labor upsurge and working in an alliance with the Communists. But once the concessions were extracted from industry, French political elites quickly and firmly pushed labor out of the ruling coalition, making the famed French industrial policy regime an affair between the state and large firms.

This is somewhat plausible as a thought experiment, but I know of no experience among LDCs that can be viewed as an exemplar. In the most well-known cases of ISI — Mexico, Brazil, Argentina, and Egypt — political elites consistently took a paternalistic attitude toward labor, never actually allying with it in "critical junctures" long enough to push through a disciplinary state apparatus.[36] This meant that, from the start, the ruling coalition in these countries kept labor at arm's length, with state elites trying to fashion an alliance with local (and sometimes multinational) capital. In all these cases the eventual quality of the state apparatus turned out to fall into what Peter Evans has called the "intermediate" range: better than the predatory kind but not as good as the East Asian developmental kind. This means that the route just mapped out must remain a conjectural one, consigned to the status of a thought experiment.

On the other hand, the quality of industrial policy in several countries employing state-led ISI does appear to have been better than in India; Brazil, Mexico, and Turkey, in the postwar period, all had higher rates of industrial growth than the subcontinent had, as well as greater success in achieving competitiveness in world markets. This suggests that, although their experience may not offer lessons on how to install a developmental apparatus through a temporary alliance with labor, it may nonetheless be instructive on how state intervention could have worked better in ISI, despite its adverse incentive structure. To make this assessment, however, research will have to turn to a carefully controlled comparative analysis of cases *within* the ISI development model and away from comparisons *between* models. As of now, when two or more cases of "intermediately successful" developmental states are analyzed, they tend to be amalgamated under the same rubric, as exemplars of a type, and then compared to the East Asian states. This has certainly enabled us to develop a sharper understanding of the spectacular achievements of that region; what is needed now, perhaps, is the generation of a typology of subtypes within ISI in order to ascertain if the differences between states using this strategy were brought about by contingent factors or if they were of a systematic kind. If this can be done, then it will be possible to assess if Indian industrial policy could have been more successful, even with import-substitution — and what it would have taken to bring about these more virtuous results.

But I have suggested that another path was open to the Indian elites, aside from using the labor movement as a temporary ally to push through a disciplinary state apparatus. This second path would have been to cement a more permanent alliance with labor and leverage a development model based on some kind of class compromise. This would have required not only a different political role for labor — for now it would not be consigned to the margins once it had done its "heavy lifting" — but almost certainly a very different economic role as well. If labor were to be further empowered, this would have called for an abandonment of the INC's paternalism toward subaltern classes and the establishment of institutions that would allow them to develop and protect their organizational autonomy. Further, this would also have required a broadening of labor's power so that it extended to the countryside as well as into the urban "informal sector." But once such commitments were made, it is highly probable that the INC would have had to abandon its overall statist model of development. The widespread empowerment of labor cannot easily coexist with a top-down, paternalistic state, conducting economic policy through a bipartite negotiation with capital; industrial strategy would have had to move in a more social-democratic direction. This, in turn, means that the discipline imposed on capital would no longer be the exclusive provenance of planners in the state apparatus. Some of that discipline could now come from employers' "political exchange" with labor, which, in social-democratic settings, has typically consisted of a greater work effort in return for a higher social wage.[37]

This may seem, perhaps, like sliding into the realm of pure speculation. Certainly I do believe that it is far-fetched. We know of no real social-democratic road to development. The experience of the Scandinavian countries can hardly be a guide, since they were more developed than India at the inception of their programs, and their internal makeup, along with the nature of their insertion into the world economy, bears almost no relation to that of India. Interestingly, however, an example of something along the lines just sketched might be closer at hand — as long as we are properly cautious in our assessments. Though it probably does not warrant the designation of a "model," the experience in the southwestern state of Kerala might offer a vision of an alternative, which, had the INC so chosen, it could have pursued. Scholars typically point to Kerala as proof positive of the virtues of significant redistribution and the provision of basic state services.[38] But recently scholars have called our attention to another component of the state's development strategy, namely, its quite successful forging of a class compromise between labor and capital.[39] The turning point in its history occurred in 1957, with the Communist Party coming into power, which initiated its development program as one based on agrarian reform but also gradually incorporating a mobilizational approach to industrial relations.

Students of the Kerala experience have carefully documented the strategy adopted by the Communist Party of India — Marxist (CPM) and its union federation, Congress of Indian Trade Unions (CITU), and contrasted it with that of the larger Indian labor movement. Crucially, whereas Indian labor, since its rapid demobilization, described in chapter 5, has largely relied on the patronage of employers or local political bosses, unions in Kerala have relied instead on an explicit strategy of political mobilization around class interests. Equally important, the unions in Kerala have found a political ally in the CPM, which, unlike the INC in 1947, has used this strategy of mobilization to further empower unions in their bargaining with employers. Employers, knowing they could not rely on a sympathetic state government (as long as the CPM was in power), had to reach agreements with labor around basic issues of wages, work conditions, tenure, and so on — again in contrast to the rest of the country, where work relations tend to be straightforwardly despotic. In turn, this has closed off many "low road" strategies of accumulation, which in turn has forced employers to give greater attention to innovating and upgrading plants and equipment.[40] Patrick Heller has called this the "democratic developmental state model" of development, though it would probably be more accurate to refer to it as the "*social-democratic* developmental state model." Of course, the comparison is more suggestive than definitive; to cast the experience of one state onto the larger canvas requires a heroic imagination. Nevertheless, the Kerala experience highlights the fact that development strategies need not be different varieties of top-down arrangements, with labor necessarily a marginal force.

These options are not merely of historical interest. In today's intellectual and political climate, in India and without, there is a sense that the era of state intervention in development is at an end. And certainly, as one witnesses the old scaffolding of the "license-permit raj" being dismantled, it is possible to feel the momentum toward freer markets as something of an inexorable force. But to take this shift as the death knell of the state is to miss the essential lessons of Marx and Polanyi — the choice is over *how* to have the state intervene in the economy, not *whether* to have it intervene. Certainly, if the arguments developed here are any guide, the increasing emphasis the state is placing on exports is most likely to occasion a *closer* relationship between the state and exporting firms. More generally, there is good reason to expect that a liberalization of markets will lead not to *less* regulation but rather to a *different regime* of regulation — which can be more dense than the one preceding it.[41] If this is the case, then the worries that animate this study — those of state capacity, internal cohesiveness, and its autonomy from social groups — remain of considerable interest. The turn away from a state-led development strategy will change the state's role, not erase it; whether the institutional capacities required for this new role in fact come about depends, as always, on politics.

The Decline of Development Models

THE FOCUS OF this book has been an analysis of the conditions under which a developmental state arose in India and Korea, with a subsidiary interest in the dynamics of state reproduction. Hence the historical period under investigation has been the first three decades or so following the installation of new state apparatuses in each country. The dynamics of recent years, when *dirigisme* has been slowly dismantled in both cases, have been left out of the analysis. In this epilogue I shall briefly attend to this, more recent period, for it raises an interesting question: is the turn away from developmental states in each country consistent with the framework offered in this book, or must it be seen as anomalous? I shall argue that, in fact, the arguments made in the preceding chapters are quite consistent with the processes under way during the past few years. More to the point, just as the orientation of business classes was central to the installation of developmental states, so has it been essential to their dismantling.

The fortunes of the Indian and Korean efforts at state building diverged in large measure because of the contrasting responses of their capitalist classes. In turn, the development models each country's political elite adopted exerted a powerful influence in shaping these responses. I have argued that ISI and ELI not only shaped capitalist preferences toward the installation of developmental states, but they also affected the dynamics of state reproduction. Hence the alliance between the Korean state and domestic industrialists remained secure so long as the latter believed that they could not succeed in export markets without state coordination; conversely, in the Indian case, local capitalists would not only resist disciplinary planning as long as ISI remained the development model, but their reluctance to turn to exports during the 1960s made a reform of the political economy all the more difficult. Once in place, ISI generated powerful incentives for capitalists to keep it in place, and thus resist reforms of the state in a disciplinary direction.

The very reproduction of the development models, however, also unleashed forces that, over time, eroded the stability of the state-class relations. In what follows I shall briefly describe these forces and chart the process through which they gradually undermined the conditions that sustained the link between development models and capitalist preferences. The core argument is that the dynamics of erosion were endogenous to the development models themselves, making their stability an inherently time-bound phenomenon. This will enable us to understand how, by the mid-1980s, both Indian and Korean capitalists were calling for a dismantling of the state apparatuses that had overseen industrialization in the postwar era.

KOREA: THE REVOLT AGAINST THE DEVELOPMENTAL STATE

That the Korean Chaebol were, by the mid-1980s, calling for a drastic scaling back of the state's regulatory powers is, by now, something of a staple among students of the country.[1] In the statist literature the growing distance between the state and the Chaebol is not seen as especially surprising. The first two decades of the developmental era, the argument goes, were a period in which the state was able simply to dominate the business class, for reasons explained in chapter 3 of this book — the putative small size of the class, the state's control of key inputs, the autonomy granted by authoritarianism, and so on. The Chaebol had little choice but to cooperate. As the size and resources of the Chaebol grew, however, the relation changed from one of outright domination by one party to a more egalitarian partnership. By the middle of the 1980s the Chaebol wielded enough power and influence to launch a successful campaign for a steady dismantling of the state's impressive regulatory apparatus. What requires explanation, on this argument, is not the *fact* of the growing rift between Korean capital and the state but its timing. It is to be expected, given statist premises, that as the Chaebol grew stronger, they would not willingly accept their subordinate position in the domestic political economy. As to the form taken by this new assertiveness, and the ends to which it was put, statists may disagree: for some, the shifting power relations heralded a change to a more consensual, symbiotic relation; for others, it paved the way for the Chaebol's capturing of state organs.[2]

So the Chaebol's call for less state discipline is not especially troublesome for much of the scholarly literature. For the arguments developed in this book, however, the apparent breakdown of the order established by Park Chung-hee does require comment. I have argued against the thesis of state dominance, insisting that the relation between the state and capital in Korea was, from the start, like a partnership — a "pact," however uneasy it may have been. And the basis for this alliance was the need each party had for the other: state managers needed local capitalists to accelerate industrialization and did not have the power simply to herd them onto the chosen investment path; industrialists needed the state to enable them to survive in export markets, which they could not do on their own. If this were so, why, then, did Korean industrialists start hammering against the state's regulatory apparatus after the first couple of decades? Why call for the dismantling of institutions that had been central to the Chaebol's own success?

The reason is not difficult to fathom. Recall from the discussion in chapter 2 that, in ELI, capitalists accept state discipline in their own self-interest. Although they may recoil at the prospect of having the state acquire its considerable monitoring and coordinating capacity— which always carries the threat of being turned against bourgeois interests—they abide by it because, without it, success in foreign markets does not appear possible. Lacking the means to acquire the inputs and the coordination called for by the highly competitive markets in industrialized countries, firms find it rational to accept the state's accretion of power to impose discipline. So long as firms lack the experience, the managerial skills, channels for technology acquisition, and financial resources that approximate those of their competitors, the alliance with a developmental state should be expected to hold. And this, I argued in chapters 2 and 7, was the case through the first twenty-five years or so after Park's ascension to power. But as firms grow in size and resources, and the need to rely on the state for survival recedes, so should the rationale for tolerating the overweening power of a disciplinary planning apparatus. Once local industrialists develop the means to acquire the inputs they need for export success without assistance, planners lose the leverage to impose conditions in exchange for their subsidies. Businesses thus are able to demand that state managers scale back the apparatus of regulations and controls that formed the teeth of the developmental state without fear of immediate losses in performance. This does not mean that firms will cease to ask for subsidization. It only means that they will now be in a position to demand that subsidies be more or less unconditional.

If we turn now to the facts of the Korean case, the changes that led to the Chaebol's defection from the developmental alliance are quite apparent. The critical period, as most commentators agree, was the second half of the 1970s, the years of the heavy and chemical industrialization drive. By the time of its completion, the Chaebol's position in the economy had become considerably stronger than in the 1970s.[3] Scholars point to their increasing control of large swathes of the economy as the basis for their newfound power against the state. But, for our purposes, this is an issue of secondary importance, since I have argued that they were sufficiently powerful to give Park pause even in the 1960s. Of far greater importance are the *qualitative* changes that came about as part of the industrialization process, which made firms more self-sufficient than before. In other words, it is not the state's increasing dependence on capital—which so much of the literature emphasizes—that merits attention but, rather, the decreasing dependence of capital on the state.

In this regard at least three developments are noteworthy. First, the reliance on the state for research and technological upgrading declined by the 1980s. In 1970 the public sector accounted for 97 percent of all Research and Development expenditures in the economy—not surprising, since there was but one corporate center for R&D in 1971! By 1980 the private sector's share of total expenditure had increased to 36 percent, and in 1990 it vastly overshadowed the public sector, accounting for 81 percent of the total, while the share of R&D in the economy had risen from .38 percent of the GNP to almost 2 percent. The number of corporate research centers in the country, meanwhile, had risen to almost one thousand.[4] All this reflected the fact that the biggest Korean firms had been frantically mastering and improving on foreign technology during the Park years, often under pressure from Park himself, who appears to have put a high priority on forcing industrialists to set up independent research centers.[5]

Second, most of the biggest Chaebol were able to acquire control over independent sources of finance. By the mid-1980s eight of the ten biggest conglomerates owned at least one non-banking financial institution (NBFI), making them far less reliant on the state for cheap finance.[6] Further, even though the Chaebol were still heavily leveraged, the system of industrial finance had undergone significant restructuring. Whereas bank loans accounted for about one-third of external finance in the late 1960s, by the early 1990s they hovered around 15–16 percent; and whereas loans from NBFIs and the sale of securities comprised less than a quarter of the external funds borrowed in the late 1960s, by the early 1990s they accounted for almost two-thirds.[7] Hence the source of indebtedness had shifted from state-owned banks to private sources, making firms more independent of planners.

Third, the Chaebol had spread into altogether new sectors of the economy, especially upstream lines, enabling them to reduce the problem of coordination with other firms. In purely quantitative terms, the average number of subsidiaries under each Chaebol rose from 4.2 in 1970 to 17.9 in 1990 to 22.3 in 1996. The numbers were even more impressive for the top five conglomerates (Hyndai, Samsung, Daewoo, Lucky-Goldstar, and Sunkyung), which, in 1994, controlled 210 affiliates between them, for an average of 42.[8] Perhaps even more important was that this rise was accompanied by a diversification into new sectors: the average number of industries in which each conglomerate owned subsidiaries rose from 7.7 in 1970 to 14 in 1989, and had reached 18.8 in 1996.[9] Although much of this diversification was horizontal, spreading into other, unrelated industries, for many of the top Chaebol it was also an index of greater vertical integration. This development had the effect of making much of the needed coordination between firms an affair internal to a conglomerate, rather than something economic planners had to arrange between conglomerates.

These changes were of considerable significance for the stability of the developmental alliance between the state and capitalists. At the new level of resources and expertise that the Chaebol wielded, the need for assistance in acquiring inputs and in inter-firm coordination was far less than it had been at the outset of ELI. This meant that the state, in turn, began losing the leverage over domestic capitalists that it once possessed. The threat of withholding assistance, or access to cheap inputs, no longer carried the grave consequences that it did during the previous two decades. Hence, by the late 1980s, Korean capitalists were in a position to start pushing back against the state, demanding a curtailment of its power over their investment and sales activities. And as many students of the Korean political economy have noted, the turn against the state at this point was made all the more potent because of the increased economic weight of the Chaebol in the economy. The dissolution of "Korea, Inc.," therefore, came about through the play of forces endogenous to the development process itself.

It is important to note that the changed resource base of the Chaebol did not signal a shift away from ELI itself. Rather, it triggered a change in the "pact" that underwrote the development model. Whereas it was rational for capitalists to support a disciplinary state at the initial stages of ELI — because of their own competitive disadvantages in world markets — the basis for the alliance eroded as the Chaebol's competitive strength grew. This is the sense in which the developmental alliance around ELI was an inherently time-bound phenomenon, as stated in the introduction to this chapter. But the dissolution of the alliance did not mean that ELI came to an end. It simply meant, instead, that the balance of power between the state and capital would now shift decisively toward the latter, bringing about a change in the terms on which the model would be reproduced — most pointedly, a change in the kind of state that would oversee export-led development. The turn away from state discipline, which was already firmly in place by the early 1990s, has only accelerated in the wake of the crisis of 1997.[10]

INDIA: THE GRADUAL IMPLOSION OF ISI

The turn away from *dirigisme* in India came from two different, but related, directions. One was from within the state itself, as a response to abuses by the ruling clique in the 1970s and 1980s. A second source of pressure was economic in nature, stemming from the emergence of new business groups, which saw the regime of internal controls as an impediment to their own ascent to power.

It is customary to refer to the years of Jawaharlal Nehru's stewardship of the Indian nation as foundational in many ways. With regard to the themes pursued in this book, this characterization of the period seems wholly accurate; one may only add that the Nehru period was critical for another reason, namely, that, with its passing, a window closed on the possibilities of building genuinely able developmental institutions. For all its shortcomings, the Nehru regime nevertheless evinced a degree of integrity that has been altogether absent in the regimes that followed. Of course, this ought not to be exaggerated — there was certainly considerable corruption, laxity in administration, and simple ineptitude. But there is no doubt that the top level of the Congress leadership was quite sincerely committed to a developmental agenda. Above all, Nehru's commanding presence in the cabinet ensured that such malfeasance as existed remained within limits.

It is this culture within the top political leadership that rapidly began to change under Indira Gandhi and, in so changing, eroded one of the essential conditions for the state to be reformed in the appropriate direction — the presence of a political elite committed to a developmental agenda. Despite her long tenure at the helm of the Indian government, which lasted almost as long as her father's, Gandhi was never able to enjoy the unquestioned supremacy that Nehru did. This was partly because of changes in the broader politics of India that were beyond her control — the most important being the rise of new social forces, especially in the countryside, which shook loose the Congress Party's political moorings. The 1970s and 1980s were simply a far more turbulent era in the subcontinent than the first two decades of Independence, and Gandhi had to retain power in this more unstable environment. But the transformation of the upper rungs of the political elite was also driven, famously, by the peculiarities of Gandhi's own personality and style of governance.

Central to this style was a reliance on fealty and unquestioning loyalty to her as criteria for selecting political allies, as well as resorting to backroom maneuvers as a way to settle political disputes. While Indira's lineage afforded her an enormous bounty of goodwill among the Indian masses, the older generation of the Congress High Command considered her a dilettante in her early years. The conflict between Gandhi and the older generation, known ominously as "the syndicate," led, as is well known, to the split in the Congress Party in 1969 and her subsequent massive electoral victory in 1971.[11] Despite this electoral triumph, however, Gandhi was, by the early 1970s, already settling into a broadly clientelistic and even conspiratorial style of functioning. The index of her insecurity was her growing reliance for advice on a small coterie surrounding her; although the members of this coterie tended to change, all had to show unquestioning personal loyalty to Indira as a condition for admittance. This dependence on personal loyalty, as against political consanguinity, found its ultimate expression, of course, in the meteoric rise to power of her son, Sanjay Gandhi. Even more so than his mother's, Sanjay Gandhi's style of functioning was entirely conspiratorial, as it had to be, since he had virtually no political experience.

As is well known, the Indira–Sanjay era in Indian politics, which lasted more than a decade, tore loose many of the traditions of governance that, under Nehru, had acted as a brake against the powerful tendencies toward political degeneration. For our purposes, two are especially relevant. First, the increasingly competitive political environment, driven largely by the rise of new social classes — particularly an increasingly assertive class of rich farmers in the northern regions — prompted a lurch toward political settlements based on payoffs to dominant classes. Pranab Bardhan and others have provided a description of the Indian state that ascribes its weak institutional capacity to its method of dispute resolution — the use of fiscal instruments to "buy off" challengers.[12] In mediating conflict in such a fashion, the state becomes drained of potentially productive resources, as well as suffering paralysis as the pitch and intensity of conflicting demands increases. Recent quantitative analysis of India's fiscal accounts suggests that the use of the exchequer to make such side payments took off starting in the mid- and late-1970s, during Gandhi's reign.[13] Of course, this meant that, far from using the state apparatus to discipline industrial firms, the Gandhi regime now used it to establish clientelistic ties with them. In this respect, the regime moved closer to the industrial policy of Syngman Rhee, as opposed to that of Park Chung-hee.

A second strategy Indira and Sanjay Gandhi used was to intervene in the normal practices of promotion and circulation of top-level bureaucrats, so that the plum posts and perquisites went to those most loyal to them personally; conversely, those who did not place such loyalty above their prescribed responsibilities were punished in sundry ways — through transfers to remote stations, delayed promotions, and the like. This was a change of momentous consequence for Indian political development. Internal conspiracy, Byzantine intrigues, shifting alliances — all this had always been a staple of Congress internal politics, even in the time of Nehru. Under Indira, although it increased in magnitude tremendously, as a phenomenon it was not altogether new. But the politicization of the bureaucracy was an innovation for which Indira and Sanjay could take all the credit. The natural consequence of such interference was a drastic demoralization of top-level bureaucrats, since, under this dispensation, the criterion on which decisions were assessed was no longer their conformity to rules but their fidelity to the ruling family. This brought the dynamics of patron-client relations into the very capillaries of the administrative structure. And, with that, another of the basic conditions of effective policy — the presence of an autonomous, rule-following bureaucracy — was irremediably eroded. Instead of being the objects of lobbying, bureaucrats now became its instrument.

In this environment, it was only natural that the industrial policy apparatus would not be guided by goals that were solely, or even mainly, developmental in nature. Much as Syngman Rhee used the instruments at his disposal to consolidate his base among Korean industrialists, so Indira — and especially Sanjay — used the licensing regime to reward their friends, and to exact punishment on their enemies.[14] With the bureaucracy already compromised by the ruling family's interventions, it was virtually inevitable that the use of the licensing system for personal gain would ramify into the administrative structure. Again, administrative corruption was not an invention of Nehru's descendents. But its sheer scale under the new regime was altogether unprecedented. In the earlier years the licensing system had been crippled by a lack of coordination and a paper-thin monitoring network; it was flawed because of inadequate institutional capacity. But in the Gandhi era, the very purpose of the system was substantially transformed, from a developmental apparatus to an instrument for the exchange of favors within patron-client networks.[15] By the end of the 1970s the industrial policy system was thoroughly compromised.[16]

It is not my intention to portray this transformation of the political culture in apocalyptic terms. While there was a noticeable, even drastic slide in the quality of governance, it did not lead to total breakdown. Indeed, one might even say that the fact that the basic state structure held together, and managed to continue administering a massive and diverse nation, was quite a remarkable achievement. The nationwide response to the Emergency, the rapid resuscitation of formal democratic institutions, the growth of social support programs during the 1970s — all these were signs that the old administrative "steel frame" and the broader political culture still had life in them. While countries in South America succumbed to prolonged authoritarianism during the 1970s and 1980s, and some parts of Sub-Saharan Africa spiraled into elite gangsterism, India managed to preserve its basic state structure. Nonetheless, it is impossible to deny that the changes the Indira–Sanjay regime wrought set into motion a process whose full implications have yet to be realized.

Under these conditions, the possibility of appropriate reform of the economic state apparatus — that is, reform in a disciplinary direction — was simply out of the question. In fact, the momentum in the decades after Nehru's death settled ever more firmly in the opposite direction. The distance between plan documents and actual policy, which was already wide in the 1960s, simply increased. On top of this, the "license quota permit raj," as it came to be known, lost political legitimacy, as its corruption became ever more visible. For critics of the system, these tendencies only provided greater proof that the basic problem was with the strategy of state-led development itself, with the solution being a greater reliance on markets. This was particularly so among younger top-level civil servants, who, by the 1980s, increasingly came to see the policy apparatus as not only inefficient but beyond the possibility of reform.[17]

Added to this spiraling disillusionment among policy elites and experts was pressure from segments of the Indian capitalist class to dismantle the regulatory regime. During the three decades after Independence, the large business houses had managed to use the licensing system to their advantage, capturing control of the lines that came to them with their license.[18] In the early years of development, when many market segments were still fairly small, the number of potential entrants who were thus shut out of these lines was still somewhat small; as income expanded, however, and with it the size of the market, so, too, did the number of aspirants to these lines. True, some of the newly emerging industrialists were able not only to break through the political barriers to entry but were even able to use these barriers to their advantage — as evidenced in the meteoric rise of the Reliance group. But for the vast majority of the class, the industrial licensing system presented a formidable barrier to entry into increasingly lucrative markets. Coeval with the growth of the capitalist class, therefore, was a general increase in the pressure for the license permit raj to be dismantled.

These trends merged in the waning years of Gandhi's rule, with the result that, once again, the issue of systemic reform was put on the agenda. And, as in the case of the mid-sixties, the call was again tilted toward a loosening of the regulatory structure. Only this time the social base for the initiative was wider and its support among elites deeper. During the earlier episode the economic performance of the preceding decade had been seen as unspectacular but respectable. Pro-market reformers could not yet credibly insist that the industrial policy regime was an actual hindrance to growth. But by the time reformers again took center stage in the mid-eighties, the situation was different. The 1970s had witnessed a marked stagnation in economic growth relative to the Nehru years, the causes of which became the subject of much debate toward the end of the decade.[19] In the wake of this slowdown, calls for a dismantling of the regulatory apparatus carried a great deal more resonance than they had at Nehru's death. So by the time of Rajiv Gandhi's ascension, the ingredients needed for an all-out attack on the old industrial policy system were in place. An irreversible course for internal liberalization was set with the budget that his finance minister, V. P. Singh, announced in 1985.

Significantly, and in line with what the preceding analysis would suggest, business pressure has mainly been for the liberalization of *internal* economic controls, so as to allow entry for hitherto excluded firms; the enthusiasm for external liberalization, however, was, and has remained, much more guarded.[20] This should not be surprising, since the decades-long insulation from international competition had made domestic firms — even many of those favoring a turn away from *dirigisme* — doubtful about their chances against foreign competitors. Indeed, very soon after the onset of liberalization, some of the largest domestic business houses organized themselves into an informal lobbying group called the "Bombay Club," which has actively called for an extremely gradual dismantling of trade barriers. The Bombay Club, throughout the nineties, was an organized opposition to rapid liberalization; its efforts have been joined at various times by other business groups, even those nurtured by the state as a support base for the policy. Hence the liberalizing regime was rocked in late 1995 when the Confederation of Indian Industries (CII) openly criticized the regime for insufficiently protecting local industry from predatory MNCs. The attack by the CII came as a shock to policy elites. It was the youngest of the major business associations, having been established in its current form in 1985, the same year V. P. Singh launched liberalization, and had been a staunch supporter of the turn away from *dirigisme*. Although, in the end, the breach was mended, it signaled that the dynamics of liberalization would generate very different kinds of reactions from Indian capitalists on the internal and external fronts.

Worth noting here is that, as in the case of ELI, ISI endogenously generated the forces gathering to dismantle the regulatory apparatus of the state. In Korea, it was the main beneficiaries of the developmental state who started calling for its diminution, as their autonomous capacity grew; in the Indian case, the demands also came from the emergence of new groups which gathered strength as industrialization progressed and which came to see the system of internal controls and artificial monopolies as an obstacle to their own expansion. Adding force to the pressure these groups exerted to dismantle the *dirigiste* regime was the rapid decay of the planning apparatus itself during the Indira–Sanjay years. The degeneration of the economic state apparatus, its transformation into a tool for consolidating the power of the Gandhi family, eased the task of legitimizing a shift away from the era of industrial planning.

A deeper analysis of these years, during which a coalition emerged around the need for liberalization, is not yet possible. I have presented its developments in extremely broad strokes, to show how the developments of the Indira era only strengthened the forces holding sway during the "reform episode" of the mid-sixties. The corruption, clientelism, and growing criminality in the policy apparatus during the later years are often taken as the root causes behind the relative failure of state-led development in India. The arguments in this book are intended to show that these phenomena, although important, were not the basic cause of the system's weakness. They formed a layer over the more basic problems, and, because they were more apparent than the latter, they were easier to hold responsible. Moreover, the idea that state-led development fails primarily because it opens the door to official corruption is a notion that resonates powerfully with the prevailing neoliberal ideology of the day. This is why an examination of the first two decades of the development effort is of central analytical importance, not only for students of the Indian experience but more widely. Such an examination shows that the weakness of the Indian developmental state subsisted at a more basic level. Even had the trends of the post-Nehru era not taken the direction they did, the state would have been crippled by the incapacities undermining industrial policy under Nehru — the fragmentation of the policy apparatus and the inability to discipline capital. These weaknesses not only blocked effective industrial policy but also, over time, drained legitimacy from the very idea of state-led development — *independently of the effects of corruption and clientelism*. The latter served to compromise the system further and to shut the door, ever more firmly, to transforming the state around the needs of disciplinary planning.

Notes

CHAPTER 1
INTRODUCTION

1. An expression attributed to the economist Raj Krishna. Unfortunately I have not been able to track down the occasion where he first introduced it.

2. Ronald Herring, "Embedded Particularism: India's Failed Developmental State," in Meredith Woo-Cumings, ed., *The Developmental State*, pp. 306–334 (Ithaca, N.Y.: Cornell University Press, 1999).

3. The concentration of industry and its implications for industrial policy are explored in detail in chapter 7.

4. The most prominent recent comparison of India and Korea is Peter Evans, *Embedded Autonomy: States and Industrial Transformation* (Princeton, N.J.: Princeton University Press, 1995). But see also Amitava Krishna Dutt, "Market Miracle and State Stagnation? The Development Experience of South Korea and India Compared," in Amitava Krishna Dutt, Kwan S. Kim, and Ajit Singh, eds., *The State, Markets, and Development: Beyond the Neoclassical Dichotomy* (Aldershot: Elgar, 1994); E. Sridharan, *The Political Economy of Industrial Promotion: Indian, Brazilian, and Korean Electronics in Comparative Perspective, 1969–1994* (Westport, Conn.: Praeger, 1996).

5. For a good overview of the crisis decade in Latin America, see John Sheahan, *Patterns of Development in Latin America* (Princeton, N.J.: Princeton University Press, 1987). For India, see the collection in Deepak Nayyar, ed., *Industrial Growth and Stagnation: The Debate in India* (Delhi: Oxford University Press, 1994).

6. See Bela Balassa, *The Newly Industrializing Countries in the World Economy* (New York: Pergamon, 1981); Anne Krueger, *Foreign Trade Regimes and Economic Development: Turkey* (New York: Columbia University Press, 1974); Anne Krueger, "Government Failures in Development," *Journal of Economic Perspectives* 4, no. 3 (1990); Jagdish Bhagwati and Padma Desai, *India: Planning for Industrialization* (New York: Oxford University Press, 1970).

7. This was indeed the conclusion endorsed by several prominent studies of the postwar experience in India. See Isher Judge Ahluwalia, *Industrial Growth in India: Stagnation since the Mid-Sixties* (Delhi: Oxford University Press, 1985); and Jagdish Bhagwati, *India in Transition: Freeing the Economy* (Oxford: Oxford University Press, 1993).

8. Alice Amsden, *Asia's Next Giant: South Korea and Late Industrialization* (Oxford: Oxford University Press, 1989); Robert Wade, *Governing the Market: Economic Theory and the Role of Government in East Asian Industrialization* (Princeton, N.J.: Princeton University Press, 1990). These works were, in fact, preceded by a small number of case studies, which did not have a comparable impact beyond area specialists. Among the earliest such works on Korea was a

series of studies released by Harvard University's Council on East Asian Studies: Leroy Jones and Il Sakong, *Government, Business, and Entrepreneurship in Economic Development: The Korean Case* (Cambridge, Mass.: Harvard University Press, 1980); Edward S. Mason et al., *The Economic and Social Modernization of the Republic of Korea* (Cambridge, Mass.: Harvard University Press, 1980); David Cole and Yung Chul Park, *Financial Development in Korea, 1945–1978* (Cambridge, Mass.: Harvard University Press, 1983). For Taiwan, an important and influential early work was Thomas Gold, "Dependent Development in Taiwan" (Ph.D. dissertation, Harvard University, 1981), a version of which was later published as *State and Society in the Taiwan Miracle* (Armonk, N.Y.: M. E. Sharpe, 1986).

9. For evidence on the regulation of trade, see Richard Luedde-Neurath, *Import Controls and Export-Oriented Development: A Reassessment of the South Korean Case* (Boulder, Colo.: Westview, 1985). See also the relevant essays in Gordon White, ed., *Developmental States in East Asia* (London: Macmillan, 1988).

10. A convenient summary on the state's interference in financial markets for the Korean case is Laurence Harris, "Financial Reform and Economic Growth: A New Interpretation of South Korea's Experience," in Laurence Harris et al., eds., *New Perspectives on the Financial System* (London: Croom Helm, 1988). See also Jung-en Woo (Meredith Woo-Cumings), *Race to the Swift: State and Finance in Korean Industrialization* (New York: Columbia University Press, 1991). For Taiwan, see the relevant chapter in Stephen Wing-Kai Chiu, *The State and the Financing of Industrialization in East Asia: Historical Origins of Comparative Divergences* (Ph.D. dissertation, Princeton University, 1992); and Tung-Jen Cheng, "Guarding the Commanding Heights: The State as Banker in Taiwan," in Stephan Haggard, Chung H. Lee, and Sylvia Maxfield, eds., *The Politics of Finance in Developing Countries*, pp. 55–92 (Ithaca, N.Y.: Cornell University Press, 1992).

11. See Alice Amsden, "Getting Relative Prices 'Wrong': A Summary," in her *Asia's Next Giant*, *chap. 6*. For additional information on domestic prices, see the studies in Harvard University's Council on East Asian Studies.

12. The work of Leroy Jones was particularly important here. See his *Public Enterprise and Economic Development: The Korean Case* (Seoul: Korea Development Institute, 1975).

13. Here, again, the earliest evidence for Korea was provided by the Harvard Council on East Asian Studies. But it has been reinforced by just about every study since then. For Taiwan, the pivotal study has been Wade, *Governing the Market*.

14. See Pranab Bardhan, "The Nature of Institutional Impediments to Economic Development," in Mancur Olson and Satu Kahkonen, eds., *A Not-So-Dismal Science: A Broader View of Economies and Societies*, pp. 245–268 (London: Oxford University Press, 2000).

15. The expression is taken from the title to Robert Wade's well-known book.

16. This has led some economic historians to try to develop a theory of how the noneconomic factors interact with the more purely economic and technological ones. In this effort Moses Abromovitz has attracted some attention by suggesting that the noneconomic factors combine to add to the "social capability"

of economic systems. By this he means the ability of national economies to utilize and absorb the technologies that are widely available. Abromovitz therefore argues that the late developers that have closed the distance between themselves and the more advanced economies are those that have inherited, or built up, greater social capabilities to absorb and utilize the best technologies. See Moses Abromovitz, "Catching Up, Forging Ahead, and Falling Behind," *Journal of Economic History* 46, no. 2 (1986): 385–406; idem., "The Search for the Sources of Growth: Areas of Ignorance, Old and New," *Journal of Economic History* 53, no. 2 (1993): 217–243.

17. This has been stressed most forcefully in recent years by Peter Evans, in his *Embedded Autonomy*.

18. Alice Amsden, "Third World Industrialization: 'Global Fordism' or a New Model?" *New Left Review*, no. 182 (July/August 1990): 23–24 (first part of quote); 16 (second part; emphasis added).

19. This is a point on which critics from the Left as well as the Right agree. See the essays in Nayyar, *Industrial Growth and Stagnation*.

20. A notable exception to this general trend has been the work of Stephan Haggard, who has devoted considerable attention to the historical roots of the developmental states in East Asia. See his *Pathways from the Periphery: The Politics of Growth in Newly Industrializing Countries* (Ithaca, N.Y.: Cornell University Press, 1990); Stephan Haggard, Byung-kuk Kim, and Chung-in Moon, "The Transition to Export-Led Growth in South Korea, 1954–1966," *Journal of Asian Studies* 50 (November 1991); and Stephan Haggard and Chien-Kuo Pang, "The Transition to Export-Led Growth in Taiwan," in Joel Aberbach, David Dollar, and Kenneth L. Sokoloff, eds., *The Role of the State in Taiwan's Development*, pp. 47–89 (Armonk, N.Y.: M. E. Sharpe, 1994). The most careful analysis of the developmental state's origins in Korea is Woo, *Race to the Swift*.

21. The works of Amsden, Wade, and Rodrik are particularly important in this regard.

22. This has not gone unnoticed. It is quite common to find students of industrial policy bemoaning the absence of scholarship that goes beyond showing *how* states are different to explain *why* they are different. See Pranab Bardhan, "Comments," in Gerald Meier, ed., *Politics and Policy-Making in Developing Countries* (San Francisco: ICS, 1991); Gustav Ranis and Syed Akhtar Mahmood, *The Political Economy of Development Policy Change* (Cambridge: Basil Blackwell, 1992), pp. v–vi.

23. I borrow this term from David Collier and Ruth Berins Collier, *Shaping the Political Arena* (Princeton, N.J.: Princeton University Press, 1993).

24. The argument from state dominance is particularly strong among some students of the Korean case. I present a critique of this tendency in chapter 3. But, for now, note that the success of the Korean state in implementing its agenda lends an intuitive plausibility to the conclusion that it was able to do so because there was no actor with the power to stop it. Success in implementation generates a bias toward overestimating the state's power.

25. The meaning of ELI has been the object of some controversy, and will be explicated and qualified in more detail shortly. For now, I present it in an extremely abbreviated form.

26. Linda Weiss has made a commendable effort to overcome this analytical divide *in her Myth of the Powerless State* (Ithaca, N.Y.: Cornell University Press, 1998); see also the essays in Atul Kohli and Vivian Shue, *The State and Social Forces* (Cambridge: Cambridge University Press, 1993).

27. For an excellent summary of recent debates on this matter, see Clyde Barrow, *Radical Theories of the State* (Madison: University of Wisconsin Press, 1993).

CHAPTER 2
LATE DEVELOPMENT AND STATE-BUILDING

1. For the role of the state in European late development, see Alexander Ger-schenkron, *Economic Backwardness in Historical Perspective* (Cambridge, Mass.: Harvard University Press, 1962); W. O. Henderson, *The Industrialization of Europe: 1780–1914* (London: Thames and Hudson, 1969); and, more recently, Paul Bairoch, *Economics and World History: Myths and Paradoxes* (Chicago: University of Chicago Press, 1993). A handy synthesis of scholarship on Japan can be found in Christopher Howe, *The Origins of Japanese Trade Supremacy* (Chicago: University of Chicago Press, 1996).

2. See Albert Hirschman, "The Political Economy of Import Substituting Industrialization in Latin America," *The Quarterly Journal of Economics* 82 (February 1968): 2–32.

3. Amsden, *Asia's Next Giant.*

4. Karl Marx, *Capital*, vol. 1 (New York: Vintage, 1977), chap. 28.

5. Karl Polanyi, *The Great Transformation* (Boston: Beacon, 1944).

6. Ibid., chap. 6.

7. See Dieter Senghaas, *The European Experience: A Historical Critique of Development Theory* (Dover: Berg, 1984).

8. Polanyi, *The Great Transformation.*

9. This idea has been enshrined by Moses Abromovitz in his well-known article, "Catching Up, Forging Ahead, and Falling Behind," *Journal of Economic History* 46, no. 2 (June 1986): 385–406. For a good collection of essays on this topic, see William Baumol, Richard R. Nelson, and Edward N. Wolff, eds., *Convergence of Productivity: Cross-National and Historical Evidence* (Cambridge: Cambridge University Press, 1994).

10. Germany and Japan are the most well-known examples of late developers that restructured agrarian relations in order to accelerate the pace of economic development. For an instructive overview of the different paths of agrarian reform, see Alain DeJanvry, *The Agrarian Question and Reformism in Latin America* (Baltimore, Md.: The Johns Hopkins University Press, 1981); and Terry Byres, "The Agrarian Question and Different Forms of Capitalist Transition: An Essay with Reference to Asia," in Sudipto Mundle and Jan Breman, eds., *Rural Transformation in Asia*, pp. 3–76 (Delhi: Oxford University Press, 1991).

11. Amsden, *Asia's Next Giant*, pp. 143–144.

12. In the developing world, this strategy has been most prominently represented in Latin America and South Asia. Interestingly, in both cases arguments in favor of state intervention were given a fillip by agencies within the United

Nations. For Latin America, it was Raul Prebisch and his coworkers in the Economic Commission for Latin America (ECLA), of course, who pioneered it, for which see Kathryn Sikkink, *Ideas and Institutions: Developmentalism in Brazil and Argentina* (Ithaca, N.Y.: Cornell University Press, 1991). For India in the postwar period, the case for positive state action was put forth by D. R. Gadgil and his associates in the United Nations' *Measures for the Economic Development of Under-Developed Countries* (Geneva, 1951). This group included W. A. Lewis and T. Schultz. But the case for planning in India was actually pioneered by M. Visvesvaraya in *A Planned Economy for India* (Bangalore: Bangalore Press, 1934).

13. The literature on tax reform in LDCs is enormous. For a good overview, see Richard Bird, *Tax Policy and Economic Development* (Baltimore, Md.: The Johns Hopkins University Press, 1992).

14. Arthur Lewis, "Economic Development with Unlimited Supplies of Labour," *The Manchester School* 22, no. 2 (1954): 139–191. The optimism in this recipe is remarkable, given that, by the 1980s, it was not uncommon for developing countries to have reached savings levels of over 20 percent, and then watch their growth rates *decelerate*.

15. For a useful presentation of fiscal policy in a developmental setting, see Ephraim Eshag, *Fiscal and Monetary Policies and Problems in Developing Countries* (Cambridge: Cambridge University Press, 1983). A more recent treatment can be found in Sudipto Mundle, "Fiscal Policy and Growth: Some Asian Lessons for Asia," *Journal of Asian Economics* 10 (1999): 15–36.

16. This is a venerable issue in development economics, which, though submerged for some time, has recently resurfaced in a new generation of scholarship. For a lucid introduction to the issue, see Debraj Ray, *Development Economics* (Princeton, N.J.: Princeton University Press, 1998).

17. A pioneering argument to this effect was made in P. N. Rosenstein-Rodan, "Problems of Industrialization in Eastern and South-Eastern Europe," *The Economic Journal* 53, nos. 210/211 (1943): 202–221; another important argument along these lines was in Hollis Chenery, "The Interdependence of Investment Decisions," in Moses Abromovitz et al., eds., *The Allocation of Economic Resources*, pp. 82–120 (Stanford: Stanford University Press, 1959). For recent elaborations of this theme, see Kevin M. Murphy, Andrei Shleifer, and Robert Vishney, "Industrialization and the Big Push," *Journal of Political Economy* 97, no. 5: 1003–1026; Andres Rodriguez-Claire, "Positive Feedback Mechanisms in Economic Development: A Review of Recent Contributions," in Istvan P. Szekely and Richard Sabot, eds., *Development Strategy and Management of the Market Economy*, vol. 2, pp. 91–145 (Oxford: Clarendon, 1997).

18. Andrew Shonfield, *Modern Capitalism* (Oxford: Oxford University Press, 1965).

19. This is most commonly associated with East Asian industrial strategy, thanks, in part, to the impact of Chalmers Johnson's work on Japan, *MITI and the Japanese Miracle: The Growth of Industrial Policy, 1925–1975* (Stanford: Stanford University Press, 1982).

20. For discussions of the divergence between private and social returns in investment, see Tibor Scitovsky, "Two Concepts of External Economies," *Journal of Political Economy* 62 (1954): 143–151; J. M. Fleming, "External Econ-

omies and the Doctrine of Balanced Growth," *Economic Journal* 65 (1955): 241–256. This theme intersects with the work on coordination failures, some of which is listed above, in note 17.

21. India is well known for its use of a licensing system, but it was a key component of Korean strategy as well. Curiously this is one dimension on which the Indian case has been much more closely studied than the Korean case. There is, to my knowledge, no serious English-language study of the Korean industrial licensing system, whereas several analyze the Indian one. I draw on these in chapters 7 and 8.

22. On the state's subsidization of enterprise in the nineteenth century, see David Landes, *The Unbound Prometheus* (Cambridge: Cambridge University Press, 1969).

23. Amsden, *Asia's Next Giant*.

24. A good discussion of the problems discipline poses for states can be found in Ben Ross Schneider, "Elusive Synergy: Business-Government Relations and Development," *Comparative Politics* (October 1998): 101–122

25. I show in chapters 6 and 7 that this was particularly so in India, where the importance of disciplining capital was recognized from the outset. Alice Amsden has shown that this was true in Brazil, too, where planners extended loans to firms with performance standards firmly attached. See her "Early Postwar Industrial Policy in Emerging Economies: Creating Competitive Assets or Correcting Market Failures?" in Hideaki Miyajima, Takeo Kikkawa, and Takashi Hikino, eds., *Policies for Competitiveness: Comparing Business-Government Relationships in the "Golden Age" of Capitalism*, pp. 133–159 (Oxford: Oxford University Press, 1999).

26. Ashok Rudra, one of the doyens of development planning in India, criticized this as the assumption of the "omnipotent planner." See Ashok Rudra, "Planning in India: An Evaluation in Terms of Its Models," *Economic and Political Weekly* 20, no. 17 (April 27, 1985). For a superb analysis of how the blinders to structural constraints among Third World planners led to developmental contradictions, and how their conservative critics were able to capitalize on this, see Abhijit Sen, "On Economic Openness and Industrialization," in Deepak Nayyar, ed., *Trade and Industrialization* (Delhi: Oxford University Press, 1997).

27. Sheahan, *Patterns of Development in Latin America*; Christian Anglade and Carlos Fortin, eds., *The State and Accumulation in Latin America*, 2 vols. (Pittsburgh: Pittsburgh University Press, 1990).

28. Deepak Lall, *The Poverty of "Development Economics"* (Cambridge, Mass.: Harvard University Press, 1985).

29. See pages 3–4 in Chapter 1.

30. Evans, *Embedded Autonomy*; Peter Evans and James Rauch, "Bureaucracy and Growth: A Cross-National Analysis of the Effects of "Weberian" State Structures on Economic Growth," *American Sociological Review* 64 (October 1999): 748–765; see also Tun-jen Cheng, Stephan Haggard, and David Kang, "Institutions and Growth in Korea and Taiwan: The Bureaucracy," *Journal of Development Studies* 37, no. 4 (October 1998): 87–111.

31. For Zaire, see Thomas Callaghy, *The State-Society Struggle: Zaire in*

Comparative Perspective (New York: Columbia University Press, 1984); for the Philippines, see Paul Hutchcroft, *Booty Capitalism* (Ithaca, N.Y.: Cornell University Press, 1998).

32. Evans, *Embedded Autonomy*, pp. 29–30, 48–49.

33. Of course, norms of recruitment and promotion are also a kind of rule-following, so whence the distinction? Rule-following, as such, typically refers to the duties attached to the individual functionary's station—her responsibilities as defined by her position in the particular bureau. This is distinct from the norms that govern movement *between* bureaus.

34. Evans, *Embedded Autonomy*, pp. 49, 71; Evans and Rauch, "Bureaucracy and Growth," pp. 751–752; Cheng, Haggard, and Kang, "Institutions and Growth in Korea and Taiwan: The Bureaucracy," passim.

35. This paragraph and the next present the skeleton of an argument that I have developed at more length elsewhere. See my "Bureaucratic Rationality and the Developmental State," *American Journal of Sociology* 107, no. 4 (January 2002): 951–989.

36. This was the very difficulty that planners ran into in Korea during the 1950s, as I briefly describe in chapter 3. Clashes between the Finance Ministry and the Planning Commission were also frequent in India in the 1950s and 1960s, for which see chapters 7 and 8 below. Also see Francine Frankel, *India's Political Economy, 1947–1977* (Princeton, N.J.: Princeton University Press, 1979).

37. This was emphasized by none other than Weber himself, who is most frequently credited for bringing to light the virtues of bureaucratic rationality. See his discussion of the "office secret" in his *Economy and Society* (Berkeley: University of California Press, 1968), 2:990–993.

38. On the difference between formal rationality and strategic rationality in state action, see Calus Offe, "The Divergent Rationalities of Administrative Action," in his *Disorganized Capitalism*, pp. 300–316 (Cambridge, Mass.: MIT Press, 1985). Offe offers this distinction in reference to the welfare state, arguing that since welfare policy is geared toward particular substantive ends, formal rule-following will offer insufficient guidance to bureaucrats. I think this argument is even more appropriate for developmental states.

39. Johnson, *MITI and the Japanese Miracle*. See also Daniel Okimoto, *Between MITI and the Market: Japanese Industrial Policy for High Technology* (Stanford: Stanford University Press, 1989).

40. See Jones and Sakong, *Government, Business, and Entrepreneurship*; Woo, *Race to the Swift*; Eun Mee Kim, *Big Business, Strong State* (Albany: State University of New York Press, 1997); Byung-Kook Kim, "Bringing and Managing Socioeconomic Change: The State in Korea and Mexico" (Ph.D. dissertation, Harvard University, 1988).

41. Bob Jessop refers to this kind of institutional capability as *state strategic capacity*, as distinct from generic administrative capacity. See Bob Jessop, *State Theory: Putting the Capitalist State in Its Place* (University Park: Pennsylvania State University Press, 1990).

42. See Evans, *Embedded Autonomy*, chaps. 1–3; Charles Sabel, " Learning by Monitoring: The Institutions of Economic Development," in Neil Smelser

and Richard Swedberg, eds., *The Handbook of Economic Sociology* (Princeton, N.J.: Princeton University Press, 1994).

43. See Moon Kyu Park, "Interest Representation in South Korea: The Limits of Corporatist Control," *Asian Survey* 27 (1987): 903–917; Karl Fields, *Enterprise and the State in Korea and Taiwan* (Ithaca, N.Y.: Cornell University Press, 1995).

44. I examine the fortunes of developmental councils in chapters 6 and 7. For a succinct presentation of their place within the larger industrial policy framework, see Sharad Marathe, *Regulation and Development: India's Policy Experience with Controls over Industry* (Delhi: Sage, 1986).

45. The literature on European corporatism is enormous. For a convenient overview, see Jukka Pekkarinen, Matti Pohkjoka, and Bob Rowthorn, eds., *Social Corporatism: A Superior Economic System?* (Oxford: Clarendon, 1992). Linda Weiss presents a synthesis of the more recent literature and relates it to the debate on developing countries — one of the few analyses to do so. See her *Myth of the Powerless State*, chap. 4.

46. For a good discussion of such bodies within the developmental state, see, in addition to Evans's book, Ben Ross Schneider, "Elusive Synergy: Business Government Relations and Development," *Comparative Politics* (October 1998): 101–122; Weiss, *The Myth of the Powerless State*, chap. 3; and Wade, *Governing the Market*, pp. 375–377.

47. The varying properties of business associations in a developmental setting have been explored recently by Ben Ross Schneider in "Relations between Government and Business and Their Consequences for Development: A Review of the Recent Literature," *Desarrollo Economico-Revista De Ciencias Sociales* 39, no. 153 (April–June 1999): 45–75.

48. How far we should press this difference, though, is not entirely clear. It may be that formal associational arrangements are well suited to the goals of a developmental state. But there are instances of informal arrangements that have worked. For example, industrial policy in France in the early postwar period seems to have been much less dependent on associational mechanisms than the East Asian one. See Shonfield, *Modern Capitalism*, chap. 7; and, for an explicit comparison with East Asia, see Vedat Milor, "Planning the Market" (unpublished ms., 1994).

49. It should be stressed that the instrumental advantage of the smaller list is secondary in relevance to its actual causal weight. If it turned out that the three elements were really no more important than, say, ten others, then I believe we would be obliged to extend the list considerably — despite the loss of parsimony. This is just to say that pragmatic or instrumental considerations take a backseat to facts about the world.

50. The main form of state assistance in these years was tariff protection. For Latin America, see Victor Bulmer-Thomas, *The Economic History of Latin America since Independence* (Cambridge: Cambridge University Press, 1994), chaps. 7–9; and Leslie Bethell, ed., *Latin America: Economy and Society since 1930* (Cambridge: Cambridge University Press, 1998); for India, where protection to local industry was, naturally, less munificent, see the account by B. R. Tomlinson in his *Economy of Modern India, 1860–1970*, in *The New Cam-*

bridge History of India, vol. 3.3, pp. 132–144 (Cambridge: Cambridge University Press, 1993).

51. For Latin America, see M. Leopoldi, "Industrial Associations and Politics in Contemporary Brazil" (Ph.D. dissertation, Oxford University, 1984); for India, see Thomas Rider, "The Tariff Policy of the Government of India and Its Development Strategy, 1894–1924" (Ph.D. dissertation, University of Minnesota, 1971), chap. 9.

52. Bethell, *Latin America*; Raghabendra Chattopadhyay, "The Idea of Planning in India, 1930–1950" (Ph.D. dissertation, Australian National University, 1985).

53. Perhaps one of the most well-known pleas for coordinated economic policy, in the form of planning, was made by the leading Indian capitalists in 1944–45 and was released in a document that came to be known as the "Bombay Plan." Industrialists in Brazil, during the first ascendancy of Vargas, had also made similar arguments in favor of taking power over economic policy away from provincial bodies and vesting it in the central government. For India, see Purshotamdas Thakurdas et al., *A Plan of Economic Development for India* (Bombay, 1944–45); for Brazil, see. Leopoldi, *Industrial Associations and Politics in Contemporary Brazil*.

54. The classic, if, in my view, overdrawn, theorization of this dynamic is Michal Kalecki, "Observations on Social and Economic Aspects of 'Intermediate Regimes,'" in *The Collected Works of Michal Kalecki*, Vol. 5: *Developing Countries*, ed. Jerzy Osiatynski, pp. 6–12 (Oxford: Oxford University Press, 1993).

55. Evans, *Embedded Autonomy*, p. 37.

56. See, for example, Barbara Geddes, *Politicians' Dilemma: Building State Capacity in Latin America* (Berkeley: University of California Press, 1994).

57. See Baldev Raj Nayyar, *India's Mixed Economy: The Role of Ideology and Interest in Its Development* (Bombay: Popular Prakashan, 1985); Prem Shankar Jha, *India: A Political Economy of Stagnation* (Delhi: Oxford University Press, 1980).

58. Many, but not all. In particular, fiscal reforms aimed at increasing the emphasis on direct, as against indirect, taxation have often crashed against the shoals of elite opposition. Two economists who played an important role in such efforts as advisers were Nicholas Kaldor and Michel Kalecki. For interesting accounts of their experiences, see John Toye, "Nicholas Kaldor and Tax Reform in Developing Countries," *Cambridge Journal of Economics* 13, no. 1 (March 1989): 183–200; A. P. Thirlwall, *Nicholas Kaldor* (New York: New York University Press, 1987); and the editor's explanatory and biographical notes in *The Collected Works of Michal Kalecki*, Vol. 5: *Developing Countries*, ed. Jerzy Osiatynski.

59. This observation is substantiated for the Indian case in some detail in chapter 6. Domestic capitalists, for the most part, accepted the initial declarations by the Indian National Congress about the future scope of public enterprises, since such enterprises were to be confined to those areas in which private capital was not interested. Even the nationalization of banks in the late 1960s did not elicit much consternation. Similarly I have come across no evidence of bourgeois opposition to Park Chung-Hee's bank nationalizations in Korea.

60. See Zysman, *Governments, Markets, and Growth*; for a discussion of French planning in the context of developmental states, see Milor, *Planning the Market*.

61. Zysman, *Governments, Markets, and Growth*; Milor, *Planning the Market*.

62. Indian planners discovered this early on. In early 1949, for example, the office of the Economic Adviser to the Government of Madras State wrote to the U.S. Embassy asking for help. It seems that the economic adviser, who was chiefly responsible for collecting firm-level data on production and investment statistics, was "experiencing difficulty in enlisting the cooperation of the various business houses . . . in obtaining the required data." He was therefore considering recommending that his government pass legislation *compelling* firms to cooperate, and was soliciting the Americans' advice on drafting such laws. See Streeper to Secretary of State, 3/24/49, Despatch #68, 845.50/3–2449, Department of State Records (DSR), Record Group 59, United States National Archives and Records Administration, College Park, Maryland.

63. See David Vogel's discussion, in this regard, of the general distrust capitalists harbor toward state managers, in his "Why Businessmen Distrust Their State: The Political Consciousness of American Corporate Executives," *British Journal of Political Science* 8 (January 1978): 45–78.

64. Jonas Pontusson has argued that this was a central reason for the Swedish bourgeoisie's unyielding resistance to the adoption of an industrial policy in Sweden at mid-century. See his "Labor, Corporatism, and Industrial Policy: The Swedish Case in Comparative Perspective," *Comparative Politics* (January 1991): 163–179.

65. The idea that particular arrangements can elicit capitalist opposition despite their benefiting from the arrangement is not a novel one. It is the linchpin, for example, of Michel Kalecki's argument for why full employment policies in industrial economies will be unstable. While full employment increases firms' profits by increasing aggregate demand and enabling full capacity utilization, the resulting tightness in labor markets also increases labor's political strength — a condition that capitalists, Kalecki argues, will typically find unacceptable. See Michal Kalecki, "Political Aspects of Full Employment," in his *Selected Essays on the Dynamics of the Capitalist Economy*, pp. 138–145 (Cambridge: Cambridge University Press, 1971).

66. For a historical discussion of this doctrine, see Douglas Irwin, *Against the Tide: An Intellectual History of Free Trade* (Princeton, N.J.: Princeton University Press, 1996); for the use of infant industry protection by early industrializers, see Dieter Senghaas, *The European Experience: A Historical Critique of Development Theory* (Dover: Berg, 1984).

67. For a lucid summary of typical policy under ISI, see James Cypher and James Dietz, *The Process of Economic Development* (London: Routledge, 1997).

68. The significance of the industrial group has been emphasized repeatedly by Alice Amsden in her work. See Amsden, *Asia's Next Giant*, chap. 5; Amsden, "South Korea: Enterprising Groups and Entrepreneurial Government," in Alfred Chandler et al., eds., *Big Business and the Wealth of Nations*, pp. 336–367 (Cambridge: Cambridge University Press, 1997); also useful is Nathaniel Leff, "Industrial Organization and Entrepreneurship in Developing Countries: The

Business Groups," *Economic Development and Cultural Change*, 26, no. 4 (1978).

69. C. P. Chandrasekhar, "Aspects of Growth and Structural Change in Indian Industry," in Nayyar, *Industrial Growth and Stagnation*, 661–675.

70. *Report of the Industrial Licensing Policy Enquiry Committee* (also known as the Dutt Committee Report) (Delhi: Government of India, 1969).

71. For a discussion of this strategy, see chapter 7 below.

72. Jagdish Bhagwati has referred to this as the "goofing off" effect. See his interview in *Challenge Magazine*, January–February 2001, pp. 6–18.

73. Evidence on India is presented in chapter 7 below; for Latin America, see Sheahan, *Patterns of Development in Latin America*, pp. 86–93. A well-known early exposition of this argument was made by Werner Baer, "Import Substitution and Industrialization in Latin America: Experiences and Interpretations," *Latin American Research Review* 7, no. 1 (1972): 95–122.

74. Note that the claim being made is that firms lack a direct reason to be efficient, not that they actually have an incentive to be inefficient. If they do not favor alternative lines for expansion, they may very well choose to use the state subsidies as directed, and increase efficiency.

75. See John Waterbury, "The Long Gestation and Brief Triumph of Import-Substituting Industrialization, *World Development* 27, no. 2 (1999): 323–341.

76. This difference between an emphasis on exports and bringing them to the core of development policy is captured by the distinction between export *promotion* and export-*led* strategy. See Cypher and Dietz, *The Process of Economic Development*, pp. 318–319.

77. Roberto Cortes Conde and Shane Hunt, *The Latin American Economies: Growth and the Export Sector, 1880–1930* (New York: Holmes and Meier, 1985); *The Cambridge History of Latin America*, Vol. 4: *Economy and Society, 1870–1930* (Cambridge: Cambridge University Press, 1986).

78. Richard Luedde-Neurath, *Import Controls and Export-Oriented Development: A Reassessment of the South Korean Case* (Boulder, Colo.: Westview, 1985); Robert Wade, "Managing Trade: Taiwan and South Korea as Challenges to Economics and Political Science," *Comparative Politics* (January 1993): 147–167.

79. Yung Whee Rhee, "Instruments for Export Policy and Administration: Lessons from the East Asian Experience," *World Bank Staff Working Papers*, #725 (1985): 184–187; Amsden, *Asia's Next Giant*, p. 69; Y. B. Rhee, B. Ross-Larson, and G. Pursell, *Korea's Competitive Edge: Managing Entry into World Markets* (Baltimore, Md.: The Johns Hopkins University Press, 1984).

80. Gary Gereffi, "Global Commodity Chains: New Forms of Coordination and Control among Nations and Firms in International Industries," *Competition and Change* 4 (1996); Sanjaya Lall, "Marketing Barriers Facing Developing Country Manufactured Exporters: A Conceptual Note," *The Journal of Development Studies* 27, no. 4 (July 1991).

81. Where producers of advanced countries could not be assumed to have an automatic advantage was in solving collective-action problems.

82. See the excellent discussion in Demostheses Pinho, "Development Strategies, Trade Policy, and State Intervention: Aspects of the Brazilian Post-War

Experience in International Perspective" (Ph.D. dissertation, University of California, Berkeley, 1991).

83. See Yeonmi Ahn, "The Political Economy of Foreign Aid: The Nature of American Aid and Its Impact on the State-Business Relationship in South Korea, 1945–1972" (Ph.D. dissertation, Yale University, 1992), chap. 3.

84. Ibid.

85. However, export of goods made by grant-in-kind aid was still prohibited. It was just that the significance of grants-in-kind was reduced dramatically after 1961. See Ahn, "The Political Economy of Foreign Aid," pp. 163–174.

86. The distinction between export-*promotion* and export-*led industrialization* is an important one, and is explained in chapter 3 below.

87. For good discussions of marketing and sales as barriers to entry in exporting, see Lall, "Marketing Barriers"; Gereffi, "Global Commodity Chains," pp. 427–429; Gary Gereffi, "Commodity Chains and Regional Divisions of Labor in East Asia," *Journal of Asian Business* 12, no. 1 (1996): 75–112.

88. Woo, *Race to the Swift*, chap. 4; Bruce Cumings, "The Origins and Development of the Northeast Asian Political Economy: Industrial Sectors, Product Cycles, and Political Consequences," in Frederic Deyo, ed., *The Political Economy of New Asian Industrialism* (Ithaca, N.Y.: Cornell University Press, 1987). Cumings places a great deal of importance on the United States, despite his apparent nod to a kind of product-cycle explanation; hence his verdict that "in both countries [i.e., South Korea and Taiwan] the export-led program was decided by the United States" (ibid., p. 70).

89. Timothy Lim, "Competition, Markets, and the Politics of Development in South Korea, 1945–1979" (Ph.D. dissertation, University of Hawaii, 1996), pp. 188–202.

90. Robert Kaufman, "How Societies Change Developmental Models or Keep Them: Reflections on the Latin American Experience in the 1930s and the Postwar World," in Gary Gereffi and Donald Wyman, eds., *Manufacturing Miracles*, pp. 110–138 (Princeton, N.J.: Princeton University Press, 1990). This was also true in India, as shown below in chapter 8.

91. For an overview, see Anne O. Krueger, *Liberalization Attempts and Consequences*, in *Foreign Trade Regimes and Economic Development*, vol. 10 (New York: National Bureau of Economic Research, 1978).

92. I discuss this in much greater detail in chapter 3.

93. The most extensive discussion of the importance of Japan for Korean export success is in Robert Castley, *Korea's Economic Miracle: The Crucial Role of Japan* (London: Macmillan, 1997).

94. The role of Japanese firms in Taiwanese industrialization and exports is brought out by Thomas Gold in his *State and Society in the Taiwanese Miracle* (Armonk, N.Y.: M. E. Sharpe, 1986).

95. The call for a truce led, in December 1947, to a massive Industrial Truce Conference. At this conference, capital and labor hammered out what appeared to be a genuine social-democratic class compromise—including the commitment to profit sharing, works committees, and a minimum wage. I discuss the conference, as well as its aftermath, in "From Class Compromise to Class Accommodation: The Origins of the Indian Industrial Relations System," in Raka Ray and Mary Katzenstein, eds., *Rethinking Class and Poverty in India*, forthcoming.

CHAPTER 3
THE ORIGINS OF THE DEVELOPMENTAL STATE IN KOREA

1. Jones and Sakong, *Government, Business, and Entrepreneurship*, p. 67.

2. Mason et al., *The Economic and Social Modernization of the Republic of Korea*, p. 263.

3. Byung-Nak Song, *The Rise of the Korean Economy* (Oxford: Oxford University Press, 1990), p. 91.

4. Kim, *Big Business, Strong State*, p. 5.

5. Alice Amsden and Robert Wade, two of the pioneers in the recent critiques of neoclassical orthodoxy, have tended to remain quite reticent on the general relation of power between the state and capital in Korea. Their analyses have focused on describing the sundry ways in which the Korean experience relied on selective state intervention while leaving aside the issue of sources of the state's power. It is not clear to me, therefore, how they would react to the position developed in this chapter.

6. Mason et al., *The Economic and Social Modernization of the Republic of Korea*, p. 265; Amsden "Third World Industrialization," p. 22.

7. Song, *The Rise of the Korean Economy*, p. 145.

8. Ibid., p. 102.

9. The most articulate exponent of this position has been Atul Kohli, in "Where do High Growth Political Economies Come From? The Japanese Lineage of Korea's 'Developmental State,'" *World Development* 22, no. 9 (1994): 1269–1293. But see also Sang-in Jun, "The Origins of the Developmental State in South Korea," *Asian Perspective* 16, no. 2 (fall–winter 1992): 181–204.

10. See their exchange with Kohli: Stephan Haggard, David Kang, and Chung-in Moon, "Japanese Colonialism and Korean Development: A Critique," *World Development* 25, no. 6 (1997): 867–881; Atul Kohli, "Japanese Colonialism and Korean Development: A Reply," *World Development* 25, no. 6 (1997): 883–888.

11. Byung-Kook Kim, "Bringing and Managing Socioeconomic Change," pp. 100–103.

12. Ahn, "The Political Economy of Foreign Aid," pp. 231, 281–283.

13. Ibid., 183–184.

14. Woo, *Race to the Swift*, chap. 2.

15. This, too, is widely recognized in the literature. For two of the best recent analyses of business strategies in the 1950s, see Ahn, "The Political Economy of Foreign Aid," and Lim, "Competition, Markets, and the Politics of Development." Analysts have sometimes attributed the absence of Schumpeterian entrepreneurs to the import-substituting strategy of the Rhee regime, which set up a dense thicket of protectionist measures and relied heavily on discretionary allocation of scarce import licenses and other subsidies; the conclusion that naturally flows from this position is that it was a turn to more market-oriented policies in the next decade—centering around the rationalization of the exchange rate—that drove Korean business into more productive activities, by closing off the ready avenues to profit through manipulation of price differentials. But the contrast drawn between the two periods along this dimension is illusory—the policy regime under Park Chung-Hee did not do away with pro-

tection and import substitution, nor did it rely any less on discretionary allocation of scarce resources. On this, see Amsden, *Asia's Next Giant*, and especially
two excellent articles by Dani Rodrik: "Getting Interventions Right: How South
Korea and Taiwan Grew Rich," *Economic Policy* (April 1995): 55–107; and
"The 'Paradox' of the Successful State," *European Economic Review* 41 (1997):
411–442.

16. This, of course, is widely recognized. For a recent mention of it, see Larry
Westphal, "The Pendulum Swings — An Apt Analogy?" *World Development* 26,
no. 12 (1998): 2223–2230 n. 14.

17. For an account of Rhee's ouster, see Quee-Young Kim, *The Fall of Synghman Rhee* (Berkeley: University of California Press, 1983); for the coup that
brought Park to power, see Se-jin Kim, *The Politics of Military Revolution in
Korea* (Chapel Hill: University of North Carolina Press, 1971).

18. Kim, "Bringing and Managing Socioeconomic Change," pp. 248–250;
David Satterwhite, "The Politics of Economic Development: Coup, State, and
the Republic of Korea's First Five Year Economic Development Plan (1962–
1966)" (Ph.D. dissertation, University of Washington, 1994), pp. 377–383.

19. Lim, "Competition, Markets, and the Politics of Development," chap. 6;
Ho-yeol Paul Yoo, "A New Political Economy of Economic Policy Change in
South Korea, 1961–1963: Crisis, Uncertainty, and Contradiction" (Ph.D. disser-
tation, Ohio State University, 1990), pp. 172–177.

20. The congruence between the junta's reforms and those Chang proposed
has led some scholars to suggest that, had he been given enough time, Chang
would have eventually pushed through the measures himself. The coup, and
hence the authoritarian regime, was thus unnecessary to the Korean experience.
This is most explicitly argued by David Satterwhite in his "Politics of Economic
Development," pp. 11–18.

21. Haggard, Kim, and Moon, "The Transition to Export-Led Growth," p.
857.

22. See David C. Kang, "South Korean and Taiwanese Development and the
New Institutional Economics," *International Organization* 49, no. 3 (summer
1995): 575. There is no detailed study of how this delicate operation was managed, for understandable reasons. Conventional sources will simply not yield the
required information for such a project. It need hardly be emphasized, however,
that one of the most promising directions of future research on the comparative
political economy of developmental states lies here. For an interesting critique of
the neoclassical and "new institutionalist" analyses of corruption from a
broadly class-analytical perspective, see Mushtaq Khan, "State Failure in Weak
States: A Critique of New Institutionalist Explanations," in John Harriss et al.,
eds., *The New Institutional Economics and Third World Development* (London: Routledge, 1995); and Mushtaq Khan, "The Efficiency Implications of
Corruption," *Journal of International Development* 8, no. 5 (1996): 683–696.

23. Kim, *Big Business, Strong State*, p. 34; Haggard, Kim, and Moon, "The
Transition to Export-Led Growth," p. 860. The formation of the EPB was
something of a relief to U.S. advisers in Seoul. Initial reports after the coup
described worrisome signs of a continuation, and even exacerbation, of the
Rhee-era dispersal of authority. Ministries seemed to be usurping a "new degree

of autonomy" that had not been possible under the previous regime, and all indications were that "strategically placed bureaucrats" were about to launch "pet projects" which the new regime would be powerless to stop. See Green to Secretary of State, May 28, 1961, 895B.00/5–2861, Department of State Records (hereafter, DSR), RG 59, United States National Archives (hereafter, USNA), College Park, Maryland.

24. The notion to establish an apex body for planning came not from Park, as has often been assumed, but from the economists in the Economic Development Council (EDC). Satterwhite stresses this point in his *Politics of Economic Development*, pp. 377–383. See also Kim, "Bringing and Managing Socioeconomic Change," pp. 248–251.

25. Chung H. Lee, "The Government, Financial System, and Large Private Enterprises in the Economic Development of South Korea," *World Development* 20 (1992): 190.

26. This episode is now a standard part of every account of Park's rise to power. For representative samples, see Jones and Sakong, *Government, Business, and Entrepreneurship*, pp. 69–70, 280–282; Kim, *Big Business, Strong State*, pp. 112–117.

27. See Lim, "Competition, Markets, and the Politics of Development," pp. 229–232.

28. Kim, *Big Business, Strong State*, p. 117 (emphasis added).

29. Karl Fields, *Enterprise and the State in Korea and Taiwan* (Ithaca, N.Y.: Cornell University Press, 1995), p. 48 (emphasis added); see also Karl Fields, "Strong States and Business Organization in Korea and Taiwan," in Sylvia Maxfield and Ben Ross Schneider, eds., *Business and the State in Developing Countries* (Ithaca, N.Y.: Cornell University Press, 1997), pp. 127–128, where he repeats this almost verbatim.

30. Ha-Joon Chang, "The Political Economy of Industrial Policy in Korea," *Cambridge Journal of Economics* 17 (1993): 152 (emphasis added). Despite the criticism that follows, I should note that Chang's is one of the very finest studies on the Korean experience. See also Ha-Joon Chang, *The Political Economy of Industrial Policy* (London: Macmillan, 1994), where he embeds his account of Korea in a wider discussion of its implications for neoclassical economics.

31. "As long as they could obtain the necessary capital inputs, both national firms and multinational subsidiaries had clear preferences for operating within the context of protected home markets — rather than assuming the risks of entering new markets and/or competing with subsidiaries established elsewhere" (Robert Kaufman, "How Societies Change Developmental Models or Keep Them: Reflections on the Latin American Experience in the 1930s and the Postwar World," in Gereffi and Wyman, *Manufacturing Miracles*, p. 129).

32. Alan Richards and John Waterbury, *The Political Economy of the Middle East* (Boulder, Colo.: Westview, 1990), p. 196; see also Abla M. Abdel-Latif, "The Non-Price Determinants of Export Success or Failure: The Egyptian Ready-made Garment Industry, 1975–89," *World Development* 21, no. 10 (1993): 1677–1684.

33. *Biweekly Economic Review*, no. 10, 895B.00/5–1961, RG 59, DSR.

34. Green to Secretary of State, 5/24/61, 895B.00/5–2461; "Developments

on the Illicit Accumulators Front," in *Biweekly Economic Review*, no. 14, 895B.00/7–1461, RG 59, DSR; for quote, see Berger to Secretary of State, 6/28/61, 895B.054/6–2861, RG 59, DSR.

35. Berger to Secretary of State, 8/1/61, 895B.00/8161, RG 59, DSR.

36. Ibid., 9/29/61, 895B.00/92961, RG 59, DSR.

37. *Biweekly Economic Review*, no. 14, 895B.00/7–1461, RG 59, DSR.

38. Ibid., no. 9, 895B.00/5–462, RG 59, DSR. See also Lim, "Competition, Markets, and the Politics of Development," pp. 251–260; and Yoo, "A New Political Economy," pp. 184–187.

39. The most detailed study of the initial plan as it related to farmers and small business is Yoo, "A New Political Economy," pp. 94–120. See also Suk-Jun Lim, "The Politics of Industrialization: Formation of Divergent Industrial Orders in Korea and Taiwan" (Ph.D. Dissertation, University of Chicago, 1997), 104–106; Inwon Choue, "The Politics of Industrial Restructuring: South Korea's Turn Toward Export-Led Heavy and Chemical Industrializtion, 1961–1974" (Ph.D. dissertation, University of Pennsylvania, 1988), pp. 155–166).

40. Lim, "Politics of Industrialization," p. 105.

41. See Haggard, *Pathways from the Periphery*, p. 68.

42. David Cole and Young Woo Nam, "The Pattern and Significance of Economic Planning in Korea," in Irma Edelman, ed., *Practical Approaches to Development Planning: Korea's Second Five-Year Plan*, p. 18 (Baltimore, Md.: The Johns Hopkins University Press).

43. Choue, "The Politics of Industrial Restructuring," p. 161. In fact, Park admitted, as did Kim Jong Pil in later years, that the junta had little understanding of the plan's operational coherence. See Satterwhite, "The Politics of Economic Development," pp. 358–364.

44. The most detailed study of this chain of events is Yoo, "A New Political Economy." The crisis was closely followed and ably reported by the *Far Eastern Economic Review* (henceforth, *FEER*). See, in particular, the issues of 3/7/63, 8/22/63, and 9/19/63.

45. *FEER*, 9/19/63, p. 737.

46. David Cole and Princeton Lyman, *Korean Development: The Interplay of Politics and Economics* (Cambridge, Mass.: Harvard University Press, 1971), p. 218. The authors, who were present in Korea at the time as advisers, recall that, as late as 1964, "planning as such was definitely not a well-established or influential process."

47. Choue, "The Politics of Industrial Restructuring," pp. 161–163; Kim, "Bringing and Managing Socioeconomic Change," pp. 261–263.

48. *Biweekly Economic Review* #3, 2/10/64, E 2–2 KOR S, Box #735, Subject-Numeric Files, RG 59, DSR; Haggard, Kim, and Moon, "The Transition to Export-Led Growth," pp. 865–866.

49. Although some scholars have pointed to the importance of Vietnam as a market for Korean goods after the mid-1960s, its role in the early years of the Park regime is less widely appreciated. Vietnam was the major destination for many iron and steel products, which were the most lucrative category for exports in 1963, bringing in $12.1 million, as against just $600,000 in 1962. In comparison, textiles and related products only garnered $7.8 million in 1963.

This also points to the precarious moorings of export success in the early years of the regime. For the statistics cited, see *Quarterly Economic Summary—October–December 1963*, 3/3/64, E 2–3 KOR S, Box #735, Subject-Numeric Files, 1964–1966, RG 59, DSR.

50. For the impending cutback on U.S. aid, see Ahn, "The Political Economy of Foreign Aid," chap. 6; and Woo, *Race to the Swift*, pp. 72–80. The American insistence on devaluation and export promotion was detailed in the so-called Dillon Letter, which embedded these demands in a larger stabilization program. This was first presented by advisers during the Chang Myon regime, and continued to be the core set of proposals for subsequent U.S pressure. On the Dillon Letter, see Satterwhite, "The Politics of Economic Development," pp. 318–330. For U.S. pressure more generally, see Woo, *Race to the Swift*, pp. 76–79; and Amsden, *Asia's Next Giant*, p. 67.

51. This distinction appears to have been proposed by Gustav Ranis and is noted by Cypher and Dietz in their excellent textbook on the subject, *The Process of Economic Development*, p. 319.

52. It may, however, require autonomy from and power over agrarian elites if the move is to promote manufacturing exports in a country with a history of exporting primary products.

53. Song, *The Rise of the Korean Economy*, pp. 90–92; John Lie, *Han Unbound: The Political Economy of South Korea* (Stanford: Stanford University Press, 1998), pp. 96–98; Martin Hart-Landsberg, *The Rush to Development* (New York: Monthly Review Press, 1993), p. 59; Alice Amsden and Takashi Hikino, "Staying Behind, Stumbling Back, Sneaking Up, Soaring Ahead: Late Industrialization in Historical Perspective," in William J. Baumol, Richard R. Nelson, and Edward N. Wolff, eds., *Convergence of Productivity: Cross-national Studies and Historical Evidence* (Oxford: Oxford University Press, 1994), p. 295. For an example of Park's punishment of a firm that refused to abide by export targets, see Mark Clifford, *Troubled Tiger: Businessmen, Bureaucrats, and Generals in South Korea* (Armonk, N.Y.: M. E. Sharpe, 1994), pp. 55–56.

54. Berger to Secretary of State, 1/8/63, 394.41/1–863, RG 59, DSR.

55. The argument offered here also implies that the success of Korean exports over time was not a simple outcome of the subsidies the state offered to exporters. It is not uncommon to find commentators pointing to state subsidization of exports as the source of the enthusiasm that business displayed for ELI. But as Dani Rodrik has pointed out, this argument fails on two counts: first, the subsidies had been in place since around 1958, whereas exports really began to take off after 1962; second, and more important, the extent of subsidies in Korea was, in fact, *lower* than in several other developing countries that were far less successful in making a switch to exports. In other words, subsidies might have encouraged Korean firms to export, but that the latter not only tried the strategy but also remained committed to it cannot be explained by the attraction of the former. See, especially, Rodrik, "The 'Paradoxes' of the Successful State," pp. 421–422. See also Mason et al., *The Economic and Social Modernization of the Republic of Korea*, pp. 134, 266.

56. This strategic relocation to neighboring countries and the use of the latter as export platforms came to be rationalized by Japanese scholars and politicians

as the "flying geese" theory of development, which bears some resemblance to Raymond Vernon's well-known product-cycle theory. In the flying geese theory, the establishment of export processing in backward countries was supposed to be the first step toward mature industrialization for those countries, as they rode the coattails of the more developed country into export markets. Although I do agree with the importance of Japan as an initial conduit to export markets, this should not be taken as an endorsement of the theory just alluded to. In particular, my account stresses the contingency of the ultimate outcome, which turns crucially on the presence of a state with sufficient capacity and autonomy to discipline capital — local, but also international. In the absence of such a state, there is no reason to assume that the requisite transfer of technology, productivity, and investment patterns will be generated. Export-orientation on its own can just as well lead to enclave economies, wildly uneven development, and financial fragility. For recent criticisms of the "flying geese" theory in the East Asian context, see Martin Hart-Landsberg and Paul Burkett, "Contradictions of Capitalist Industrialization in East Asia: A Critique of 'Flying Geese' Theories of Development," *Economic Geography* 74, no. 2 (April 1998): 87–110; more generally, see Michael Mortimore, "Flying Geese or Sitting Ducks? Transnationals and Industry in Developing Countries," *CEPAL Review* 51 (December 1993): 15–34.

57. The most notable exception to this is the fine work by Robert Castley, *Korea's Economic Miracle: The Crucial Role of Japan* (London: Macmillan, 1997), to which I am greatly indebted. But, more recently, John Lie has also drawn attention to the importance of the Japanese as a conduit to U.S. markets. Though he does not spend a great deal of time examining its significance for the rise of the developmental state, Lie's analysis is, in important respects, quite close to the one developed here. See Lie, *Han Unbound*, esp. pp. 86, 129.

58. Sanjaya Lall, "Marketing Barriers"; Castley, *Korea's Economic Miracle.*

59. Gary Gereffi has analyzed markets for such goods as "buyer-driven" commodity chains, as against "producer-driven" chains, exemplified most clearly by the automobile industry. See Gereffi, "Global Comodity Chains," pp. 427–429; and Gary Gereffi, "Commodity Chains and Regional Divisions."

60. MacArthur to Secretary of State, 12/10/60, 494.95B41/12–1060; see also his telegrams of 1/2/61 and 1/24/61, in 494.95B41/1–261 and 494.95B41/1–2461, respectively, all in RG 59, DSR.

61. McConnaughy to Secretary of State, 1/26/61, 494.95B41/1–2661, RG 59, DSR.

62. Reischauer to Secretary of State, 11/20/61, 895B.05194/11–2061, RG 59, DSR; Berger to Secretary of State, 12/13/61, 895B.05194/12–1361, RG 59, DSR. Note that Park's assent suggests he was already committed to normalization jut a few months after taking power, although it took another four years to achieve it. More on this below.

63. Reischauer to Secretary of State, 494.95B41/12–1361, RG 59, DSR; Reischauer to SS, 494.95B41/2–1662, RG 59, DSR.

64. Reischauer to SS, 895B.05194/3–2662, RG 59, DSR; Reischauer to SS, 895B.05194/2–2162, RG 59, DSR.

65. *Oriental Economist* (March 1963): 146–149.

66. *Biweekly Economic Review* #9, 5/4/64, E2–2, KOR S, Box# 735, Subject Numeric Files, 1964–1966, RG 59, DSR.

67. *FEER*, 1/3/63, p. 11; "Textile Industry Report," 6/13/65, INCO-FIBERS, KOR S, Box #1141, Subject-Numeric Files, 1964–1966, RG 59, DSR.

68. Pappeno to Department of State, 4/23/62, 895B.00/4–2362.

69. Berger to Secretary of State, 1/2/63, 394.41/1–263, RG 59, DSR.

70. Reischauer to Department of State, 2/21/62, 895B.05194/2–2162, RG 59, DSR.

71. Quick to Department of State, 5/23/62, 895B.35/5–2362, RG 59, DSR.

72. *Quarterly Economic Summary (July–September)*, 1964, E2–3 KOR S, Box #735, Subject-Numeric Files, 1964–1966, RG 59, DSR.

73. "Textile Industry Report," 6/13/65, INCO-FIBRES, KOR S, Box #1141, Subject-Numeric Files, 1964–1966, RG 59, DSR.

74. *Quarterly Economic Summary*, 8/17/64, E2–3, KOR S, Box #735, Subject Numeric Files, 1964–1966, RG 59, DSR.

75. Byoung Doo Lee, "The Politics of Industrialization: The Textiles Industry in South Korea and the Philippines" (Ph.D. dissertation, Northwestern University, 1990), p. 353; see also Castley, *Korea's Economic Miracle*, pp. 235–36.

76. Castley, *Korea's Economic Miracle*, Table 8.25, p. 241.

77. Byoung Doo Lee, "The Politics of Industrialization," pp. 293–296, 307–308.

78. Barbara Stallings conjectured on the likely importance of foreign capital for Korean export success, particularly of the availability of marketing facilities, in "The Role of Foreign Capital in Economic Development," Gereffi and Wyman, *Manufacturing Miracles*, p. 76. In a perceptive passage, she notes that while U.S. advisers may have been important in applying pressure for a turn toward exports, "it was clear that foreign capital had to participate *in order to make it a success*" (ibid.; emphasis added). This distinction between *proposing* a strategy and *sustaining* it over time is typically elided by statists.

79. Other commentators have drawn attention to the importance of the Normalization Treaty of 1965; see Woo, *Race to the Swift*; Hart-Landsberg, *The Rush to Development*; Haggard, *Pathways from the Periphery*; and Haggard, Kim, and Moon, "The Transition to Export-Led Growth." But in these accounts the treaty is seen as a means of securing development loans from Japan, which eased the financial burden on the state, especially since the United States was scaling down its loan commitments. The treaty's consequences for trade are noted, but not emphasized, and its link to the growing ties between the business classes from the two countries is rarely even noted. That said, I should mention that it is not clear how important Haggard regards the treaty, even on his more limited grounds. While he gives it some prominence for export success in his *Pathways from the Periphery*, it recedes in importance in Haggard, Kim, and Moon's "Transition to Export-Led Growth." Similarly, although Woo includes the business pressure for the treaty in her account of the early Park years, the significance she attaches to it is not clear. As mentioned earlier, the works of Castley and Lie are closest to the analysis presented here.

80. In Young Kim, "The Political Economy of a Chaebol's Capital Accumulation in South Korea: The Case of Samsung, 1938–1987" (Ph.D. dissertation, University of Hawaii, 1996), pp. 209–210. Chol, like Park himself, had been educated in Japan (ibid., 205–207).

81. Kwan Bong Kim, *The Korea-Japan Treaty Crisis and the Instability of the*

Korean Political System (New York: Praeger, 1971), pp. 87–90. See also Haggard, *Pathways from the Periphery*, pp. 73–74.

82. Kim, *The Korea-Japan Treaty Crisis*, p. 88.

83. Woo, *Race to the Swift*, p. 86.

84. Castley, *Korea's Economic Miracle*, p. 136.

85. Ibid., p. 137.

86. Ibid., pp. 140–141.

87. Chung H. Lee, "United States and Japanese Direct Investment in Korea: A Comparative Study," Hitotsubashi Journal of Economics 20, no. 2 (February 1980): 39. This article is an excellent study of the Japanese connection during Park's rule.

88. Ibid., p. 33.

89. Castley, *Korea's Economic Miracle*, p. 143.

90. Ibid., p. 144. But see also 141–145. The importance of trading companies for access to markets is also pointed out in Mason et al., *The Economic and Social Modernization of the Republic of Korea*, p. 139.

91. Gereffi, "Global Comodity Chains," pp. 427–429; Gereffi, "Commodity Chains and Regional Divisions."

92. Castley, *Korea's Economic Miracle*, 119–130.

93. Pappano to Dept. of State, 5/31/62, 895B.00/5–3162, RG 59, DSR.

94. *Biweekly Economic Report*, #9, 9/18/64, E2–2 KOR S, Box #735, Subject-Numeric Files 1964–1966, RG 59, DSR.

95. Doherty to Dept. of State, 4/10/62, 494.95B41/4–1062, RG 59, DSR

96. *Quarterly Economic Summary*, 12/17/64, E 2–3 KOR S, Box #735, Subject-Numeric Files 1964–1966, RG 59, DSR.

97. Gilbert T. Brown, *Korean Pricing Policies and Economic Development in the 1960s* (Baltimore, Md.: The Johns Hopkins University Press, 1973), p. 143; Haggard, Kim, and Moon, "The Transition to Export-Led Growth," p. 865.

98. Yung Whee Rhee, Bruce Ross Larson, and Gary Pursell, *Korea's Competitive Edge: Managing Entry into World Markets* (Baltimore, Md.: The Johns Hopkins University Press, 1984), pp. 29–31; Brown, *Korean Pricing Policies*, p. 145.

99. Clifford, *Troubled Tiger*, p.63.

100. Brown, *Korean Pricing Policies*, p. 145.

101. There is no a priori answer to what this stage is. It has to be discovered through careful comparative analysis. I am certain that states can impose themselves on business classes up to a certain point of the latter's growth—after which their strategic position in the economy makes such ambitions exceedingly difficult. My guess is that Taiwan was probably a case in which the arguments statists make about Korea—arguments about state dominance—may, in fact, hold.

CHAPTER 4
PRECURSORS TO PLANNING IN INDIA:
THE MYTH OF THE DEVELOPMENTAL BOURGEOISIE

1. For samples, see B. R. Tomlinson, *The Economy of Modern India, 1860–1970* (New York: Cambridge University Press, 1993), p. 166; A. H. Hanson,

The Process of Planning: A Study of India's Five-Year Plans (London: Oxford University Press, 1966), pp. 41–44; Dalip Swamy, *The Political Economy of Indian Development* (New Delhi: Sage, 1994), p. 45; Sumit Sarkar, *Modern India: 1870–1947* (Delhi: Macmillan, 1983), pp. 407–408. National historians hold the document in particular esteem. See Rajat Ray, *Industrialization in India: Growth and Conflict in the Private Corporate Sector, 1900–1947* (Delhi: Oxford University Press, 1982), pp. 332–338; and Aditya Mukherjee, "The Indian Capitalist Class and Congress on National Planning and the Public Sector, 1930–1947," *Economic and Political Weekly*, September 2, 1978, passim.

2. Ray, *Industrialization in India*, p. 334.

3. Ibid. p. 337–338.

4. Marathe, *Regulation and Development*, p. 28.

5. The story behind the passing of the act and its provisions is ably summarized in Sarkar, *Modern India*, chap. 6. Despite the space opened to popularly elected government, the center would still wield considerable influence through its control over state finance and through the power of provincial governors, who were directly answerable to Delhi.

6. For the most extensive account of the debate within Congress, see Shashi Joshi and Bhagwan Josh, *The Struggle for Hegemony in India, 1920–47: The Colonial State, the Left, and the National Movement* (Delhi: Sage, 1992), vol. 2, chap. 7.

7. Sarkar, *Modern India*, p. 350.

8. A detailed account of the formation and fortunes of the National Planning Committee can be found in Chattopadhyay, "The Idea of Planning in India."

9. The membership consisted of *four businessmen* (A. D. Shroff, Purshotamdas Thakurdas, Walchand Hirachand, and Ambalal Sarabhai); *seven intellectuals* (Meghnad Saha, A. K. Saha, Nazir Ahmad, V. S. Dubey, J. C. Ghosh, Radhakamal Mukherjee, and K. T. Shah); *one labor leader* (N. M Joshi); *one "Gandhian"* (J. C. Kumarappa); and *one businessman/politician* (M. Visvesvaraya). Actually the functional presence of business within the NPC was greater than this list suggests. Once the actual work began, a large number of subcommittees were created to develop sectorally specific proposals. On these latter bodies, the business presence increased radically as new members were brought in on an ad-hoc basis.

10. The disagreements between the members were probably made more severe because of their realization that the plans being devised were really more of a template for future, and not present, policy. It would have been difficult for the provincial ministries to install meaningful planning while control over their pursestrings remained in the hands of the Viceroy in Delhi. Indeed, Nehru had made the forward-looking orientation explicit in an early circular to the NPC, in which he enjoined the members to proceed on the assumption that the plans would be implemented by a sovereign state. This clearly suggested that what was at stake was the direction of future, and not just present, policy. See Nehru's "Note circulated to members of the National Planning Committee," June 4, 1939, JNSW, ser. 1, vol. 9.

11. Chattopadhyay, "The Idea of Planning in India," p. 115.

12. For a list of what came under the designation of "key industries," see

ibid., chap. 3 n. 136. It included such items as machine tools, chemicals, heavy engineering, shipbuilding, and so on

13. See, in particular, National Planning Committee, *Report of the Sub-Committee on Industrial Finance* (Delhi: Government of India, 1948); and National Planning Committee, *Report of the Sub-Committee on Public Finance* (Delhi: Government of India, 1949). The exception to this trend was the *Report of the Sub-Committee on Manufacturing Industries* (Delhi: Government of India, 1948), which came out in favor of heavy state regulation of industry, despite the fact that it was chaired by Ambalal Sarabhai, a prominent industrialist.

14. Chattopadhyay, "The Idea of Planning in India," p. 116.

15. Ibid., 119–120.

16. Ibid., 124–127.

17. Ibid., p. 120.

18. Claude Markovits, *Indian Business and Nationalist Politics, 1931–1939: The Indigenous Capitalist Class and the Rise of the Congress Party* (Cambridge: Cambridge University Press, 1985), p. 170.

19. W. H. Lewis (Governor of Orissa) to Viceroy Linlithgow, November 14, 1942 (Document #8) in QIMBSD, vol. 2. The Birlas had tried to obtain permission earlier, but the government, although willing to give them permission, was not amenable to the extremely generous conditions they requested.

20. Markovits, *Indian Business and Nationalist Politics*, pp. 151–171.

21. Johannes H. Voigt, *India in the Second World War* (New Delhi: Arnold-Heinemann, 1987), pp. 107–111.

22. For a standard account of the movement's course, see Sarkar, *Modern India*, pp. 388–405.

23. Ibid., pp. 395–397.

24. Ibid., pp. 394–398. The ebb in working-class participation should not come as a surprise, considering that the most powerful union federation in the country, the All-India Trade Union Congress, was heavily Communist. And the Communist Party had, since Hitler's invasion of the Soviet Union in 1941, been averse to any disruption of the war effort. Indeed, the extend of labor participation is something of a surprise, as it had to go against the advice of its leadership.

25. Pandey, introduction to *The Indian Nation in 1942*, (ed.) Gyan Panday (Calcutta: K. P. Bagchi, 1988), p. 5. Gandhi himself, it seems, had had no intention of spending his time in prison while the movement progressed. His arrest on August 9 seems to have taken him by surprise; indeed, it seems that Birla caught wind of the impending arrest and passed the information on to Gandhi the night before the event. But Gandhi refused to believe it, expecting that no arrest would be forthcoming until he had had a chance to write to the Viceroy. Hence, at least for the initial stages of the movement, Gandhi had expected to remain at large. See Secret Letter from C.I.D. Bombay to Deputy Director Intelligence Bureau, Home Department, New Delhi, dated September 9, 1942 (Appendix #5) in QIMSBD, vol. 2.

26. Ibid. See also I. Kamtekar, "The End of the Colonial State in India" (Ph.D. dissertation, Cambridge University, 1988), pp. 26–27. Note that this goes against the grain of the established historiography of the movement, which

shares the view of the colonial authorities that it was largely a Congress conspiracy throughout.

27. Sarkar, *Modern India*, pp. 394–398.

28. Viceroy's Circular Letter to all Provincial Governors, November 2, 1942 (Document #2) in QUIMSBD, vol. 2. See also letter from the Resident for States of Western India to Secretary to the Crown Representative, August 20, 1942 (Appendix II) in ibid. This suspicion seems to have been fueled by initial reports from the provinces, most of it secondhand. See Intelligence Report, August 17, 1942 (Document #10) in QIMBSD, vol. 1.; Intelligence Report, September 17, 1942 (Document #9) , QUIMSBD, vol. 2.

29. "Summary of Information Regarding Congress and Big Business Generally," n.d. (probably spring 1943) (Document #21), in ibid.

30. Bihar Governor to Viceroy, February 1, 1942 (Document #14), in ibid.

31. "Congress and 'Big Business,'" note by Intelligence Department, May 18, 1943 (Document #22) in ibid. This note summarized the information collected by the colonial authorities on business support for Quit India. For more testimony about the capitalist attitude toward the movement, see also U. P. Governor to Viceroy, November 9, 1942 (Document #6); Orissa Governnor to Viceroy, November 14, 1942 (Document #8); Orissa Governor to Viceroy, November 27, 1942 (Document #12); Central Provinces Governor to Viceroy, February 26, 1943 (Document #15), all in QIMSBD, vol. 2.

32. See the press communiqué issued by the Federation of Indian Chambers of Commerce and Industry, September 13, 1942, in PT Papers, File 267. See also the letter sent by Birla, Tata, Thakurdas, and others to Personal Secretary of the Viceroy on August 5, 1942, PT Papers, File 239 part 4, NMML.

33. U. P. Governer to Viceroy, November 9, 1942 (Document #6), in ibid.

34. Shri Ram to Thakurdas, August 24, 1942, PT Papers, file 239, part 4, NMML.

35. Shri Ram to Thakurdas, August 31, 1942, ibid.

36. Thakurdas to Shri Ram, August 26, 1942, ibid.

37. Ibid. As Thakurdas wrote regarding the relations between British and Indian leaderships, "The mist of suspicion is getting deeper and darker, and no man trusts another."

38. The Hindi word for "Hooligans."

39. Shri Ram to Thakurdas, August 31, 1942, ibid. Emphasis added.

40. In late September Thakurdas wrote to Birla, "Tata spoke to me yesterday about his talk with you, and he is trying to organize a Secretariat, as he said, for the purposes discussed by you both. He asked me if I would join and I said that it is real constructive work and has my heartiest co-operation." Thakurdas does not say explicitly that the Secretariat in question refers to the one intended to work on the Bombay Plan, but it is the likely reference. Thakurdas to Birla, September 25, 1942, PT Papers, File 239 Part 4, NMML See also Tata's recollections on the importance of Birla to the initiative in Lala, *Beyond the Last Blue Mountain* (New York: Viking, 1988).

41. Proceedings of the First Meeting of the Committee on Post-War Economic Development, December 11, 1942, PT Papers, File 291, part 1, NMML.

42. General Note, enclosed in Mathai to Thakurdas, December 8, 1942, ibid.

43. Ibid.

44. Here Thakurdas added in the margin: "*into the capitalist structure*"; ibid.

45. Ibid.

46. See File 291, part 2, PT Papers, NMML.

47. Thakurdas et al., *A Plan of Economic Development for India* (1944), passim.

48. For the government's reaction, see the correspondence in File 13(2)-P/45, Finance Department, NAI.

49. Birla to Thakurdas, January 21, 1944, PT Papers, File 291, part 1, NMML

50. For the declaration by the Federation, see ibid.

51. Exceptions to this trend were exceedingly rare. For an exception among the intelligentsia, see P.S.N. Prasad, "Some Arguments in the Bombay Plan," *Indian Journal of Economics* (1945): 25–40. Outside the intellectual community, doubts were raised by labor representatives; see the remarks by V. B. Karnik, a leader of M. N. Roy's Indian Federation of Labour, at the meeting of the East India Association in July 1944, published in *The Asiatic Review* (1944). Both Prasad and Karnik raised similar points, pertaining mainly to the issue of implementation. How were the plans to be put into effect? And since they would obviously require a great degree of state control, what kind of state did they presume? Karnik pointed out the oddity of not having a discussion of distribution in a document hinging its appeal on the income effects of its recommendations. Interestingly, these two issues — state control and distribution — were the very ones taken up in the second volume published a year later. Some possible reasons for this sequencing will be addressed below.

52. See the clippings gathered in PT Papers, File 291 and File 260; in the business press, the flag for planning was carried by the *Eastern Economist*, which Birla owned. There was some movement in this direction in 1942, but, interestingly, the real barrage of articles and editorials in favor of planning started in December 1943, a month before the publication of the Bombay Plan. The magazine issued a four-part series on the necessity of planned economic development, the last installment coming out on December 31. After this, the flow of such articles in this magazine was virtually unceasing. This stands in sharp contrast to the line taken by the other major business organ of the time, *Capital*, which took a decidedly more aloof attitude toward the issue. *Capital* was much closer to the British business concerns in the country.

53. The Plan was the subject of a large number of articles in the *Indian Journal of Economics* in the years 1944–46.

54. Here, too, as with the Bombay Plan, it was the Quit India uprising that seems to have goaded the state into action. Although suggestions for designing postwar plans were already in the air before its launching, it was only after the shock of its force that London made such plans a priority. See the documents in the *Transfer of Power* series, vol. 3, chap. 7.

55. The work of these committees is ably described in Chattopadhyay, "The Idea of Planning in India," pp. 178–198.

56. The lack of progress was a source of frustration to some in London, especially to Stafford Cripps. But he was unable to prod Viceroy Linlithgow to

greater effort. On his part, Linlithgow found an able ally in Secretary of State for India Amery, who was quite skeptical about the value of London initiating development plans for India. For the scuffle between Cripps, on one side, and Amery and Linlithgow, on the other, see the *Transfer of Power* series, vol. 3, chap. 7.

57. This was facilitated by the arrival of Archibald Wavell as new the Viceroy in October 1943. Wavell appears to have had a more firm grasp of the Indian situation than did his predecessor, Linlithgow.

58. File 8(5)-P/45, Finance Department, Planning Section, NAI.

59. See the letters from Birla to Mathai in PT Papers, File 291, part 1, and Kasturbhai Lalbhai Papers, File K-135, both in NMML.

60. See the correspondence between Viceroy Wavell and Secretary of State for India in the *Transfer of Power* series, vol. 4, documents #438 (Wavell to Amery, 3/23/44) and #439 (Amery to Wavell, 3/24/44).

61. See the analysis of the colonial state's relation to Indian business and, in particular, the latter's overshadowing of British business in the final years of colonial rule, in Anna-Maria Misra, "Entrepreneurial Decline and the End of Empire: British Business in India, 1919–1949" (Ph.D. dissertation, Oxford University, 1992), chaps. 5–7.

62. "Brief Record of an informal conference with authors of *A Plan of Economic Development for India*, on Thursday, the 20th April," PT Papers, File 260, NMML.

63. Here there was a hint of discord, along lines that persisted from the time of the National Planning Committee: it was agreed that control would extend from restrictions on form, location, and degree of investment to outright state ownership. Less clear was the scope of the state ownership and the principles that would guide its extension. The Bombay planners suggested that so long as private initiative was forthcoming in any sector, investment ought to be left to private capital therein; their interlocutors pointed out that this amounted to the public being saddled with only the least remunerative fields for state enterprise. After discussion, it was decided that, apart from public utilities and defense industries, "it would not be possible or desirable to set out in advance the industries or enterprises which should be owned by Government" (see "Point #5 in ibid.); instead, it was determined that "each case should be decided on merits." This was, of course, a hopelessly unstable formula and left the state delegation in a bind: so long as the domain of state ownership was not clearly laid out, private capital could — and would, as we shall see — cavil at all exhortations to it to step up its investments, pointing out the uncertainty induced by such gaps in policy statements; but once it was actually formulated, if any such policy exceeded business perceptions of what was proper, the latter could cry foul. For the time being, however, Raisman and his colleagues took solace in the fact that the planners did not simply rule out the possibility altogether.

64. See point #8 in ibid.

65. On the decision to place Dalal in charge of the Planning Department, see Wavell to Amery, March 24, 1944 (#439), Wavell to Amery, March 29, 1944 (#447), Amery to Wavell, April 5, 1944 (#451), all in *Transfer of Power* series, vol. 4.

66. Chattopadhyay, "The Idea of Planning in India," p. 215.

67. See, for example, the following notes: "State Assistance of Industry," "Licensing of Industry," "State Ownership and Management of Industry," "Control over Industry," all in File 8(5)-P/45, Finance Department, Planning Section, NAI.

68. See the comments of Sir Theodore Gregory and Ram Chandra in "Minutes of a Meeting Held on 21 October 1944 . . .," in ibid.

69. In particular, Akbar Hydari expressed optimism in this regard; see ibid.

70. Thus Ramaswamy Mudaliar met with L. N. Birla, G. D. Birla's brother, urging him to rally the class around the efforts of the Planning Department. See the report by Birla in L. N. Birla to Thakurdas, December 29, 1944; L. N. Birla to Thakurdas, January 6, 1945, File 336, PT Papers, NMML.

71. *A Plan for the Economic Development of India, Part 2*, January 1945, Paragraphs 40–42.

72. Ibid., Paragraph 46.

73. Ibid., Paragraphs 47–48.

74. Ironically the initial draft for part 2, penned by John Mathai, had been even more elaborate and concessive in the powers it would concede to the state. But the discussion in the final product was much more condensed and fleeting. The difference between the draft and the final version was probably occasioned by the concern to avoid tilting toward state control any more than necessary. See Mathai's draft and Birla's "Note" of October 3, 1944, on the draft, in File K-135, Kasturbhai Lallbhai Papers, NMML.

75. Dalal was not one of the signatories to part 2, as he was by that time in the employ of the government.

76. *Statement of Government Industrial Policy*, Planning Department, 1945.

77. Ibid., Paragraph 2.

78. Ibid., Paragraph 3.

79. Ibid., Paragraphs 5–9.

80. Ibid., Paragraphs 10–12.

81. Ibid., Paragraph 14.

82. Emphasis added. Note that this was a step back from the position the government took in the April meeting, where it had pointed out that this would confine public investment to the least remunerative fields.

83. All three conditions are enumerated in Paragraph 7 of the *Statement*.

84. See "The Organization of Controls," February 2, 1945, and "A Functioning Directed Economy," February 9, 1945. In both, the editor, for the first time in the year he had been writing on the need for planning, explicitly mentioned the need for extensive state intervention. Until this point the magazine had stuck to the strategy of part 1 of the Plan, defending planning because of its income effects and its importance in helping industry recover after the war. To the extent that state intervention had been broached, it was kept at the most general level, and always accompanied with cautionary tales of the ineptitude of the state. It is, in fact, remarkable how closely the magazine followed Birla's own shifting positions. After Independence, when Birla turned decisively against state control, the magazine followed suit, contradicting its wartime advocacy of state control as coolly as Birla did himself.

85. Merrell to Secretary of State, February 2, 1945, 845.50/2–245, RG 59, DSR; Lane to Secretary of State, January 10, 1945, 845.50/1–1045, RG 59, DSR. Through January and February of 1945 Dalal went on tour throughout the country, meeting with businessmen in an attempt to drum up support for the recommendations of part 2 of the plan, while officials from the Planning Department were assigned the more public forums, like radio.

86. G. L. Mehta, address to the Annual Session of the Federation of Indian Chambers of Commerce and Industry, March 4, 1945, File 336, PT Papers, NMML.

87. Memorandum from the Indian Chamber of Commerce to the Secretary, Finance Department, 9/13/45, File 14 (37) P/45, Finance Department, Planning I Branch, NAI.

88. Donovan to Secretary of State, 5/15/45, Dispatch #2041, 845.60/5–1545, DSR.

89. This was the case according to Mathai, as he said in a conversation with an U.S. Embassy official; in ibid.

90. *Bombay Free Press Journal*, 4/24/45.

91. Donovan to Secretary of State, 5/15/45, Dispatch #2041, 845.60/5–1545, DSR; G. L Mehta, address to the Annual Session of the Federation of Indian Chambers of Commerce and Industry, March 4, 1945, File 336, PT Papers, NMML.

92. Misra, "Entrepreneurial Decline and the End of Empire," chaps. 5–7.

93. Michael Kidron, *Foreign Investments in India* (Oxford: Oxford University Press, 1965), p. 53.

94. Ibid., p. 54.

95. Misra, "Entrepreneurial Decline and the End of Empire," chap. 7.

96. This was also reported by U.S. consulate officials in their reports at the time. See "Conversation with Sir Chunilal B. Mehta Regarding Indian Finance," Donovan to Secretary of State, Dispatch # 3039, 845.5/8–1446, DSR.

97. Donovan to Secretary of State, 5/15/45, Dispatch #2041, 845.60/5–1545, DSR.

98. See his speeches from this period in G. D. Birla, *The Path to Prosperity* (Bombay, 1946).

99. An important exception is Michael Kidron's superb book, *Foreign Investments in India*.

100. See, for example, Aditya Mukherjee, "The Indian Capitalist Class and Congress on National Planning and the Public Sector, 1930–1947," *Economic and Political Weekly*, September 2, 1978.

CHAPTER 5
THE DEMOBILIZATION OF THE LABOR MOVEMENT

1. See Barrow, *Radical Theories of the State*. For a superb exemplification of this argument in an underdeveloped country, see Nora Hamilton, *The Limits of State Autonomy* (Princeton, N.J.: Princeton University Press, 1982).

2. Industrial peace was broken only at the end of 1950, in a massive strike in Bombay. But soon after the strike labor activity declined again to anemic levels.

3. Quoted in Chattopadhyay, "The Idea of Planning in India," p. 83.

4. Ibid., p. 82.

5. Despite this nod to state control, there was still no explicit mention of planning. Only in 1937 was the INC to openly endorse the idea of planning.

6. Though he was sympathetic, Nehru never joined the CSP.

7. It also needs to be said that it was Gandhi's patronage that kept the CSP sheltered from right-wing attacks. It is doubtful that the CSP could have survived in the Congress without Gandhi's protection.

8. Sarkar, *Modern India*, pp. 343–344.

9. For the most thorough account of this crucial episode, and especially the attempt at worker-peasant representation, see D. A. Low, *Rearguard Action: Selected Essays on Indian Colonial History* (Cambridge: Cambridge University Press, 1996), chap. 5: "Congress and 'Mass Contacts', 1936–1937."

10. This change will be explored more deeply in chapter 6.

11. Historians have just about entirely ignored the war years as a subject of study, so the contemporary researcher is forced to fall back on the works published contemporaneously with the events. Among these, see N. V. Sovani, *Post-War Inflation in India — A Survey* (Pune: Gokhale Institute of Politics and Economics, 1949).

12. Not only did merchants thrive in the black market. Industrialists, too, worked to limit supplies to the market so as to divert them to the black market. For accounts of this activity, see the various articles in the *Harijan* during this period.

13. For the most thorough analysis, see Shreekant Palekar, *Problems of Wage Policy for Economic Development* (Bombay: Asia Publishing House, 1962).

14. Ibid., p. 174.

15. For this early history, see V. B. Karnik, *Indian Trade Unions: A Survey.* (Bombay: Labour Education Service, 1960).

16. Ibid.

17. See the articles in *Capital*, one of the main organs of the business community, for 1946–47. In particular, see *Capital*, 1/10/46, p. 44; "Ditcher's Diary, 7/25/46, p. 145; "The Present Wave of Industrial Unrest," 8/1/46; and "The Steel Industry in Britain and India," 9/12/46, p. 337. The attitude to concessions is also reflected in the business criticisms of calls to shorten the working day to forty-eight hours. See the speech by Homi Mody to the Employers Federation of India in ibid., 1/3/46, p. 2.

18. Another line that business took sometimes was to concede that there may be some legitimacy to the idea that labor was in a bad way but that this notion was being distorted and illegitimately amplified by "outside elements," that is, Communists. See the speech by M. A. Master, President of the Federation of Indian Chambers of Commerce and Industry, July 9, 1947, in File 336, PT Papers, NMML.

19. Master recalls this in his speech, referred to in the previous note.

20. Interestingly the business press attributed the strike wave not to the manifest fall in real wages but rather as an attempt by a coddled and bloated work-

ing class to hold onto its wartime *gains*. In this, it appears that attention was being riveted to movements in money wages, not real wages, which, as we have seen, had fallen precipitously. For the aforementioned complaints and diagnoses, see *Capital*, "A Ditcher's Diary," 7/25/46, p. 145; and ibid., "The Present Wave of Industrial Unrest," 8/1/46. Industrial unrest, in this view, was being fomented by the worker, who, after the war, "sees his good time coming to an end." And strikes were being forced onto the country by "ignorant workers [who] continue to hug the delusion that the most effective solvent to industrial disputes is the strike" (*Capital*, 1/10/46, p. 44).

21. The forum for such interventions was Gandhi's magazine, the *Harijan*. See, for example, Desai's broadside against the owners of the textile mills in "Indian Textile Industry," January 19, 1947; three articles by J. C. Kumarappa — "Our Economic Policy," January 26, 1947; "Controls and Controls," November 7, 1948; and "Profit Sharing," November 7, 1948; and S. N. Aggarwal, "National Government's Industrial Policy," May 2, 1948.

22. See the following articles by Gandhi in the *Harijan*: "Some Labour Questions," February 17, 1946, in which Gandhi urged arbitration onto railway workers; "Capitalism and Strikes," March 31, 1946; "Sweepers Strike," March 21, 1946, in which Gandhi opposes a sweepers strike because it deprives citizens of clean streets; "Strikes," August 11, 1946, in which Gandhi opposes the postal workers strike because it should only have been resorted to after thorough consultation with the government (i.e., the workers' employer).

23. Indeed, by mid-1948 it fell to the Gandhians — led by Shankarrao Deo — to oppose the rightward swing of the Congress.

24. The resolution is reproduced in a longer document, "Labour Unrest in the Post-War Period," contained in File 26/1946, AICC Papers, NMML.

25. See the discussion in "Memorandum on present labour policy and conciliation-arbitration machinery of the U.P. Government," submitted by AITUC to the U.P. Labour Inquiry Committee, 1947, AITUC Papers, File 190, NMML. The observations made in this memorandum closely anticipate the findings in the industrial relations literature on India, such as it is.

26. See the discussion in E. A. Ramaswamy, *Power and Justice: The State in Industrial Relations* (Delhi: Oxford University Press, 1984), pp. 44–48.

27. See "Memorandum of B. T. Ranadive on the Government Proposals Regarding Trade Disputes" and "Draft Views of Com. N. M. Joshi on the Government Proposals Regarding Trade Disputes," both in File 278, AITUC Papers; "Views on the Industrial Disputes Bill," File 286, AITUC Papers, NMML.

28. See Joshi's intervention in *Constituent Assembly Debates*, February 10, 1947, pp. 380–381.

29. Ibid., pp. 442–443.

30. In particular, the bill provided that works committees in any particular plant would be set up "in consultation with" the local union. Maniben Kara moved that it be amended, so that the clause "in consultation with" could be replaced by "with the consent of." This would ensure that the union would not be undermined by a rival power center. But her motion was voted down, and the clause stood. See *Assembly Debates*, February 12, 1947, pp. 519–522.

31. Quoted in Harold Crouch, *The Indian Trade Union Movement* (Bombay:

Asia Publishing House, 1966), p. 83. In a pamphlet issued later that same month, Nanda took the high road, omitting all mention to arbitration and relying instead on the generic anti-Communism that was to become the stock of much of the Congress Left: "It is obvious that the Communists are the perpetual enemy of any established authority in this country and that they will seek to keep the country in a disturbed state in order to suit the international aims of a foreign power. . . . Whenever and wherever we associate ourselves with the Communists we incur loss or liability for ourselves. Therefore, the need for creating a separate Central Organization of Labour is immediate and imperative" (Gulzarilal Nanda, *Future of Indian Labour*, May 1947, pp. 7–8). This pamphlet can be found in File 123, Jayprakash Narayan Papers, Inst. II, NMML.

32. Pant, the Premier of the United Provinces, considered it an "urgent matter" that the Congress have a "close-knit labour organization" of its own. See G. B. Pant to Patel, September 23, 1947, Patel Papers, Reel 48, NAI. Of course, Patel needed no convincing on this, as he was one of the most implacable of the anti-Communists in the High Command.

33. Quoted in "Postwar Developments in the Indian Labor Movement," Report #5 by Office of Intelligence Research, U.S. Department of State.

34. *People's Age*, May 11, 1947, p. 6.

35. In exchange, labor was to be given significant concessions in the form of wage increases, considerable voice at the level of the shop floor, through such agencies as works committees, and even moves toward profit-sharing with management. Employers, through the business offensive discussed in the next chapter, soon scuttled almost all these concessions. Unfortunately the actual dynamics of this aspect of the postwar dispensation are beyond the purview of this book and are therefore not discussed hereafter.

36. The only exception to this was the massive strike in Bombay textile mills in the fall of 1950. Other than this, strike activity rapidly dissipated.

37. For LDCs, an outstanding book remains Nora Hamilton's study of Mexico in the 1930s: see her *Limits of State Autonomy*.

CHAPTER 6
THE BUSINESS OFFENSIVE AND THE RETREAT OF THE STATE

1. The Industries (Development and Regulation) Act was first proposed under the name of the Industries (Development and Control) Bill in 1949; the name was changed when the legislation was finally passed in 1951.

2. See the first section in chapter 4 above.

3. Purshotamdas Thakudas et al., *A Plan of Economic Development for India, Part II* (Bombay, 1944), p. 32.

4. See the memo entitled "State Assistance to Industry" by the Department of Planning and Development, in File 8(5) P/45, Planning Department, Finance Ministry, NAI.

5. *Statement of Government Industrial Policy*, New Delhi, April 1945.

6. See Chattopadhyay, "The Idea of Planning in India," pp. 255–258.

7. Ibid., 258–268.

8. The deliberations of the Advisory Planning Board are contained in File 12(12)-P1/46, Part 1, Planning I, Finance Ministry, NAI.

9. *Report of the Advisory Planning Board* (1947), p. 17. The board was disbanded soon after the publication of the *Report*.

10. *Report of the Fiscal Commission* (Delhi: Government of India, 1950).

11. The fact that firms had no reason to accept discipline does not establish that the institutionalization of the requisite instruments would have been impossible — only that they would have to be established over the resistance of the business class. But in the absence of the mobilized labor movement, the state's autonomy to impose this on domestic capital was drastically reduced.

12. Apart from Nehru, the committee included Jayprakash Narayan, Maulana Azad, Shankarrao Deo, Achyut Patwardhan, N. G. Ranga, Gulzarilal Nanda, and J. C. Kumarappa. For the proceedings and draft documents, see File ED-7, Parts 1 and 2/1947–48, All-India Congress Committee Papers, First Inst., NMML.

13. See the section on Industry in the *Report*, File ED-7, Part 1/1947–48, AICC Papers, NMML. The section was drafted by a subcommittee consisting of Jayprakash Narayan, Shankarrao Deo, Gulzarilal Nanda, and, interestingly, John Mathai, who had been recruited on an ad-hoc basis.

14. The primary change in this regard was Nehru's declaration that the government wing of the party — those of its members who were in the Cabinet — would not be directly accountable to the party leadership. This issue crystallized in a conflagration between Nehru and J. B Kripalani, the Congress Party president. Kripalani, a stalwart of the Congress Left, insisted that the Congress members in the Cabinet work in tandem with the party organization when formulating policy, since the party was the link to the government's base. Nehru strenuously objected, demanding independence from the direct hold by the party. Not surprisingly, Nehru won, and, in protest, Kripalani resigned as party president in late 1947. This outcome represented a dramatic increase in the Congress government representatives' independence from party control and hence, indirectly, from popular pressure. For an account of the confrontation between Nehru and Kripalani, see Stanley Kochanek, *The Congress Party of India: The Dynamics of One-Party Democracy* (Princeton, N.J.: Princeton University Press, 1968), chap. 1.

15. H. P. Mody to M. A. Master, January 28, 1948, File 1060, M.A. Master Papers, NMML; statement by the Indian Merchants Chamber, February 13, 1948, in File 1138, IMC Papers, NMML. Mody organized a meeting of major industrialists in Bombay on January 30, who also released a statement denouncing the document, which can be found in ibid.

16. The trigger for the exit was a canny move by Patel, who proposed a resolution in early 1948 that made it illegal for organized groups to remain within the Congress Party. As the Congress Socialists were the only such group, this was an obvious invitation to leave, which the group obligingly accepted. However, Patel's move was not a basic cause of the split; the growing disenchantment in the group with the Congress's rightward slide was likely to have occasioned a split sooner rather than later. Narayan, in his speech at Poona on

November 27, 1947, announced that the Socialists would constitute an opposition party to Congress. See also Macdonald to Secretary of State, 10/7/47, #523, 845.00/10–747, DSR, USNA; the comments by Jayprakash Narayan to embassy officers in Donovan to Secretary of State, #277, 845.00/10–2047, DSR.

17. The conviction that Patel, not Nehru, was the power in the Congress leadership is virtually universal among their contemporaries. See the transcripts of the oral interviews with A. P. Jain, H. K. Mahtab, Jayprakash Narayan, and others, in NMML. See also Philips Talbot to Walter Rogers, April 22, 1947, H. V. Johnson Papers, Box 5, India File, Harry S. Truman Library, Independence, Missouri, where Talbot lists the sources of Patel's power; and the remarks of K. M. Munshi reported in Donovan to Secretary of State, #293, 10/28/47, 845.00/10–2847, DSR. Munshi, a member of the Legislative Assembly of Bombay and later a central cabinet minister, was of the view that Nehru could not even survive as prime minister without Patel's willingness to mobilize the Congress machinery on his behalf.

18. A copy of the *Industrial Policy Statement* can be found in *India Information*, May 15, 1948.

19. See Chattopadhyay, "The Idea of Planning in India," pp. 300–301.

20. *Industrial Policy Statement*.

21. Ibid., Paragraph 2. These were coal, iron and steel, aircraft manufacture, shipbuilding, telephone and telegraph services, and mineral oils.

22. Ibid.

23. Ibid.

24. Speech by G. D. Birla at the Fifth Ordinary General Meeting of the United Commercial Bank, April 22, 1948, contained in Despatch #255, 845.516/5–448, 5/4/48, DSR.

25. Quoted in Kidron, *Foreign Investments in India*, p. 86.

26. Nehru's assurances had started much earlier. In early 1948, before the *IPS* was released, Nehru led the charge against a proposed resolution in Parliament endorsing a socialist path for Indian development. Central to his reply was an argument against nationalization and the disruption it was likely to cause. See *Constituent Assembly (Legislative) Debates*, February 17, 1948. Nehru's public position now became one urging that existing industry be left alone and that future industry be reserved for the state. See also his speech to the Federation of Indian Chambers of Commerce and Industry on March 28, 1948, in *JNSW*, 2nd series, vol. 5, and his speech to the Central Advisory Council on Industry, January 24, 1949, in ibid., vol. 9. This apparently was the reasoning behind the wording of the *IPS* with regard to the second category of industries, that is, the one in which existing firms would be allowed to expand but future investment would be the state's prerogative. But here, too, as we saw, a loophole was left to allow private capital to come in when deemed appropriate.

27. *Capital*, 12/22/49, p. 11.

28. "Indian Parliament and the Future of Industry," *Capital*, 4/15/48.

29. The significance of the *IPS* as a barometer for the party/government tussle was astutely realized by the American officials in Delhi. See the excellent reporting in Macdonald to Secretary of State, #292, 5/10/48, 845.60/5–1048, DSR. Mac-

donald observed that, although the *IPS* still carried some trappings of radicalism, this was mainly an attempt by Nehru to keep the Gandhians and the remnants of the Left onboard. The thrust of the *IPS*, however, bore the imprint of the business offensive and reflected the constraints this imposed on the state: "Nehru . . . being at the head of a government, has felt the full pressure of such necessities as increasing production from an established and going industrial organization. . . The Congress ideologists do not feel these pressures in the same way since they do not have to contend with the industrial community or with the day-to-day necessities of production." It is hard to imagine a better statement on the different structurally defined interests of the party and the state!

30. See above, chapter 4.

31. For the continuity between the two statements, see Marathe, *Regulation and Development*, pp. 41–45. Raghabendra Chattopadhyay has argued that, in some ways, the 1948 statement was far more timid than its colonial predecessor of 1945. See Chattopadhyay, "The Idea of Planning in India," pp. 298–300.

32. See the report on the meetings of the Development and Priorities Sub-committee of the reconstituted NPC, 10/3/45 and 10/12/45, File 11, M. O. Mathai Papers, NMML.

33. Chattopadhyay, "The Idea of Planning in India," p. 120.

34. The initial draft was prepared by S. Bhoothalingam, Joint Secretary in the Industry Ministry. See File I(4)/1(9)/48, Department of Industrial Policy and Promotion (DIPP), Industry Ministry. Bhoothalingam set to work on the draft by late June 1948.

35. See the note, "Legislation for the regulation of certain industries by the Central government" by Bhoothalingam, in ibid.

36. Reference to the Korean use of industrial licensing can be found in Amsden, *Asia's Next Giant*, pp. 14, 73, 103, 133.

37. Amsden noted in 1989 that, despite its extensive use, there was no detailed study of the industrial licensing procedure in Korea (ibid., p. 133 n. 17). Myong-hon Kang, in *The Korean Business Conglomerate: Chaebol Then and Now* (Berkeley: Institute of East Asian Studies, 1996), p. 40, maintains that licensing was, along with credit policy, one of the two main forms of control over capital. See also Jong-chan Rhee, *The State and Industry in Korea: The Limits of the Authoritarian State* (London: Routledge, 1994), pp. 64, 80, 81, for its use in the Heavy and Chemical Industrialization drive.

38. However, it should be noted that, by the 1960s, business dependence on bank credit had greatly increased.

39. This title was later changed to the Industrial (Development and Regulation) Act when it was finally passed in 1951.

40. I have used the copy of the bill published in the *Hindustan Times*, March 24, 1949. See Clauses 5, 6, 7, 10, 12, and 15.

41. Ibid., Clause 7, section 2.

42. Ibid., Clause 9.

43. It met before the IDR bill was enacted because its appointment had already been called for by the *Industrial Policy Statement* of April 1948.

44. K. D. Jalan to S. P. Mookerjee (Industry Minister), 5/24/49, in File 1063, M. A. Master Papers, NMML.

45. Business had been in favor of this change since the 1930s. For samples of such support, see text of the Quarterly Meeting of the All-India Manufacturers Association, May 8, 1949, Resolution 1 (Central Control and Regulation of Industries); memorandum from the U.P. Chamber of Commerce to Secretary, Ministry of Industry and Supply, July 18, 1949, both in File 1(4)–1(44)/49, Industrial Policy and Promotion Department, Industry Ministry, Udyog Bhavan, New Delhi.

46. See the letter from G. D. Birla to Industry Minister Mookerjee, April 18, 1949, in File 1063, M. A. Master Papers, NMML. See also the record of the meeting on August 5, 1949, between FICCI representatives and the Select Committee, in File 1065, ibid.

47. See the plea for postponing the passage of the bill, contained in a letter of April 2, 1949, from K. D. Jalan, President of FICCI, to Finance Minister John Mathai, File 1(4)–1(44)/49, Records of the Industry Ministry, Udyog Bhavan, New Delhi.

48. This can be surmised from an examination of the papers of the IMC held in NMML, which contain elaborate correspondence with various other organizations.

49. This was conveyed by G. D. Birla to a U.S. Embassy officer, for which see "Conversation with Mr. G. D. Birla," Despatch #859, 10/3/49, 845.5151/10–349, RG 59, DSR.; see also the comments made by S. Bhoothalingam, also underscoring the governments openness to modification, in Despatch A-698, 7/16/49, 845.60/7–1649, RG 59, DSR.

50. The Industry Minister Shyama Prasad Mookerjee assured Loy Henderson, the American ambassador, that he was doing everything in his power to make the bill more acceptable to both domestic and foreign business, but was constrained by having to avoid appearing like the government had capitulated to business pressure. He asked Henderson to explain the situation quietly to "leading American firms in India like General Motors, Firestone, etc." See Henderson to Department of State, #1157, 12/19/49, 845.60/12–1949, DSR.

51. Cf. Tulsidas Kilachand's intervention as reported in the FICCI Circular, "Report regarding the meeting of the Federation's representatives with the Select Committee on August 5, 1949," File 1065, M. A. Master Papers, NMML; memorandum from G. L. Bansal, Secretary of FICCI, to Syama Prasad Mookerjee, 9/26/49, in File 1(4)–1(57)/49, Industrial Policy and Promotion Department, Industry Ministry.

52. "Comments of Shri B. M. Birla on the Industries (Development and Control) Bill," FICCI Circular, File 1063, M. A. Master Papers, NMML.

53. Circular, "Report regarding the meeting of the Federation's representatives with the Select Committee on August 5, 1949," File 1065, M. A. Master Papers, NMML.

54. Ibid.

55. Ibid.

56. Ibid.

57. "Comments of Lala Shri Ram on the Industries (Development and Control) Bill, 1949," FICCI Circular, August 27, 1949, File 1063, M. A. Master Papers, NMML.

58. G. L. Bansal, Secretary to the Federation of Indian Chambers of Commerce and Industry, to Syama Prasad Mookerjee, 9/26/49, File I(4)–1(57)/49, Industrial Policy and Promotion Department, Industry Ministry. See remarks on Clauses 5, 6, 7, and 8.

59. These would be Coal, Iron and Steel, Aircraft Manufacture, Shipbuilding, manufacture of telephones and related equipment, and Mineral Oils. See ibid., remarks on Clause 3.

60. Presumably because the council was to be appointed by the state. See ibid., remarks on Clause 9.

61. Ibid., Clause 9.

62. "The [Industries] Development Board should be the main executive of the Government of India in administering the various provisions of the Bill" (ibid.).

63. The only restriction that the memo was willing to countenance was that, in cases where the state deemed it necessary, new undertakings in the six industries could be prohibited "for a period not exceeding 12 months at a time" (ibid., Clause 6). Hence, even where applicable, state regulation of investment flows was to be strictly temporary.

64. Interestingly, this was not the most strident position coming out of the Federation. In the meetings leading up to the drafting of the memo, B. M. Birla proposed to do away with the idea of a board as well as to rescind all powers to license investment. Industrial policy would be confined to the registration of all undertakings, the collection of statistics, and temporary power to restrict the entry of capital into sectors with over-capacity (Clause 6). It was a more moderate position, which Lala Shri Ram presented, that allowed for the formation of a board at all. The final memo was a compromise between the Birla and Shri Ram lines. See the memos by Birla and Shri Ram in File 1063, M.A. Master Papers, NMML.

65. For a lucid theoretical discussion of these two dimensions of capitalist power, see Erik Wright, "Class and Politics," in his *Interrogating Inequality: Essays on Class Analysis, Socialism, and Marxism*, chap. 5 (London: Verso, 1994).

66. See H. Venkatasubbiah, *The Indian Economy since Independence* (Bombay: Asia Publishing House, 1961).

67. The occasion for the strike was the first budget of the new government, which came in the spring of 1947 and which capital found wholly unacceptable. As T. Shone relayed to the India Office, "an early result [of the budget] has been the decision of some leading firms to abandon proposals for fresh developments which were under consideration" (T. Shone to N. Brook, April 23, 1947 [#204], TOP, vol. 10).

68. See "Many Industrial Plans Abandoned," *Times of India*, April 11, 1947; "Market Slump," *Indian News Chronicle*, June 25, 1948; "Sentiment of the Bombay Business Community at the Beginning of 1949," Dispatch #5, 1/5/49, 845.5017/1–549, RG 59, DSR, John J. Macdonald to Secretary of State, April 14, 1947, 845.60/4–1447, RG 59, DSR; Macdonald to Secretary of State, September 6, 1947, 845.6511/9–647, RG59, DSR; Speech by D.M. Khatau, President of the Bombay Millowners Association at the Annual General Meeting, May 16, 1947, in Dispatch #204, 845.60/5–2647, RG 59, DSR; E. A. Gilmore

to Secretary of State, "Memorandum of Conversation with B. L. Jalan, President, Marwari Chamber of Commerce," December 5, 1947, 845.00/12–847, RG 59, DSR.

69. Statement of Jagjivandas Dosabhai to the IMC on March 4, 1947, File 67, IMC Papers, NMML.

70. Secretary, Madras Chamber of Commerce to Percival Groffiths, April 9, 1949, Enclosure 2 in Despatch #83, 4/16/49, 845.60/4–1649, DSR; emphasis added.

71. K. D. Jalan (FICCI President), to John Mathai, April 2, 1949, File I(4)–1(44)/49, Industrial Policy and Promotion Department, Industry Ministry.

72. The U.P. Chamber of Commerce to Industry Ministry, July 18, 1949, File 1(4)–1(44)/49, Industrial Policy and Promotion Department, Industry Ministry.

73. Hence, in his recommendation of talking points made to the Industry Ministry in a meeting in January 1949, the vice president of the All-India Manufacturers Association listed the following as the very first imperative: "The Need for Inspiring Confidence among Industrialists and Investors in the Industrial Future." See also "Memorandum to Members of the Central Advisory Council of Industries," File 181, Walchand Hirachand Papers, NMML, New Delhi.

74. See, for example, the document produced by the Industry Ministry in mid-1949, "Suggestions for the Formulation of a Short-Term Economic Policy by the Government of India," contained in Dispatch #365, 5/2/49, 845.50/5–249, RG 59, DSR.

75. For a brief analysis of the 1947 budget and its modification, see Raghabendra Chattopadhyay, "Liaquat Ali Khan's Budget of 1947–48: The Tryst with Destiny," *Social Scientist* (June/July 1988): 77–89.

76. See Kochanek, *The Congress Party of India*, pp. 138–145.

77. See, for example, his letter to K. T. Shah, May 13, 1939, JNSW, ser. 1, vol. 9.

78. Nehru to B. C. Roy, 8/2/48, JNSW, 2nd series, vol. 7.

79. Speaking to business representatives at a meeting in early 1949, Nehru pleaded that "this business of capital being sullen will not do great credit to the holders of capital" (Speech to the Central Advisory Council for Industries, 1/24/49, JNSW, 2nd series, vol. 10; later that year, at a FICCI annual meeting, Nehru sarcastically complained in a speech that "[our industrialists] are frightfully delicate persons and if any wrong word is said or some speech is delivered, their temperature goes up" (Speech to FICCI, 3/4/49, ibid.).

80. Nehru to John Mathai. 2/16/50, JNSW, 2nd series, vol. 14, part 1.

81. Note to Cabinet, 6/18/49, File 15(40)ECC/49, Records of the Economic Committee of the Cabinet, Cabinet Secretariat, National Archives of India, New Delhi; emphasis added.

82. The matter was handed over to the business-dominated Central Advisory Council for Industries, which did not meet for another five months and which dutifully reported that there was nothing to be concerned about. See the correspondence in File 15(111)P/49, Records of the Economic Committee of the Cabinet, Cabinet Secretariat, National Archives of India, New Delhi.

83. G. D. Birla to V. Shankar, 4/18/49, Reel 11, Patel Papers, NAI. V. Shankar was Patel's personal secretary. Much of this correspondence between Birla and Patel went throughShankar.

84. Birla to Patel, 5/5/49; Birla to John Mathai (Copy to Patel), 5/12/49 and 5/17/49; Birla to Mathai (Copy to Patel), 7/18/49, all in Reel 11, Patel Papers, NAI. Much of this anxiety in the letters was also directed to the ongoing income-tax investigations against businessmen.

85. Patel to Birla, 5/13/49, ibid.

86. Shankar to Birla, 7/4/49, ibid.

87. Ibid.

88. Stanley Kochanek's *Congress Party of India* is still the best analysis of the internal configuration of power.

89. See above, chapter 4.

90. Venkatsubbiah, *The Indian Economy since Independence*.

91. The most important source of capital imports to India was still the United Kingdom. In late 1945 the director of the British Chemical Plant Manufacturers' Association surveyed India's capital needs and informed prospective buyers that British suppliers had such a backlog of orders that importing from them was not a realistic option in the near future. See *Capital*, 11/29/45, p. 740.

92. Venkatsubbiah, *The Indian Economy since Independence*.

93. For coal, see *Capital*, 2/14/46, 3/14/46, and 3/6/47; for the chemicals, machine tools, and steel industries, see the minutes to the meetings of the Sub-Committees of the CACI in 1949, in File 188, Walchand Hirachand Papers, NMML.

94. Immediately after the war, G. D. Birla called for economic planning as a means for increasing the Indian market for automobiles! See the report on his speech on All-India Radio in *Capital*, 12/6/45.

95. Thus *Capital* endorsed the Indian Coalfield Committee's Report, quoting favorably that to ensure an orderly growth of the industry, "the responsibility . . . must rest with the state and that can be achieved only with an orderly plan" (*Capital*, 1/30/47, p. 168).

96. Witness *Capital*'s praise of the *Report of the Advisory Planning Board*, "Super-Plan for Indian Development," in the issue dated 2/13/47.

97. "Development Plans of Government," released by K. D. Jalan on 1/15/50, in File 70, IMC Papers, NMML. See also the commentary on the paper by *Commerce and Industry*, 1/25/50, which endorses the Federation's call for a more planned approach to development.

98. See the *Report of the Advisory Planning Board* (1947), pp. 14–15.

99. See his "Notes," particularly "Machinery for Planning," and the shorter "Note on the Future Machinery for Planning," in 12(12)-PI/46, part 1, Finance Department, Planning Division, NAI. Shah, it should be mentioned, was on four of the five subcommittees appointed by the APB to draft its report.

100. The relevant section in the *Report* is Section IV, which is taken from the shorter or Shah's two notes, namely, "Note on the Future Machinery for Planning," in 12(12)-PI/46, part 1, Finance Department, Planning Division, NAI.

101. *Report of the Advisory Planning Board* (1947), p. 24, Paragraph 87.

102. Nanda, "Note to the Working Committee," 1/19/50, quoted in Kochankek, *The Congress Party of India*, p. 142.

103. See his comments to a U.S. Embassy officer in the spring of 1950, where he reiterated this belief; Timberlake to Department of State, #366, 4/1/50, 791.00/4–150, DSR.

104. The Economic Committee of the Cabinet (ECC) was formed in late 1947. The ministries it included were Commerce; Industry; Works, Mines, and Power; Transport; and Finance. Notice that the Labor and Agriculture ministries were not included at first, reflecting the enormous weight being given to the business climate ("Economic Conditions Becoming Chaotic," 10/9/47, *Capital*).

105. "Planning Commission or Super-Cabinet," *Economic Weekly*, 3/25/50.

106. Kochanek, *The Congress Party of India*, pp. 140–144.

107. Ibid., p. 142.

108. "Planning Commission or Super-Cabinet," *Economic Weekly*, 3/25/50.

109. *Gazette of India*, March 15, 1950.

110. Ibid., Paragraph 6.

111. Hence, a week after its appointment was announced, Nanda was still expressing the hope that it would be endowed with strong executive powers. See "Conversation with Mr. Gulzarilal Nanda on March 23," Timberlake to Department of State, #366, 4/1/50, 791.00/4–150, DSR.

112. "Wanted: A Holiday from Planning," *Economic Weekly*, 4/29/50.

113. Ibid.

114. See the correspondence between Mathai and Nehru in JNSW, 2nd series, vol. 14, part 2, pp. 227–250.

115. Nehru to Patel, 5/25/50, JNSW, 2nd series, vol. 14, part 2.

116. S. Gopal, *Jawaharlal Nehru, Volume Two* (Cambridge, Mass.: Harvard University Press, 1979), p. 99.

117. See Nehru's complaint about this matter to C. Rajagopalachari, in a letter dated 10/7/50, JNSW, 2nd series, vol. 15, part 1.

118. *Gazette of India*, March 15, 1950.

119. I argue in the next chapter that even such patronage could never substitute for institutional powers of the kind that the Economic Planning Board held in Korea.

120. See, for example, Evans, *Embedded Autonomy*.

121. See above, the section in this chapter entitled "The Institutional Outcome (1) — The Planning Commission."

122. See Non-Ferrous Metals Manufacturers Association to Industry Ministry, April 11, 1949; Bombay Millowners' Association to Industry Ministry, May 18, 1949; U.P. Chamber of Commerce to Industry Ministry, July 18, 1949, FICCI to Industry Ministry, September 26, 1949, all in File I(4)–1(44)/49, Industrial Policy and Promotion Department, Industry Ministry.

123. See the foreword by D. R. Gadgil to N. V. Sovani's *Post-War Inflation in India — A Survey* (Pune: Gokhale Institute of Politics and Economics, 1949).

124. Ibid., pp. 54–55.

125. Communiqué issued by the Government of India on textile policy, 7/30/48, quoted by Sovani in ibid.

126. See the excellent analyses in *Economic Weekly* during these months, especially "Millowners on Textile Control," 4/8/50; "The Cold War for Decontrol," 5/20/50; "Controls to Stay, but Ceilings May Be Raised," 6/17/50.

127. See Rajnarayan Chandavarkar, *The Origins of Industrial Capitalism in India* (Cambridge: Cambridge University Press, 1994).

128. Sanjay Baru, *The Political Economy of Sugar in India* (Delhi: Oxford University Press, 1990).

129. Ibid., pp. 134–136.

130. See the description in my Ph.D. dissertation, Locked in Place: State-Building and the Failure of Industrial Policy in India, 1940–1970 (University of Wisconsin-Madison, 1999), chap. 6, section 6.7.

131. "Schedule A" in "The Industries (Development and Regulation) Act, 1951," *Gazette of India (Extraordinary)*, part 2 — section 1, November 1, 1951.

132. See ibid., chap. 2, section 6.

133. Ibid.

134. Evans, *Embedded Autonomy*, passim.

135. Ibid., chap. 2, section 5.

136. H. K. Mahtab, speech on October 11, 1951, *Constituent Assembly Debates* (Delhi: Government of India, 1951), column 4649.

137. Ibid., columns 4649–4650. See also the G. L. Nanda's speech, October 12, followed by Mahtab's intervention, both of which repeatedly stressed this function of the two bodies.

138. See chap. 2, section 6, and "The Second Schedule" in "The Industries (Development and Regulation) Act, 1951," *Gazette of India (Extraordinary)*, part 2 — section 1, November 1, 1951.

139. Moon Kyu Park, "Interest Representation in South Korea: The Limits of Corporatist Control," *Asian Survey* 27 (1987): 903–917; Karl Fields, *Enterprise and the State in Korea and Taiwan* (Ithaca, N.Y.: Cornell University Press, 1995).

140. Wade, *Governing the Market*.

141. Indeed, Gadgil criticized the whole approach to dealing with the private sector as a fantasy. See his remarks in the Summary Record of the First Meeting of the Planning Commission Advisory Board," August 21–23, 1950, in File LSR/PC-2, Lala Shri Ram Archives, New Delhi.

142. See Gadgil's remarks in the Summary Record of the First Meeting of the Planning Commission Advisory Board," August 21–23, 1950, in File LSR/PC-2, Lala Shri Ram Archives, New Delhi.

143. This was in reply to Gadgil in a later meeting of the Advisory Board. See the "Summary Record of the Second Meeting of the Planning Commission Advisory Board," July 24–25, 1951, in LSR/PC-2, Lala Shri Ram Archives, New Delhi.

CHAPTER 7
STATE STRUCTURE AND INDUSTRIAL POLICY

1. Evans, *Embedded Autonomy*.

2. Ibid., p. 69.

3. For a more detailed presentation of this argument, see my "Bureaucratic Rationality and the Developmental State," *American Journal of Sociology* 107 (January 2002): 4.

4. Again, the claim is for relative, not absolute, failure. A claim to absolute failure would be justified if investment decisions had been wholly, or even largely, unaffected by policy. Such was clearly not the case. But an argument *can* be made that policy was ineffectual in *many respects*, which can then be specified.

5. On the importance of non-discretionary controls, see Jones and Sakong, *Government, Business, and Entrepreneurship*, chap. 4.

6. Amsden, *Asia's Next Giant*, pp. 14, 17, 73, 103, 133; Kang, in *The Korean Business Conglomerate*, pp. 40–42, says that licensing was one of the two major forms of control over private capital. Unfortunately there is no real study of the licensing system in Korea, unlike in India, where it has been studied extensively.

7. Kang, *The Korean Business Conglomerate*, p. 42.

8. Song, *The Rise of the Korean Economy*, p. 96.

9. Amsden, *Asia's Next Giant*, p. 133 n. 17.

10. Ibid.

11. Ahn, "The Political Economy of Foreign Aid," pp. 287–288.

12. Dani Rodrik, "The 'Paradoxes' of the Successful State," *European Economic Review* 41 (1997): 411–442.

13. Rhee, *The State and Industry in Korea*, pp. 60–65.

14. Ahn, "The Political Economy of Foreign Aid," pp. 183–184, 281–283.

15. Paul Kuznets, "Indicative Planning in Korea," *Journal of Comparative Economics* 14 (1990): 657–676; see also pp. 667, 671.

16. Woo, *Race to the Swift*.

17. Ahn, "The Political Economy of Foreign Aid," p. 231.

18. Kuznets, "Indicative Planning in Korea," pp. 666–668.

19. Ibid., pp. 665–666.

20. Ibid., p. 666.

21. Y. B. Rhee, B. Ross-Larson, and G. Pursell, *Korea's Competitive Edge: Managing Entry into World Markets* (Baltimore, Md.: The Johns Hopkins University Press, 1984).

22. Haggard, Kim, and Moon, "The Transition to Export-Led Growth," pp. 860–861.

23. Kuznets, "Indicative Planning in Korea," p. 666.

24. Perhaps the most famous such involvement was with the building of the Posco steel plant. See Clifford, *Troubled Tiger*, chap. 5.

25. For an extremely interesting discussion of the tension between formal rationality and instrumental rationality within a bureaucratic setup, see Clus Offe, "The Divergent Rationalities in Administrative Action," in his *Disorganized Capitalism* (Cambridge, Mass.: MIT Press, 1985), pp. 300–316.

26. Harrgard, Kim, and Moon, "The Transition to Export-Led Growth," p. 865.

27. Jeon-Ro Yoon, "The State and the Electronics Industry in Korea" (Ph.D. dissertation, Brown University, 1989), pp. 52–53, 94.

28. Yun-han Chu, "The State and the Development of the Automobile Industry in South Korea and Taiwan," in *The Role of the State in Taiwan's Development*, ed. Joel Aberbach, pp. 125–169 (Armonk, N.Y.: M. E. Sharpe, 1994).

29. For Park's launching of this drive, see Clifford, *Troubled Tiger*, p. 63. For the corporatist aims, see Moon Kyu Park, "Interest Representation in South Korea: The Limits of Corporatist Control," *Asian Survey* 27 (August 1987): 903–917.

30. Clifford, *Troubled Tiger*, p. 63. Clifford gives the Korea Highway Corporation and the Korea Cement Industry Association as examples.

31. Brown, *Korean Pricing Policies and Economic Development*, p. 145.

32. A good brief overview of the Chaebols, their place in the economy, and their use for industrial policy is Alice Amsden, "South Korea: Enterprising Groups and Entrepreneurial Government," in Alfred Chandler, Franco Amatori, Takahashi Hikino, eds., *Big Business and the Wealth of Nations* (Cambridge: Cambridge University Press, 1997). The most detailed study is Seok Ki Kim, "Business Concentration and Government Policy: A Study of the Phenomenon of Business Groups in Korea, 1945–1985" (Ph.D. dissertation: Harvard University, 1987).

33. Amsden has highlighted the advantages of a highly concentrated industrial sector for industrial policy: "only if a group succeeded in one industry would it be rewarded with a license and credit to enter yet another industry" ("South Korea," p. 364). Of course, the most important such yardstick was performance in export markets.

34. This opinion is virtually unanimous and, I think, largely correct. For examples, see Dalip Swamy, *The Political Economy of Industrialization* (Delhi: Sage, 1995); the various essays in Terry Byres, ed., *The State and Planning in India* (Delhi: Oxford University Press, 1994).

35. See S. L. Shetty, "Structural Retrogression in the Indian Economy since the Mid-Sixties," *Economic and Political Weekly*, Annual Number (February 1978): 101–122; reprinted in Nayyar, *Industrial Growth and Stagnation*, pp. 176–177.

36. Ben Ross Schneider, "Elusive Synergy: Business-Government Relations and Development," *Comparative Politics* (October 1998).

37. Pranab Bardhan, *The Political Economy of Development in India* (Oxford: Oxford University Press, 1983), Table 15.

38. See the speeches by H. K. Mahtab (Industry Minister), and G. L. Nanda (Minister for Planning) on October 11 and 12, 1951, in *Constituent Assembly (Legislative) Debates* (1951).

39. The place of the Central Advisory Council for Industries and the Development Councils in industrial policy is explained well by Marathe in *Regulation and Development*.

40. See the speech delivered by H. K. Mahtab on October 12, 1951, *Constituent Assembly (Legislative) Debates*.

41. Ibid., 4757–4758.

42. See Section 6(4) and Schedule II in the text of the IDRA, published in the *Gazette of India Extraordinary*, part 2, section 1, November 1, 1951.

43. Venkatasubbiah, *The Indian Economy since Independence*, pp. 174–175.

44. Interview with Ajit Mazumdar (Ex-Chairman of the Licensing Committee), 7/22/97; interview with Arun Ghosh (Ex-Member, Licensing Committee), 8/10/97. This was also the verdict rendered by A. H. Hansen, in *The Process of Planning: A Study of India's Five-Year Plans* (Oxford: Oxford University Press, 1966), p. 485.

45. Hanson, *The Process of Planning*, p. 454.

46. Interview with Arun Ghosh, 8/10/97.

47. H. K. Mahtab explicitly defended the final face of the IDRA on these grounds. See his speech to the Constituent Assembly, October 12, 1951.

48. Ibid., pp. 4755–4756.

49. "Memorandum by the Bengal Chamber of Commerce on the Planning Commission's Report," File LSR/PC-4, Lala Shri Ram Archives, New Delhi. This memo is not dated, but it was written soon after the Planning Commission submitted its draft of the first plan.

50. See above, chap. 6, section entitled "The Institutional Outcome (1)—The Planning Commission.

51. This was the view of D. R. Gadgil, who criticized the whole approach of dealing with the private sector as a fantasy. See his remarks in the "Summary Record of the First Meeting of the Planning Commission Advisory Board," August 21–23, 1950, in File LSR/PC-2, Lala Shri Ram Archives, New Delhi.

52. This was in reply to Gadgil in a later meeting of the Advisory Board. See the "Summary Record of the Second Meeting of the Planning Commission Advisory Board," July 24–25, 1951, in LSR/PC-2, Lala Shri Ram Archives, New Delhi.

53. See the "Summary Record of the Sixth Meeting of the Central Advisory Council for Industry," 1954?, File LSR/M/C&I-15, Lala Shri Ram Archives, New Delhi. See also the "Minutes of the Second Meeting of the CACI, 10/2/52," File LSR/M/C&I-13, Lala Shri Ram Archives, in which the decision to establish the first DCs was reached.

54. Remarks by S. Bhoothalingam, Joint Secretary, Industry Ministry, in "Summary Record of the Second Meeting of the Steering Committee of the CACI," File LSR/PC-6, Lala Shri Ram Archives, New Delhi.

55. One bureaucrat I interviewed said that the meetings were so useless that he spent most of the time doodling in his notebook.

56. Letter to Paul Hoffman, June 23, 1953, Hoffman Papers, Box 73, India (Miscellaneous Correspondence, 1951–1956), Harry S. Truman Presidential Library, Independence, Missouri.

57. See the verdict in the various reports of the Administrative Reforms Commission of the Government of India, especially *Report of the Study Team on Economic Administration (1967), Report of the Study Team on the Machinery of Planning* (1968), and *Report of the Working Group on Developmental, Control, and Regulatory Organizations* (1968); also useful is *Report of the Industrial Licensing Policy Enquiry Committee* (1969).

58. Hence the oddity that, in the plan document, one finds a plea that the IDRA—which was to be the central arm for implementing industrial planning—be passed quickly! See the *First Five-Year Plan* (Delhi: Government of India, 1950).

59. This was recognized by leading economists and advisers to the Planning Commission at the time. See the discussion on the plan document in the "Proceedings of the Meeting of the Advisory Board on Planning," October 23, 1952, File 222, Jayaprakash Narayan Papers, NMML, New Delhi. As usual, D. R. Gadgil was the most eloquent on this point.

60. One can get an idea of this by examining the projects listed in *Industrial Projects in the First Plan* (Delhi: Government of India, 1956).

61. Interview with K. B. Lall, an ex-chair of the Licensing Committee, 7/15/96.

62. Oddly Stephan Haggard and others have suggested that the EPB was modeled after the Indian Planning Commission. But, in fact, the scope of the EPB's power and authority was qualitatively greater than its Indian counterpart. Haggard and his colleagues do not mention how they arrive at their conclusion, but it is mistaken. See Haggard, Kim, and Moon, "The Transition to Export-Led Growth," p. 856.

63. For an overall description, see *Report of the Study Team on Economic Administration* (1967).

64. Administrative Reforms Commission, *Report on the Machinery for Planning* (Delhi: Government of India, 1968), pp. 13–14.

65. For the (theoretical) relation between licensing and the plans, see *Report of the Industrial Licensing Policy Enquiry Commission*.

66. Administrative Reforms Commission, *Report of the Study Team on the Machinery for Planning* (Delhi: Government of India, 1967), pp. 13–15.

67. *Report on the Machinery for Planning* (1968), p. 13.

68. This was confirmed in all my interviews with bureaucrats.

69. *Report of the Study Team on the Machinery for Planning (1967)*, p. 12.

70. Ibid., p. 15.

71. *Report on the Machinery for Planning* (1968), p. 16.

72. *Report of the Working Group on Developmental, Control, and Regulatory Organizations*, p. 41.

73. Ibid.

74. *Report of the Study Team on Economic Administration* (1967), pp. 16, 82.

75. This was most visibly manifested in the foreign exchange crisis of 1957, which I will address presently.

76. *Nineteenth Report of the Estimates Committee (1971–72), Fifth Lok Sabha* (Delhi: Government of India, 1971), p. 134.

77. See Arun Shourie's incisive analysis in "Controls and the Current Situation: Why Not Let the Hounds Run?" *Economic and Political Weekly* 8, Annual Number (August 1973): 31–33.

78. Hanson, *The Process of Planning*, p. 304.

79. Ibid., p. 291.

80. *Report of the Working Group on Developmental, Control, and Regulatory Organizations*, p. 6.

81. *Report of the Study Team on the Directorate-General of Technical Development, Part 2* (Delhi: Government of India, 1966), pp. 5, 7.

82. See the discussion of ministerial autonomy in Shourie, "Controls and the Current Situation," p. 1483.

83. Evans, *Embedded Autonomy*; Weiss, *The Myth of the Powerless State*.

84. *Report of the Industrial Licensing Policy Enquiry Committee* (1969), pp. 30–31.

85. For a description of this design, see ibid.

86. Again, this was confirmed in interviews with bureaucrats.

87. *Report of the Study Team on the Machinery for Planning* (1967), p. 12.

88. For evidence, see the Dutt Committee Report, chaps. 3 and 6.

89. Shourie, "Controls and the Current Situation," p. 1483.

90. *Report of the Study Team on Economic Administration* (1967), Appendix 1.

91. Dutt Committee Report, p. 100.

92. This was to have serious implications for the public sector, which I discuss in the next chapter.

93. Dutt Committee Report, p. 100.

94. *Report of the Study Team on the Directorate-General of Technical Development* (1966), part 2, pp. 30–32.

95. Interview with K. B. Lall, 7/15/96. Lall, who had been the chairman of the Licensing Committee, told me that he would approve licenses on the assumption that 25 percent would not fructify. This elicited complaints from Penderal Moon, a high-ranking official in the Planning Commission, to the effect that this was nullifying all the calculations of the plans. But Lall would simply ignore Moon, and Moon had no means to enforce compliance. Over-licensing is one of the most well-known aspects of the industrial policy regime in India.

96. The process is described in *Report of the Study Team on the Directorate-General of Technical Development* (1966), part 2, chap. 3.

97. *Report of the Study Team on the Machinery for Planning* (1967), p. 83.

98. Interview, Ajit Mazoomdar, 7/22/97. Arun Shourie also makes this distinction, though in a puzzled way, in "The Allocation of Foreign Exchange in India" (Ph.D. dissertation, Syracuse University, 1967), pp. 81, 165.

99. The administrative reforms commission found that "action against defaulters is seldom taken and extensions of time are given as a matter of routine" (*Report of the Study Team on the Machinery for Planning* (1967), p. 20).

100. Shourie reported that in their allocative decisions bureaucrats were concerned not with "maximizing any particular variable but with minimizing complaints" ("The Allocation of Foreign Exchange in India," p. 81).

101. The strategic orientation of firms is often ignored in neoclassical critiques of industrial policy, which stress only the failure of state strategy. The role of firms' strategy, however, should not be ignored as a factor in the failure of state strategy.

102. This is well known, but its logic was most pointedly revealed by R. K. Hazari in *Report on Industrial Planning and Licensing Policy (Final Report)*, vol. 1 (Delhi: Government of India, 1966).

103. See the analysis in Aurobindo Ghosh, "Investment Behavior of Monopoly Houses" [in three parts], *Economic and Political Weekly*, October 26, November 2, November 9, 1974.

104. Ibid., part 1, October 26, 1974, p. 1820.

105. For evidence, see the Corporate Studies Group, *Functioning of the Industrial Licensing System: A Report* (New Delhi: Government of India, 1983), pp. 70–78.

106. Ghosh, "Investment Behavior of Monopoly Houses," part 2, November 2, 1974, pp. 1872–1873.

107. For evidence of production in excess of sanctioned capacity, see the Corporate Studies Group, *Functioning of the Industrial Licensing System*, pp. 35–39.

108. For a superb explication of this logic, see C. P. Chandrashekhar, "As-

pects of Growth and Structural Change in Indian Industry," in Nayyar, *Industrial Growth and Stagnation*, pp. 318–345.

109. This was first pointed out in the Hazari Committee Report.

110. Ghosh, "Investment Behavior of Monopoly Houses," part 2, Table 6.

111. The obsession with making the process faster is evidenced in every report on the policy apparatus that I have seen.

CHAPTER 8
LOCKED IN PLACE: EXPLAINING THE NON-OCCURRENCE OF REFORM

1. This is most pointedly the case with neoclassical critics of planning, such as Jagdish Bhagwati and Padma Desai. See their *India: Planning for Industrialization* (London: Oxford University Press, 1970).

2. Baldev Raj Nayar, *India's Mixed Economy: The Role of Ideas and Interests in Its Development* (Bombay: Popular Prakashan, 1985).

3. These arguments tend to build on the New Political Economy, and its emphasis on "rent-seeking." See, for example, Prem Shankar Jha, *India: A Political Economy of Stagnation* (Delhi: Oxford University Press, 1980).

4. Nayar's book, *India's Mixed Economy* (Bombay: Popular Prakashan, 1988) is the most glaring example of this tendency.

5. I should say, however, that I do not think this was the case at all. There is scant evidence, in my view, that most of the top Indian bureaucrats and policy makers were *ideologically* opposed to markets, even in the early years of planning. In fact, they were very open to allowing markets the maximum possible latitude *compatible* with the goals of accelerated development. The commitment was to an accelerated pace of development, not to regulations. I merely entertain the possibility here for the sake of argument.

6. By way of illustration, one scholar in Delhi told me the following anecdote: he once asked a minister in the Indian government did he not realize the implications of making decisions based on who gave him the highest bribe. The minister said of course he did but there was no reason for concern: "I simply find out who the most efficient producer is—and then I take the bribe from *him*." The story may be apocryphal, but it illustrates nicely that corruption need not eliminate appropriate developmental decisions.

7. On these questions, see the emerging work by Mushtaq Khan, "State Failure in Weak States: A Critique of New Institutionalist Explanations," in Harriss, *The New Institutional Economics and Third World Development*; and Mushtaq Khan, "The Efficiency Implications of Corruption," *Journal of International Development* 8, no. 5 (1996): 683–696.

8. Hazari, *Report on Industrial Planning and Licensing Policy (Final Report)*, vol. 1 (1966), p. 19.

9. Ibid.

10. See his correspondence with Nehru in the years of the First Five-Year Plan, contained in his Correspondence Files with Nehru, 1953–54, TTK Papers, NMML. Also useful are the summaries of events given in Dispatch #908, Bartlett to Dept. of State, 2/24/55, 791.13/2–2455, DSR.

11. Note on fall in exchange reserves by the Planning Commission, C. D. Deshmukh Papers, Subject File 88, NMML.

12. Note by TTK to Nehru, January 11, 1958. The pages of this note are dispersed across three files in the TTK collection: page 1 is in the Correspondence File with Nehru, 1958–59; page 2 is in Subject File 14; and pages 3–4 are in File 8B, all in TTK Papers, NMML.

13. B. K. Nehru, *Nice Guys Finish Second* (Delhi: Viking, 1997), p. 260 (emphasis added).

14. Ibid., pp. 261, 282.

15. A. H. Hanson, *The Process of Planning: A Study of India's Five-Year Plans, 1950–1964* (London: Oxford University Press, 1966), pp. 155–163.

16. Kidron, *Foreign Investment in India*, pp. 141–142.

17. See the correspondence between Nehru, TTK, and C. D. Deshmukh in the TTK papers, Correspondence File (Jawaharlal Nehru), 1957, 1958; TTK papers, File 8B; C. D. Deshmukh Papers, Subject File 88, all in NMML.

18. Statement in Parliament, in late March 1958, quoted by Kirdon in *Foreign Investment in India*, p. 125.

19. Dutt Committee Report, p. 100.

20. Kidron, *Foreign Investment in India*, p. 127.

21. Thus the third plan document observed, "one of the main drawbacks in the past has been that the programme for exports has not been regarded as an integral part of the country's development effort under the five year plans" (*Third Five-Year Plan* [Delhi: Government of India, 1961], p. 137).

22. Ibid., pp. 137–141.

23. Note that this need not have meant that the firms in question produce *exclusively* for the export market. In Korea and even in Japan, this was not the case; in India, it would have actually been undesirable, given its huge size and the crushing need for serving the domestic market. What would have been desirable is for firms to be forced to use international standards as *benchmarks* for their own productivity. For this, all that would have been required was that they export a certain portion of their product or one of the several products they manufactured. This was the condition to which Korean and Japanese firms were often subjected.

24. Martin Wolf, *India's Exports* (London: Oxford University Press, 1982), pp. 122–123; Deepak Nayyar, *India's Exports and Export Policies in the 1960s* (Cambridge: Cambridge University Press, 1976), p. 261.

25. Wolf, *India's Exports*, pp. 66–67.

26. Ibid., pp. 92, 124.

27. *Foreign Collaboration in Indian Industry: Survey Report* (Bombay: Reserve Bank of India, 1968), p. 11.

28. Ibid., p. 107.

29. *Report of the Industrial Licensing Policy Enquiry Committee* (1969), p. 135. See also Kidron, *Foreign Investments in India*, chap. 6, but esp. pp. 245–246.

30. The Indian case thus fits well with the experience of Latin America, which was also subject to an MNC strategy oriented toward local markets. See Michael Mortimore, "Flying Geese or Sitting Ducks? Transnationals and Industry in Developing Countries," *CEPAL Review* 51 (December 1993): 15–34.

31. See the excellent analysis in Robert Castley, *Korea's Economic Miracle: The Crucial Role of Japan* (London: Macmillan, 1997). See also Lee, "United States and Japanese Direct Investment in Korea."

32. For a description, see *Report of the Study Team on Economic Administration* (1967), chap. 8; Nayyar, *India's Exports and Export Policies*, chap. 10.

33. Ibid.

34. *Estimates Committee (1963–64, Third Lok Sabha), 48th Report, Ministry of International Trade*, p. 21.

35. For a review of some of these committees, see *Estimates Committee (1971–72, Fifth Lok Sabha), 14th Report, Ministry of Foreign Trade.*

36. *Estimates Committee (1963–64, Third Lok Sabha), 48th Report*, pp. 4–5.

37. Nayyar, *India's Exports and Export Policies*, chap. 10.

38. Ibid., pp. 226, 259.

39. C. P. Chandrasekhar, "Growth and Technical Change in the Indian Cotton-Mill Industry," *Economic and Political Weekly*, Annual Number (January 1984): PE34–PE35.

40. Nayyar, *India's Exports and Export Policies*, pp. 257–258, 262.

41. *Estimates Committee (1961–62, Third Lok Sabha), 166th Report, Ministry of Commerce and Industry, Office of the Textile Commissioner, Part V: Export Promotion of Cotton Textiles*, p. 6 (emphasis added).

42. *Estimates Committee (1963–64, Third Lok Sabha), 48th Report, Ministry of International Trade*, p. 5.

43. *Report of the Industrial Licensing Policy Enquiry Committee* (1969), p. 73. The discussion of export obligations is on pages 72–73.

44. *Report of the Industrial Licensing Policy Enquiry Committee* (1969), p. 137.

45. Ibid.

46. D. R. Gadgil, as usual, immediately noticed the implications of the 1957 crisis for the public sector. See his address to the Planning Commission's Panel of Economists in January 1958, "On Re-phasing the Second Five-Year Plan," published in D. R. Gadgil, *Planning and Economic Policy in India* (Poona: Asia Publishing House, 1961).

47. Aurobino Ghosh and Arvind Vyas, "Industrial Structure and Industrial Policy," in *Alternative Policies for the Fourth Five-Year Plan* (Kerala: State Planning Board, 1968), p. 235; Frankel, *India's Political Economy*, pp. 148,152.

48. Ghosh and Vyas, "Industrial Structure and Industrial Policy."

49. Frankel, *India's Political Economy*, p. 217

50. Michael Kidron gives an extensive list of such concessions in his *Foreign Investments in India*, pp. 141–152.

51. Ibid., p. 315.

52. For a general treatment, see Amiya Bagchi, "Public Sector Industry and the Quest for Self-Reliance in India," *Economic and Political Weekly*, Annual Number (April 1982): 615–628; for Steel, see Bernard D'Mello, "Soviet Collaboration in Indian Steel Industry, 1954–84," *Economic and Political Weekly*, March 5, 1988; for petrochemicals, see Sushil Khanna, "Transnational Corporations and Technology Transfer: Contours of Dependence in Indian Petrochemical Industry," *Economic and Political Weekly*, Annual Number (August 1984)

(also see Francine Frankel, *India's Political Economy*, pp. 267–268); for fertilizers, see Biswajit Dhar, "Factors Influencing Technology Selection: Case Study of Thal-Vaishet and Hazira Fertiliser Projects," *Economic and Political Weekly*, Annual Number (August 1984).

53. Leading the charge in this offensive were Morarji Desai (Finance Minister), S. K. Patil (Food and Agriculture Minister), and C. Subramaniam (Steel Minister and later Food Minister).

54. P. B. Medhora, *Industrial Growth since 1950: An Assessment* (Bombay: University of Bombay Press, 1968), chap. 3.

55. See above, chapter 7, the second section: "State Structure and Industrial Policy in India."

56. Interview with K. B. Lall, 7/15/96.

57. Shourie, "The Allocation of Foreign Exchange in India," p. 6.

58. Medhora, *Industrial Growth since 1950*, pp. 55–58.

59. Indeed, once the crisis was at hand, the PC could only plead to the ministries that, in the future, it "be kept fully in the picture," as one source put it. Bunker to Department of State, Deptel #7586, 11/14/57, 891.00/11–1357, DSR.

60. For Shastri's doubts about the PC, see Frankel, *India's Political Economy*, pp. 247–250; Michael Brecher, *Nehru's Mantle* (New York: Praeger, 1966), p. 119.

61. Frankel, *India's Political Economy*, p. 250.

62. Brecher, *Nehru's Mantle*, p. 119.

63. Ibid.

64. Frankel, *India's Political Economy*, p. 251.

65. Ibid., pp. 251, 256.

66. Ibid., pp. 268–269.

67. Ibid., pp. 269–288.

68. The deputy chairman is the highest officer within the PC. The post of chair is held by the prime minister.

69. This view was expressed early on in "Planning without a Policy Frame," which is published in *Planning and Economic Policy in India* (Pune: Gokhale Institute of Economics, 1962).

70. "After the Five Year Plans," *London Financial Times*, 1/29/68, attachment to Bowles to Department of State, Dispatch # A-801, File E-5 India, Box 636, DSR.

71. Bowles to Department of State, 4/25/68, Dispatch # A-1028, File E-5 India, Box 636, DSR. The quote is the reporting officer's.

72. See also the remarks of R. Venkataraman, Member (Industries Group) of the PC, to M. Gordon Tiger in Dispatch # A-1375, 8/9/68, File INCO-10, Box 966, DSR.

73. That this was the motivation should not come as a surprise to anyone familiar with Gadgil's career, which began in the 1930s. Throughout the period of industrial planning in India, Gadgil had been, without question, the most astute critic of the policy regime, and the common thread running through all his work was the imperative to discipline private capital coupled with the lamentable *inability* to do so. That he chose to voluntarily concede greater scope to private capital goes against the grain of his entire career. It could only have

come about with the greatest hesitation and on the realization that building up state capacity was simply not in the cards.

74. See above, chapter 7, the second section, "State Structure and Industrial Policy in India."

75. Frankel, *India's Political Economy*, pp. 310–311.

76. Ibid.

77. Administrative Reforms Commission, *Report of the Study Team on the Machinery of the Government of India and Its Procedures of Work*, part 1 (Delhi: Government of India, 1967), pp. 19–28.

78. Ibid., p. 21 (emphasis added).

79. *Report of the Study Team on Economic Administration*, p. 89 (emphasis added).

80. Frankel, *India's Political Economy*, pp. 305–306.

81. All my interviewees, who were in the economic bureaucracy at the time, confirmed that Indian capitalists were not enamored with external liberalization.

82. The most detailed accounts of the role of the World Bank–U.S. combine are in John P. Lewis, *India's Political Economy* (Delhi: Oxford University Press, 1995), and Frankel, *India's Political Economy*, chaps. 7 and 8.

83. Frankel, *India's Political Economy*, pp. 269–271, 280–281.

84. For an account of the Johnson administration's India policy, and Johnson's own interest in it, see Robert J. McMahon, *The Cold War in the Periphery: The United States, India, and Pakistan* (New York: Columbia University Press, 1994), chap. 9.

85. Frankel, *India's Political Economy*.

86. At the heart of the proposed liberalization measures was a greater reliance on the new agricultural technologies that produced the Green Revolution.

87. Frankel, *India's Political Economy*.

88. See the relevant chapter in *The Department of State during the Administration of President Lyndon B. Johnson*, vol. 3, a part of "Historical Reports Relating to Diplomacy during the Lyndon B. Johnson Administration," Office of the Executive Secretariat, RG 59, DSR, USNA, College Park.

89. Frankel, *India's Political Economy*, pp. 314–315.

90. Uma Lele and Manmohan Agarwal, "Four Decades of Economic Assistance in India and the Role of External Assistance," in Uma Lele and Ijaz Nabi, eds., *Transitions in Development: The Role of Aid and Commercial Flows* (San Francisco: ICS Press, 1991), p. 32.

91. Ibid., pp. 20–21.

92. Vijay Joshi and I.M.D. Little, *India: Macroeconomics and Political Economy, 1964–1991* (Delhi: Oxford University Press, 1994), chap. 11.

CHAPTER 9
CONCLUSION

1. Here I am referring to capitalists in the industrial sector. The importance of agrarian classes, and the rise of a class of a kulak farmers, has received enormous attention in India.

2. Honorable mention must be made here of Michael Kidron's superb book, *Foreign Investments in India*, which has been virtually alone in noting and describing the business attack on the emerging policy apparatus after Independence.

3. A notable recent exception to this is Amit Kumar Gupta, *The Agrarian Drama: 1934–1951* (Delhi: Manohar, 1996). But Gupta's book is among the exceedingly few efforts by historians to cross the divide.

4. Karl Fields, *Enterprise and the State in Korea and Taiwan* (Ithaca, N.Y.: Cornell University Press, 1995), p. 68.

5. *Ibid.*

6. This weakness is analyzed well by Thomas Gold in his Ph.D. dissertation, "Dependent Development in Taiwan" (Ph.D. dissertation, Harvard University, 1981).

7. Richard Kuisel, *Capitalism and the State in France* (Cambridge: Cambridge University Press, 1981), p. 191.

8. In 1945 the index of industrial activity in France was at 48 percent of its level in 1938. See Milor, *Planning the Market*, p. 72.

9. Kuisel, *Capitalism and the State in France*, p. 191.

10. *Ibid.*

11. A good overview of these years, and the moral ascendance of the Left, can be found in Donald Sassoon's massive *One Hundred Years of Socialism* (New York: New Press, 1996), pp. 117–136.

12. Geoff Eley, *Forging Democracy: The History of the Left in Europe, 1850–2000*, p. 289.

13. Kuisel, *The State and Capitalism in France*, pp. 257–258.

14. Peter Hall, *Governing the Economy: The Politics of State Intervention in Britain and France* (Oxford: Oxford University Press, 1986), p. 140.

15. The classic English-language description of the wartime accretion of state capacity is, of course, Johnson, *MITI and the Japanese Miracle*. See, in particular, chapters 5 and 6.

16. Takeo Kikkawa, "The Relationship between the Government and Companies in Japan during and after World War II," in Jun Sakudo and Takao Shiba, eds., *World War II and the Transformation of Business Systems* (Tokyo: University of Tokyo Press, 1993), pp. 59–80.

17. Seiichiro Yonekura, "The Functions of Industrial Associations," in *The Japanese System and Its Historical Origins*, ed. Tetsuji Okazaki and Masahiro Okuno-Fujiwara, pp. 180–207 (Oxford: Oxford University Press, 1999).

18. Details are provided in ibid., pp. 190–195. See also Johnson, *MITI and the Japanese Miracle*, chap. 6.

19. Elizabeth Payne Tsunoda, "Rationalizing Japan's Political Economy: The Business Initiative, 1920–1955" (Ph.D. dissertation, Columbia University, 1993).

20. Ibid., chap. 6, esp. pp. 268–291.

21. Ibid., pp. 269–270.

22. Johnson, *MITI and the Japanese Miracle*, chap. 5.

23. There are many studies of Japan's postwar economic difficulties. A good short account is in Yotaka Kosai, *The Era of High-Speed Growth: Notes on the Postwar Japanese Economy* (Tokyo: University of Tokyo Press, 1986), chap. 2.

24. See the extensive discussion in Gregory Tilton, "The Political Development of Japan's Postwar Economy" (Ph.D. dissertation, Ohio State University, 1997).

25. Though there was a brief bout with price and distribution controls during the war that the state could and did build on in the years to follow, absent was any experience with economic coordination of firms or even of state agencies.

26. This is stressed by Chalmers Johnson in his retrospective look at *MITI and the Japanese Miracle*: "The Developmental State: Odyssey of a Concept," in Woo-Cumings, *The Developmental State*, pp. 32–60.

27. The differences between Western and Japanese FDI persisted even within Korea, as shown in Lee, "United States and Japanese Direct Investment in Korea."

28. In 1955, 65 percent of exports were in labor-intensive sectors. The single largest item in all exports was textiles, which stood at 36 percent. By 1973 labor-intensive goods stood at 43 percent of the total, with textiles down to an amazing 6.3 percent. See Lawrence Krause and Sueo Sekiguchi, "Japan and the World Economy," in Hugh Patrick and Henry Rosovsky, eds., *Asia's New Giant: How the Japanese Economy Works* (Washington D.C.: The Brookings Institute, 1976), p. 409, Tables 6–9.

29. Christopher Howe, *The Origins of Japanese Trade Supremacy* (Chicago: University of Chicago Press, 1996), pp. 205–220.

30. For the statistic about the United States, see Howe, Table 8.5; for the information about India, see ibid., pp. 220–225.

31. Takafusa Nakamura, *The Postwar Japanese Economy: Its Development and Structure* (Tokyo: University of Tokyo Press, 1981), p. 42, Table 2.7.

32. John Dower, *Embracing Defeat: Japan in the Wake of World War II* (New York: Norton, 1999), p. 543.

33. See Laura Hein, *Fueling Growth: The Energy Revolution and Economic Policy in Postwar Japan* (Cambridge, Mass.: Harvard University Press, 1990), pp. 278–280.

34. William Borden, *The Pacific Alliance: United States Foreign Economic Policy and Japanese Trade Recovery, 1947–1955* (Madison: University of Wisconsin Press, 1984), p. 187.

35. Ibid., pp. 170–172.

36. For Mexico in the Cardenas years, see Hamilton, *The Limits of State Autonomy*; for Brazil during the critical Vargas years, see Collier and Collier, *Shaping the Political Arena* (Princeton, N.J.: Princeton University Press, 1992); for Egypt, see Marsha Pripstein Posusney, *Labor and the State in Egypt: Workers, Unions, and Restructuring* (New York: Columbia University Press, 1997); for Argentina, see Daniel James, *Resistance and Integration: Peronism and the Argentine Working Class, 1946–1976* (Cambridge: Cambridge University Press, 1988).

37. The analysis of this exchange in social-democratic settings by Adam Przeworski is still one of the most lucid. See "Material Interests, Class Compromise, and the State," which is chapter 5 in his *Capitalism and Social Democracy* (Cambridge: Cambridge University Press, 1985).

38. The work of Amartya Kumar Sen and Jean Dreze has been particularly important in heralding the region's achievements. See, inter alia, their book,

India: Economic Development and Social Opportunity (Delhi: Oxford University Press, 1995).

39. Patrick Heller, *The Labor of Development: Workers and the Transformation of Capitalism in Kerala, India* (Ithaca, N.Y.: Cornell University Press, 1999).

40. Ibid., chap. 7.

41. See Steven K. Vogel, *Freer Markets, More Rules: Regulatory Reform in Advanced Countries* (Ithaca, N.Y.: Cornell University Press, 1996). Vogel presents this argument with explicit reference to Polanyi on p. 3.

EPILOGUE

1. For a representative account, see Kim, *Big Business, Strong State*.

2. For an example of the former, see ibid.; for the latter, see David C. Kang, *Crony Capitalism: Corruption and Development in South Korea and the Philippines* (Cambridge: Cambridge University Press, 2002). I should note that while Kang's analysis of the post-Park era does emphasize the state's shrinking power relative to capital, his arguments regarding the Park era do not sit easily with the statist canon.

3. See Kang, *The Korean Business Conglomerate*.

4. Linsu Kim, *Imitation to Innovation: The Dynamics of Korea's Technological Learning* (Cambridge, Mass.: Harvard Business School Press, 1997), Table 2.3, pp. 54–55.

5. Ibid. Linsu Kim's book, *Imitation to Innovation*, is a superb account of this process.

6. Kim, *Big Business, Strong State*, p. 189.

7. Soo Chan Jang, "Driving Engine or Rent-Seeking Super-Cartel? The Business-State Nexus and Economic Transformation in South Korea, 1960–1999" (Ph.D. dissertation, Michigan State University, 2000), Table 3.11, p. 275.

8. Ibid. p. 352.

9. Ibid., Table 3.28, p. 294.

10. Several scholars have argued that the decline in the state's power was one of the factors that increased Korea's vulnerability to crisis. The most consistent analysis along these lines is Ha-Joon Chang, "Korea: The Misunderstood Crisis," *World Development* 26, no. 8 (1998): 1555–1561; idem, "The Hazard of Moral Hazard: Untangling the Asian Crisis," *World Development* 28, no. 4 (2000): 775–788; Chang and Chul-gyue Yoo, "The Triumph of the Rentiers?" *Challenge* 43, no. 1 (January/February 2000): 105–124.

11. See Frankel, *India's Political Economy*, chap. 10.

12. Pranab Bardhan, *The Political Economy of Development in India* (Oxford: Basil Blackwell, 1984).

13. Rathin Roy, "The Politics of Fiscal Policy: Some Reflections on Fiscal Policy and State Intervention in Developing Economies, with Special Reference to India" (Ph.D. dissertation, University of Cambridge, 1994).

14. The licensing apparatus was not only used to reward friends. Sanjay Gandhi utilized it to block the entrance of potential rivals into the small car market,

so he could develop his own pet project. See the details in the *Interim Report: Shah Commission* (Delhi: Government of India, 1978).

15. See the account by Nitish K. Sengupta, *Inside the Steel Frame: Reminiscences and Reflections of a Former Civil Servant* (New Delhi: Vikas, 1995).

16. See Brewer Stevenson Stone, "Governmental Corruption in India and China" (Ph.D. dissertation, Harvard University, 1994).

17. For a study of the emergence of a market-oriented "reform team" in the bureaucracy, see Vanita Shastri, "The Political Economy of Policy Formation in India: The Case of Industrial Policy, 1948–1994" (Ph.D. dissertation, Cornell University, 1995), chaps. 4 and 5.

18. See above, chapter 7, the third section: "The Rationality of Non-Disciplinary Industrial Policy."

19. See the essays collected in Nayyar, *Industrial Growth and Stagnation*.

20. Supriya Roychowdhury, "The State and Business in India: The Political Economy of Liberalization, 1984–1989" (Ph.D. dissertation, Princeton University, 1992), pp. 133–135.

Bibliography

UNPUBLISHED ARCHIVAL SOURCES
I. New Delhi, India

1. National Archives of India

A. GOVERNMENT FILES
Finance Department, Planning Branch, 1944–47
Finance Department, Planning Branch I, 1945–46
Finance Department, Planning Branch II, 1946
Ministry of Finance, Planning Department, 1947–48
Home Ministry Files, 1947–51
Cabinet Secretariat, Economic Committee of the Cabinet, 1945–51

B. PRIVATE PAPERS
Vallabhai Patel Papers
Rajendra Prasad Papers

2. Nehru Memorial Museum and Library

A. PRIVATE PAPERS
G. D. Birla
C. D. Deshmukh
Walchand Hirachand
A. P. Jain
T. T. Krishnamachari
J. C. Kumarappa
Kasturbhai Lalbhai
H. K. Mahtab
H. D. Malaviya
M. A. Master
M. O. Mathai
G. L. Mehta
Syama Prasad Mookerjee
Jayprakash Narayan
Jawaharlal Nehru
Pitambar Pant
C. Rajagopalachari
Purshotamdas Thakurdas

B. INSTITUTIONAL COLLECTIONS
All-India Congress Committee Papers
All-India Trade Union Congress Papers
Indian Merchants Chamber

3. Lala Shri Ram Archives

Commerce and Industry Ministry Series
Finance Ministry Series
Planning Commission Series
Food and Agriculture Ministry Series
Indian Finance Corporation Series
Reserve Bank of India Series
Personal Correspondence

4. Ministry Archives

A. GOVERNMENT OF INDIA, INDUSTRY MINISTRY, DEPARTMENT OF INDUSTRIAL POLICY
AND PROMOTION FILES [UDYOG BHAVAN, NEW DELHI]

B. GOVERNMENT OF INDIA, COMMERCE MINISTRY FILES [UDYOG BHAVAN, NEW DELHI]

II. College Park, Maryland: National Archives of the United States
1. State Department records, Record Group 59

A. DECIMAL FILES, 1950–62

B. SUBJECT-NUMERIC FILES, 1963–69

C. LOT FILES
  i. Office of the Executive Secretariat
  ii. Policy Planning Staff, Subject and Country Files

2. Records of the Foreign Agricultural Service, Record Group 166

A. NARRATIVE REPORTS OF SPECIAL AGENTS, CONSULAR OFFICES, AND AGRICULTURAL
ATTACHÉS

B. FORMERLY CONFIDENTIAL NARRATIVE REPORTS OF SPECIAL AGENTS, CONSULAR
OFFICES, AND AGRICULTURAL ATTACHÉS

3. Files of the Agency for International Development, Record Group 286

A. OFFICE OF THE EXECUTIVE SECRETARIAT
  i. Subject Country and Chronological Files, 1962–64
  ii. Subject Country and Chronological Files, 1964–65

B. OFFICE OF THE ADMINISTRATOR
  i. Office of the Executive Secretary, Regional and Country Files, 1961–66
  ii. Office of the Executive Secretary, Regional and Country Files, 1966–69

4. Files of U.S. Foreign Assistance agencies, 1948–61, Record Group 469

A. OFFICE OF NEAR EAST, SOUTH ASIA, AND AFRICA — SUBJECT FILES

B. PROGRAM FILES

III. Independence, Missouri, USA: Harry S. Truman Presidential Library

Harry S. Truman Papers
Henry S. Grady Papers
Charles Brannon Papers
Dean Acheson Papers
H. V. Johnson Papers
Paul Hoffman Papers
White House Central Files
Office Files
President's Secretary's Files

PUBLISHED ARCHIVAL SOURCES

Foreign Relations of the United States series, various volumes
State Department Confidential Central Files on the Internal Affairs of India, 1945–49
State Department Confidential Central Files on the Internal Affairs of India, 1950–54
National Security Council Files, Lyndon B. Johnson Presidential Library
Transfer of Power series, Penderal Moon, ed.

PUBLISHED GOVERNMENT DOCUMENTS

166th Report of the Estimates Committee, Ministry of Commerce and Industry, Office of the Textile Commissioner. Part 5: *Export Promotion of Cotton Textiles (1961–62), Third Lok Sabha.* Delhi: Government of India, 1961.
Administrative Reforms Commission. *Report on Economic Administration.* Delhi: Government of India 1968.
———. *Industrial Projects in the First Plan.* Delhi: Government of India, 1956.
———. *Interim Report: Shah Commission.* Delhi: Government of India, 1978.
———. *Report of the Advisory Planning Board.* Delhi: Government of India, 1947.
———. *Report of the Fiscal Commission.* Delhi: Government of India, 1950.
———. *Report on the Machinery for Planning.* Delhi: Government of India, 1968.
———. *Report of the Study Team on Economic Administration.* Delhi: Government of India, 1967.
———. *Report of the Study Team on the Machinery of the Government of India and Its Procedures of Work.* Part 1. Delhi: Government of India, 1967.
———. *Report of the Study Team on the Machinery of Planning.* Delhi: Government of India, 1967.
———. *Report of the Working Group on Developmental, Control, and Regulatory Organizations.* Delhi: Government of India, 1968.
"Cabinet Resolution on the Establishment of a Planning Commission." *Gazette of India*, March 15, 1950.
Constituent Assembly (Legislative) Debates. Delhi: Government of India, 1951.

First Five-Year Plan. Delhi: Government of India, 1950.

Forty-eighth Report of the Estimates Committee, Ministry of International Trade (1963–64), Third Lok Sabha. Delhi: Government of India, 1963.

Fourteenth Report of the Estimates Committee, Ministry of Foreign Trade, Fifth Lok Sabha. (Delhi: Government of India, 1971–72.

Hazari, R. K. *Report on Industrial Planning and Licensing Policy (Final Report).* Vol. 1. Delhi: Government of India, 1966.

National Planning Committee. *Report of the Sub-Committee on Industrial Finance.* Delhi: Government of India, 1948.

————. *Report of the Sub-Committee on Manufacturing Industries.* Delhi: Government of India, 1948.

————. *Report of the Sub-Committee on Public Finance.* Delhi: Government of India, 1949.

Nineteenth Report of the Estimates Committee (1971–72), Fifth Lok Sabha. Delhi: Government of India, 1971.

Report of the Monopolies Enquiry Commission. Delhi: Government of India, 1965.

Report of the Industrial Licensing Policy Enquiry Committee (Dutt Committee Report). Delhi: Government of India, 1969.

Report of the Study Team on the Directorate-General of Technical Development. Delhi: Government of India, 1966.

Reserve Bank of India. *Foreign Collaboration in Indian Industry: Survey Report.* Bombay: Reserve Bank of India, 1968.

BOOKS, ARTICLES, AND DISSERTATIONS

Abdel-Latif, Abla M. "The Non-Price Determinants of Export Success or Failure: The Egyptian Ready-made Garment Industry, 1975–89." *World Development* 21, no. 10 (1993): 1677–1684.

Abromovitz, Moses. "Catching Up, Forging Ahead, and Falling Behind." *Journal of Economic History* 46, no. 2 (1986): 385–406.

————. "The Search for the Sources of Growth: Areas of Ignorance, Old and New." *Journal of Economic History* 53, no. 2 (1993): 217–243.

Ahluwalia, Isher Judge. *Productivity and Growth in Indian Manufacturing.* Delhi: Oxford University Press, 1991.

————. *Industrial Growth in India: Stagnation since the Mid-Sixties.* Delhi: Oxford University Press, 1985.

Ahn, Yeonmi. "The Political Economy of Foreign Aid: The Nature of American Aid and Its Impact on the State-Business Relationship in South Korea, 1945–1972." Ph.D. dissertation, Yale University, 1992.

Amsden, Alice. *Asia's Next Giant: South Korea and Late Industrialization.* Oxford: Oxford University Press, 1989.

————. "Third World Industrialization: 'Global Fordism' or a New Model?" *New Left Review,* no. 182 (July/August 1990): 5–31.

————. "A Theory of Government in Late Industrialization." In Louis Putterman and Dietrich Rueschemeyer, eds., *State and Market in Development: Synergy or Rivalry?* (Boulder, Colo.: Westview, 1992).

———. "Like the Rest: South-East as 'Late' Industrialization." *Journal of International Development* 7, no. 5 (1995): 791–799.

———. "South Korea: Enterprising Groups and Entrepreneurial Government." In Alfred Chandler et al., eds., *Big Business and the Wealth of Nations*, pp. 336–367 (New York: Cambridge University Press, 1997).

———. "Early Post-War Industrial Policy in Emerging Economies: Creating Competitive Assets or Correcting Market Failures?" In Hideaki Miyajima, Takeo Kikkawa, and Takashi Hikino, eds., *Policies for Competitiveness: Comparing Business-Government Relationships in the 'Golden Age' of Capitalism*, pp. 133–159 (Oxford: Oxford University Press, 1999).

Amsden, Alice, and Takashi Hikino. "Staying Behind, Stumbling Back, Sneaking Up, Soaring Ahead: Late Industrialization in Historical Perspective." In William J. Baumol, Richard R. Nelson, and Edward N. Wolff, eds., *Convergence of Productivity* (Oxford: Oxford University Press, 1994), pp. 285–315.

Baer, Werner. "Import Substitution and Industrialization in Latin America: Experiences and Interpretations." *Latin American Research Review* 7, no. 1 (1972): 95–122.

Bagchi, Amiya. "Public Sector Industry and the Quest for Self-Reliance in India." *Economic and Political Weekly*, Annual Number (April 1982): 615–628.

Bairoch, Paul. *Economics and World History: Myths and Paradoxes.* Chicago: University of Chicago Press, 1993.

Balassa, Bela. *The Newly Industrializing Countries in the World Economy.* New York: Pergamon, 1981.

Bardhan, Pranab. *The Political Economy of Development in India.* Oxford: Oxford University Press, 1983.

———. Bardhan, Pranab. "Comments." In Gerald Meier, ed., *Politics and Policy-Making in Developing Countries.* San Francisco: ICS Press, 1991.

———. "The Nature of Institutional Impediments to Economic Development." In Mancur Olson and Satu Kahkonen, eds., *A Not-So-Dismal Science: A Broader View of Economies and Societies*, pp. 245–268 (London: Oxford University Press, 2000).

Barrow, Clyde. *Radical Theories of the State.* Madison: University of Wisconsin Press, 1993.

Baru, Sanjay. *The Political Economy of Sugar in India.* Delhi: Oxford University Press, 1990.

Baumol, William, Richard R. Nelson, and Edward N. Wolff, eds. *Convergence of Productivity: Cross-National and Historical Evidence.* Cambridge: Cambridge University Pres, 1994.

Bethell, Leslie, ed. *Latin America: Economy and Society since 1930.* Cambridge: Cambridge University Press, 1998.

Bhagwati, Jagdish. *Protectionism.* Cambridge: MIT Press, 1988.

———. *India in Transition: Freeing the Economy.* Oxford: Oxford University Press, 1993.

Bhagwati, Jagdish, and Padma Desai. *India: Planning for Industrialization.* London: Oxford University Press, 1970.

Bird, Richard. *Tax Policy and Economic Development*. Baltimore, Md.: The Johns Hopkins University Press, 1992.

Block, Fred. *Revising State Theory*. Philadelphia: Temple University Press, 1987.

Borden, William. *The Pacific Alliance: United States Foreign Economic Policy and Japanese Trade Recovery, 1947–1955*. Madison: University of Wisconsin Press, 1984.

Brecher, Michael. *Nehru's Mantle*. New York: Praeger, 1966.

Brown, Gilbert T. *Korean Pricing Policies and Economic Development in the 1960s*. Baltimore, Md.: The Johns Hopkins University Press, 1973.

Bulmer-Thomas, Victor. *The Economic History of Latin America since Independence*. Cambridge: Cambridge University Press, 1994.

Byres, T. J., ed. *The State and Planning in India*. Delhi: Oxford University Press, 1994.

Byres, Terry. "The Agrarian Question and Different Forms of Capitalist Transition: An Essay with Reference to Asia." In Sudipto Mundle and Jan Breman, eds., *Rural Transformation in Asia*, pp. 3–76 (Delhi: Oxford University Press, 1991).

Callaghy, Thomas. *The State-Society Struggle: Zaire in Comparative Perspective*. New York: Columbia University Press, 1984.

Castley, Robert. *Korea's Economic Miracle: The Crucial Role of Japan*. London: Macmillan, 1997.

———. "Korea's Export Growth: An Alternative View." *Canadian Journal of Development Studies* 18, no. 2 (1997): 187–212.

Chandavarkar, Rajnarayan. *The Origins of Industrial Capitalism in India: Business Strategies and the Working Class in Bombay, 1900–1940*. Cambridge: Cambridge University Press, 1994.

Chandrasekhar, C. P. "Growth and Technical Change in the Indian Cotton-Mill Industry." *Economic and Political Weekly*, Annual Number (January 1984): PE34–PE35.

———. "Aspects of Growth and Structural Change in Indian Industry." In Deepak Nayyar, *Industrial Growth and Stagnation: The Debate in India*, pp. 318–345 (Delhi: Oxford University Press, 1994).

Chang, Ha-Joon. "The Political Economy of Industrial Policy in Korea." *Cambridge Journal of Economics* 17 (1993): 131–157.

———. *The Political Economy of Industrial Policy*. London: Macmillan, 1994.

———. "Korea: The Misunderstood Crisis." *World Development* 26, no. 8 (1998): 1555–1561.

———. "The Hazard of Moral Hazard: Untangling the Asian Crisis." *World Development* 28, no. 4 (2000): 775–788.

Chang, Ha-Joon, and Chul-Gyue Yoo. "The Triumph of the Rentiers?" *Challenge* 43, no. 1 (January/February 2000): 105–124.

Chattopadhyay, Raghabendra. "The Idea of Planning in India, 1930–1950." Ph.D. dissertation, Australian National University, 1985.

Chenery, Hollis. "The Interdependence of Investment Decisions." In Moses Abromovitz et al., eds., *The Allocation of Economic Resources*, pp. 82–120 (Stanford: Stanford University Press, 1959).

Cheng, Tung-jen. "Guarding the Commanding Heights: The State as Banker in

Taiwan." In Stephan Haggard, Chung H. Lee, and Sylvia Maxfield, eds., *The Politics of Finance in Developing Countries*, pp. 55–92 (Ithaca, N.Y.: Cornell University Press, 1992).

Cheng, Tung-jen, Stephan Haggard, and David Kang. "Institutions and Growth in Korea and Taiwan: The Bureaucracy." *Journal of Development Studies* 37, no. 4 (October 1998): 87–111.

Chibber, Vivek. "Locked in Place: State-Building and the Failure of Industrial Policy in India, 1940–1970." Ph.D. dissertation, University of Wisconsin–Madison, 1999.

———. "Building a Developmental State: The Korean Case Reconsidered." *Politics and Society* 27, no. 3 (September 1999): 309–346.

———. "Bureaucratic Rationality and the Developmental State." *American Journal of Sociology* 107, no. 4 (January 2002): 951–989.

———. "From Class Compromise to Class Accommodation: The Origins of the Indian Industrial Relations System." In Raka Ray and Mary Katzenstein, eds., *Rethinking Class and Poverty in India*, (Cambridge: Cambridge University Press, forthcoming).

Choue, Inwon. "The Politics of Industrial Restructuring: South Korea's Turn Toward Export-Led Heavy and Chemical Industrializtion, 1961–1974." PhD dissertation, University of Pennsylvania, 1988.

Chu, Yun-Han. "The State and the Development of the Automobile Industry in South Korea and Taiwan." In Joel Aberbach, ed., *The Role of the State in Taiwan's Development*, pp. 125–169 (Armonk, N.Y.: M. E. Sharpe, 1994).

Clifford, Mark. *Troubled Tiger: Businessmen, Bureaucrats, and Generals in South Korea*. Armonk, N.Y.: M. E. Sharpe, 1994.

Cole, David, and Princeton Lyman. *Korean Development: The Interplay of Politics and Economics*. Cambridge, Mass.: Harvard University Press, 1971.

Cole, David, and Young Woo Nam. "The Pattern and Significance of Economic Planning in Korea." In Irma Edelman, ed., *Practical Approaches to Development Planning: Korea's Second Five-Year Plan* (Baltimore, Md.: The Johns Hopkins University Press, 1970).

Cole, David, and Yung Chul Park. *Financial Development in Korea, 1945–1978*. Cambridge, Mass.: Harvard University Press, 1983.

Collier, David, and Ruth B. Collier. *Shaping the Political Arena*. Princeton, N.J.: Princeton University Press, 1992.

Corporate Studies Group, *Functioning of the Industrial Licensing System: A Report*. New Delhi: Government of India, 1983.

Cortes Conde, and Roberto and Shane Hunt. *The Latin American Economies: Growth and the Export Sector, 1880–1930*. New York: Holmes and Meier: 1985.

Crouch, Harold. *The Indian Trade Union Movement*. Bombay: Asia Publishing House, 1966.

Cumings, Bruce. "The Origins and Development of the Northeast Asian Political Economy: Industrial Sectors, Product Cycles, and Political Consequences." In Frederic Deyo, ed., *The Political Economy of New Asian Industrialism*, pp. 44–83 (Ithaca, N.Y.: Cornell University Press, 1987).

Cypher, James, and James Dietz. *The Process of Economic Development*. London: Routledge, 1997.

D'Mello, Bernard. "Soviet Collaboration in Indian Steel Industry, 1954–84." *Economic and Political Weekly*, March 5, 1988.

DeJanvry, Alain. *The Agrarian Question and Reformism in Latin America*. Baltimore, Md.: The Johns Hopkins University Press, 1981.

Deyo, Frederick, ed. *The Political Economy of New Asian Industrialism*. Ithaca, N.Y.: Cornell University Press, 1987.

Dhar, Biswajit. "Factors Influencing Technology Selection: Case Study of Thal-Vaishet and Hazira Fertilizer Projects." *Economic and Political Weekly*, Annual Number (August 1984).

Dower, John. *Embracing Defeat: Japan in the Wake of World War II*. New York: Norton, 1999.

Dutt, Amitava Krishna. "Market Miracle and State Stagnation? The Development Experience of South Korea and India Compared." In Amitava Krishna Dutt, Kwan S. Kim, and Ajit Singh, eds., *The State, Markets, and Development: Beyond the Neoclassical Dichotomy* (Aldershot: Elgar, 1994).

Eley, Geoff. *Forging Democracy: The History of the Left in Europe, 1850–2000*. Oxford: Oxford University Press, 2002.

Eshag, Ephraim. *Fiscal and Monetary Policies and Problems in Developing Countries*. Cambridge: Cambridge University Press, 1983.

Evans, Peter. *Embedded Autonomy: States and Industrial Transformation*. Princeton, N.J.: Princeton University Press, 1995.

Evans, Peter, and James Rauch. "Bureaucracy and Growth: A Cross-National Analysis of the Effects of "Weberian" State Structures on Economic Growth." *American Sociological Review* 64 (October 1999): 748–765.

Fields, Karl. *Enterprise and the State in Korea and Taiwan*. Ithaca, N.Y.: Cornell University Press, 1995.

———. "Strong States and Business Organization in Korea and Taiwan." In Sylvia Maxfield and Ben Ross Schneider, eds., *Big Business and the State in Developing Countries* (Ithaca, N.Y.: Cornell University Press, 1997).

Fleming, J. M. "External Economies and the Doctrine of Balanced Growth." *Economic Journal* 65 (1955): 241–256.

Fortin, Carlos, and Christian Anglade. "Accumulation, Adjustment, and the Autonomy of the State in Latin America," in Christian Anglade and Carlos Fortin, eds., *The State and Capital Accumulation in Latin America*, 2: 211–341 (Pittsburgh: Pittsburgh University Press, 1990).

Frankel, Francine. *India's Political Economy, 1947–1977*. Princeton, N.J.: Princeton University Press, 1978.

Gadgil, D. R. "On Re-phasing the Second Five-Year Plan." In D. R. Gadgil, *Planning and Economic Policy in India* (Poona: Asia Publishing House, 1961).

———. "Planning without a Policy Frame." In D. R. Gadgil, *Planning and Economic Policy in India* (Pune: Gokhale Institute of Economics, 1962).

Geddes, Barbara. *Politician's Dilemma: Building State Capacity in Latin America*. Berkeley: University of California Press, 1994.

Gereffi, Gary. "Global Commodity Chains: New Forms of Coordination and Control among Nations and Firms in International Industries." *Competition and Change* 4 (1996): 427–439.

———. "Commodity Chains and Regional Divisions of Labor in East Asia." *Journal of Asian Business* 12, no. 1 (1996): 75–112.

Gereffi, Gary, and Donald Wyman, eds. *Manufacturing Miracles: Paths of Industrialization in Latin America and East Asia*. Princeton, N.J.: Princeton University Press, 1990.

Gerschenkron, Alexander. *Economic Backwardness in Historical Perspective*. Cambridge, Mass.: Harvard University Press, 1962.

Ghosh, Aurobindo. "Investment Behavior of Monopoly Houses" (in three parts). *Economic and Political Weekly*, October 26, November 2, November 9, 1974.

Ghosh, Aurobindo, and Arvind Vyas. "Industrial Structure and Industrial Policy." In *Alternative Policies for the Fourth Five-Year Plan* (Kerala: State Planning Board, 1968).

Gold, Thomas. "Dependent Development in Taiwan." Ph.D. dissertation, Harvard University, 1981.

———. *State and Society in the Taiwan Miracle*. Armonk, N.Y.: M. E. Sharpe, 1986.

Goldsmith, Raymond. *The Financial Development of India, 1869–1977*. New Haven: Yale University Press, 1977.

Gopal, Sarvepalli. *Jawaharlal Nehru*. Vol. 2. Cambridge, Mass.: Harvard University Press, 1979.

Goswami, Omkar. *Industry, Trade, and Peasant Society: The Jute Economy of Eastern India, 1900–1947*. Delhi: Oxford University Press, 1990.

Haggard, Stephan. *Pathways from the Periphery: The Politics of Growth in Newly Industrializing Countries* (Ithaca, N.Y.: Cornell University Press, 1990).

Haggard, Stephan, David Kang, and Chung-In Moon. "Japanese Colonialism and Korean Development: A Critique." *World Development* 25, no. 6 (1997): 867–881.

Haggard, Stephan, and Chien-Kuo Pang. "The Transition to Export-Led Growth in Taiwan." In Joel Aberbach, David Dollar, and Kenneth L. Sokoloff, eds., *The Role of the State in Taiwan's Development*, pp. 47–89 (Armonk, N.Y.: M. E. Sharpe, 1994).

Haggard, Stephan, Byung-kuk Kim, and Chung-in Moon. "The Transition to Export-Led Growth in South Korea, 1954–1966." *Journal of Asian Studies* 50 (November 1991): 850–873.

Hall, Peter. *Governing the Economy: The Politics of State Intervention in Britain and France*. Oxford: Oxford University Press, 1986.

———, ed. *The Political Power of Economic Ideas*. Princeton, N.J.: Princeton University Press, 1992.

Hamilton, Clive. *Capitalist Industrialization in Korea*. Boulder, Colo.: Westview, 1986.

Hamilton, Nora. *The Limits of State Autonomy*. Princeton, N.J.: Princeton University Press, 1982.

Hansen, A. H. *The Process of Planning: A Study of India's Five-Year Plans*. Oxford: Oxford University Press, 1966.

Harris, Laurence. "Financial Reform and Economic Growth: A New Interpretation Of South Korea's Experience." In Laurence Harris et al., eds., *New Perspectives on the Financial System*, pp. 368–388 (London: Croom Helm, 1988).

Hart-Landsberg, Martin. *The Rush to Development*. New York: Monthly Review Press, 1993.

Hart-Landsberg, Martin, and Paul Burkett. "Contradictions of Capitalist Industrialization in East Asia: A Critique of 'Flying Geese' Theories of Development." *Economic Geography* 74, no. 2 (April 1998): 87–110.

Hein, Laura. *Fueling Growth: The Energy Revolution and Economic Policy in Postwar Japan.* Cambridge, Mass.: Harvard University Press, 1990.

Heller, Patrick. *The Labor of Development: Workers and the Transformation of Capitalism in Kerala, India.* Ithaca, N.Y.: Cornell University Press, 1999.

Henderson, W. O. *The Industrialization of Europe: 1780–1914.* London: Thames and Hudson, 1969.

Herring, Ronald. "Embedded Particularism: India's Failed Developmental State." In Meredith Woo-Cumings, ed., *The Developmental State*, pp. 306–334 (Ithaca, N.Y.: Cornell University Press, 1999).

Hirschman, Albert. "The Political Economy of Import Substituting Industrialization in Latin America." *The Quarterly Journal of Economics* 82 (February 1968): 2–32.

Howe, Christopher. *The Origins of Japanese Trade Supremacy.* Chicago: University of Chicago Press, 1996.

Hutchcroft, Paul. *Booty Capitalism.* Ithaca, N.Y.: Cornell University Press, 1998.

Irwin, Douglas. *Against the Tide: An Intellectual History of Free Trade.* Princeton, N.J.: Princeton University Press, 1996.

James, Daniel. *Resistance and Integration: Peronism and the Argentine Working Class, 1946–1976.* Cambridge: Cambridge University Press, 1988.

Jang, Soo Chan. "Driving Engine or Rent-Seeking Super-Cartel? The Business-State Nexus and Economic Transformation in South Korea, 1960–1999." Ph.D. dissertation, Michigan State University, 2000.

Jessop, Bob. *State Theory: Putting the Capitalist State in Its Place.* University Park: Penn State Press, 1990.

Jha, Prem Shankar. *India: A Political Economy of Stagnation.* Delhi: Oxford University Press, 1980.

Johnson, Chalmers. *MITI and the Japanese Miracle: The Growth of Industrial Policy, 1925–1975.* Stanford: Stanford University Press, 1982.

———. "The Developmental State: Odyssey of a Concept." In Meredith Woo-Cumings, ed., *The Developmental State*, pp. 32–60 (Ithaca, N.Y.: Cornell University Press, 1999).

Jones, Leroy. *Public Enterprise and Economic Development: The Korean Case.* Seoul: Korea Development Institute, 1975.

Jones, Leroy, and Il Sakong. *Government, Business, and Entrepreneurship in Economic Development: The Korean Case.* Cambridge, Mass.: Harvard University Press, 1980.

Joshi, Shashi, and Bhagwan Josh. *Struggle for Hegemony in India, 1920–47: The Colonial State, the Left, and the National Movement.* Delhi: Sage, 1992.

Joshi, Vijay, and I.M.D. Little. *India: Macroeconomics and Political Economy, 1964–1991.* Delhi: Oxford University Press, 1994.

Jun, Sang-In. "The Origins of the Developmental State in South Korea." *Asian Perspective* 16, no. 2 (fall/winter 1992): 181–204.

Kalecki, Michel. "Political Aspects of Full Employment." In his *Selected Essays on the Dynamics of the Capitalist Economy*, pp. 138–145 (Cambridge: Cambridge University Press, 1971).

———. "Observations on Social and Economic Aspects of 'Intermediate Regimes.'" In *The Collected Works of Michal Kalecki*, Volume 5: *Developing Countries*, ed. Jerzy Osiatynski, pp. 6–12 (Oxford: Oxford University Press, 1993).

Kamtekar, I. "The End of the Colonial State in India." Ph.D. dissertation, Cambridge University, 1988.

Kang, David C. "South Korean and Taiwanese Development and the New Institutional Economics." *International Organization* 49, no. 3 (summer 1995): 555–587.

———. *Crony Capitalism: Corruption and Development in South Korea and the Philippines*. Cambridge: Cambridge University Press, 2002.

Kang, Myong-Hon. *The Korean Business Conglomerate: Chaebol Then and Now*. Berkeley: Institute of East Asian Studies, 1996.

Karnik, V. B. *Indian Trade Unions: A Survey*. Bombay: Labour Education Service, 1960.

Kaufman, Robert. "How Societies Change Developmental Models or Keep Them: Reflections on the Latin American Experience in the 1930s and the Postwar World." In Gary Gereffi and Donald Wyman, eds., *Manufacturing Miracles: Paths of Industrialization in Latin America and East Asia*, pp. 110–138 (Princeton, N.J.: Princeton University Press, 1990).

Keynes, John Maynard. *The General Theory of Employment, Interest, and Money*. New York: Harcourt, Brace, and World, 1937.

Khan, Mushtaq. "State Failure in Weak States: A Critique of New Institutionalist Explanations." In John Harriss et al., eds., *The New Institutional Economics and Third World Development*, pp. 71–87 (London: Routledge, 1995).

———. "The Efficiency Implications of Corruption." *Journal of International Development* 8, no. 5 (1996): 683–696.

Khanna, Sushil. "Transnational Corporations and Technology Transfer: Contours of Dependence in Indian Petrochemical Industry." *Economic and Political Weekly*, Annual Number (August 1984).

Kidron, Michael. *Foreign Investments in India*. Oxford: Oxford University Press, 1965.

Kikkawa, Takeo. "The Relationship between the Government and Companies in Japan during and after World War II." In Jun Sakudo and Takao Shiba, eds., *World War II and the Transformation of Business Systems*, pp. 59–80 (Tokyo: University of Tokyo Press, 1993).

Kim, Byung Kook. "Bringing and Managing Socioeconomic Change: The State in Korea and Mexico." Ph.D. dissertation, Harvard University, 1988.

Kim, Eun Mee. *Big Business, Strong State*. Albany: State University of New York Press, 1997.

Kim, In Young. "The Political Economy of a Chaebol's Capital Accumulation in South Korea: The Case of Samsung, 1938–1987." Ph.D. dissertation, University of Hawaii, 1996.

Kim, Kwan Bong. *The Korea-Japan Treaty Crisis and the Instability of the Korean Political System*. New York: Praeger, 1971.

Kim, Linsu. *Imitation to Innovation: The Dynamics of Korea's Technological Learning*. Cambridge, Mass.: Harvard Business School Press, 1997.

Kim, Quee-Young. *The Fall of Synghman Rhee*. Berkeley: University of California Press, 1983.

Kim, Se-Jin. *The Politics of Military Revolution in Korea*. Chapel Hill: University of North Carolina Press, 1971.

Kim, Seok Ki. "Business Concentration and Government Policy: A Study of the Phenomenon of Business Groups in Korea, 1945–1985." Ph.D. dissertation, Harvard University, 1987.

Kochanek, Stanley. *The Congress Party of India: The Dynamics of One-Party Democracy*. Princeton, N.J.: Princeton University Press, 1968.

Kohli, Atul, and Vivian Shue. *The State and Social Forces*. Cambridge: Cambridge University Press, 1993.

Kohli, Atul. "Where Do High Growth Political Economies Come From? The Japanese Lineage of Korea's 'Developmental State.'" *World Development* 22, no. 9 (1994): 1269–1293.

Kohli, Atul. "Japanese Colonialism and Korean Development: A Reply." *World Development* 25, no. 6 (1997): 883–888.

Kosai, Yotaka. *The Era of High-Speed Growth: Notes on the Postwar Japanese Economy*. Tokyo: University of Tokyo Press, 1986.

Krause, Lawrence, and Sueo Sekiguchi. "Japan and the World Economy." In Hugh Patrick and Henry Rosovsky, eds., *Asia's New Giant: How the Japanese Economy Works* (Washington, D.C.: The Brookings Institute, 1976).

Krueger, Anne. *Foreign Trade Regimes and Economic Development: Turkey* (New York: Columbia University Press, 1974.

———. *Liberalization Attempts and Consequences*. Volume 10 of *Foreign Trade Regimes and Economic Development*. New York: National Bureau of Economic Research, 1978.

———. "Government Failures in Development." *Journal of Economic Perspectives* 4, no. 3 (1990): 9–23.

Kuisel, Richard. *Capitalism and the State in France*. Cambridge: Cambridge University Press, 1981.

Kuznets, Paul. "Indicative Planning in Korea." *Journal of Comparative Economics* 14 (1990): 657–676.

Lala, R.M. *Beyond the Last Blue Mountain: A Life of J.R.D. Tata*. New York: Viking, 1992.

Lall, Deepak. *The Poverty of "Development Economics."* Cambridge, Mass.: Harvard University Press, 1985.

Lall, Sanjaya. "Marketing Barriers Facing Developing Country Manufactured Exporters: A Conceptual Note." *Journal of Development Studies* 27, no. 4 (July 1991): 137–150.

Landes, David. *The Unbound Prometheus: Technological Change and Industrial Development in Western Europe from 1750 to the Present*. Cambridge: Cambridge University Press, 1969.

Lee, Byoung Doo. "The Politics of Industrialization: The Textiles Industry in South Korea and the Philippines." Ph.D. dissertation, Northwestern University, 1990.

Lee, Chung H. "United States and Japanese Direct Investment in Korea: A Comparative Study." *Hitosubashi Journal of Economics* 20, no. 2 (February 1980): 26–41.

———. "The Government, Financial System, and Large Private Enterprises in the Economic Development of South Korea." *World Development* 20 (1992).

Leff, Nathaniel. "Industrial Organization and Entrepreneurship in Developing Countries: The Business Groups." *Economic Development and Cultural Change* 26, no. 4 (1978): 661–675.

Lele, Uma, and Manmohan Agarwal. "Four Decades of Economic Assistance in India and the Role of External Assistance." In Uma Lele and Ijaz Nabi, eds., *Transitions in Development: The Role of Aid and Commercial Flows* (San Francisco: ICS Press, 1991).

Leopoldi, Maria. "Industrial Associations and Politics in Contemporary Brazil." Ph.D. dissertation, Oxford University, 1984.

Lewis, Arthur. "Economic Development with Unlimited Supplies of Labour." *The Manchester School* 22, no. 2 (1954): 139–191.

Lewis, John P. *India's Political Economy*. Delhi: Oxford University Press, 1995.

Lie, John. *Han Unbound: The Political Economy of South Korea*. Stanford: Stanford University Press, 1998.

Lim, Suk-Jun. "Politics of Industrialization: Formation of Divergent Industrial Orders in Korea and Taiwan." Ph.D. dissertation, University of Chicago, 1997.

Lim, Timothy. "Competition, Markets, and the Politics of Development in South Korea, 1945–1979." Ph.D. dissertation, University of Hawaii, 1996.

Low, D. A. *Rearguard Action: Selected Essays on Indian Colonial History*. Cambridge: Cambridge University Press, 1996.

Luedde-Neurath, Richard. *Import Controls and Export-Oriented Development: A Reassessment of the South Korean Case*. Boulder, Colo.: Westview, 1985.

Marathe, Sharad. *Regulation and Development: India's Policy Experience with Controls over Industry*. Delhi: Sage, 1986.

Markovits, Claude. *Indian Business and Nationalist Politics, 1931–1939: The Indigenous Capitalist Class and the Rise of the Congress Party*. Cambridge: Cambridge University Press, 1985.

Mason, Edward, et al. *The Economic and Social Modernization of the Republic of Korea*. Cambridge, Mass.: Harvard University Press, 1980.

Maxfield, Sylvia, and Ben Ross Schneider, eds. *Business and the State in Developing Countries* (Ithaca, N.Y.: Cornell University Press, 1997).

McMahon, Robert J. *The Cold War in the Periphery: The United States, India, and Pakistan*. New York: Columbia University Press, 1994.

Measures for the Economic Development of Underdeveloped Countries. Geneva: United Nations, 1951.

Medhora, P. B. *Industrial Growth since 1950: An Assessment*. Bombay: University of Bombay Press, 1968.

Miliband, Ralph. *Class Power and State Power: Political Essays*. London: Verso, 1983.

Milor, Vedat. "Planning the Market: Structural Transformation of the Economy in France, Turkey, and Korea, 1950–1990." Unpublished MS., 1995.

Misra, Anna-Maria. "Entrepreneurial Decline and the End of Empire: British Business in India, 1919–1949." Ph.D. dissertation, Oxford University, 1992.

Mortimore, Michael. "Flying Geese or Sitting Ducks? Transnationals and Industry in Developing Countries." *CEPAL Review* 51 (December 1993): 15–34.

Mukherjee, Aditya. "The Indian Capitalist Class and Congress on National Planning and the Public Sector, 1930–1947." *Economic and Political Weekly*, September 2, 1978.

Mundle, Sudipto. "Fiscal Policy and Growth: Some Asian Lessons for Asia." *Journal of Asian Economics* 10 (1999): 15–36.

Mundle, Sudipto. "Growth, Disparity, and Capital Reorganization in Indian Economy." *Economic and Political Weekly*, Annual Number (March 1981).

Murphy, Kevin M., Andrei Shleifer, and Robert Vishney. "Industrialization and the Big Push." *Journal of Political Economy* 97, no. 5: 1003–1026.

Nakamura, Takafusa. *The Postwar Japanese Economy: Its Development and Structure*. Tokyo: University of Tokyo Press, 1981.

Nayar, Baldev Raj. *India's Mixed Economy: The Role of Ideas and Interests in Its Development*. Bombay: Popular Prakashan, 1985.

Nayyar, Deepak. *India's Exports and Export Policies in the 1960s*. Cambridge: Cambridge University Press, 1976.

———, ed. *Industrial Growth and Stagnation: The Debate in India*. Delhi: Oxford University Press, 1994.

Nehru, B. K. *Nice Guys Finish Second*. Delhi: Viking, 1997.

Nelson, Richard R., and Edward N. Wolff, eds. *Convergence of Productivity: Cross-National Studies and Historical Evidence*. Oxford: Oxford University Press, 1994.

Offe, Claus. *Disorganized Capitalism*. Cambridge: MIT Press, 1985.

Okimoto, Daniel. *Between MITI and the Market: Japanese Industrial Policy for High Technology*. Stanford: Stanford University Press, 1989.

Palekar, Shreekant. *Problems of Wage Policy for Economic Development*. Bombay: Asia Publishing House, 1962.

Pandey, Gyan. *The Indian Nation in 1942*. Calcutta: K. P. Bagchi, 1988.

Park, Moon Kyu. "Interest Representation in South Korea: The Limits of Corporatist Control." *Asian Survey* 27 (August 1987): 903–917.

Pekkarinen, Jukka, Matti Pohkjoka, and Bob Rowthorn, eds. *Social Corporatism: A Superior Economic System?* Oxford: Clarendon, 1992.

Pinho, Demosthenes. "Development Strategies, Trade Policy, and State Intervention: Aspects of the Brazilian Post-War Experience in International Perspective." Ph.D. dissertation, University of California–Berkeley, 1991.

Polanyi, Karl. *The Great Transformation: The Political and Economic Origins of Our Time*. Boston: Beacon, 1944.

Pontusson, Jonas. "Labor, Corporatism, and Industrial Policy: The Swedish Case in Comparative Perspective." *Comparative Politics* (January 1991): 163–179.

Posusney, Marsha Pripstein. *Labor and the State in Egypt: Workers, Unions, and Restructuring*. New York: Columbia University Press, 1997.

Przeworski, Adam. *Capitalism and Social Democracy*, chap. 5: "Material Interests, Class Compromise, and the State." Cambridge: Cambridge University Press, 1985.

Ramaswamy, E. A. *Power and Justice: The State in Industrial Relations*. Delhi: Oxford, 1984.

Ranis, Gustav, and Syed Akhtar Mahmood. *The Political Economy of Development Policy Change.* Cambridge: Basil Blackwell, 1992.

Ranis, Gustav, and Theodore Schultz, eds. *The State of Development Economics.* Oxford: Basil Blackwell, 1988.

Rathin Roy. "The Politics of Fiscal Policy: Some Reflections on Fiscal Policy and State Intervention in Developing Economies, with Special Reference to India." Ph.D. dissertation, Cambridge University, 1994.

Ray, Debraj. *Development Economics.* Princeton, N.J.: Princeton University Press, 1998.

Ray, Rajat. *Industrialization in India: Growth and Conflict in the Private Corporate Sector, 1900–1947.* Delhi: Oxford University Press, 1982.

Rhee, Jong-Chan. *The State and Industry in Korea: The Limits of the Authoritarian State.* London: Routledge, 1994.

Rhee, Y. B., B. Ross-Larson, and G. Pursell. *Korea's Competitive Edge: Managing Entry into World Markets.* Baltimore, Md.: The Johns Hopkins University Press, 1984.

Rhee, Yung Whee. "Instruments for Export Policy and Administration: Lessons from the East Asian Experience." *World Bank Staff Working Papers,* no. 725 (1985).

Richards, Alan, and John Waterbury. *The Political Economy of the Middle East.* Boulder, Colo.: Westview, 1990.

Rider, Tomas. "The Tariff Policy of the Government of India and Its Development Strategy, 1894–1924." Ph.D. dissertation, University of Minnesota, 1971.

Rodriguez-Claire, Andrez. "Positive Feedback Mechanisms in Economic Development: A Review of Recent Contributions." In Istvan P. Szekely and Richard Sabot, eds., *Development Strategy and Management of the Market Economy,* vol. 2, pp. 91–145 (Oxford: Clarendon, 1997).

Rodrik, Dani. "Getting Interventions Right: How South Korea and Taiwan Grew Rich." *Economic Policy* (April 1995): 55–107.

———. "The 'Paradoxes' of the Successful State." *European Economic Review* 41 (1997): 411–442.

Rosenstein-Rodan, P. N. "Problems of Industrialization in Eastern and South-Eastern Europe." *The Economic Journal* 53, nos. 210/211 (1943): 202–221.

Roychowdhury, Supriya. "The State and Business in India: The Political Economy of Liberalization, 1984–1989." Ph.D. dissertation, Princeton University, 1992.

Rudra, Ashok. "Planning in India: An Evaluation in Terms of Its Models." *Economic and Political Weekly* 20, no. 17 (April 27, 1985): 758–674.

Sabel, Charles. "Learning by Monitoring: The Institutions of Economic Development." In Neil Smelser and Richard Swedberg, eds., *The Handbook of Economic Sociology* (Princeton, N.J.: Princeton University Press, 1994).

Sarkar, Sumit. *Modern India: 1870–1947.* Delhi: Macmillan, 1983.

Sassoon, Donald. *One Hundred Years of Socialism.* New York: New Press, 1996.

Satterwhite, David. "The Politics of Economic Development: Coup, State, and the Republic of Korea's First Five-Year Economic Development Plan (1962–1966)." Ph.D. dissertation, University of Washington, 1994.

Schneider, Ben Ross. "Elusive Synergy: Business Government Relations and Development." *Comparative Politics* (October 1998): 101–122.

Schneider, Ben Ross. "Relations Between Government and Business and Their Consequences for Development: A Review of the Recent Literature." *Desarrollo Economico-Revista De Ciencias Sociales* 39, no. 153 (April–June 1999): 45–75.

Schneider, Ben Ross. *Politics within the State: Elite Bureaucrats and Industrial Policy in Authoritarian Brazil.* Pittsburgh: Pittsburgh University Press, 1991.

Scitovsky, Tibor. "Two Concepts of External Economies." *Journal of Political Economy* 62 (1954): 143–151.

Sen, A. K., and Jean Dreze. *India: Economic Development and Social Opportunity.* Delhi: Oxford University Press, 1995.

Sen, Abhijit. "On Economic Openness and Industrialization." In Deepak Nayyar, ed., *Trade and Industrialization*, pp. 88–168 (Delhi: Oxford University Press, 1997).

Senghaas, Dieter. *The European Experience: A Historical Critique of Development Theory.* Dover, Berg, 1984.

Sengupta, Nitish K. *Inside the Steel Frame: Reminiscences and Reflections of a Former Civil Servant.* New Delhi: Vikas, 1995.

Shastri, Vanita. "The Political Economy of Policy Formation in India: The Case of Industrial Policy, 1948–1994." Ph.D. dissertation, Cornell University, 1995.

Sheahan, John. *Patterns of Development in Latin America.* Princeton, N.J.: Princeton University Press, 1987.

Shetty, S. L. "Structural Retrogression in the Indian Economy since the Mid-Sixties." *Economic and Political Weekly*, Annual Number (February 1978); reprinted in Deepak Nayyar, ed., *Industrial Growth and Stagnation: The Debate in India*, 131–218 (Delhi: Oxford University Press, 1994).

Shonfield, Andrew. *Modern Capitalism.* Oxford: Oxford University Press, 1965.

Shourie, Arun. "The Allocation of Foreign Exchange in India." Ph.D. dissertation, Syracuse University, 1967.

———. "Controls and the Current Situation: Why Not Let the Hounds Run?" *Economic and Political Weekly* 8, Annual Number (August 1973): 31–33.

Sikkink, Kathryn. *Ideas and Institutions: Developmentalism in Brazil and Argentina.* Ithaca, N.Y.: Cornell University Press, 1991.

Skidelsky, Robert. *John Maynard Keynes: The Economist as Savior, 1920–1937.* New York: Penguin, 1992.

Song, Byung-Nak. *The Rise of the Korean Economy.* Oxford: Oxford University Press, 1990.

Sovani, N. V. *Post-War Inflation in India—A Survey.* Pune: Gokhale Institute of Politics and Economics, 1949.

Sridharan, E. *The Political Economy of Industrial Promotion: Indian, Brazilian, and Korean Electronics in Comparative Perspective 1969–1994.* Westport: Praeger, 1996.

Stallings, Barabara. "The Role of Foreign Capital in Economic Development." In Gary Gereffi and State in Latin America," in Gary Gereffi and Donald

Wyman, eds., *The State and Capital Accumulation in Latin America*, pp. 211–340 (Pittsburgh: University of Pittsburgh Press, 1990).

Stone, Brewer Stevenson. "Governmental Corruption in India and China." Ph.D. dissertation, Harvard University, 1994.

Swamy, Dalip. *The Political Economy of Industrialization*. Delhi: Sage, 1995.

Thakurdas, Purshotamdas, et al. *A Plan of Economic Development for India*. Bombay, 1944–45.

Thirlwall, A. P. *Nicholas Kaldor*. New York: New York University Press, 1987.

Tilton, Gregory. "The Political Development of Japan's Postwar Economy." Ph.D. dissertation, Ohio State University, 1997.

Tomlinson, B. R. *The Economy of Modern India, 1860–1970*. New York: Cambridge University Press, 1993.

Toye, John. "Nicholas Kaldor and Tax Reform in Developing Countries." *Cambridge Journal of Economics* 13, no. 1 (March 1989): 183–200.

Tsunoda, Elizabeth Payne. "Rationalizing Japan's Political Economy: The Business Initiative, 1920–1955." Ph.D. dissertation, Columbia University, 1993.

Venkatasubbiah, H. *The Indian Economy since Independence*. Bombay: Asia Publishing House, 1961.

Visvesvaraya, M. *A Planned Economy for India*. Bangalore: Bangalore Press, 1934.

Vogel, David. "Why Businessmen Distrust Their State: The Political Consciousness of American Corporate Executives." *British Journal of Political Science* 8 (January 1978): 45–78.

Vogel, Steven K. *Freer Markets, More Rules: Regulatory Reform in Advanced Countries*. Ithaca, N.Y.: Cornell University Press, 1996.

Voigt, Johannes H. *India in the Second World War*. New Delhi: Arnold-Heinemann, 1987.

Wade, Robert. *Governing the Market*. Princeton, N.J.: Princeton University Press, 1990.

Waterbury, John. "The Long Gestation and Brief Triumph of Import-Substituting Industrialization." *World Development* 27, no. 2 (1999): 323–341.

Weber, Max. *Economy and Society*. Berkeley: University of California Press, 1968.

Weiss, Linda. *The Myth of the Powerless State*. Ithaca, N.Y.: Cornell University Press, 1998.

Westphal, Larry. "The Pendulum Swings—An Apt Analogy?" *World Development* 26, no. 12 (1998): 2223–2230

White, Gordon, ed. *Developmental States in East Asia*. London: Macmillan, 1988.

Wing-kai Chiu, Stephen. "The State and the Financing of Industrialization in East Asia: Historical Origins of Comparative Divergences." Ph.D. dissertation, Princeton University, 1992.

Wolf, Martin. *India's Exports*. Oxford: Oxford University Press, 1982.

Woo, Jung-en. *Race to the Swift: The State and Finance in Korean Industrialization*. New York: Columbia University Press, 1991.

Woo-Cumings, ed. *The Developmental State*. Ithaca, N.Y.: Cornell University Press, 1999.

Wright, Erik. Review of *Embedded Autonomy: States and Industrial Transformation* by Peter Evans, in *Contemporary Sociology* 25, no. 2 (March 1996): 176–179.

Wright, Erik Olin. *Interrogating Inequality: Essays on Class Analysis, Socialism, and Marxism*. London: Verso, 1994.

Yonekura, Seiichiro. "The Functions of Industrial Associations." In Tetsuji Okazaki and Masahiro Okuno-Fujiwara, eds., *The Japanese System and Its Historical Origins*, pp. 180–207 (Oxford: Oxford University Press, 1999).

Yoo, Ho-yeol Paul. "A New Political Economy of Economic Policy Change in South Korea, 1961–1963: Crisis, Uncertainty, and Contradiction." Ph.D. dissertation, Ohio State University, 1990.

Yoon, Jeon-Ro. "The State and the Electronics Industry in Korea." Ph.D. dissertation, Brown University, 1989.

Zysman, John. *Governments, Markets, and Growth: Financial Systems and the Politics of Industrial Change*. Ithaca, N.Y.: Cornell University Press, 1983.

Index